M000107307

Rethinking Commodification

CRITICAL AMERICA

General Editors: Richard Delgado and Jean Stefancic

Rethinking Commodification

*Cases and Readings in
Law and Culture*

EDITED BY
Martha M. Ertman and
Joan C. Williams

NEW YORK UNIVERSITY PRESS
New York and London

NEW YORK UNIVERSITY PRESS
New York and London
www.nyupress.org

© 2005 by Martha M. Ertman and Joan C. Williams
All rights reserved

Library of Congress Cataloging-in-Publication Data
Rethinking commodification : cases and readings in law & culture /
edited by Martha M. Ertman and Joan C. Williams.
p.   cm. — (Critical America)
Includes index.
ISBN 0-8147-2228-8 (cloth : alk. paper)
ISBN 0-8147-2229-6 (pbk. : alk. paper)
1. Culture and law—Cases. 2. Consumption (Economics).
3. Free enterprise.   I. Ertman, Martha M. II. Williams, Joan C.
III. Series.
K487.C8A52 2005
344'.09—dc22   2005006139

New York University Press books are printed on acid-free paper,
and their binding materials are chosen for strength and durability.

Manufactured in the United States of America

c 10 9 8 7 6 5 4 3 2 1
p 10 9 8 7 6 5 4 3 2 1

To my parents, Mary Jane and Gardner Ertman
And to Oscar (MME)

To Pastora Sandoval and the memory of
Mari Barron (JCW)

Contents

Acknowledgments

As with any project spanning half a decade, we cannot begin to thank everyone who helped shape this book into its ultimate form. However, some institutions and individuals stand out.

First the institutions: The University of Denver, the University of Utah, and the Washington College of Law at American University, as well as the Hughes-Rudd Research and Development Fund at the University of Denver and WorkLife Law at American University, granted generous support by sponsoring two workshops to brainstorm new ways to think about commodification and vet papers implementing those new ideas. In addition, these institutions gave us summer research grants to work on this book, and both faculty and students at the University of Utah generously contributed insights about the book's structure and content, the former through two faculty workshops, and the latter in a seminar, The Role of Markets in Love, Sex, and Other Things, that used an early draft of the book as its text.

In addition, we are grateful to the following individual friends, colleagues, and family members for their support, perspective, and insight during the process of writing and editing this book: Jay Brown, Alan Chen, Christine Cimini, Susan Clinkenbeard, James X. Dempsey, Sue Donnelly, Nancy Ehrenreich, John Flynn, Leslie Francis, Jane Garrity, Erika George, Sarah Williams Golhagen, Dan Greenwood, Claudio Grossman, Karen Jacobs, Leslie Francis, Laura Kessler, Lisa Kieda, Terry Kogan, Ruth Lemansky, Dennis Lynch, Amy Lyndon, Beth Lyndon-Griffith, Nell Jessup Newton, Scott Matheson, Julie Nice, Kate Regan, Dorothy Ross, Teemu Ruskola, Gerda Saunders, Natascha Seidneck, Reva Siegel, Kate Silbaugh, Mary Simon, Pat Standley, Joyce Sterling, Debora Threedy, Manuel Utset, Leti Volpp, Jessica West, Alyssa Wolf-Velarde, Mary Westby, Marilyn Winokur, Bob Yegge, and Viviana Zelizer. We extend especially warm thanks to Madhavi Sunder and Peggy

Radin for recommending this project to the editors of NYU Press's Critical America series, and also thank them, along with Carol Rose, for writing incisive chapters synthesizing the book's original and reprinted material, a task which called for patience and good humor in adapting their chapters to an ever-changing table of contents.

Moreover, this book could not have taken shape without the intelligence and enthusiasm of the participants in the Second Feminist Theory Workshop: Identities, Intimacies & Ca$h: Retheorizing Commodification at American University's Washington College of Law and the Commodification Futures conference at the University of Denver. Many of these participants wrote chapters for this volume, and the authors of previously published material generously granted permission to reproduce their work here. Richard Delgado and Jean Stefancic contributed to the volume as editors of the Critical America series; Debbie Gershenowitz and Despina Papazoglou Gimbel with thoughtful editorial work; Sean Graff through his expert creation of the cover photograph; Stephanie Gaynor with precise proofreading and indexing; Sandra Black, Cynthia Lane, Joan Pope, and Sharon Wolfe with able administrative assistance; Michael Haukedalen with strong research assistance; and Theresa Sheridan with the painstaking work of obtaining copyright permissions. Most crucially, Tiffany Pezzulo brought the fierceness and dedication of an Amazon to this project, providing outstanding all-around research assistance for two solid years and often responding on a dime to last minute requests.

On top of all these personal and professional debts, Martha Ertman wishes to acknowledge the ways she has been sustained by the matchless friendship of a number of good souls in various cities as this volume reached its completion. In Salt Lake City Melanee Cherry, Faye Jensen, Sylvia Lesser, Kathryn Stockton (also an outstanding editor) and Shelley White brought laughter and insight, as did the members of the interdisciplinary writing group: Beth Clement, Chris Talbot, and Margaret Toscano (who, as a group, contributed invaluable editorial advice alongside tea and cookies). Family members Mary Jane, Gardner, Eric, Anne, Susie and Andy Ertman, as well as Betsy Ertman Bahn, proffered substantive and emotional support at key times, as did Provincetown friends Mary Beth Caschetta, David Chambers, Meryl Cohn, John Crane, Marylyn Donahue, Lisa Gonsalves, Alison Hyder, and Amy O'Hara. Sam Korsak conveyed superlative kindness from New Hampshire, as did Katherine Franke and Renée Römkens from New York, and Jennifer Levi from

Massachusetts. Especially priceless and personal contributions of time and wisdom came from two extraordinary, spirited people. First, Victor Flatt swooped in to aid in completing a draft of this book when it looked like Baby Oscar was going to arrive sooner than anticipated, and also provided sage advice on many topics, from the book's cover to the topics covered in it. Second, and equally crucial, Kathryn Casull brought a newcomer's enthusiasm to the project in its final stages, along with medical aid, loving kindness, and tons of help with all kinds of things that competed with the task of finishing this book.

Finally, and perhaps most important, we thank one another for a fabulous collaboration, as well as two more people. First, Adrienne Davis for her invaluable contributions to this book in its early stages, brainstorming about the state of commodification theory, co-organizing two conferences, invariably bringing humor and imaginative flair to identify the threads of commodification theory that, if absent, would render this book woefully incomplete. Second, Oscar Ertman, for timing his arrival to coincide perfectly with this book's completion.

Bibliographic Note

We have chosen thirty-five cases, articles, and book excerpts that illustrate various commodification themes; many excellent pieces and cases could not be included. In tightly editing the excerpted materials for readability, we have omitted many of the extensive footnotes that characterize law review articles, renumbered footnotes as necessary, and conformed all pieces to legal citation conventions. While deletions within paragraphs are generally not indicated, asterisks indicate where larger portions of the text have been deleted.

Preface

Freedom, Equality, and the Many Futures of Commodification

Martha M. Ertman and Joan C. Williams

Most people think that some things—parenthood, human body parts and people, to name a few—are not for sale. However, despite formal legal prohibitions, people routinely buy and sell all of these things. Three times in the past three years, *New York Times* Sunday Magazine cover stories documented thriving international markets in parenthood, kidneys, and young women.[1] The most legal of these markets is the one in which American parents pay to adopt third world children, believing the children to be either abandoned or orphaned, when in fact brokers often bribe, coerce, or trick birth mothers into giving up their children. This market could be described as a gray market. The markets in kidneys and sexual slaves, in contrast, are black markets. Despite legal and cultural condemnation, traffickers purchase and resell kidneys. They also purchase, trick, or abduct girls and young women from impoverished areas of Mexico or eastern Europe and, after "breaking them in," force them to engage in as many as twenty fifteen-minute sessions of sex a day, resulting in a profit of $20,000–$30,000 a week. Less obvious examples of things that are routinely sold include religious standing (through regular monetary payments to a church known as tithing) and racial identity (through things like FUBU clothing, which is made by, and signals identity within, the African-American community).

Is everything for sale? Or is there a realm of sacred things and relationships outside the market? "Commodification" is the term scholars use to describe the process of something becoming understood as a commodity, as well as the state of affairs once this has taken place.[2]

Classic texts tend to fall into two camps. People who support the recognition of legal markets in adoption, human organs, military service, votes, and everything else generally feel they are defending freedom of contract—people's freedom to buy and sell whatever they wish. In contrast, people who question whether markets in parental rights or body parts (as well as intellectual property, identity, religious standing, or homemaking labor) worry about other values, notably equality, dignity, and solidarity.

In both pro- and anticommodification camps, the instinct is to frame discussions in terms of an on-off decision about whether or not to commodify. The result is a discussion that follows fixed rails, forever trying to pinpoint the proper boundary between market and nonmarket transactions.

This book first familiarizes readers with the traditional commodification debate then offers a solution to the impasse in sharp new writings that move beyond the on-off question of whether or not to commodify. But before describing the structure, substance, and goals of the book, we should define some key terms: "market" and "marketization"; "commodity" and "commodification."

A market exists whenever buyers and sellers come together to exchange things or services and the laws of supply and demand determine price.[3] When there are willing buyers and willing sellers, anything and everything will be in the market, regardless of legal rules forbidding the practice. For example, slavery has long been banned around the world, yet the international slave trade continues to flourish,[4] and the same holds true for illegal drugs and stolen art. In short, if a sale is prohibited despite the existence of both supply and demand, the market for these things simply will be a black market, or perhaps a gray market, depending on the breadth of the ban and the effectiveness of its enforcement. The core question in the commodification debate concerns what social relationships should be handled by market institutions and governed by market norms; in short, what should be the scope of marketization.

While the newer term "marketization" has distinct advantages—as we will see, the older terminology proves confusing in crucial contexts— most existing discussions use the more traditional terminology of "commodity" and "commodification." Like any important concept, "commodity" has various definitions. Karl Marx defined it as something that has both use value and exchange value.[5] As such, it is "an object outside us, a thing that by its properties satisfies human wants of some sort or another," ultimately tied to money and an impersonal market.[6] Friedrich

Engels concisely summarized this line of thinking by stating that "[t]o become a commodity a product must be transferred to another, whom it will serve as a use-value, by means of an exchange."[7]

Classic examples of commodities are fungible items such as wheat and services such as labor. But these definitions do not tell us whether everything that has use value and exchange value is, or should be, for sale. The dictionary definition sheds further light on what we mean when we talk about commodities, defining "commodity" as "an economic good," an "article of commerce," any "mass-produced unspecialized product," and, most expansive, "something useful or valued."[8] Perhaps statutes most precisely define what counts as a commodity, as in Uniform Commercial Code Article 2's definition of "goods" as "things that are moveable at the time of identification to the contract," including, among other things, the unborn young of animals.[9] Yet other statutes, known as blood shield statutes, narrow this definition to exclude human body parts, such as blood, as goods in order to shield providers from warranty claims asserted under the U.C.C.[10] Synthesizing this analysis, we might define commodities as goods or services that are, or could be, bought and sold at some point. Seeing things in this marketized way is known as commodification.

The classic justification of the market is the idea of freedom of contract. Building on John Locke's assertion that "life, liberty, and property" are, or should be, of utmost importance,[11] classical liberal thinkers have emphasized the importance of freedom in ordering one's affairs (stressing, for example, the difference between slavery and working for wages). The leading pieces supporting marketization, some of which are excerpted in this volume, situate themselves within this classical liberal tradition.[12] But Marx complicated the industrialist enthusiasm for freedom of contract by raising questions of power and equality, in particular exposing the ways that power struggles between capitalists, the bourgeoisie, and workers resulted in more freedom for some contracting parties than others. In other words, while classical liberals emphasized the freedom of lifting feudal restraints on alienating property, Marx revealed ways that labor becomes alienated when workers exchange their time and effort for a pittance, leaving capital to enjoy the surplus value created by the difference between the cost of producing a commodity and the price at which it is sold. Unionization and other forms of collective action, under this line of thinking, represent workers' efforts to obtain for themselves some of the benefits of exchange that classical liberals are more likely to situate in autonomous individualism than in solidarity. The excerpt by Michael Sandel represents this focus on equality and community, articulating concerns that often are raised to oppose commodification.[13]

But scholars across the ideological spectrum use the term "commodification" to discuss only certain kinds of sales. They generally do not worry (let alone write) about the commodification of milk, garbage collection, or soybean futures. Instead, people use the term "commodification" to challenge the understanding of things, services, or relationships in market terms. This challenge asserts boundary issues, asking what is, and should be, in and out of the market.

In the classic commodification debate, the most important question is how to define that boundary, accounting for either liberty or concerns about equality, dignity, and solidarity in deciding what to do about *existing* markets in contested commodities and the related question of what *should be* in and out of the market. This book seeks to change that debate. It seeks to replace the traditional on-off question of whether or not to commodify with an approach that examines and rejects the basic premises of that traditional question.

The conventional assumption is of hostile worlds: that the world is bifurcated into an economic arena dominated by rational self-interest and self-interest alone ("the market"), and a sharply different arena of intimacy and altruism that must be protected from the kind of instrumental behavior that is appropriate in market contexts.[14] This imagery, of two hostile worlds whose overlap can bring only corruption, underlies *both* the law-and-economics enthusiasm for markets (for example, Richard Posner and Elisabeth Landes's proposed market for babies) *and* the classic skepticism of marketization (for example, Margaret Jane Radin's worry that "conceiving of any child in market rhetoric harms personhood").[15]

In fact, this way of construing what's at issue in proposals to expand marketization is just one way of looking at these issues. It is, we think, a flawed way. The new materials in this book, taken as a whole, argue against the vision of a world bifurcated into separate hostile spheres whose boundary is policed by commodification anxiety.[16] In fact, intimate relations typically have economic dimensions, and market relations often do not adhere to the model of self-interest and self-interest alone. Thus the lines between strategic dating and marriage are often blurrier than we like to admit, and the capitalist elite commonly build personal relationships to cement deals. Indeed, this book grew out of our efforts to find theoretical justification for remunerating homemakers for their contributions to family wealth.[17] One of us (Ertman) has taken this argument even further to contend that marriage itself is analogous to a close corporation and cohabitation is akin to a business partnership.[18]

Once we abandon the Hamlet question of "to commodify or not to commodify," where do we go? This book seeks to answer that question, using the best available tools from anthropology, law, sociology, geography, political theory, philosophy, and gender studies. In Part I, we reprint a selection of the best existing literature on commodification, which we call the classic texts. In Part II, we present a selection of outstanding new work suggesting innovative ways to rethink commodification. These new pieces come out of a workshop and conference in which we brought together widely disparate scholars who have developed robust discussions about commodification but have rarely engaged with each other.[19] One of the strengths of bringing together the diverse conversations in queer theory, racial and ethnic studies, feminism, Marxism, and intellectual property is that it enables us to examine how various theories fit together. Consequently, this book represents an attempt to refocus social inquiry about economics, intimacy, and identity by melding the diverse debates for—and against—commodification in this wide range of contexts and intellectual communities. Bringing together new voices helped crystallize a growing critique of the existing commodification debate, on the grounds that

- the traditional debate misdescribes the commodified market sphere; and
- it also misdescribes the noncommodified spheres of family and intimacy.

Finally, by misdirecting our attention to the on-off question of whether or not to commodify, the traditional debate deflects attention away from more useful inquiries into the interactions between marketization proposals and the distribution of social power.

In the belief that the right tool is half the job, we hope that this book will help crystallize a new approach to commodification.

NOTES

1. Michael Finkel, *This Little Kidney Went to Market*, NY Times Magazine, May 27, 2001, at 26; Sara Corbett, *Baby Laundering: Where Do Babies Come*

From?, NY Times Magazine, June 16, 2002, at 44; Peter Landesman, *Sex Slaves on Main Street*, NY Times Magazine, Jan. 25, 2004, at 30. For examples of the far reach of markets, see Don Oldenburg, *Ringing Up Baby: Companies Yawned at Child Naming Rights, But Was It an Idea Ahead of Its Time?*, Wash. Post, Sept. 11, 2001; and Edward L. Andrews, *New Scale for Toting Up Lost Freedom vs. Security Would Measure in Dollars*, NY Times, Mar. 10, 2003, at A11. Academic investigations of commodification include Michael F. Brown, Who Owns Native Culture (2003) and Note, *The Price of Everything, The Value of Nothing: Reframing the Commodification Debate*, 117 Harv. L. Rev. 689 (2003).

2. Margaret Jane Radin, Contested Commodities 95 (1996), excerpted in this volume.

3. Merriam-Webster's Collegiate Dictionary 712 (10th ed. 1993).

4. Kevin Bales, Disposable People: New Slavery in the Global Economy 8–9 (1999); Landesman, *supra* note 1.

5. Igor Kopytoff, *The Cultural Biography of Things: Commoditization as Process, in* The Social Life of Things: Commodities in Cultural Perspective 68 (Arjun Appadurai, ed., 1986).

6. *See* Arjun Appadurai, *Introduction: Commodities and the Politics of Value, in* The Social Life of Things, supra note 5, excerpted in this volume.

7. *Id.* (quoting Marx 1971:48).

8. Merriam-Webster's Collegiate Dictionary, *supra* note 3, at 231–32).

9. U.C.C. §2-105 (2000).

10. *See, e.g.,* Colo. Rev. Stat. §13-22-104 (2001).

11. Edward J. Eberle, Dignity and Liberty: Constitutional Visions in Germany and the United States 16 (2002).

12. *See, e.g.,* Richard A. Posner, *Community and Conscription*, The New Republic, May 19, 2003, at 27, this volume.

13. Michael J. Sandel, *What Money Can't Buy: The Moral Limits of Markets*, excerpted in this volume.

14. Viviana A. Zelizer, *The Purchase of Intimacy*, 25 L & Soc. Inq. 817 (2000).

15. Elisabeth M. Landes & Richard A. Posner, *The Economics of the Baby Shortage*, 7 J. Leg. Stud. 323 (1978); Radin, Contested Commodities supra note 2, at 139, both excerpted in this volume.

16. Joan C. Williams, Unbending Gender 117–18 (2000), excerpted in this volume.

17. Joan C. Williams, *Is Coverture Dead? Beyond a New Theory of Alimony*, 82 Geo. L. J. 2227 (1994); Martha M. Ertman, *Commercializing Marriage: A Proposal for Valuing Women's Work Through Premarital Security Agreements*, 77 Tex. L. Rev. 17 (1998).

18. Martha M. Ertman, *Marriage as a Trade: Bridging the Private/Private Distinction*, 36 Harv. Civ. R.-Civ. Lib. L. Rev. 79 (2001).

19. We would like to thank Adrienne Davis, without whose partnership we could not have staged the workshop Identities, Intimacies, and Ca$h: Retheorizing Commodification, and the conference Commodification Futures, cosponsored by the Program on Gender, Work and Family at American University, Washington College of Law, and the University of Denver College of Law. Her insights were crucial to forming the structure of this book.

Introduction

The Subject and Object of Commodification

Margaret Jane Radin and Madhavi Sunder

In the latter part of the twentieth century, academic attention to commodification grew in response to increasing calls to turn over more and more of human life to the invisible hand of the market. Where some saw freedom in markets, others sensed despairing capitulation or inexorable dehumanization. Contrary to the liberatory economic rhetoric, the ability to sell anything and everything might—commodification theorists argued—prove ultimately disempowering. When this discourse entered the legal arena, the question was to what extent legal limits on commodification should exist. Commodification scholars focused our attention on the choices made, and consequences felt, of reducing aspects of our lives to market exchange.

Viewed this way, the topic of commodification is reduction of the person (subject) to a thing (object). Viewed in terms of society as a whole, the inquiry is who would be the subjects of commodification—controlling the terms of the sale—and who would be its objects—turned into mere commodities in a global trade? The answers to these crucial questions determine the distribution of wealth in society, and indeed throughout the world. They also determine how we conceive of ourselves (and others) as persons, and therefore bear deeply on the meaning of human life itself. Often, those whom commodification objectifies become entrenched as society's subordinated class.[1] Conversely, those who control the terms of commodification secure their position as society's ruling class. Market relations reflect, create, and reinforce social relations. But they are not the whole of those relations.

This book reveals the changing subject(s) and object(s) of commodification. It traces how the academic discourse evolved, both in its treatment of commodification as an academic topic (subject) of study and in its views of the purpose (object) of commodification, as well as how the discourse evolved in its views of the subject in a relationship of commodification (the owner) and the object in a relationship of commodification (the thing owned). The book begins by establishing a canon of commodification discourse. In legal academia, the marketplace finds its champions in Elisabeth Landes and Richard Posner, who modestly propose to assist childless couples through a free market in babies.[2] Scholars and courts resisted their approach, and the tendency of the Chicago school of economics to embrace an archetype of "universal commodification."[3] Court rulings in this volume range from declaring a surrogacy contract void for public policy reasons where a mother has contracted to sell her parental rights,[4] to denying one Mr. John Moore property ownership in his spleen and blood cells (although research doctors were free to profit from medical discoveries derived therefrom).[5]

The Thirteenth Amendment forms the backdrop of these cases. Our nation's long and bitter history of subjugating an entire racialized group of people to slavery offered a devastating critique of commodification—here, the reduction of persons to things. Indeed, the first wave of commodification scholars reminded us that human flourishing depends upon the *separation* of these two categories. Persons are harmed when they are, in whole or in part, commodified.[6] The harms of commodification take many forms—from dignitary to economic exploitation, from changes in people's material lives to changes in the discourse through which their self-conception is constructed and survives.

In the Information Age, knowledge, ideas, and culture are the hot commodities. Intellectual property is America's most important export. It is not surprising, then, that traditional knowledge and genetic resources in the developing world stand at the center of global struggles for control of these valuable resources.[7] Corporations mine everything from forests to medical patients for "raw materials" for their lucrative patents. Supermodel Christy Turlington, for example, offers Sundāri, a "collection of Ayurvedic-inspired luxury skin care products suited to meet the needs of contemporary women."[8]

Cyberspace intensifies the concerns of traditional commodification theorists.[9] From an economic perspective, the Internet deeply reduces the costs of transacting with others around the world. With the click of a mouse, individuals as far apart as Argentina and Zimbabwe can correspond and, perhaps what is more important, *trade* via sites such as eBay. Where search and information costs would have prohibited exchanges between such parties in the past, the Internet makes a truly global marketplace more possible and at the same time more valuable. Indeed, on the Internet nearly everything—from the eggs of female models[10] to mail order brides[11] and Nazi paraphernalia[12]—is posted for sale.[13]

The Canon: Economics and Cultural Studies

Debates over commodification have occurred primarily within two disciplinary frameworks: economics and cultural studies. Beginning with Gary Becker's work, the Chicago school of economics made a basic claim: everything is already commodified—exchanged in marketplaces for a price, even if that price exists only implicitly in the "shadows," not subject to discussion in the light of day.[14] But the Chicago economic view goes further yet, arguing (as a matter of utilitarian ethics) that explicit and universal commodification is *good,* and that efforts to prevent it through *legal* rules that prohibit the sale of certain goods and services are prima facie bad. To this end, Posner and Landes, seek (in the absence of market failures) unregulated markets in *everything*—even human babies.[15]

This argument for expanded laissez-faire markets is grounded in a defense of private culture. These Chicago school economists tend to view individual preferences as exogenous to the market and the market as merely a neutral mechanism for maximizing satisfaction of those preferences. Universal commodifiers trust the preexisting preferences of private actors (as expressed through supply, demand, and the resulting price structure) and distrust the paternalism of the state, which would seek to discipline those preferences. Markets, then, offer the mechanism through which culture is realized, by definition: culture is tastes and distastes expressed— or, as the Chicago school sees it, revealed—through markets.

When one of us (Radin) published *Market-Inalienability* in 1987, the apparent hegemony of the Chicago school's economic discourse in law was interrupted.[16] The paper criticized the use of economic categories and analytical procedures as the only language and medium through which to explain, organize, and make our world.[17] Questioning the moral neutrality of markets, it argued that the archetype of "universal commodification" is itself a "worldview"—a conceptual scheme—that, if left unchecked, might threaten to vitiate competing ways of understanding and creating our world. Focusing on the rhetoric of commodification, it reasoned that conceiving of and speaking of everything from sex to babies in the market terms of goods with exchange value would coarsen our world, slowly chipping away at the nonmonetizable aspects of life.[18] This is the feared corruptive influence of commodification. If everything that humans value becomes conceivable only in terms of gains from trade, human life as we now know it no longer can exist. The worry for legal theorists, moreover, is that without legal support for alternative conceptualizations, commodification of some important things of value could have a "domino effect"[19] on others, and overrun nonmarket cultures in which some parts of life—including love, babies, sex, and freedom—are not for sale.

Market-Inalienability also questioned the economic neutrality of markets. Markets affect the rich and the poor differently. The poor are more likely to be the sellers, and the rich, the buyers, of questionable commodities such as sexual services or body parts. Unequal distributions of wealth make the poorest in society, with little to offer in the marketplace, more likely to commodify themselves—their bodies for sex, their reproductive capabilities, their babies, and parental rights. Such "desperate exchanges"[20] raise moral and legal concerns about the coercive nature of markets, and challenge the economists' understanding of "voluntary" market transactions.[21] Notably, the article asked whether certain things should be "market-inalienable"—that is, aspects of life that may be given away but not sold in markets.[22] Thus, conventional wisdom would have it that while donations of human organs and an adoption regime for babies would be acceptable, free markets in organs and babies would not.

At the same time, *Market-Inalienability* recognized the way elites who use this reasoning are simply deepening the misery and powerlessness of those who have nowhere to turn but to attempted sales of their bodies. Pragmatically, the article asked whether foreclosing markets to the poorest in order to protect them and society in fact harms them even more by denying them a source of revenue. This was the "double bind" implicit in commodification controversies.[23]

Market-Inalienability formed the germ of a book, *Contested Commodities*.[24] The book goes further than the article, trying to conceptualize the indicia of commodification; the relationship between commodification, objectification, and subordination; and the consequences of commodifying politics and speech. In short, one of us (Radin) worried about the effects of commodification—or the denial thereof—on the poor but also about the effects of commodification on everyone, through the shifting understanding of human relationships it entailed.[25] Each of us has argued since then that the only way to make progress is to restructure the way we think about commodification so as not to let it polarize into these two views that are both unacceptable for the powerless.[26] That is, it is unacceptable for society to embrace commodification of aspects of the self when it is in practice the only avenue of survival for the powerless, and equally unacceptable for society to heap opprobrium and further oppression on those who try to create and enter such markets under those conditions.

Simultaneous to the legal and economic discourse on commodification, cultural studies theorists delved into the cultural significance of commodification. A volume edited by Arjun Appadurai published in 1986 sought to understand "The Social Life of Things."[27] How are cultures constituted through things, and in opposition to them? On the one hand, cultures seek to build communities of meaning through shared commodities. On the other hand, commodification—with its attendant homogeneity and fungibility of the commodified good or service—can work against the impulse of culture to differentiate.[28] France seeks to rebuff Hollywood by legislating local media content rules. Towns seek to preserve their local character by zoning out McDonalds. Wal-Mart chills the blood of local shopkeepers the world over. India kicks out Coca-Cola in favor of domestic drinks (though two decades later Coca-Cola is back, and now the owner of the local competition).

This view of culture and commodities in *opposition*—with culture as a differentiating impulse and commodification as a homogenizing one—evokes a deeper tension between meaning and markets. Under one view, commodification aids culture-building—individuals express and create commonality through markets. Under another view, markets strip away local meanings and contexts, universalizing a good and making it common, rather than unique. And when global markets are controlled by powerful, Western corporations, their universalizing goods and services overrun local ones: cultural and market imperialism converge. And yet, placing cultural commodities outside the market by declaring them sacrosanct can also impede cultural evolution. As Appadurai warns, "enclaving" cultural resources—controlling culture through select guardians of culture—favors the powerful members of society.[29] Thus, these scholars, too, highlighted the potential ill effects of both commodification and non-commodification.

The sociologist Viviana Zelizer offered another important contribution to the cultural understanding of commodification during this time. In her 1985 book *Pricing the Priceless Child: The Changing Social Value of Children,* Zelizer showed that, contrary to the writings of Becker and other economists, children over time were perceived less and less as commodities with exchange value and more and more as "priceless."[30] Zelizer's findings challenged the "domino theory"—she argued that markets do not overrun cultures but, rather, are themselves defied and influenced by culture.[31]

Emergent Voices: Compensation and Control

In the two decades since these foundational works surfaced, the subject and object of commodification have taken a distinctly cultural turn.

What might broadly be called a "cultural studies" approach animates much of the new commodification scholarship published herein. Cultural studies theorists observe the circulation of peoples, capital, and commodities in an age characterized by globalization, liberalization, the Internet, mass markets, and increasing freedom of movement.[32] Above all, the cultural studies approach centers on the production and circulation of "meanings" in modern society, markets, and culture.[33] For these scholars, commodification and culture are indelibly linked. The cultural study of "commodities in motion"[34] focuses on the changing meaning of the commodity as it passes through various local and global circuits, including markets. Cultural studies theorists argue that, in many cases, individual agents—and not just the hegemonic market—control those meanings. Thus, commodities are in motion both literally and figuratively. As they pass through various physical spaces, they also undergo semiotic changes.

Like the approach of commodification scholars who came before,[35] this approach is postmodern in that it is skeptical of the binary and totalizing categories of traditional Western theory (e.g., commodified versus noncommodified, gift versus sale, market versus family, material versus spiritual). The new commodification scholars intensify the claim that "[t]hese oppositions parody both poles and reduce human diversities artificially."[36] That is, the diverse and shifting cultural life of things is an expression of human life, not its rejection.

But the new theorists perhaps go further with this observation than the original commodification critics did, arguing that the unstable meanings of commodities make them potentially or actually liberating, and not just potentially or actually subjugating. A central claim animating many of these papers is that moral agents are not the mere victims of commodification and markets. Far from it, they can—and do—appropriate the chains that bind them.

Take a few examples. Madonna Ciccone appropriates female sexuality but retains cultural and market dominance.[37] African Americans market their own holiday, Kwanzaa, during the heavily commercial Christmas season.[38] Lesbians make babies by buying sperm on an open market.[39] American women pay for romance in Latin America.[40] Female sex workers in the United States increasingly set the terms of the trade.[41] Indigenous peoples seek royalties for others' use of their native symbols and remedies.[42]

A new age of freedom through commodification, or what Appadurai has termed "commodity resistance"?[43] According to some, yes. Read as a whole, the essays in the latter half of this volume suggest an emerging new conception of human flourishing itself: today, demands for equality include a right to compensation and control in the world's markets. This market-liberationist rhetoric hearkens back to old-style market liberationism. The question is if—and how—they are different. On the one hand, this contemporary liberationist claim may be more consonant with changes in our understanding of rights elsewhere. For example, in the international human rights field, we have witnessed a similar shift from first-generation rights—civil and political rights to speech and political participation—to second-generation rights—namely, social and economic rights.

On the other hand, the focus on commodification as a means to social and economic parity is more controversial. Early commodification theorists recognized that poor and disempowered peoples are more likely to engage in "desperate exchanges." Taking a pragmatic approach to such situations, ideal theory (leaning toward inalienability of personal attributes) may have to give way to nonideal theory, allowing for some commodification in certain, regulated exchanges.

But thinking that commodification is sometimes strategically necessary is different from the normative claims to commodify that we hear in the latter half of this volume. Where early commodification theorists may have viewed commodification as nonideal but necessary, many of the emergent commodification theorists see freedom itself in the ability to commodify. The worry here is that the poor have neither the ability nor the right to commodify. Thus, the role of law is quite different in this new context: rather than calling on law to *regulate* trades, many authors in this volume seek law to *facilitate* trades, in everything from sex work to sperm to indigenous intellectual property. Again, the underlying theme of these commodification authors is welcoming commodification—more commodification can mean more *equality,* not inequality.[44]

Here is where we begin to see the changing discourse of commodification more clearly. The new commodification scholarship is focused less on the traditional object (in the sense of objectification) of commodification: it does not dwell on women, blacks, gays, and the victims of the market; nor does it suppose that the only object (in the sense of purpose) of commodification is subordination. To the contrary, the object of commodification can be liberty and equality, and the feared objectification can be discounted, they contend. Indeed, whether this is possible depends on the subject of commodification, that is, on who controls the terms of the sale and the meaning of the exchange.

So are the new commodification theorists liberal laissez-faire apologists in new garb? Politically, at least, they do not see themselves in the same camp as the Chicago school economists.[45] But just how different they are from traditional free-market liberals is a question calling for investigation. Does the focus on control and compensation require further structuring by law? Or will laissez-faire markets be preferred? The answers, this book reveals, differ by author and context.

One thing is certain. Early on, one of us (Radin) called for a nuanced, case-by-case analysis of commodification as it shifts in culture and in time. The new commodification theorists have taken up this task with insight and vigor.

Agency, Meaning, and the "Multivalent" Commodity

Williams and Zelizer's contribution to this volume exemplifies the "cultural studies" approach to commodification. Williams and Zelizer reject Michael Walzer's "separate spheres" view of the commodified and non-commodified worlds as distinct,[46] and the "hostile worlds" view that "when such separate spheres come into contact they contaminate each other."[47] "Instead of living in segregated spheres, people participate in networks of social relations that span a variety of settings," they write. "They manage different ties simultaneously rather than moving from one sealed chamber to another."[48] Destabilizing the traditional categories, Williams and Zelizer write that "many market transactions have elements of emotion and sociability, and . . . many intimate transactions have economic dimensions." Teemu Ruskola makes a similar observation in his comparative study of Chinese clan corporations.[49] Carol Rose describes a reality in which categorizations dissolve so that gift-giving may be understood as market exchange, or worse, theft.[50]

All of the above offer concrete examples of what Miranda Joseph terms the "multivalent commodity"[51]—the idea that any given object has multiple meanings—sometimes commodified, sometimes noncommodified, and sometimes both—depending upon the context. This concept questions the hegemony of a hostile worlds or domino theory,[52] which perceives the commodified world as threatening the existence of the noncommodified world. Zelizer argues that many commodities are in fact able to retain their multiple meanings. Ann Lucas agrees, arguing in her chapter that "commodified and noncommodified sexuality can coexist."[53] Deborah Stone, too, suggests that the market does not denigrate care work, either, but bureaucracy does—through the loss of agency on the part of the care worker.[54] These contributions suggest that, increasingly, the central issue of commodification is who has the power to control the meaning of the commodity. As Regina Austin writes in her chapter on the black holiday Kwanzaa, "Commodification per se is not the problem . . . the real struggle is over the meaning that is embedded in" black cultural objects.[55]

Controlling the meaning of commodification is where agency, another foundational concept in cultural studies, comes in. Writing about female sex workers, Ann Lucas rejects arguments for criminalizing prostitution as paternalistic, contending that female prostitutes have much more agency than they are perceived to have. For Lucas, the harm of commodifying sex work is neither its effect on noncommodified[56] sex relationships (i.e., the "domino theory") nor the immorality of such a trade.[57] That is, what matters is not the sale but the autonomy of the seller. Legalizing prostitution, she argues, would have the beneficial effect of reducing forced sex work and enhancing sex workers' autonomy.[58] Martha Nussbaum similarly urges that autonomy, not morality, should be at the center of our consideration of prostitution's future.[59]

Highlighting the mere presence of agency and multivalent meanings, however, is not to say that the market does not matter. As Miranda Joseph writes herein, while the market is not destiny, we must nonetheless be vigilantly conscious of how it shapes us.[60] Surely there must be some contexts—perhaps pornography?—in which the emergent writers would agree that commodification affects the noncommodified commitments of human value that we feel must be maintained. While the postmodern resistance to the idea of the market as a totalizing, hegemonic force among the emergent voices is strong, scholars must also contend with existing material and social inequalities that reinforce dominant meanings over subversive ones. In such contexts, laissez-faire markets will often entrench further existing structures of domination. Thus, while the two of us agree that contested meanings exist, we disagree that we can take the plurality of meanings for granted.[61] Without more, market forces threaten to wipe out noncommodified understandings of the world that many of us hold dear.[62] Thus, regulatory approaches facilitating autonomy of sellers and a plurality of meanings may go further toward achieving both liberty and equality.

Commodification and Subordination

But the optimism of the emergent authors should not be mistaken for naiveté. Having studied the lessons of their predecessors, they, too, recognize commodification's dangers. To this end, their work continues to ask an important question: What is the relationship between commodification, objectification, and subordination?[63]

Whether the formerly dispossessed who become owners of new commodities will exercise power in the same old ways remains to be seen. Tanya Hernández is concerned that the predominantly white, Western female sex tourist market subordinates poor, Third World men who are the objects of the women's desire.[64] Here we have an apparent case of equality for women: they can wield a power that has previously belonged to men, achieved through commodification, objectification, and subordination premised on differences of race and class. At the same time, Hernández suggests that the Third World men, too, have power—and perhaps even more power—than do the women in these trades. At first glance, female sex tourism appears to subvert traditional gender relations, figuratively if not literally putting the "women on top." But in fact, Hernández argues, these relationships ultimately exploit and reinscribe traditional gender relationships, rather than subvert them: The male locals make the women feel powerful by making them feel *feminine*.[65] The female tourists, in turn, accord the men power by giving them sex.[66] Interestingly, Hernández describes how the male sex workers attempt to avoid the "feminization" of their identities by recasting "their activities within a masculine narrative."[67] Commodification, she argues, leads to a "staged authenticity" of reified—not subversive—gender relations.[68] Hernández calls this view of women's equality "disquieting."[69]

Others are self-consciously critical of the by-products of commodification but, as nonideal theorists would recommend, argue that the good may outweigh the bad. Ertman, for example, is concerned that white lesbians buying male sperm may be enriching themselves at others' expense. She is not sympathetic to the male donors (like Hernández, she believes they are in the driver's seat because of traditional gender hierarchies).[70] Rather, Ertman worries, as does Patricia Williams in the earlier part of this volume,[71] that white lesbians will "prefer" white babies—and thereby reinforce traditional *racial* hierarchies.[72] Here, the problem is not commodification per se but, rather, the failure to regulate or temper private preferences. At the same time, Ertman points out that markets offer an important vehicle for the expression of what she calls "good" preferences that the more conservative state may otherwise disallow (e.g., adoption and parenting by gays).[73] The question arises, then, whether all private preferences—à la Landes and Posner—ought to be allowed, and not just what she terms "good" ones.

While individuals may come out differently on these questions, and for different reasons (some propelled by "pragmatic" concerns, others by "equality," and still others by "liberty"), there is an important point of commonality among most of the authors in this volume. Early commodification scholarship worried about commodification when "[r]elationships between people are disguised as relationships between commodities, which appear to be governed by abstract market forces."[74] But the new authors keep a concern about social relations at the forefront of their analyses. In essay after essay, they ask whether the liberating aspects of commodification can be harnessed without releasing commodification's subordinating impulses. Some of them think, in certain specific temporal and cultural contexts, that the answer, at least provisionally, is yes.

Culture as Commodity

Another central insight of this volume is that economic empowerment and cultural empowerment are indelibly linked.[75] As Salman Rushdie has observed, "[T]hose who do not have power over the story that dominates their lives, power to retell it, rethink it, deconstruct it, joke about it, and change it as times change, truly are powerless. . . ."[76] This is the essence of what Appadurai means when he calls commodities political. Controlling culture—the arena through which we represent ourselves—is essential for attaining power. For better or worse, markets are a primary means of distributing and debating cultural representations. Thus, cultural control requires some market control.

This is an important new turn in progressive theorizing; many progressives have previously resisted the commodification of culture, worried in particular about the appropriation of cultural forms and knowledge by outsiders. But the new authors deploy commodification as a strategy for both economic and cultural growth. Regina Austin's contribution best exemplifies this approach. Austin describes the frustration in the black community when white artists (from yesterday's Elvis and Benny Goodman to today's Eminem) appropriate black cultural forms for profit.[77] For Austin, economic empowerment for blacks depends upon their reclaiming market control of their cultural representations.[78]

Significantly, Austin is concerned not just about the loss of compensation but also about the misrepresentation of black culture. Commodification of black culture by whites, she writes, is a form of "mummification"—it freezes black culture and reifies it into artificial forms, creating a "staged authenticity" that threatens the organic, dynamic nature of black culture.[79] In contrast, Austin is optimistic about commodification of black culture by African Americans in the form of the holiday Kwanzaa. Austin recognizes the corrupting influence of markets. She observes, for example, hip-hop's tendency toward a misogynist, homophobic, and crassly materialistic culture.

But Kwanzaa offers a model for good commodification, Austin argues. To begin with, she is not troubled by the fact that Kwanzaa is a "made up" holiday, invented by African Americans in recent times. While some would call the holiday inauthentic, Austin believes the invention illustrates the dynamism of culture, and how the African American diaspora appropriates and changes traditional cultures to suit its own needs.

Austin's contribution highlights the political importance of commodities. Black control of culture enhances both the economy and the dignity of the community. Through the production and distribution of Kwanzaa, African Americans, now the *subjects* of commodification, wrest some compensation for their work and, perhaps more important, cultural and market control, from their commodifying counterparts.

At the same time, we may do well to think about commodity resistance *and its limits*. Vesting control over cultural representations in particular communities raises difficult questions. Which members of a community will exercise such rights? How will dissenters within the community fare?[80] In a multicultural, diasporic world, how do we define the relevant community?[81] How will we decide who is "inside" or "outside" a community? How do we best resolve the inherent tension between intellectual property rights in culture and freedom of speech? Dereka Rushbrook's contribution critically assessing queerness as "an object of consumption" raises other important concerns.[82] Consuming common material objects, and even gay "spaces" in cities, is central to the development of a gay identity, as well as an acceptance of gays among cosmopolitan, chic nongays, Rushbrook writes.[83] But paradoxically, commodified gay identity may ultimately vitiate gay community and political activism, Rushbrook argues, once gay is reduced to a mere commodity for the consumption of all rather than a living, dynamic community.[84] bell hooks expresses yet another concern about "eating the other": the insatiable hunger for stories and images of the Other.[85] Commentators make similar arguments about the new hit reality TV show *Queer Eye for the Straight Guy*, which features five gay men (the "Fab 5") who make over "frumpy" straight men and win the hearts of American TV viewers along the way.[86] While some worry that the show symbolizes how "gay people have become complicit in their own oppression"[87] others rejoice that the show has endeared gay men to the American public at a time when the issues of gay marriage and gay bishops are front and center in public debates.[88]

The existence of these questions and concerns do not, by themselves, counsel against cultural commodification. Rather, they remind us that the goal is not commodification or noncommodification, per se, but rather, the "semiotic democracy" that Rushdie describes—that is, a world in which all individuals and groups have rights to make their cultural worlds. On that score, we see many successes, from the 1998 movie *Smoke Signals*, which was written, directed, and coproduced by Native

Americans,[89] to the 2002 black independent film *Barbershop*,[90] and the 2003 surprise hit *Bend It Like Beckham,* directed by a diasporic Indian filmmaker.[91]

Cultural theory helps us to see better these cultural commodities as means of economic and cultural resistance. It highlights cultures—and commodities—as interrelated, dynamic, and tainted rather than pure. In short, commodified culture is culture nonetheless.

Culture and Markets

This volume's interdisciplinary account of the changing subject and object of commodification—bringing together both economic and cultural theorists under the same roof—helps to deconstruct both markets and culture, separately, and to reconstruct them in relation to one another.

Culture is a paradox. In the modern world today we more and more hear claims to "rights" to culture. Indeed, despite globalization and the liberalization of choice the world over, modern individuals want and demand cultural community. At the same time, we wish to avoid the constraining aspects of culture. Stated differently, we prefer the roots that culture affords yet at the same time want to be able to spread our wings and be free.[92]

Markets evince a similar paradox. Some theorists herein, in the spirit of traditional liberalism, recognize our need for markets and their liberating aspects. At the same time, the authors caution against the market's constraining features, asking: Do markets really afford freedom or just the appearance of it? How do markets alienate us from our communities[93] and reduce us to cultural caricatures—that is, branded things rather than peoples?[94] Property rights in cultural intangibles such as Native stories or Kwanzaa raise other troubling concerns. If, as Salman Rushdie writes, freedom lies in being able "to have power over the story that dominates their lives, power to retell it, rethink it, deconstruct it, joke about it, and change it as times change," do not property rights in cultural ideas prevent others—cultural outsiders, despised members of the culture, and new generations—from accessing the very resources they need to be free? To be sure, such concerns animate the crucial balances struck in traditional intellectual property laws in the United States (from disfavoring moral rights to allowing for "fair use" of otherwise protected material), which help to wrest control from a select few guardians of culture.

What emerges, then, from these pages is a more nuanced understanding of the effects of too much—and too little—commodification on both culture and markets. Too much protection of cultures through commodification can lead to cultural ossification and mummification (by cultural outsiders as well as insiders). Too little protection, however, can make cultures too unstable, the easy prey of Western corporate culture or control by others. In the same vein we hear that inalienability of some resources—from traditional knowledge to the genetic resources in our own bodies—could reinforce social relations in which some are the privileged holders of property and others the mere suppliers of "raw materials."[95] In this view markets might facilitate cultural democracy (making the goods available to all). Going further, commodification might spur cultural *change*.

At the same time, reinscribing the doctrines of traditional liberalism is not the answer. As the Great Mahele in Hawaii illustrated, private property rights may impoverish, not enrich, a community coerced by economic circumstance to sell away all of its rights to the highest (usually white and Western) bidder.[96] While history cannot foreclose options today and tomorrow, it does remind us that commodification remains a nonideal approach in a context of inequality. The continuing challenge, then, for commodification theorists is to find a way to express the human needs for freedom and flexibility outside the terms of contract and markets, as well as within them.[97]

Commodification's Present and Future

The changing subjects and objects of commodification unfold between these pages as they do in our increasingly complex world. As this book goes to press, an administrator at the University of California, Los Angeles has been arrested for allegedly stealing and selling body parts of cadavers donated to the university's medical school.[98] And the *New York Times* follows its reporter's purchase of freedom of two teenage girls who had been sold into sexual slavery in Cambodia. Tragically, in a world with ever-widening gaps between the haves and have nots, commodification of human beings—indeed, even human slavery[99]—persists. In Cambodia today men buy sex with girls for as little as $3,[100] while expressing a "preference" for virgins, who command prices ranging from $500 to $1,000.[101] The girls are ensnarled in a chain of commodification: first, they are often commodified by their families, sold to brothels out of desperation; the brothel owner commodifies them in turn.

It is unsurprising that the freedom of these girls, too, can be purchased. Indeed, the *New York Times* reporter "bought" the freedom of two girl sex workers for as little as $200 a person.[102] A happy ending for commodification? Perhaps. But as the essays—old and new—in this volume make too clear, commodification exists within a complicated cultural and economic landscape. In truth, the subject of commodification is an unfinished story, just as the story of these girls remains to be told. At the time of this writing, after she had been reunited with her family, one of the two girls had returned to the brothels.

But the failure of commodity resistance to "answer" her plight is not the only reason the reporter's "purchase" feels not quite right. The Nature Conservancy raises funds to purchase land to protect it from development—the perfect act of commodification to protect the object of the commodification. Imagine now an analogous organization—a nongovernmental organization for sex workers, raising funds to purchase the freedom of girls in the Third World. The essays in this volume push us to understand better why we are disturbed by such a league.

The commodification of rights is particularly troubling. If a girl's freedom can be purchased, her freedom can also be sold. The very existence of a group purchasing the freedom of girls makes a market for girls, perhaps encouraging the very thing it is intended to eliminate. The Declaration of Independence guarantees that the rights to "life, liberty, and the pursuit of happiness" are inalienable.[103] But our connection to this foundation seems to have become unhinged. More and more public rights to speech, equality, and access—once guaranteed through the traditional law of intellectual property—are becoming alienable today, through the combined regimes of technology, property, and contract.[104]

At the same time, the optimistic stories of agency and contested meanings herein hearten us. They show that resistance to the hegemonic market is not only possible but sometimes an empirical reality; that is, that markets may not be as hegemonic as they seem. Indeed, the optimism of the new commodification theory—more so than its postmodern deconstruction—may be precisely what makes this approach progressive. We cannot be progressive if we do not have some optimism—that we can get from here (not so good) to there (better). Of course, the way we conceptualize the here and the there are intertwined and interdependent. Also, the transition is important—how idealistic can we be and still make progress rather than going nowhere—or worse, going backward? But if we are not idealistic enough we can cement current structures, naturalizing them. And as one of us (Sunder) has written, reform from within is normatively important; it is the process through which we claim a home in the world.[105] In sum, we are hopeful that the approaches outlined in this volume—nonideal and optimistic—just may work, but we should recognize that they always harbor a potential for backlash. Commodification remains a two-edged sword, even while its meaning is continually evolving and being transformed, both by actions and relations in the world and by the discourse of those who observe and theorize about them —the writers in this volume.

NOTES

1. See Margaret Jane Radin, Contested Commodities 154–63 (1996).

2. See Elizabeth M. Landes & Richard A. Posner, *The Economics of the Baby Shortage*, 7 J. Leg. Stud. 323 (1978). *Cf.* Kenneth J. Arrow, *Invaluable Goods*, XXXV J. of Econ. Lit. 757–765 (June 1997) (reviewing Margaret Jane Radin, Contested Commodities (1996)) (implying that Landes and Posner do not reflect economists as a whole).

3. Radin, Contested Commodities, *supra* note 1, at 2.

4. *In re* Baby M, 537 A.2d 1227 (N.J. 1988). *Cf.* Johnson v. Calvert, 19 Cal. Rptr. 2d 494 (1993).

5. Moore v. Regents of Univ. of Cal., 793 P.2d 479, 497 (Cal. 1990).

6. See Anita L. Allen, *Slavery and Surrogacy, in* Subjugation and Bondage: Critical Essays on Slavery and Social Philosophy 229–254 (Tommy L. Lott ed., 1998).

7. See Madhavi Sunder, *Property in Personhood*, this volume.

8. *About Sundāri, at* http://www.sundari.com/about_frameset.cfm (last visited Feb. 27, 2004).

9. See Margaret Jane Radin, *Incomplete Commodification in the Computerized World, in* The Commodification of Information (Niva Elkin-Koren & Neil Weinstock Netanel eds., 2002). See also Sunder, *Property in Personhood*, this volume.

10. See http://www.ronsangels.com/index2.html (last visited Feb. 20, 2004).

11. See, e.g., http://www.bridesbymail.com/ (last visited Feb. 20, 2004); http://www.goodwife.com/ (last visited Feb. 20, 2004).

12. See Yahoo! Inc. v. La Ligue Contre Le Racisme et L'Antisemitisme, 169 F. Supp.2d 1181, 1184 (N.D. Cal. 2001).

13. See, e.g., Michael L. Rustad, *Private Enforcement of Cybercrime on the*

Electronic Frontier, 11 S. Cal. Interdisc. L.J. 63, 100–101 (2001) (discussing the sale of kidneys on eBay); Brian J. Caveney, *Going, Going, Gone . . . The Opportunities and Legal Pitfalls of Online Surgical Auctions,* 103 W. Va. L. Rev. 591, 593 (2001) (discussing eBay's sale of drug-free urine).

14. Gary Stanley Becker, The Economic Approach to Human Behavior (1978).

15. See Elisabeth M. Landes and Richard A. Posner, *The Economics of the Baby Shortage,* 7 J. Leg. Stud. 323 (1978).

16. Margaret Jane Radin, *Market-Inalienability,* 100 Harv. L. Rev. 1849 (1987). The article was upsetting to some, and it was unclear whether the oversimplified schematic of universal commodification was something economists wanted to uphold or defend against. I (Radin) recall that my esteemed mentor, Mike Levine, came to my office after receiving the manuscript, and argued passionately both that he wasn't a universal commodifier and that there is nothing wrong with universal commodification. For some time I have been convinced that my most useful scholarly contribution is likely to be having made the word "commodification" speakable in legal academic discourse.

17. *Id.* at 1851.

18. *Id.* at 1918–1919.

19. *Id.* at 1914.

20. Michael Walzer, Spheres of Justice 100–103 (1983).

21. See Radin, Contested Commodities, *supra* note 1, at 154. *Cf.* Martha C. Nussbaum, *Taking Money for Bodily Services,* J. of Legal Studies 693, 723 (Jan. 1998).

22. *Compare* Guido Calabresi & A. Douglas Melamed, *Property Rules, Liability Rules, and Inalienability, One View of the Cathedral,* 85 Harv. L. Rev. 1089 (1972) *with* Radin, *Market-Inalienability, supra* note 16, at 1851.

23. Radin, Contested Commodities, *supra* note 1, at 124.

24. See *Id.*

25. See Radin, *Market-Inalienability, supra* note 16, at 1945–1946.

26. Radin, Contested Commodities, *supra* note 1, at 102–114; Margaret Jane Radin, *The Pragmatist and the Feminist,* 63 S. Cal. L. Rev. 1699 (1990); Sunder, *Property in Personhood,* this volume; Anupam Chander & Madhavi Sunder, *The Romance of the Public Domain,* 92 Cal. L. Rev. (forthcoming 2004).

27. See Arjun Appadurai, *Introduction: Commodities and the Politics of Value, in* The Social Life of Things: Commodities in Cultural Perspective 3 (Arjun Appadurai, ed., 1986).

28. See Igor Kopytoff, *The Cultural Biography of Things: Commoditization as Process, in* The Social Life of Things: Commodities in Cultural Perspective (Arjun Appadurai, ed., 1986).

29. See Appadurai, *supra* note 27, at 25.

30. Joan Williams & Viviana Zelizer, *To Commodify or Not to Commodify: That Is Not the Question,* this volume.

31. *Id.*

32. See generally Cary Nelson et al., *Cultural Studies: An Introduction, in* Cultural Studies (Lawrence Grossberg et al. eds., 1992); Richard Johnson, *What Is Cultural Studies, Anyway?,* 16 Social Text 38 (Winter 1986/87); John Fiske, *Cultural Studies and the Culture of Everyday Life, in* Cultural Studies 154 (Lawrence Grossberg et al. eds., 1992).

33. Claudia Strauss & Naomi Quinn, A Cognitive Theory of Cultural Meaning 5 (1997) (quoting Ulf Hannerz, Cultural Complexity: Studies in the Social Organization of Meaning (1992)). *See also* Clifford Geertz, The Interpretation of Cultures 5 (1973).

34. Appadurai, *supra* note 27, at 16.

35. See, e.g., Radin, Contested Commodities, *supra* note 1, at 102–114.

36. Appadurai, *supra* note 27, at 13.

37. Cf. Duncan Kennedy, Sexy Dressing Etc. 192–208 (1993).

38. Regina Austin, *Kwanzaa and the Commodification of Black Culture,* this volume.

39. Martha M. Ertman, *What's Wrong with a Parenthood Market?,* this volume.

40. Tanya Hernández, *Sex in the [Foreign] City: Commodification and the Female Sex Tourist,* this volume.

41. Ann Lucas, *The Currency of Sex: Prostitution, Law, and Commodification,* this volume.

42. Sarah Harding, *Culture, Commodification, and Native American Cultural Patrimony,* this volume; Madhavi Sunder, *Property in Personhood,* this volume.

43. Appadurai, *supra* note 27, at 30.

44. Williams & Zelizer, *supra* note 30.

45. Ertman, *supra* note 39.

46. Michael Walzer, *Spheres of Justice* (1983), this volume. For a different critique of Walzer's "separate spheres" model, see Radin, Contested Commodities, *supra* note 1, at 46.

47. Williams & Zelizer, *supra* note 30.

48. *Id.*

49. Teemu Ruskola, *Home Economics: What Is the Difference between a Family and a Corporation?,* this volume.

50. Carol M. Rose, *Giving, Trading, Thieving, and Trusting: How and Why Gifts Become Exchanges, and (More Importantly) Vice Versa,* 44 Fla. L. Rev. 295 (1992), this volume.

51. See Miranda Joseph, *The Multivalent Commodity: On the Supplementarity of Value and Values,* this volume.

52. See Radin, Contested Commodities, *supra* note 1, at 101 (asking whether the domino theory is in fact true); see *id.* at 102–114.

53. Lucas, *supra* note 41.

54. Deborah Stone, *For Love nor Money: The Commodification of Care*, this volume.

55. Austin, *supra* note 38.

56. We use this word noting that a realm of pure, noncommodified sex likely does not exist; that is, noncommodified sex relationships may not actually be all that noncommodified.

57. Lucas, *supra* note 41.

58. *Id.*

59. See Martha C. Nussbaum, *Taking Money for Bodily Services*, 27 J. of Legal Studies 693, 723 (1998), this volume.

60. See Joseph, *supra* note 51.

61. See Radin, Contested Commodities, *supra* note 1, at 120–122; Madhavi Sunder, *Piercing the Veil*, 112 Yale L. J. 1399, 1466–1471 (2003).

62. Radin, Contested Commodities, *supra* note 1, at 223.

63. See generally *id.* at 154–163.

64. Hernández, *supra* note 40.

65. *Id.*

66. *Id.*

67. *Id.*

68. *Id.*

69. *Id.*

70. Ertman, *supra* note 39.

71. Patricia J. Williams, *In Search of Pharaoh's Daughter, in* The Rooster's Egg: The Persistence of Prejudice (1995), this volume.

72. Ertman, *supra* note 39.

73. *Id.*

74. Radin, *Market-Inalienability, supra* note 16, at 1873.

75. See, e.g., Williams & Zelizer, *supra* note 30.

76. Salman Rushdie, *Excerpts from Rushdie's Address: 1,000 Days 'Trapped Inside a Metaphor,'* N.Y. Times, Dec. 12, 1991, at B8 (excerpts from speech delivered at Columbia University).

77. As the white rapper, Eminem, happily sings of how he makes his living:
Though I'm not the first king of controversy
I am the worst thing since Elvis Presley
To do Black Music so selfishly
And use it to get myself wealthy
Hey, there's a concept that works[.]
Eminem, "Without Me," on *The Eminem Show* (Aftermath Records 2002), available at http://homepage.ntlworld.com/alan.stuart/music/uslyrics/withoutm.html.

78. Austin lauds Kwanzaa because it is about blacks "building [their] own businesses" and "control[ling] the economics of [their] community." Kwanzaa "accepts the market as a site of conflict and recognizes that if blacks do not compete and consume, they will die." Austin concludes that creating and controlling markets is necessary for blacks to break "the economic and social bonds of white supremacy." Austin, *supra* note 38.

79. *Id.*

80. Madhavi Sunder, *Cultural Dissent,* 54 Stan. L. Rev. 495 (2001).

81. Madhavi Sunder, *Intellectual Property and Identity Politics: Playing with Fire,* 4 J. Gender Race & Just. 69 (2000).

82. Dereka Rushbrook, *Cities and Queer Space: Staking a Claim to Global Cosmopolitanism,* this volume.

83. *Id.*

84. *Id.*

85. bell hooks, *Eating the Other: Desire and Resistance,* this volume.

86. Anne Neville, *Fashion Police Meet the Frumpy,* Buffalo News, Mar. 5, 2004, at B1.

87. Christopher Kelly, *Gay TV Making Great Strides in Exactly the Wrong Direction,* Miami Herald, Aug. 26, 2003. *See also* Josh Ferris, *Gay Presence in the Media Helpful, Stereotypes Harmful,* Pitt News, Dec. 4, 2003; Neil Steinberg, *Closer Look at "Queer Eye" Reveals An Ugly Stereotype,* Chicago Sun-Times, Oct. 10, 2003, at 24; Lisa de Moraes, *The TV Column,* Wash Post, July 9, 2003.

88. See David Teather, *Gay Team Flings TV Closet Door Wide Open: A Hit Reality Show Seems to be Changing Attitudes to Homosexuality on American TV. Is This the Dawn of a New Era?,* The Guardian, Aug. 11, 2003, at 5.

89. See Timothy Egan, *An Indian Without Reservations,* NY Times, Jan. 18, 1988, at 16.

90. See, e.g., *'Barbershop' Attacked by Reverend Jesse Jackson,* available at http://www.mtv.com/news/articles/1457788/09252002/ice_cube.jhtml (last visited Jan. 8, 2004) (describing the Reverend Jesse Jackson's outrage at the film's critical and comical discussion of such black luminaries as Martin Luther King, Jr., Rosa Parks, and Jackson himself). Lead actor Ice Cube responded, "Just because we talk about people doesn't mean we don't love these people too." *Id.*

91. *Bend It Like Beckham* (Twentieth Century Fox 2003). See also *Fire* (New Yorker Pictures 2000) (highlighting lesbian relationship within middle-class Indian family); *Monsoon Wedding* (Universal Studios 2003) (exploring theme of sexual abuse by family members in Indian family).

92. See generally Sunder, *Cultural Dissent, supra* note 87, at 499.

93. Michael J. Sandel, *What Money Can't Buy: The Moral Limits of Markets,* this volume.

94. Alexandra Chasin, Selling Out: The Gay and Lesbian Movement Goes to Market (2001), this volume.

95. See Appadurai, *supra* note 27, at 25.

96. See generally Sally Engle Merry, Law and Empire in the Pacific: Fiji and Hawaii (2003).

97. Radin, Contested Commodities, *supra* note 1, at 62.

98. *Head of UCLA Cadaver Program Is Arrested,* Mar. 7, 2004, available at http://news.yahoo.com/news?tmpl=story2&cid=519&u=/ap/20040307/ap_on_ re_us/body_p... (last visited Mar. 7, 2004).

99. Nicholas D. Kristof, *Loss of Innocence,* N.Y. Times, Jan. 28, 2004, at A25.

100. *Id.*

101. Nicholas D. Kristof, *Stopping the Traffickers,* N.Y. Times, Jan. 31, 2004, at A17.

102. *Id.*

103. The Declaration of Independence para. 2 (U.S. 1776).

104. See Margaret Jane Radin, *Regulation by Contract, Regulation by Machine,* 160 J. Instit. & Theoretical Econ. 1 (2004).

105. See Sunder, *Cultural Dissent, supra* note 80, at 551.

PART I

Classic Texts of Commodification Theory

A.

Definitions
Commodity and Commodification

Commodities and the Politics of Value

Arjun Appadurai[1]

Economic exchange creates value. Value is embodied in commodities that are exchanged. Focusing on the things that are exchanged, rather than simply on the forms or functions of exchange, makes it possible to argue that what creates the link between exchange and value is *politics,* construed broadly. This argument justifies the conceit that commodities, like persons, have social lives.

* * *

The Spirit of the Commodity

If my argument holds water, it will follow that it is definitionally useful to regard commodities as existing in a very wide variety of societies (though with a special intensity and salience in modern, capitalist societies).

Marx's own reanalysis of the concept of commodity was a central part of his critique of bourgeois political economy and a fulcrum for the transition from his own earlier thought[2] on capitalism to the full-fledged analysis of *Capital.* Today, the conceptual centrality of the idea of commodity has given way to the neoclassical, marginalist conception of "goods," and the word "commodity" is used in neoclassical economics only to refer to a special subclass of primary goods and no longer plays a central analytic role. [I]n most modern analyses of economy (outside anthropology), the meaning of the term commodity has narrowed to reflect only one part of the heritage of Marx and the early political economists. That is, in most contemporary uses, commodities are special kinds of manufactured goods (or services), which are associated only with capitalist modes of production and are thus to be found only where capitalism has penetrated.

Yet it is clear that this is to draw on only one strand in Marx's own understanding of the nature of the commodity.

* * *

[I]n his famous discussion of the fetishism of commodities, Marx does note, as he does elsewhere in *Capital,* that the commodity does not emerge whole-cloth from the product, under bourgeois production, but makes its appearance "at an early date in history, though not in the same predominating and characteristic manner as nowadays."[3]

Let us start with the idea that a commodity is *any thing intended for exchange.* For comparative purposes, then, the question becomes *not* "What is a commodity?" but rather "What sort of an exchange is commodity exchange?" Here we need to deal with two kinds of exchange that are conventionally contrasted with commodity exchange. The first is barter (sometimes referred to as direct exchange), and the other is the exchange of gifts. Let us start with barter.

I would suggest that barter is the exchange of objects for one another *without* reference to money and *with* maximum feasible reduction of social, cultural, political, or personal transaction costs.

* * *

Though Marx ran into difficulties in his own analysis of the relationship between barter and commodity exchange, he was right to see that there was a *commonality of spirit* between barter and capitalist commodity exchange, a commonality tied (in this view) to the object-centered, relatively impersonal, asocial nature of each. In the various simple forms of barter, we see an effort to exchange things without the constraints of sociality on the one hand, and the complications of money on the other. Barter in the contemporary world is on the increase: one estimate has it that an estimated $12 billion a year in goods and services is bartered in the United States alone. International barter (Pepsico syrup for Russian vodka, Coca-Cola for Korean toothpicks, and Bulgarian forklifts are examples) is also developing into a complex alternative economy. In these latter situations, barter is a response to the growing number of barriers to international trade and finance, and has a specific role to play in the larger economy. Barter, as a form of trade, thus links the exchange of commodities in widely different social, technological, and institutional circumstances. Barter may thus be regarded as a special form of commodity exchange, one in which, for any variety of reasons, money plays either no role or a very indirect role (as a mere unit of account). By this definition of barter, it would be difficult to locate any human society in which commodity exchange is completely irrelevant. Barter appears to be the form of commodity exchange in which the circulation of things is most divorced from social, political, or cultural norms.

* * *

calculated?

Gifts, and the spirit of reciprocity, sociability, and spontaneity in which they are typically exchanged, usually are starkly opposed to the profit-oriented, self-centered, and calculated spirit that fires the circulation of commodities. Further, where gifts link things to persons and embed the flow of things in the flow of social relations, commodities are held to represent the drive—largely free of moral or cultural constraints—of goods for one another, a drive mediated by money and not by sociality. [T]his is a simplified and overdrawn series of contrasts.

* * *

Part of the difficulty with a cross-cultural analysis of commodities is that, as with other matters in social life, anthropology is excessively dualistic: "us and them"; "materialist and religious"; "objectification of persons" versus "personification of things"; "market exchange" versus "reciprocity"; and so forth. These oppositions parody both poles and reduce human diversities artificially. One symptom of this problem has been an excessively positivist conception of the commodity, as being a certain *kind* of thing, thus restricting the debate to the matter of deciding *what kind* of thing it is. But, in trying to understand what is distinctive about commodity exchange, it does not make sense to distinguish it sharply either from barter on the one hand, or from the exchange of gifts on the other. [I]t is important to see the calculative dimension in all these forms of exchange, even if they vary in the form and intensity of sociality associated with them.

Let us approach commodities as things in a certain situation, a situation that can characterize many different kinds of thing, at different points in their social lives. This means looking at the commodity potential of all things rather than searching fruitlessly for the magic distinction between commodities and other sorts of things. It also means breaking significantly with the production-dominated Marxian view of the commodity and focusing on its *total* trajectory from production, through exchange/distribution, to consumption.

But how are we to define the commodity situation? I propose that *the commodity situation in the social life of any "thing" be defined as the situation in which its exchangeability (past, present, or future) for some other thing is its socially relevant feature.* Further, the commodity situation, defined this way, can be disaggregated into: (1) the commodity phase of the social life of any thing; (2) the commodity candidacy of any thing; and (3) the commodity context in which any thing may be placed. Each of these aspects of "commodity-hood" needs some explication.

[Regarding the commodity phase] let us note for the moment that things can move in *and* out of the commodity state, that such movements can be slow or fast, reversible or terminal, normative or deviant. Though the biographical aspect of some things (such as heirlooms, postage stamps, and antiques) may be more noticeable than that of some others (such as steel bars, salt, or sugar), this component is never completely irrelevant.

The commodity *candidacy* of things is less a temporal than a conceptual feature, and it refers to the standards and criteria (symbolic, classificatory, and moral) that define the exchangeability of things in any particular social and historical context. It is true that in most stable societies, it would be possible to discover a taxonomic structure that defines the world of things, lumping some things together, discriminating between others, attaching meanings and values to these groupings, and providing a basis for rules and practices governing the circulation of these objects.
* * *
We may speak, thus, of the cultural framework that defines the commodity candidacy of things, but we must bear in mind that some exchange situations are characterized by a shallower set of shared standards of value than others. I therefore prefer to use the term *regimes of value,* which does *not* imply that every act of commodity exchange presupposes a complete cultural sharing of assumptions, but rather that the degree of value coherence may be highly variable from situation to situation, and from commodity to commodity.

Finally, the commodity *context* refers to the variety of *social* arenas, within or between *cultural* units, that help link the commodity candidacy of a thing to the commodity phase of its career. Thus in many societies, marriage transactions might constitute the context in which women are most intensely, and most appropriately, regarded as exchange values. Dealings with strangers might provide contexts for the commoditization of things that are otherwise protected from commoditization. Auctions accentuate the commodity dimension of objects (such as paintings) in a manner that might well be regarded as deeply inappropriate in other contexts. Bazaar settings are likely to encourage commodity flows as domestic settings may not. The variety of such contexts, within and across societies, provides the link between the social environment of the commodity and its temporal and symbolic state. [T]he commodity context, as a social matter, may bring together actors from quite different cultural systems who share only the most minimal understandings (from the conceptual point of view) about the objects in question and agree *only* about the terms of trade.

Thus, commoditization lies at the complex intersection of temporal, cultural, and social factors. To the degree that some things in a society are frequently to be found in the commodity phase, to fit the requirements of commodity candidacy, and to appear in a commodity context, they are its quintessential commodities. To the degree that many or most things in a society sometimes meet these criteria, the society may be said to be highly commoditized. In modern capitalist societies, it can safely be said that more things are likely to experience a commodity phase in their own careers, more contexts to become legitimate commodity contexts, and the standards of commodity candidacy to embrace a large part of the world of things than in noncapitalist societies. Though Marx was therefore right in seeing modern industrial capitalism as entailing the most intensely commoditized type of society, the comparison of societies in regard to the degree of "commoditization" would be a most complex affair given the definitional approach to commodities taken here.

Three additional sets of distinctions between commodities are worth making here. The first divides commodities into the following four types: (1) commodities by *destination,* that is, objects intended by their producers principally for exchange; (2) commodities by *metamorphosis,* things intended for other uses that are placed into the commodity state; (3) a special, sharp case of commodities by metamorphosis are commodities by *diversion,* objects placed into a commodity state though originally specifically protected from it; (4) *ex-commodities,* things retrieved, either temporarily or permanently, from the commodity state and placed in some other state. It also seems worthwhile to distinguish "singular" from "homogeneous" commodities in order to discriminate between commodities whose candidacy for the commodity state is precisely a matter of their class characteristics (a perfectly standardized steel bar, indistinguishable in practical terms from any other steel bar) and those whose candidacy is precisely their uniqueness *within* some class (a Manet rather than a Picasso; one Manet rather than another).

* * *

Paths and Diversions

By drawing on certain ethnographic examples, I hope to show in this section that the flow of commodities in any given situation is a shifting compromise between socially regulated paths and competitively inspired diversions.

* * *

The kula is an extremely complex regional system for the circulation of particular kinds of valuables, usually between men of substance, in the Massim group of islands off the eastern tip of New Guinea. The main objects exchanged for one another are of two types: decorated necklaces (which circulate in one direction) and armshells (which circulate in the other). These valuables acquire very specific biographies as they move from place to place and hand to hand, just as the men who exchange them gain and lose reputation as they acquire, hold, and part with these valuables. The term *keda* (road, route, path, or track) is used in some Massim communities to describe the journey of these valuables from island to island. But keda also has a more diffuse set of meanings, referring to the more or less stable social, political, and reciprocal links between men that constitute these paths. In the most abstract way, keda refers to the path (created through the exchange of these valuables) to wealth, power, and reputation for the men who handle these valuables.[4]

* * *

The path taken by these valuables is thus both reflective and constitutive of social partnerships and struggles for preeminence. But a number of other things are worth noting about the circulation of these valuables. The first is that their exchange is not easily categorized as simple reciprocal exchange, far from the spirit of trade and commerce. Though monetary valuations are absent, both the nature of the objects and a variety of sources of flexibility in the system make it possible to have the sort of calculated exchange that I maintain is at the heart of the exchange of commodities. [P]artners negotiate what Firth calls "exchange by private treaty," a situation in which something like price is arrived at by some negotiated process other than the impersonal forces of supply and demand.[5] What Firth here calls "indebtedness engineering" is a variety of the sort of calculated exchange that, by my definition, blurs the line between commodity exchange and other, more sentimental, varieties. The most important difference between the exchange of these commodities and the exchange of commodities in modern industrial economies is that the increment being sought in kula-type systems is in reputation, name, or fame, with the critical form of capital for producing this profit being people rather than other factors of production.[6] Pricelessness is a luxury few commodities can afford.

* * *

The kula system gives a dynamic and processual quality to Mauss's ideas regarding the mingling or exchange of qualities between men and things, as Munn[7] has noted with regard to kula exchange in Gawa: "Although men appear to be the agents in defining shell value, in fact, without shells, men cannot define their own value; in this respect, shells and men are reciprocally agents of each other's value definition." But in the reciprocal construction of value, it is not only paths that play an important role, but diversions as well.

* * *

Desire and Demand

Part of the reason why demand remains by and large a mystery is that we assume it has something to do with desire, on the one hand (by its nature assumed to be infinite and transcultural) and need on the other (by its nature assumed to be fixed). I suggest that we treat demand, hence consumption, as an aspect of the overall political economy of societies. Demand, that is, emerges as a function of a variety of social practices and classifications, rather than a mysterious emanation of human needs, a mechanical response to social manipulation (as in one model of the effects of advertising in our own society), or the narrowing down of a universal and voracious desire for objects to whatever happens to be available.

* * *

One mechanism that frequently translates political control into consumer demand is that of the "sumptuary laws" that characterize complex premodern societies, but also characterize small-scale, preindustrial, and preliterate societies. Wherever clothing, food, housing, body decoration, number of wives or slaves, or any other visible act of consumption is subject to external regulation, we can see that demand is subject to social definition and control. From this point of view, the plethora of "taboos" in primitive societies, which forbid particular kinds of marriage, food consumption, and interaction can be seen as strict moral analogues to the more explicit, legalized sumptuary laws of more complex and literate societies.

What modern money is to primitive media of exchange, fashion is to primitive sumptuary regulations. There are clear morphological similarities between the two, but the term *fashion* suggests high velocity, rapid turnover, the illusion of total access and high convertibility, the assumption of a democracy of consumers and of objects of consumption. Primitive media of exchange, like primitive sumptuary laws and taboos, on the other hand, seem rigid, slow to move, weak in their capacity to commensurate, tied to hierarchy, discrimination, and rank in social life. But the establishments that control fashion and good taste in the contemporary West are no less effective in limiting social mobility, marking social rank and discrimination, and placing consumers in a game whose ever-shifting rules are determined by "taste makers" and their affiliated experts who dwell at the top of society.

Modern consumers are the victims of the velocity of fashion as surely as primitive consumers are the victims of the stability of sumptuary law. The demand for commodities is critically regulated by this variety of taste-making mechanisms, whose social origin is more clearly understood (both by consumers and by analysts) in our own society than in those distant from us. In both cases demand is a socially regulated and generated impulse, not an artifact of individual whims or needs.

Thus we can state as a general rule that those commodities whose consumption is most intricately tied up with critical social messages are likely to be *least* responsive to crude shifts in supply or price, but most responsive to political manipulation at the societal level.

* * *

Demand is thus neither a mechanical response to the structure and level of production nor a bottomless natural appetite. It is a complex social mechanism that mediates between short- and long-term patterns of commodity circulation. Short-term strategies of diversion might entail small shifts in demand that can gradually transform commodity flows in the long run. Looked at from the point of view of the reproduction of patterns of commodity flow (rather than their alteration), however, long-established patterns of demand act as constraints on any given set of commodity paths.

* * *

Conclusion: Politics and Value

Apart from learning some moderately unusual facts, and regarding them from a mildly unconventional point of view, is there any general benefit in looking at the social life of commodities in the manner proposed in this essay? What does this perspective tell us about value and exchange in social life that we did not know already, or that we could not have discovered in a less cumbersome way? Is there any point in taking the heuristic position that commodities exist everywhere and that the spirit of commodity exchange is not wholly divorced from the spirit of other forms of exchange?

* * *

Politics (in the broad sense of relations, assumptions, and contests pertaining to power) is what links value and exchange in the social life of commodities. In the mundane, day-to-day, small-scale exchanges of things in ordinary life, this fact is not visible, for exchange has the routine and conventionalized look of all customary behavior. But these many ordinary dealings would not be possible were it not for a broad set of agreements concerning what is desirable, what a reasonable "exchange of sacrifices" comprises, and who is permitted to exercise what kind of effective demand in what circumstances. What is political about this process is not just the fact that it signifies and constitutes relations of privilege and social control. What is political about it is the constant tension between the existing frameworks (of price, bargaining, and so forth) and the tendency of commodities to breach these frameworks. This tension itself has its source in the fact that not all parties share the same *interests* in any specific regime of value, nor are the interests of any two parties in a given exchange identical.

At the top of many societies, we have the politics of tournaments of value, and of calculated diversions that might lead to new paths of commodity flow. As expressions of the interests of elites in relation to commoners we have the politics of fashion, of sumptuary law, and of taboo, all of which regulate demand. Yet since commodities constantly spill beyond the boundaries of specific cultures (and thus of specific regimes of value), such political control of demand is always threatened with disturbance. In a surprisingly wide range of societies, it is possible to witness the following common paradox. It is in the interests of those in power to completely freeze the flow of commodities, by creating a closed universe of commodities and a rigid set of regulations about how they are to move. Yet the very nature of contests between those in power (or those who aspire to greater power) tends to invite a loosening of these rules and an expansion of the pool of commodities. This aspect of elite politics is generally the Trojan horse of value shifts. So far as commodities are concerned, the source of politics is the tension between these two tendencies.

Ever since Marx and the early political economists, there has not been much mystery about the relationship between politics and production. We are now in a better position to demystify the demand side of economic life.

NOTES

1. From Arjun Appadurai, *Introduction, in The Social Life of Things: Commodities in Cultural Perspective* 3, 6–7, 9–20, 29, 31–33, 40–41, 56–58 (1986). Reprinted with the permission of Cambridge University Press.

2. See especially Karl Marx, Capital: Vol. I. A Critical analysis of capitalist production (1971); Grundrisse: Foundations of the critique of political economy (1973).

3. Capital, *supra* note 2, at 86.

4. Shirley F. Campbell, *Kula in Vakuta: The Mechanics of keda, in* The Kula: New Perspectives on Massim Exchange, 203–4 (J. W. Leach & E. Leach eds. 1983).

5. Raymond Firth, *Magnitudes and Values in Kula Exchange, in* The Kula, *supra* note 4, at 91.

6. Marilyn Strathern, *The Kula in Comparative Perspective, in* The Kula, *supra* note 4, at 73, 80; Frederick H. Damon, *What Moves the Kula, in* The Kula, *supra* note 4, at 339.

7. Nancy D. Munn, *Gawan kula: Spatiotemporal Control and the Symbolism of Influence, in* The Kula, *supra* note 4, at 283.

B.

Contested Commodities
Babies/Parental Rights and Obligations

The Economics of the Baby Shortage

Elisabeth M. Landes and Richard A. Posner[1]

Although economists have studied extensively the efforts of government to regulate the economy, public regulation of social and personal life has largely escaped economic attention. With the rapid development of the economic analysis of nonmarket behavior, the conceptual tools necessary for the economic study of social (as distinct from narrowly economic) regulation are now at hand. Nor is there any basis for a presumption that government does a good job of regulating nonmarket behavior; if anything, the negative presumption created by numerous studies of economic regulation[2] should carry over to the nonmarket sphere. An example of nonmarket regulation that may be no less perverse than the widely criticized governmental efforts to regulate imports, transportation, new drugs, bank entry, and other market activities is the regulation of child adoptions—the subject of this paper.

Sometimes natural parents do not want to raise their child; the typical case is where the birth is illegitimate. And in some cases where the natural parents do raise the child initially, their custody is later terminated for one reason or another—death or other incapacity, abuse, or extreme indigence. In either case—the unwanted infant or the abused, neglected, or abandoned child—there are potential gains from trade from transferring the custody of the child to a new set of parents.

Ordinarily, potential gains from trade are realized by a process of voluntary transacting—by a sale, in other words. Adoptions could in principle be handled through the market and in practice, as we shall see, there is a considerable amount of baby selling. But because public policy is opposed to the sale of babies, such sales as do occur constitute a "black market."

* * *

Disequilibrium in the Adoption Market: The Baby Shortage and the Baby Glut

Students of adoption agree on two things. The first is that there is a shortage of white babies for adoption; the second is that there is a glut of black babies, and of children who are no longer babies (particularly if they are physically or mentally handicapped), for adoption.

* * *

The principal suppliers of babies for adoption are adoption agencies. Restrictive regulations governing nonagency adoption have given agencies a monopoly (though not a complete one) of the supply of children for adoption. However, while agencies charge fees for adoption, usually based on the income of the adoptive parents, they do not charge a market-clearing (let alone a monopoly-profit-maximizing) price. This is shown by the fact that prospective adoptive parents applying to an agency face waiting periods of three to seven years.[3] And the (visible) queue understates the shortage, since by tightening their criteria of eligibility to adopt a child the agencies can shorten the apparent queue without increasing the supply of babies. Thus some demanders in this market must wait for years to obtain a baby, others never obtain one, and still others are discouraged by knowledge of the queue from even trying. Obtaining a second or third baby is increasingly difficult.

The picture is complicated, however, by the availability of independent adoptions. An independent adoption is one that does not go through an agency. Most independent adoptions are by a relative, for example a stepfather, but some involve placement with strangers and here, it would seem, is an opportunity for a true baby market to develop. However, the operation of this market is severely curtailed by a network of restrictions, varying from state to state (a few states forbid independent adoption by a nonrelative) but never so loose as to permit outright sale of a baby for adoption.[4]

Just as a buyer's queue is a symptom of a shortage, a seller's queue is a symptom of a glut. The thousands of children in foster care are comparable to an unsold inventory stored in a warehouse. Child welfare spe-

cialists attribute this "oversupply" to such factors as the growing incidence of child abuse, which forces the state to remove children from the
custody of their natural parents, and the relatively small number of
prospective adoptive parents willing to adopt children of another race,
children who are no longer infants, or children who have a physical or
mental handicap. No doubt these factors are important. However, some
children are placed in foster care as infants and remain there until they
are no longer appealing to prospective adoptive parents. We believe that
the large number of children in foster care is, in part, a manifestation of
a regulatory pattern that (1) combines restrictions on the sale of babies
with the effective monopolization of the adoption market by adoptive
agencies, and (2) fails to provide effectively for the termination of the natural parents' rights.

A Model of the Adoption Market

Here we present a simple analytical model of the adoption market as it
exists today in the United States. Queues for some children (mainly white
infants) in the legal market, overstocks of others (older, nonwhite, or
physically or mentally handicapped children), and black-market activity
in infants are all shown to be the result of the peculiar market structure
in adoption that has been brought about by public regulation.

Whereas in 1957 only 53 percent of all nonrelative adoptions went
through adoption agencies, in 1971 the proportion was almost 80 percent.[5] This would be a matter of limited significance from the economic
standpoint if adoption agencies were both numerous and free from significant restrictions on their ability to operate as efficient profit-maximiz-
ing firms. The first condition is more or less satisfied but not the second.
While agencies are generally not limited in the fees they may charge
prospective adoptive parents, they are constrained to other inefficient restrictions. For example, they are constrained to operate as "nonprofit"
organizations, which presumably retards, perhaps severely, their ability
to attract capital, and may have other inefficient effects as well.[6] The most
significant restriction is the regulation of the price at which the agencies
may transact with the natural parents. Adoption agencies that are also
general child-welfare agencies must accept all children offered to them at
a regulated price (but may place them in foster care rather than for adoption); and they may offer no additional compensation to suppliers (the

natural parents) in order to increase the supply of babies. The regulated price is generally limited to the direct medical costs of pregnant women plus (some) maintenance expenses during the latter part of the pregnancy. To be sure, agencies have some flexibility in the kinds of services they may offer the natural parents, such as job counseling, but they cannot thereby transfer to the natural parents anything approaching the free-market value of the child.

* * *

The Effects of the Baby Shortage

* * *

In independent adoption, normally the only payments that may be made are (1) compensation to the natural mother for her medical, and some maintenance, costs plus (2) compensation to the obstetrician and the lawyer for their professional (i.e., medical and legal) services, excluding any search costs they may have incurred in arranging for the adoption. The included items represent only a part of the costs of producing and selling a baby. The major omitted items are (1) the opportunity costs of the natural mother's time during the period of pregnancy or hospitalization when she is precluded from working, over and above her maintenance costs, (2) any pain or other disutility of the pregnancy and delivery to her, (3) any value which she attaches to keeping the child rather than putting it up for adoption, and (4) the costs of search of the middleman —usually an obstetrician or lawyer—in locating and bringing together the supplier and demander.

In practice the constraints on full compensation to producer and middleman are less rigid than suggested. The difficulties of monitoring the fees and activities of the attorney, obstetrician, and natural mother enable these individuals to charge somewhat more than the technically permitted amounts without running any appreciable risk of punishment. This is why independent placement of babies for adoption (other than to relatives) is often referred to as the "gray market." However, the constraints placed on independent adoption are sufficiently stringent to prevent it from approximating a free market. Women have little or no incentive to put a child up for adoption rather than retain or abort it (since abortions are relatively inexpensive, and public assistance is ordinarily available to cover their medical expenses and maintenance costs regardless of whether they keep or give up the child). At the same time, the constraints on payment discourage the emergence of an effective middleman function to match up the prospective sellers and buyers—the middleman activity *per se* cannot be compensated. This is particularly serious in a market of this sort where the sellers and buyers tend to be geographically and socially remote, are not professional businessmen, do not participate in this market on a regular basis, and are dealing in a highly individualized commodity.

In these circumstances, the economist expects a black market to emerge. Some fraction—we do not know what—of the 17,000 independent adoptions are indeed black-market adoptions in the sense that the compensation paid either the natural parents or the middlemen, or both, exceeds the lawful limits.[7] However, the potential criminal and professional sanctions for the individuals involved in baby selling not only drive up the costs and hence the price of babies (and so reduce demand) but necessarily imply a clandestine mode of operation. This imposes significant information costs on both buyers and sellers in the market, which further raise the (real) price of black-market babies to buyers and reduce the net price to sellers.

The legally permissible compensation to the natural parents is unlikely to exceed $3,000.[8] However, prices for babies in the black market are alleged to range between $9,000 and $40,000.[9] To some extent these prices reflect search costs and other middleman expenses that would be found in a free market, but they may to a greater extent reflect the expected penalties suppliers face and the additional costs of search entailed by operating in a clandestine market.

A further consideration is that there will be more fraud in a black market for babies than in a lawful market, so fear of being defrauded will further deter potential demanders. In lawful markets the incidence of fraud is limited not only by the existence of legal remedies against the seller but also by his desire to build a reputation for fair dealing. Both the clandestine mode of operation of current baby sellers and the lack of a continuing business relationship between seller and buyer reduce the seller's market incentives to behave reputably. To summarize, we cannot, simply by observing the black market, estimate the market-clearing prices and quantities of babies in a lawful baby market.

The constraints on the baby market may also be responsible in part for the glut of children in foster care—and this quite apart from the possible incentives of adoption agencies to place children in foster care rather than for adoption. Since the natural parents have no financial incentive to place a child for adoption, often they will decide to place it in foster care instead. This is proper so long as they seriously intend to reacquire custody of the child at some later date. But when they do not the consequence of their decision to place the child in foster care may be to render the child unadoptable, for by the time the parents relinquish their parental rights the child may be too old to be placed for adoption. This would happen less often if parents had a financial incentive to relinquish their rights at a time when the child was still young enough to be adoptable.

* * *

Objections to a Free Baby Market

The foregoing analysis suggests that the baby shortage and black market are the result of legal restrictions that prevent the market from operating freely in the sale of babies as of other goods. This suggests as a possible reform simply eliminating these restrictions. However, many people believe that a free market in babies would be undesirable. The objections to baby selling must be considered carefully before any conclusion with regard to the desirability of changing the law can be reached.

Criticisms Properly Limited to the Black Market

We begin with a set of criticisms that in reality are applicable not to the market as such but only, we believe, to the *black* market. The first such criticism is of the high price of babies and the bad effects that are alleged to flow from a high price, such as favoring the wealthy.[10] This criticism of the use of the price system is based on the current prices in the black market. There is no reason to believe that prices would be so high were the sale of babies legalized. On the contrary, prices for children of *equivalent quality* would be much lower.

The current black-market price is swollen by expected punishment costs which would not be a feature of a legalized baby market. In a legal and competitive baby market, price would be equated to the marginal costs of producing and selling for adoption babies of a given quality. These marginal costs include certain well-known items, such as the natural mother's medical expenses and maintenance during pregnancy and the attorney's fee for handling the legal details of the adoption proceeding, that are unlikely to exceed $3,000 in the aggregate. The question marks are the additional fees that would be necessary (1) to compensate a woman either for becoming pregnant or, if she was pregnant already, for inducing her to put the baby up for adoption rather than abort or retain it, and (2) to cover the search costs necessary to match baby and adoptive parents.

* * *

Another prevalent criticism of the market, and again one that pertains primarily to the operations of the black market, is that fraud and related forms of dishonesty and overreaching pervade the market method of providing children for adoption. It is contended, for example, that the health of the child or of the child's mother is regularly misrepresented and that frequently after the sale is completed the seller will attempt to blackmail the adoptive parents.[11] Such abuses are probably largely the result of the fact that the market is an illegal one. Sellers cannot give legally enforceable guarantees of genealogy, health, or anything else to the prospective parents, and even the seller's adherence to the negotiated price is uncertain given the buyer's inability to enforce the contract of sale by the usual legal procedures. Any market involving a complex and durable good (i.e., one that yields services over a substantial period of time) would probably operate suboptimally in the absence of legally enforceable contracts or, at a minimum, regular, repetitive business relations between (the same) sellers and (the same) buyers. Both conditions are absent from the illegal baby market and this is the likeliest explanation for the number of complaints about the honesty of the sellers in that market.

To be sure, there are probably inherent limitations on the use of legal remedies to protect purchasers even in a legal baby market. For example, consideration of the welfare of the child might lead courts to refuse to grant rescission to a buyer as a remedy for breach of warranty (i.e., allow him to return the child). And courts might be reluctant to order specific performance of a contract to put up a child for adoption. However, similar limitations are a traditional feature of remedies for personal-service contracts.

* * *

This analysis suggests a qualification to our earlier conclusion that legalizing the baby market would result in a reduction in the price of babies below the current black market level: the conclusion refers to a *quality-adjusted* price. The current illegality of baby selling reduces the bene-

fits of transacting to the buyer by depriving him of the contractual protections that buyers in legal markets normally receive. Prospective adoptive parents would presumably be willing to pay more for a child whose
health and genealogy were warranted in a legally enforceable instrument
than they are willing to pay under the present system where the entire risk
of any deviation from expected quality falls on them. Thus the effect of
legalizing the baby market would be not only to shift the marginal cost of
baby production and sale downward but to move the demand curve for
adoptive children upward.

Criticisms of a Legal Market

We now consider criticisms of baby selling that are applicable to a legal
market rather than just to the present illegal market. The first is that the
rationing of the supply of babies to would-be adoptive parents by price is
not calculated to promote the best interests of the children, the objective
of the adoption process.[12] This criticism cannot be dismissed as foolish.
The ordinary presumption of free-enterprise economics is no stronger
than that free exchange will maximize the satisfaction of the people trading, who in this case are the natural and adoptive parents. There is no presumption that the satisfactions of the thing traded, in most instances a
meaningless concept, are also maximized. If we treat the child as a member of the community whose aggregate welfare we are interested in maximizing, there is no justification for ignoring how the child's satisfactions
may be affected by alternative methods of adoption.

Very simply, the question is whether the price system would do as good
a job as, or a better job than, adoption agencies in finding homes for children that would maximize their satisfactions in life. While there is no direct evidence on this point, some weak indirect evidence is provided in a
follow-up study of independent adoptions which suggests that children
adopted privately do as well as natural children. Witmer and her coau-
thors find that the distribution of I.Q. and a measure of school achievement, both at age 11, between children adopted privately and natural
children of comparable socioeconomic backgrounds are virtually identical, although they also find that the adopted children did not perform as
well on certain psychological tests as did the natural children.[13] It is true
that some, perhaps most, independent adoptions do not involve price rationing, but the most important thing is that independent adoption in-

volves a minimum of the sort of screening of prospective parents that the adoption agencies do. If children adopted without the screening seem nevertheless to do about as well as natural children, then one is entitled to be skeptical of the need for or value of the screening.

* * *

One valuable function agencies may perform is screening out people whose interest in having children is improper in an uncontroversial sense —people who wish to have children in order to abuse or make slaves of them. The criminal statutes punishing child abuse and neglect would remain applicable to babies adopted in a free market, but the extreme difficulty of detecting such crimes makes it unlikely, at least given current levels of punishment, that the criminal statutes alone are adequate. This may make some prescreening a more effective method of prevention than after-the-fact punishment. But the logical approach, then, is to require every prospective baby buyer to undergo some minimal background investigation. This approach would be analogous to licensing automobile drivers and seems as superior to the agency monopoly as licensing is to allocating automobiles on a nonprice basis.

Moreover, concern with child abuse should not be allowed to obscure the fact that abuse is not the normal motive for adopting a child. And once we put abuse aside, willingness to pay money for a baby would seem on the whole a reassuring factor from the standpoint of child welfare. Few people buy a car or a television set in order to smash it. In general, the more costly a purchase, the more care the purchaser will lavish on it. Recent studies suggest that the more costly it is for parents to obtain a child, the greater will be their investment in the child's quality attributes, such as health and education.[14]

A further point is that today some fetuses are probably aborted because the cost to the mother of carrying them to term and placing them for adoption exceeds the permissible return. In a free adoption market, some of the 900,000 fetuses aborted in 1974 would have been born and placed for adoption. If the welfare of these (potential) children is included in the calculation of the welfare of adopted children, both actual and potential, the heavy costs imposed on the market by adoption regulation may actually decrease child welfare.

Another objection to the market for babies is the alleged vulnerability of both natural and adoptive parents to overreaching by middlemen. Parenthood is thought to be so emotional a phenomenon that people cannot reason about it in the same way they reason about the goods and services normally traded in the market.[15] But many of those goods and services, such as medical care, also involve a strong emotional component, yet it has rarely been thought appropriate to exclude such goods from market exchange. And studies of marriage and procreation have shown that people in fact calculate in family matters, whether implicitly or explicitly, in the same way they do when purchasing ordinary goods and services.[16]

Other objections to legalizing the market in babies are more symbolic than pragmatic. For example, to accord a property right in the newborn child to the natural parents seems to some observers to smack of slavery.[17] But allowing a market in adoptions does not entail giving property rights to natural parents for all purposes. Laws forbidding child abuse and neglect would continue to be fully applicable to adoptive parents even if baby sales were permitted. Further, we are speaking only of sales of newborn infants, and do not suggest that parents should have a right to sell older children. The creation of such a right would require identification of the point at which the child is sufficiently mature to be entitled to a voice in his placement. However, the question is largely academic given the lack of any significant market for adopting older children.

* * *

The antipathy to an explicit market in babies may be part of a broader wish to disguise facts that might be acutely uncomfortable if widely known. Were baby prices quoted as prices of soybean futures are quoted, a racial ranking of these prices would be evident, with white baby prices higher than nonwhite baby prices. [A]nyone who thinks about the question will realize that prices for babies are racially stratified as a result of different supply and demand conditions in the different racial groups, but perhaps bringing this fact out into the open would exacerbate racial tensions in our society.

Some people are also upset by the implications for the eugenic alteration of the human race that are presented by baby selling. Baby selling may seem logically and inevitably to lead to baby breeding,[18] for any market will generate incentives to improve the product as well as to optimize the price and quantity of the current quality level of the product. In a regime of free baby production and sale there might be efforts to breed children having desirable characteristics and, more broadly, to breed children with a *known* set of characteristics that could be matched up with those desired by prospective adoptive parents. Indeed, one can imagine, though with some difficulty, a growing separation between the production and rearing of children. No longer would a woman who wanted a child but who had a genetic trait that might jeopardize the child's health have to take her chances on a natural birth. She could find a very close genetic matchup to her and her husband's (healthy) genetic endowment in the baby market. However, so long as the market for eugenically bred babies did not extend beyond infertile couples and those with serious genetic disorders, the impact of a free baby market on the genetic composition and distribution of the human race at large would be small.

* * *

[handwritten: wouldn't "acceptable" parents have babies to make money?]

Interim Steps toward a Full-Fledged Baby Market

We close by speculating briefly on the possibility of taking some tentative and reversible steps toward a free baby market in order to determine experimentally the social costs and benefits of using the market in this area. Important characteristics of a market could be simulated if one or more adoption agencies, which typically already vary their fees for adoption according to the income of the prospective parents, would simply use the surplus income generated by the higher fees to make side payments to pregnant women contemplating abortion to induce them instead to have the child and put it up for adoption.

[handwritten: doesn't that eliminate free choice?]

This experiment would yield evidence with respect to both the demand and supply conditions in the adoption market and would provide information both on the value that prospective adoptive parents attach to being able to obtain a baby and on the price necessary to induce pregnant women to substitute birth for abortion. Follow-up studies of the adopted children, comparing them with children that had been adopted by parents paying lower fees, would help answer the question whether the payment of a stiff fee has adverse consequences on the welfare of the child.

Some states appear not to limit the fees that adoption agencies pay to natural parents. The experiment we propose could be implemented in such states without new legislation.

NOTES

1. Reprinted with permission from Elisabeth M. Landes and Richard A. Posner, *The Economics of the Baby Shortage*, 7 J. Leg. Stud. 323–28, 337–45, 347–48 (1978). Copyright 1978 by The University of Chicago. All rights reserved.

2. See, *e.g.,* William A. Jordan, *Producer Protection. Prior Market Structure and the Effects of Government Regulation,* 15 J. Law & Econ. 151 (1972).

3. Adoption and Foster Care, 1975: Hearings before the Subcomm. On Children & Youth of the Senate Comm. On Labor & Public Welfare, 94th Cong., 1st Sess. 6 (1975) [hereinafter cited without cross-reference as Adoption and Foster Care]. A further round of hearings on baby selling began on March 22, 1977, before the Criminal Justice Subcommittee of the House Judiciary Committee, in connection with a bill to make the sale of babies in interstate commerce a federal crime. See Chicago Sun-Times, March 3 1977, at 55 col. 3.

4. The relevant state laws are described in *Note: Black-Market Adoptions,* 22 Catholic Lawyer 48 (1976), and in Daniel R. Grove, *Independent Adoption: The Case for the Gray Market,* 13 Vill. L. Rev. 116 (1967).

5. See U.S. Dep't of Health, Education, & Welfare, Nat'l Center for Social Statistics, Adoptions in 1971 (1973).

6. In particular, it may lead the agencies to dissipate their profits in expenditures that reduce welfare—*e.g.,* unnecessarily intrusive inspections of the home of the adoptive parents.

7. Regardless of how obtained-whether lawfully or in the black market-most babies are formally adopted and hence most black-market activities show up in the statistics of independent adoption. In some cases, however, where an adoption is arranged prior to the birth of the adopted child, the adoptive parents' name may simply be entered directly on the birth certificate, thus obviating any formal adoptive procedure.

8. See Adoption and Foster Care 132, 139.

9. See Adoption and Foster Care 160, 165–66, 175, 182; Chicago Tribune, March 22, 1977, sec. 1, at 3.

10. See, *e.g.,* Adoption and Foster Care 11, 27.

11. Adoption and Foster Care 20–21.

12. Adoption and Foster Care 7.

13. Helen L. Witmer, Elizabeth Herzog, Eugene A. Weinstein, & Mary E. Sullivan, Independent Adoptions: A Followup Study (1963).

14. Gary S. Becker & H. Gregg Lewis, *Interaction between Quality and Quantity of Children, in* Economics of the Family, 81 (Theodore W. Schultz ed. 1974); Gary S. Becker & Nigel Tomes, *Child Endowments and the Quantity and Quality of Children,* 84 J. Pol. Econ. S143–S162 (August 1976). Even critics of baby selling seem generally satisfied with the quality of the families who obtain children in the black market. *See* Adoption and Foster Care 13.

15. See Adoption and Foster Care 12, 44.

16. See studies in Economics of the Family, *supra* note 14.

17. See Adoption and Foster Care 2–3.

18. See Adoption and Foster Care 22–23.

In the Matter of Baby M

537 A.2d 1227 (N.J. 1988)

Wilentz, C.J.

In this matter the Court is asked to determine the validity of a contract that purports to provide a new way of bringing children into a family. For a fee of $10,000, a woman agrees to be artificially inseminated with the semen of another woman's husband; she is to conceive a child, carry it to term, and after its birth surrender it to the natural father and his wife. The intent of the contract is that the child's natural mother will thereafter be forever separated from her child. The wife is to adopt the child, and she and the natural father are to be regarded as its parents for all purposes. The contract providing for this is called a "surrogacy contract," the natural mother inappropriately called the "surrogate mother."

We invalidate the surrogacy contract because it conflicts with the law and public policy of this State. While we recognize the depth of the yearning of infertile couples to have their own children, we find the payment of money to a "surrogate" mother illegal, perhaps criminal, and potentially degrading to women. Although in this case we grant custody to the natural father, the evidence having clearly proved such custody to be in the best interests of the infant, we void both the termination of the surrogate mother's parental rights and the adoption of the child by the wife/stepparent. We thus restore the "surrogate" as the mother of the child. We remand the issue of the natural mother's visitation rights to the trial court, since that issue was not reached below and the record before us is not sufficient to permit us to decide it *de novo*.

We find no offense to our present laws where a woman voluntarily and without payment agrees to act as a "surrogate" mother, provided that she is not subject to a binding agreement to surrender her child. Moreover, our holding today does not preclude the Legislature from altering the current statutory scheme, within constitutional limits, so as to permit surrogacy contracts. Under current law, however, the surrogacy agreement before us is illegal and invalid.

Facts

In February 1985, William Stern and Mary Beth Whitehead entered into a surrogacy contract. It recited that Stern's wife, Elizabeth, was infertile, that they wanted a child, and that Mrs. Whitehead was willing to provide that child as the mother with Mr. Stern as the father.

The contract provided that through artificial insemination using Mr. Stern's sperm, Mrs. Whitehead would become pregnant, carry the child to term, bear it, deliver it to the Sterns, and thereafter do whatever was necessary to terminate her maternal rights so that Mrs. Stern could thereafter adopt the child. Mrs. Whitehead's husband, Richard,[1] was also a party to the contract; Mrs. Stern was not. Mr. Whitehead promised to do all acts necessary to rebut the presumption of paternity under the Parentage Act.[2] Although Mrs. Stern was not a party to the surrogacy agreement, the contract gave her sole custody of the child in the event of Mr. Stern's death. Mrs. Stern's status as a nonparty to the surrogate parenting agreement presumably was to avoid the application of the baby-selling statute to this arrangement.[3]

* * *

After several artificial inseminations over a period of months, Mrs. Whitehead became pregnant. The pregnancy was uneventful and on March 27, 1986, Baby M was born.

* * *

The struggle over Baby M began when it became apparent that Mrs. Whitehead could not return the child to Mr. Stern. Due to Mrs. Whitehead's refusal to relinquish the baby, Mr. Stern filed a complaint seeking enforcement of the surrogacy contract. He alleged, accurately, that Mrs. Whitehead had not only refused to comply with the surrogacy contract but had threatened to flee from New Jersey with the child in order to avoid even the possibility of his obtaining custody. The court papers asserted that if Mrs. Whitehead were to be given notice of the application for an order requiring her to relinquish custody, she would, prior to the hearing, leave the state with the baby. And that is precisely what she did.

After the order was entered, *ex parte*, the process server, aided by the police, in the presence of the Sterns, entered Mrs. Whitehead's home to execute the order. Mr. Whitehead fled with the child, who had been handed to him through a window while those who came to enforce the order were thrown off balance by a dispute over the child's current name.

* * *

Invalidity and Unenforceability of Surrogacy Contract

We have concluded that this surrogacy contract is invalid. Our conclusion has two bases: direct conflict with existing statutes and conflict with the public policies of this State, as expressed in its statutory and decisional law.

One of the surrogacy contract's basic purposes, to achieve the adoption of a child through private placement, though permitted in New Jersey "is very much disfavored."[4] Its use of money for this purpose—and we have no doubt whatsoever that the money is being paid to obtain an adoption and not, as the Sterns argue, for the personal services of Mary Beth Whitehead—is illegal and perhaps criminal. In addition to the inducement of money, there is the coercion of contract: the natural mother's irrevocable agreement, prior to birth, even prior to conception, to surrender the child to the adoptive couple. Such an agreement is totally unenforceable in private placement adoption.[5] Even where the adoption is through an approved agency, the formal agreement to surrender occurs only *after* birth (as we read N.J.S.A. 9:2–16 and 17, and similar statutes), and then, by regulation, only after the birth mother has been offered counseling.[6] Integral to these invalid provisions of the surrogacy contract is the related agreement, equally invalid, on the part of the natural mother to cooperate with, and not to contest, proceedings to terminate her parental rights, as well as her contractual concession, in aid of the adoption, that the child's best interests would be served by awarding custody to the natural father and his wife—all of this before she has even conceived, and, in some cases, before she has the slightest idea of what the natural father and adoptive mother are like.

* * *

Conflict with Statutory Provisions

The surrogacy contract conflicts with: (1) laws prohibiting the use of money in connection with adoptions; (2) laws requiring proof of parental unfitness or abandonment before termination of parental rights is ordered or an adoption is granted; and (3) laws that make surrender of custody and consent to adoption revocable in private placement adoptions.

1. Our law prohibits paying or accepting money in connection with any placement of a child for adoption.[7]

* * *

Considerable care was taken in this case to structure the surrogacy arrangement so as not to violate this prohibition. The arrangement was structured as follows: the adopting parent, Mrs. Stern, was not a party to the surrogacy contract; the money paid to Mrs. Whitehead was stated to be for her services—not for the adoption; the sole purpose of the contract was stated as being that "of giving a child to William Stern, its natural and biological father"; the money was purported to be "compensation for services and expenses and in no way . . . a fee for termination of parental rights or a payment in exchange for consent to surrender a child for adoption"; the fee to the Infertility Center ($7,500) was stated to be for legal representation, advice, administrative work, and other "services." Nevertheless, it seems clear that the money was paid and accepted in connection with an adoption.

The Infertility Center's major role was first as a "finder" of the surrogate mother whose child was to be adopted, and second as the arranger of all proceedings that led to the adoption. Its role as adoption finder is demonstrated by the provision requiring Mr. Stern to pay another $7,500 if he uses Mary Beth Whitehead again as a surrogate, and by ICNY's agreement to "coordinate arrangements for the adoption of the child by the wife." The surrogacy agreement requires Mrs. Whitehead to surrender Baby M for the purposes of adoption. The agreement notes that Mr. *and* Mrs. Stern wanted to have a child, and provides that the child be "placed" with Mrs. Stern in the event Mr. Stern dies before the child is born. The payment of the $10,000 occurs only on surrender of custody of the child and "completion of the duties and obligations" of Mrs. Whitehead, including termination of her parental rights to facilitate adoption by Mrs. Stern. As for the contention that the Sterns are paying only for services and not for an adoption, we need note only that they would pay nothing in the event the child died before the fourth month of pregnancy, and only $1,000 if the child were stillborn, even though the "services" had been fully rendered. Additionally, one of Mrs. White-head's estimated costs, to be assumed by Mr. Stern, was an "Adoption Fee," presumably for Mrs. Whitehead's incidental costs in connection with the adoption.

Mr. Stern knew he was paying for the adoption of a child; Mrs. White-head knew she was accepting money so that a child might be adopted; the Infertility Center knew that it was being paid for assisting in the adoption of a child. The actions of all three worked to frustrate the goals of the statute. It strains credulity to claim that these arrangements, touted by those in the surrogacy business as an attractive alternative to the usual route leading to an adoption, really amount to something other than a private placement adoption for money.

* * *

Baby-selling potentially results in the exploitation of all parties involved. Conversely, adoption statutes seek to further humanitarian goals, foremost among them the best interests of the child. The negative consequences of baby-buying are potentially present in the surrogacy context, especially the potential for placing and adopting a child without regard to the interest of the child or the natural mother.

2. The termination of Mrs. Whitehead's parental rights, called for by the surrogacy contract and actually ordered by the court fails to comply with the stringent requirements of New Jersey law.

* * *

In this case a termination of parental rights was obtained not by proving the statutory prerequisites but by claiming the benefit of contractual provisions. From all that has been stated above, it is clear that a contractual agreement to abandon one's parental rights, or not to contest a termination action, will not be enforced in our courts. The Legislature would not have so carefully, so consistently, and so substantially restricted termination of parental rights if it had intended to allow termination to be achieved by one short sentence in a contract.

* * *

3. The provision in the surrogacy contract stating that Mary Beth Whitehead agrees to "surrender custody . . . and terminate all parental rights" contains no clause giving her a right to rescind. It

is intended to be an irrevocable consent to surrender the child for adoption—in other words, an irrevocable commitment by Mrs. Whitehead to turn Baby M over to the Sterns and thereafter to allow termination of her parental rights.

* * *

This statutory pattern, providing for a surrender in writing and for termination of parental rights by an approved agency, is generally followed in connection with adoption proceedings and proceedings by [The Department of Youth and Family Services] to obtain permanent custody of a child. The statute speaks of such surrender as constituting "relinquishment of such person's parental rights in or guardianship or custody of the child *named therein* and consent by such person to adoption of the child." (emphasis supplied). We emphasize "named therein," for we construe the statute to allow a surrender only after the birth of the child. The formal consent to surrender enables the approved agency to terminate parental rights.

* * *

The provision in the surrogacy contract whereby the mother irrevocably agrees to surrender custody of her child and to terminate her parental rights conflicts with the settled interpretation of New Jersey statutory law. There is only one irrevocable consent, and that is the one explicitly provided for by statute: a consent to surrender of custody and a placement with an approved agency or with DYFS. The provision in the surrogacy contract, agreed to before conception, requiring the natural mother to surrender custody of the child without any right of revocation [signals] the creation of a contractual system designed to circumvent our statutes.

Public Policy Considerations

[handwritten: would it make a difference if the surrogate was not a natural parent?]

* * *

The surrogacy contract guarantees permanent separation of the child from one of its natural parents. Our policy, however, has long been that to the extent possible, children should remain with and be brought up by both of their natural parents. That was the first stated purpose of the previous adoption act: "it is necessary and desirable (a) to protect the child from unnecessary separation from his natural parents." While not so stated in the present adoption law, this purpose remains part of the public policy of this State. This is not simply some theoretical ideal that in practice has no meaning. The impact of failure to follow that policy is nowhere better shown than in the results of this surrogacy contract. A child, instead of starting off its life with as much peace and security as possible, finds itself immediately in a tug-of-war between contending mother and father.

The surrogacy contract violates the policy of this State that the rights of natural parents are equal concerning their child, the father's right no greater than the mother's. The whole purpose and effect of the surrogacy contract was to give the father the exclusive right to the child by destroying the rights of the mother.

* * *

Under the contract, the natural mother is irrevocably committed before she knows the strength of her bond with her child. She never makes a totally voluntary, informed decision, for quite clearly any decision prior to the baby's birth is, in the most important sense, uninformed, and any decision after that, compelled by a pre-existing contractual commitment, the threat of a lawsuit, and the inducement of a $10,000 payment, is less than totally voluntary. Her interests are of little concern to those who controlled this transaction.

Although the interest of the natural father and adoptive mother is certainly the predominant interest, realistically the *only* interest served, even they are left with less than what public policy requires. They know little about the natural mother, her genetic makeup, and her psychological and medical history. Moreover, not even a superficial attempt is made to determine their awareness of their responsibilities as parents.

Worst of all, however, is the contract's total disregard of the best interests of the child. There is not the slightest suggestion that any inquiry will be made at any time to determine the fitness of the Sterns as custodial parents, of Mrs. Stern as an adoptive parent, their superiority to Mrs. Whitehead, or the effect on the child of not living with her natural mother.

This is the sale of a child, or, at the very least, the sale of a mother's right to her child, the only mitigating factor being that one of the purchasers is the father. Almost every evil that prompted the prohibition on the payment of money in connection with adoptions exists here.

First, and perhaps most important, all parties concede that it is unlikely that surrogacy will survive without money.

Second, the use of money in adoptions does not *produce* the problem —conception occurs, and usually the birth itself, before illicit funds are offered. With surrogacy, the "problem," if one views it as such, consisting of the purchase of a woman's procreative capacity, at the risk of her life, is caused by and originates with the offer of money.

Third, [adoptions] do not lead the mother to the highest paying, ill-suited, adoptive parents. She is just as well off surrendering the child to an approved agency. In surrogacy, the highest bidders will presumably become the adoptive parents regardless of suitability, so long as payment of money is permitted.

* * *

In the scheme contemplated by the surrogacy contract in this case, a middle man, propelled by profit, promotes the sale. Whatever idealism may have motivated any of the participants, the profit motive predominates, permeates, and ultimately governs the transaction. The demand for children is great and the supply small. The situation is ripe for the entry of the middleman who will bring some equilibrium into the market by increasing the supply through the use of money.

Intimated, but disputed, is the assertion that surrogacy will be used for the benefit of the rich at the expense of the poor.[8] In response it is noted that the Sterns are not rich and the Whiteheads not poor. Nevertheless, it is clear to us that it is unlikely that surrogate mothers will be as proportionately numerous among those women in the top twenty percent income bracket as among those in the bottom twenty percent. Put differently, we doubt that infertile couples in the low-income bracket will find upper income surrogates.

* * *

The point is made that Mrs. Whitehead *agreed* to the surrogacy arrangement, supposedly fully understanding the consequences. Putting aside the issue of how compelling her need for money may have been, and how significant her understanding of the consequences, we suggest that her consent is irrelevant. There are, in a civilized society, some things that money cannot buy. In America, we decided long ago that merely because conduct purchased by money was "voluntary" did not mean that it was good or beyond regulation and prohibition. Employers can no longer buy labor at the lowest price they can bargain for, even though that labor is "voluntary,"[9] or buy women's labor for less money than paid to men for the same job,[10] or purchase the agreement of children to perform oppressive labor,[11] or purchase the agreement of workers to subject themselves to unsafe or unhealthful working conditions.[12] There are, in short, values that society deems more important than granting to wealth whatever it can buy, be it labor, love, or life.

The long-term effects of surrogacy contracts are not known, but feared —the impact on the child who learns her life was bought, that she is the offspring of someone who gave birth to her only to obtain money; the impact on the natural mother as the full weight of her isolation is felt along with the full reality of the sale of her body and her child; the impact on the natural father and adoptive mother once they realize the consequences of their conduct. Literature in related areas suggests these are substantial considerations, although, given the newness of surrogacy, there is little information.

* * *

Beyond that is the potential degradation of some women that may result from this arrangement. In many cases, of course, surrogacy may bring satisfaction, not only to the infertile couple, but to the surrogate mother herself. The fact, however, that many women may not perceive surrogacy negatively but rather see it as an opportunity does not diminish its potential for devastation to other women.

* * *

They have choices

Custody

Having decided that the surrogacy contract is illegal and unenforceable, we now must decide the custody question without regard to the provisions of the surrogacy contract that would give Mr. Stern sole and permanent custody.

* * *

There were eleven experts who testified concerning the child's best interests, either directly or in connection with matters related to that issue. Our reading of the record persuades us that the trial court's decision awarding custody to the Sterns (technically to Mr. Stern) should be affirmed since "its findings . . . could reasonably have been reached on sufficient credible evidence present in the record."[13] More than that, on this record we find little room for any different conclusion.

NOTES

1. Subsequent to the trial court proceedings, Mr. and Mrs. Whitehead were divorced, and soon thereafter Mrs. Whitehead remarried. Nevertheless, in the

course of this opinion we will make reference almost exclusively to the facts as they existed at the time of trial, the facts on which the decision we now review was reached.

2. N.J. Stat. Ann. tit. 9, §§ 17-43a(1)–44a.

3. N.J. Stat. Ann. tit. 9, §§ 3–54.

4. Sees v. Baber, 74 N.J. 201, 217 (1977).

5. Sees, 74 N.J. at 212–14.

6. N.J. Stat. Ann. tit. 10, § 121A-5.4(c).

7. N.J. Stat. Ann. tit. 9, §§ 3–54a.

8. See, *e.g.,* Margaret Jane Radin, *Market Inalienability,* 100 Harv. L. Rev. 1849, 1930 (1987).

9. 29 U.S.C. § 206 (1982).

10. 29 U.S.C. § 206(d).

11. 29 U.S.C. § 212.

12. 29 U.S.C. §§ 651 to 678. (Occupational Safety and Health Act of 1970).

13. Beck v. Beck, 86 N.J. 480, 496 (1981).

In Search of Pharaoh's Daughter

Patricia J. Williams[1]

When I decided to adopt, I was unprepared for the reality that adoption is already a pretty straightforward market.

"Describe yourself," said the application form. *Oh lord,* I remember thinking, *this is worse than a dating service. What's appealing about me, and to whom'? Responsible nonsmoking omni-vore seeks . . . what? Little person for lifetime of bicycle rides, good education, and peanut butter sandwiches? Forty and fading fast so I thought I'd better get a move on?* "You can't tell them you're forty," a friend advised. "No one will ever pick you." Okay, I sighed. "Very well rounded," I wrote.

* * *

"What age, what sex?" asked the social worker. "Doesn't matter," I said, "though I'd like to miss out on as little as possible."

"If you're willing to take a boy, you'll get younger," she replied. "There's a run on girls."

"What races would you accept?" asked the adoption agency. "And what racial combinations?" There followed a whole menu of evocative options, like Afro-Javanese, Sino-Germanic, and just plain "white." I assume that this list, so suggestive of the multiple combinations of meat offered at, say, Kentucky Fried Chicken, would make Elizabeth Landes [*sic*] and Richard Posner very happy indeed. They advise:

> The genetic characteristics of natural children are highly correlated with their parents' genetic characteristics, and this correlation could conceivably increase harmony within the family compared to what it would be with an adopted child. Nevertheless, there is considerable suitability between natural and adopted children and it might be much greater if better

genetic matching of adopted children with their adoptive parents were feasible—as might occur, we shall see, under free market conditions.

"Any," I wrote, knowing that harmony genes abound in my ancestral bloodlines—yet wondering if the agency really meant to address that question to black parents. Would they truly consider placing "any" child with me if this agency happened to have a "surplus" of white babies? Would I get a Korean baby if I asked? And for all of the advertised difficulties, what does it mean that it is so relatively easy for white American families not just to adopt black children but to choose from a range of colors, nationalities, and configurations from around the world?

* * *

"What color?" asked the form. *You've got to be kidding.* I looked quizzically at the social worker. "Some families like to match," she said. *You mean, like color-coordinated? You mean like the Louisiana codes?*

"I don't care," I wrote. And with that magical stroke of the pen, the door to a whole world of plentiful, newborn, brown-skinned little boys with little brown toes and big brown eyes and round brown noses and fat brown cheeks opened up to me from behind the curtain marked "Doesn't Care."

"This is a cheap shot," says my friend the economist. "How can anyone criticize or take scholarly issue with the breathy mother-love of such descriptions? And what does any of this have to do with the price of tea in China?" It's a good question, I guess, and all I can do is remind the reader that I am trying, quite intentionally, to explode the clean, scientific way in which this subject is often discussed. And if it has little to do with tea or soybeans, just maybe the positioning of mother-or-any-other-love as some kind of irrelevant externality has a little something to do with the price of children in America.

My son, because he is a stylish little character, arrived at my home in a limousine. (Credit for this must be shared with the social worker, who was a pretty jazzy sort herself.) I had a big party and a naming ceremony and invited everyone I knew. I was so happy that I guess I missed that price tag hanging from his little blue knitted beanie. A few weeks later I got a call from the agency: "Which fee schedule are you going to choose?"

"What's this?" I asked the adoption agent, flipping madly through Landes and Posner for guidance: "Prospective adoptive parents would presumably be willing to pay more for a child whose health and genealogy were warranted in a legally enforceable instrument than they are willing to pay under the present system where the entire risk of any deviation from expected quality falls on them."

"Are you going with the standard or the special?" came the reply. There followed a description of a system in which adoptive parents paid a certain percentage of their salaries to the agency, which fee went to administrative costs, hospital expenses for the birth mother, and counseling. Inasmuch as it was tied exclusively to income, in a graduated scale, it clearly met the definition of a fee for services rendered. This, it was explained to me, was the standard price list.

"And the special?" I asked. After an embarrassed pause, I was told that that referred to "older, black, and other handicapped children," and that its fees were exactly half of those on the standard scale. Suddenly what had been a price system based on services rendered became clearly, sickeningly, a price system for "goods," a sale for chattel, linked not to services but to the imagined quality of the "things" exchanged. Although, as the agency asserted, this system was devised to provide "economic incentives" for the adoption of "less requested" children, in our shopping-mall world it had all the earmarks of a two-for-one sale.

* * *

How will my son's "price" at birth relate to what value doctors put on his various parts if he ever stubs his toe and shows up at a hospital? Will he be valued more as a series of parts in the marketplace of bodies or more as a whole, as a precious social being with not just a body or a will but a soul? Will his fate be decided by a fellow human being who cares for him, or will his "outcome" be negotiated by some formulaic economic tracking policy based on his having health insurance or a job? Who will rule the fate of this most precious bit of "living property," as Harriet Beecher Stowe called the status of blacks?

* * *

I was unable to choose a fee schedule. I was unable to conspire in putting a price on my child's head.

NOTE

1. Reprinted with the permission of the publisher from The Rooster's Egg: The Persistence of Prejudice by Patricia J. Williams, pp. 218–225, Cambridge, Mass.: Harvard University Press, Copyright © 1995 by the President and Fellows of Harvard College.

Johnson v. Calvert

851 P.2d 776 (Cal. 1993)

Panelli, J.

* * *

Mark and Crispina Calvert are a married couple who desired to have a child. Crispina was forced to undergo a hysterectomy in 1984. Her ovaries remained capable of producing eggs, however, and the couple eventually considered surrogacy. In 1989 Anna Johnson heard about Crispina's plight from a coworker and offered to serve as a surrogate for the Calverts.

On January 15, 1990, Mark, Crispina, and Anna signed a contract providing that an embryo created by the sperm of Mark and the egg of Crispina would be implanted in Anna and the child born would be taken into Mark and Crispina's home "as their child." Anna agreed she would relinquish "all parental rights" to the child in favor of Mark and Crispina. In return, Mark and Crispina would pay Anna $10,000 in a series of installments, the last to be paid six weeks after the child's birth. Mark and Crispina were also to pay for a $200,000 life insurance policy on Anna's life.

The zygote was implanted on January 19, 1990. Less than a month later, an ultrasound test confirmed Anna was pregnant.

Unfortunately, relations deteriorated between the two sides. Mark learned that Anna had not disclosed she had suffered several stillbirths and miscarriages. Anna felt Mark and Crispina did not do enough to obtain the required insurance policy. She also felt abandoned during an onset of premature labor in June.

In July 1990, Anna sent Mark and Crispina a letter demanding the balance of the payments due her or else she would refuse to give up the child.

71

The following month, Mark and Crispina responded with a lawsuit, seeking a declaration they were the legal parents of the unborn child. Anna filed her own action to be declared the mother of the child, and the two cases were eventually consolidated.

* * *

In this case the factual basis of each woman's claim is obvious. Thus, there is no need to resort to an evidentiary presumption to ascertain the identity of the natural mother. Instead, we must make the purely legal determination as between the two claimants.

* * *

Anna, not Crispina, gave birth to the child and Crispina, not Anna, is genetically related to him. Both women thus have adduced evidence of a mother and child relationship as contemplated by the [Parentage] Act.[1] Yet for any child California law recognizes only one natural mother, despite advances in reproductive technology rendering a different outcome biologically possible.

* * *

Because two women each have presented acceptable proof of maternity, we do not believe this case can be decided without enquiring into the parties' intentions as manifested in the surrogacy agreement. Mark and Crispina are a couple who desired to have a child of their own genes but are physically unable to do so without the help of reproductive technology. They affirmatively intended the birth of the child, and took the steps necessary to effect in vitro fertilization. But for their acted-on intention, the child would not exist. Anna agreed to facilitate the procreation of Mark's and Crispina's child. The parties' aim was to bring Mark's and Crispina's child into the world, not for Mark and Crispina to donate a zygote to Anna. Crispina from the outset intended to be the child's mother. Although the gestative function Anna performed was necessary to bring about the child's birth, it is safe to say that Anna would not have been given the opportunity to gestate or deliver the child had she, prior to implantation of the zygote, manifested her own intent to be the child's mother. No reason appears why Anna's later change of heart should vitiate the determination that Crispina is the child's natural mother.

We conclude that although the Act recognizes both genetic consanguinity and giving birth as means of establishing a mother and child relationship, when the two means do not coincide in one woman, she who intended to procreate the child—that is, she who intended to bring about the birth of a child that she intended to raise as her own—is the natural mother under California law.

* * *

In deciding the issue of maternity under the Act we have felt free to take into account the parties' intentions, as expressed in the surrogacy contract, because in our view the agreement is not, on its face, inconsistent with public policy.

* * *

Anna urges that surrogacy contracts violate several social policies. Relying on her contention that she is the child's legal, natural mother, she cites the public policy embodied in Penal Code section 273, prohibiting the payment for consent to adoption of a child. She argues further that the policies underlying the adoption laws of this state are violated by the surrogacy contract because it in effect constitutes a prebirth waiver of her parental rights.

* * *

We disagree. Gestational surrogacy differs in crucial respects from adoption and so is not subject to the adoption statutes. The parties voluntarily agreed to participate in in vitro fertilization and related medical procedures before the child was conceived; at the time when Anna entered into the contract, therefore, she was not vulnerable to financial inducements to part with her own expected offspring. As discussed above, Anna was not the genetic mother of the child. The payments to Anna under the contract were meant to compensate her for her services in gestating the fetus and undergoing labor, rather than for giving up "parental" rights to the child. Payments were due both during the pregnancy and after the child's birth. We are, accordingly, unpersuaded that the contract used in this case violates the public policies embodied in Penal Code section 273 and the adoption statutes. For the same reasons, we conclude these contracts do not implicate the policies underlying the statutes governing termination of parental rights.

* * *

Finally, Anna and some commentators have expressed concern that surrogacy contracts tend to exploit or dehumanize women, especially women of lower economic status.

* * *

We are unpersuaded that gestational surrogacy arrangements are so likely to cause the untoward results Anna cites as to demand their invalidation on public policy grounds. Although common sense suggests that women of lesser means serve as surrogate mothers more often than do wealthy women, there has been no proof that surrogacy contracts exploit poor women to any greater degree than economic necessity in general exploits them by inducing them to accept lower-paid or otherwise undesirable employment.

The argument that a woman cannot knowingly and intelligently agree to gestate and deliver a baby for intending parents carries overtones of the reasoning that for centuries prevented women from attaining equal economic rights and professional status under the law. To resurrect this view is both to foreclose a personal and economic choice on the part of the surrogate mother, and to deny intending parents what may be their only means of procreating a child of their own genes. Certainly in the present case it cannot seriously be argued that Anna, a licensed vocational nurse who had done well in school and who had previously borne a child, lacked the intellectual wherewithal or life experience necessary to make an informed decision to enter into the surrogacy contract.

* * *

Dissenting Opinion

Kennard, J. . . . Unlike the majority, I do not agree that the determinative consideration should be the intent to have the child that originated with the woman who contributed the ovum. In my view, the woman who provided the fertilized ovum and the woman who gave birth to the child both have substantial claims to legal motherhood. Pregnancy entails a unique commitment, both psychological and emotional, to an unborn child. No less substantial, however, is the contribution of the woman from whose egg the child developed and without whose desire the child would not exist.

* * *

Policy Considerations

* * *

This case presents a difficult issue. The majority's resolution of that issue deserves serious consideration. Ultimately, however, I cannot agree that "intent" is the appropriate test for resolving this case.

* * *

The majority's resort to "but-for" causation is curious. The concept of "but-for" causation is a "test used in determining tort liability. . . ."[2] In California, the test for causation is whether the conduct was a "substantial factor" in bringing about the event.[3] Neither test for causation assists the majority, as I shall discuss.

The proposition that a woman who gives birth to a child after carrying it for nine months is a "substantial factor" in the child's birth cannot reasonably be debated. Nor can it reasonably be questioned that "but for" the gestational mother, there would not be a child.

* * *

The "originators of the concept" rationale seems comfortingly familiar. The reason it seems familiar, however, is that it is a rationale that is frequently advanced as justifying the law's protection of intellectual property. As stated by one author, "an idea belongs to its creator because the idea is a manifestation of the creator's personality or self."[4]

The problem with this argument, of course, is that children are not property. Unlike songs or inventions, rights in children cannot be sold for consideration, or made freely available to the general public. Our most fundamental notions of personhood tell us it is inappropriate to treat children as property. Although the law may justly recognize that the originator of a concept has certain property rights in that concept, the originator of the concept of a child can have no such rights, because children cannot be owned as property.

Next, the majority offers as its third rationale the notion that bargained-for expectations support its conclusion regarding the dispositive significance of the genetic mother's intent.

It is commonplace that, in real or personal property transactions governed by contracts, "intentions that are voluntarily chosen, deliberate, express and bargained-for" ought presumptively to be enforced and, when one party seeks to escape performance, the court may order specific performance. But the courts will not compel performance of all contract obligations. For instance, even when a party to a contract for personal services (such as employment) has willfully breached the contract, the courts will not order specific enforcement of an obligation to perform that personal service. Just as children are not the intellectual property of their parents, neither are they the personal property of anyone, and their delivery cannot be ordered as a contract remedy on the same terms that a court would, for example, order a breaching party to deliver a truckload of nuts and bolts.

* * *

I would reverse the judgment of the Court of Appeal, and remand the case to the trial court for a determination of disputed parentage on the basis of the best interests of the child.

NOTES

1. Civ. Code, § 7003, subd. (1), 7004, subd. (a), 7015; Evid. Code, § 621, 892.
2. Black's Law Dict. 200 (6th ed. 1990).
3. Mitchell v. Gonzales 54 Cal.3d 1041, 1049, 1054, 1056 (1991).
4. Justin Hughes, *The Philosophy of Intellectual Property* 77 Geo. L.J. 287, 330 (1988).

C.

Defaulting to Freedom
or to Equality
Treating Some Things as Inalienable

Property Rules, Liability Rules, and Inalienability

One View of the Cathedral

Guido Calabresi and A. Douglas Melamed[1]

[*Editors' Note*: The following article is a highly influential piece of law and economics scholarship. It provides a foundational framework for understanding different kinds of legal rules by examining who owns entitlements and how those entitlements are protected. The authors identify two kinds of entitlements: property rules, under which an entitlement is transferred only with the consent of the entitlement holder; and liability rules, under which an entitlement holder receives compensation after an involuntary transfer (for example, eminent domain or nuisance claims). But most relevant for purposes of commodification theory is the article's discussion of what kinds of entitlements are not transferable at all—in other words, what kinds of things are inalienable. This section on inalienability is excerpted below.]

Inalienable Entitlements

* * *

[One] instance in which external costs may justify inalienability occurs when external costs do not lend themselves to collective measurement which is acceptably objective and nonarbitrary. Such external costs are often called moralisms.

If Taney is allowed to sell himself into slavery, or to take undue risks of becoming penniless, or to sell a kidney, Marshall may be harmed, simply because Marshall is a sensitive man who is made unhappy by seeing slaves, paupers, or persons who die because they have sold a kidney. Again Marshall could pay Taney not to sell his freedom to Chase the slaveowner; but again, because Marshall is not one but many individuals, freeloader and information costs make such transactions practically impossible. Again, it might seem that the state could intervene by objectively valuing the external cost to Marshall and requiring Chase to pay that cost. But since the external cost to Marshall does not lend itself to an acceptable objective measurement, such liability rules are not appropriate.

* * *

Obviously we will not always value the external harm of a moralism enough to prohibit the sale.[2] And obviously also, external costs other than moralisms may be sufficiently hard to value to make rules of inalienability appropriate in certain circumstances; this reason for rules of inalienability, however, does seem most often germane in situations where moralisms are involved.[3]

There are two other efficiency reasons for forbidding the sale of entitlements under certain circumstances: self paternalism and true paternalism. Examples of the first are Ulysses tying himself to the mast or individuals passing a bill of rights so that they will be prevented from yielding to momentary temptations which they deem harmful to themselves. This type of limitation is not in any real sense paternalism. It merely allows the individual to choose what is best in the long run rather than in the short run, even though that choice entails giving up some short run freedom of choice.

True paternalism brings us a step further toward explaining such prohibitions and those of broader kinds—for example the prohibitions on a whole range of activities by minors. Paternalism is based on the notion that at least in some situations the Marshalls know better than Taney what will make Taney better off. Here we are not talking about the offense to Marshall from Taney's choosing to read pornography, or selling himself into slavery, but rather the judgment that Taney was not in the position to choose best for himself when he made the choice for erotica or servitude. The first concept we called a moralism and is a frequent and important ground for inalienability. The second, paternalism, is also an important economic efficiency reason for inalienability: the most efficient pie is no longer that which costless bargains would achieve, because a person may be better off if he is prohibited from bargaining.

NOTES

1. Reprinted with permission from Guido Calabresi and A. Douglas Melamed, *Property Rules, Liability Rules, and Inalienability: One View of the Cathedral*, 85 Harv. L. Rev. 1089, 1111–14 (1972).

2. For example, I am allowed to buy and read whatever books I like, or to sell my house to whomever I choose, regardless of whether my doing so makes my neighbors unhappy.

3. The fact that society may make an entitlement inalienable does not, of course, mean that there will be no compensation to the holder of the entitlement if it is taken from him. Thus even if a society forbids the sale of one's kidneys it will still probably compensate the person whose kidney is destroyed in an auto accident.

Contested Commodities

Margaret Jane Radin[1]

[handwritten note: argues that commodities can be both commodified & Non-commodified Simultaneously]

The contemporary arena of moral and political debate is full of painful and puzzling controversies about what things can properly be bought and sold: babies? sexual services? kidneys and corneas? environmental pollution permits? These things are contested commodities. They challenge us to try to understand the appropriate scope of the market. This book presents a pragmatic philosophical and legal approach to thinking about some of our contested commodities—those that are related to persons and the nature of human life.

* * *

The ungainly word "commodification" denotes a particular social construction of things people value, their social construction as commodities. Commodification refers to the social process by which something comes to be apprehended as a commodity, as well as to the state of affairs once the process has taken place. "Contested commodification"—the focus of this book—refers to instances in which we experience personal and social conflict about the process and the result.

The word "commodity," as I use it, is a conception embedded in modern market society. There are other ways of understanding the word "commodity" that are outside the culture of the market society or that antedate its historical era. I am concerned with the connotations of something's being treated as a commodity against the background of our contemporary common understanding of organized markets.

Although there are affinities between my use of the term "commodity" and Marx's, I do not adopt the notion, which some derive from Marx, that commodification is always wrong. Nor do I find, as many Marxists would, that commodified understandings of social interactions cannot coexist with noncommodified ones.

Instead I believe there can be coexistent commodified and noncommodified understandings of various aspects of social life. The questions I believe need to be asked are in what instances there actually is such coexistence, and whether that coexistence is unstable, threatening to decay into a monolithic structure of commodification.

These questions arise from the pragmatic methodology I favor. This book reflects a pragmatist's take on the social meaning(s) of market trading and of the attendant notions of property entitlements alienable through freedom of contract. True to the pragmatic spirit, the explorations in this book are relatively retail rather than wholesale—sticking fairly close to the details of context and not engaging in a search for a grand theory. In my view, no one theory is suitable for all cases of contested commodification.

* * *

Considering commodification as a worldview involves confronting one influential strand of contemporary economic analysis. The Chicago school of economics tends to conceive of everything people may value as a scarce commodity with a price. Economic journals are full of studies treating as market commodities aspects of life and love that the rest of us are used to thinking of as noneconomic. Policy analysts ask us to make monetized trade-offs about the length and quality of life in order to allocate health care resources; they ask us to value life in dollars in order to find out the "right" level of occupational safety risk. Is anything wrong with reasoning that way? If there are realms of social life that are or should be off-limits to the market, how should we delineate those realms, and what kind of analysis could we use in them? What (if anything) is wrong with commodification of everything?

Because these questions ask about the appropriate relationship of particular things to the market, it looks as if we need a normative theory about the appropriate social role of the market to answer it. Theories about the role of the market can be imagined as ordered on a continuum stretching from universal noncommodification (nothing in markets) to universal commodification (everything in markets). On this continuum, Karl Marx's theory can represent the theoretical pole of universal noncommodification. The views of Gary Becker, a Nobel laureate who applies economic analysis to family life, and of Judge Richard Posner, author of an economic theory of sex, can be seen as close to the opposite theoretical pole. In this book I explore the theoretical poles, but I find matters too complex to be captured adequately by one of these wholesale theories.

If both theoretical poles are inadequate, what is in the middle? A traditional middle way has been a kind of market compartmentalization. Many theorists in the liberal political tradition see a normatively appropriate but limited realm for commodification coexisting with one or more nonmarket realms. They partition the social world into markets and politics, markets and rights, markets and families, and so on. For a compartmentalizer, the crucial question is how to conceive of the permissible scope of the market. An acceptable answer would solve problems of contested commodification. Nevertheless, I argue that traditional liberal compartmentalization is at best oversimplified and cannot lead to the kind of answer envisioned. Worse, it may tempt us to overlook the ways in which market and nonmarket conceptualizations of social interactions can and do coexist, and it fails to give us a theoretical handle on how to evaluate these cultural crosscurrents.

I want to argue for a different kind of middle way. In this book I develop a notion of incomplete commodification that I hope will help us deal better with the complexities of commodification as we experience it. These complexities include the plurality of meanings of any particular interaction, the dynamic nature of these meanings (their instability), and the possible effects (good or ill) in the world of either promoting or trying to forestall a commodified understanding of something that we have previously valued in a noneconomic way. I give no wholesale argument that commodified understandings—market conceptualizations—are bad no matter where and how they occur. Instead I try to work through these complexities with respect to a number of salient issues, among them prostitution [and] baby-selling. I [also] consider the ramifications of understanding free expression as a laissez-faire marketplace of ideas, and of understanding democracy as merely a species of economics.

* * *

Contagious Commodification? A Domino Theory

[I]t becomes natural to wonder whether commodification is contagious and monolithic. If it is both, then once some commodification enters the arena, there is a slippery slope—a domino effect—leading to market domination.

The domino theory assumes that for some things, the noncommodified version is morally preferable; it also assumes that the commodified
and noncommodified versions of some interactions cannot coexist.
Under this theory, the existence of some commodified sexual interactions
will contaminate or infiltrate everyone's sexuality so that all sexual relationships will become commodified. If it is morally required that noncommodified sex be possible, market-inalienability of sexuality would be
justified. This result can be conceived of as the opposite of a prohibition:
there is assumed to exist some moral requirement that a certain "good"
be socially available. The domino theory thus supplies an answer (as the
prohibition theory does not) to the liberal question why people should
not be permitted to choose both market and nonmarket interactions: the
noncommodified version is morally preferable when we cannot have
both.

* * *

If, however, conflicting understandings of an interaction are not well crys-
tallized, each can characterize one of its aspects. The same person can understand an interaction in different, and conflicting, ways, as, analo-
gously, she can both feel a painting is priceless and yet have it appraised
for insurance purposes. Then neither commodification nor noncommodification can accurately describe the way such a person conceives of an interaction. That second kind of coexistence of market and nonmarket understandings also can be denominated a species of incomplete commodification.

Where different meanings coexist in society as a whole or in persons
themselves, it becomes simplistic to think of our social policy as binary;
either complete commodification or complete noncommodification. Instead, it becomes important to recognize both our social division over
commodification and the nonmarket aspect of many transactions that
can be conceived of in market terms.

The domino theory assumes that anytime we find market and nonmarket understandings coexisting, either as a contested concept or as internally plural meanings, it is inevitable that the market understandings
will win out.

I want to urge, on the contrary, that such a preordained victory of market understandings should not be presumed. If we do presume it, we are
implicitly subscribing to the commodified theory of human nature that
makes market understandings more powerful than their possible alternatives. Such an implicit and broad-based commitment must be avoided if

we wish to achieve a more nuanced understanding of where we stand with respect to commodification.

* * *

As an alternative to compartmentalization, I think we should recognize a continuum reflecting degrees of commodification that will be appropriate in a given context. An incomplete commodification—a partial market inalienability—can sometimes reflect the conflicted state of affairs in the way we understand an interaction. And an incomplete commodification can sometimes substitute for a complete noncommodification that might accord with our ideals but cause too much harm in our nonideal world.

* * *

The Double Bind: Nonideal Justice and Never-Ending Transition

There is always a gap between the ideals we can formulate and the progress we can realize. Hence there is always an ambiguity about theorizing about justice, and there is always an ambiguity about seeking justice. Does justice refer to the best general ideals we can formulate? We can call this ideal justice. Or does justice refer to a theoretical working out of what changes would now count as social improvements? We can call this nonideal justice. When we seek justice, should we pursue ideal or nonideal justice?

* * *

Pursuing nonideal justice is linked with a dilemma of transition from where we are now to a better world. If we compromise our ideals too much because of the difficulties of our circumstances, we may reinforce the status quo instead of making progress. Some would argue that giving welfare entrenches recipients in an underclass rather than helping them to escape from it. On the other hand, if we are too utopian about our ideals given our circumstances, we may also make no progress. Granted that an underclass in need of welfare would not exist in an ideal state, it still may worsen the situation to abolish welfare now. This practical dilemma of nonideal justice is what I call the double bind.

* * *

The double bind is omnipresent in the pursuit of justice because the problem of transition that generates it is simply an artifact of the interdependence of theory and practice. Nonideal justice is the process by which we try to make progress (effect a transition) toward our vision of the good world. In the transition all decisions about justice—as opposed to theories about it—are pragmatic decisions. Ideal theory is equally necessary because we need to know what we are trying to achieve; and ideal theory metamorphoses as our decisions take effect. In other words, our visions and nonideal decisions, our theory and practice, paradoxically constitute each other.

With respect to commodification, the double bind has two main consequences. First, if we sometimes cannot respect personhood either by permitting sales or by banning sales, justice requires that we consider changing the circumstances that create the dilemma. We must consider wealth and power redistribution. Second, we still must choose a regime for the meantime, the transition, in nonideal circumstances. To resolve the double bind, we have to investigate particular problems separately. Decisions must be made (and remade) for each thing that some people desire to sell. At the same time, each separate decision must be made in light of a reevaluation of both our ideals and our circumstances.

Social Justice in Context

* * *

The personhood argument that people should not be allowed to sell, for example, their organs because to do so is degrading to personhood calls attention to a more pervasive problem of social justice. If people are so desperate for money that they are trying to sell things we think cannot be separated from them without significant injury to personhood, we do not cure the desperation by banning sales. Nor do we avoid the injury to personhood. Perhaps the desperation is the social problem we should be looking at, rather than the market ban. Perhaps worse injury to personhood is suffered from the desperation that caused the attempt to sell a kidney or cornea than would be suffered from actually selling it. The would-be sellers apparently think so. Then justice is not served by a ban on "desperate exchanges."

These considerations change the arena of argument from considerations of appropriateness to the market to explicit considerations of social justice. If neither commodification nor noncommodification can put to rest our disquiet about harm to personhood in conjunction with certain specific kinds of transactions-if neither commodification nor noncommodification can satisfy our aspirations for a society exhibiting equal respect for persons—then we must rethink the larger social context in which this dilemma is embedded. We must think about wealth and power redistribution.

* * *

Thus the double bind: both commodification and noncommodification may be harmful. Harmful, that is, under our current social conditions. Neither one need be harmful in an ideal world. The fact that money changes hands need not necessarily contaminate human interactions of sharing. Nor must the fact that a social order makes nonmonetary sharing its norm necessarily deprive or subordinate anyone. That commodification now tends toward fungibility of women, and that noncommodification now tends toward their domination and continued subordination are artifacts of the current social hierarchy. In other words, the fact of oppression is what gives rise to the double bind.

[handwritten margin note: Social Norms are what make it harmful]

* * *

Then how can we make progress? The other half of the problem is the nonideal problem of transition from the present situation toward our ideal. The pragmatist solution is to confront each dilemma as it occurs and choose the alternative that will hinder empowerment the least and further it the most. Appropriate solutions may all differ, depending on the current stage of women's empowerment, and how the proposed solution might move the current social conception of gender and our vision of how gender should be reconceived for the future. Indeed, the "same" double bind may demand a different solution tomorrow from the one we find best today.

* * *

Prostitution and Baby-Selling: Contested Commodification and Women's Capacities

Payment in exchange for sexual intercourse and payment in exchange for relinquishing a child for adoption are nodal cases of contested commodification. They express the double bind for women especially clearly. They implicate issues of race and class. They show how our culture stubbornly insists on conceiving of the person as a moral agent, as a subject distinct from a world of objects, yet how at the same time our culture persistently commodifies and objectifies.

* * *

Prostitution

Start with the traditional ideal of sexual interaction as equal nonmon-etized sharing. In an ideal theory of justice, we might hold that the "good" commodified sexuality ought not to exist: that sexual activity should be market-inalienable. But considerations of nonideal justice might tell us that prohibiting sale of sexual services in order to preserve sexuality as nonmonetized sharing is not justified under current circum-stances. One reason to say this is that sex is already commodified. Legal-ized prostitution has existed in many places, and there has always been a large black market of which everyone is well aware. Those who purchase prostitutes' services are often not prosecuted, at least in traditional male-female prostitution.[2] This practice tolerates commodification of sexuality, at least by the purchasers.

Moreover, in our nonideal world, market-inalienability—especially if enforced through criminalization of sales—may cause harm to ideals of personhood instead of maintaining and fostering them, primarily because it exacerbates the double bind. Poor women who believe that they must sell their sexual services in order to survive are subject to moral oppro-brium, disease, arrest, and violence. The ideal of sexual sharing is related to identity and contextuality, but the identity of those who sell is under-mined by criminalization and powerlessness, and their contextuality, their ability to develop and maintain relationships, is stunted in these cir-cumstances.

Despite the double bind and the harms of the black market to prosti-tutes, fear of a domino effect—the discourse contagion of market rhetoric —might be thought to warrant market-inalienability as an effort to ward off conceiving of all sexuality as commodified. To this suggestion many people would protest that the known availability of commodified sex does not by itself render noncommodified sexual interactions impossible or even more difficult. They would say that the prevalence of ideals of in-terpersonal sexual sharing despite the widespread association of sex and money, is proof that the domino effect in rhetoric is not to be feared.

But we must evaluate the seriousness of the risk if commodification proceeds. What if sex were fully and openly commodified? Suppose news-papers, radio, TV, and billboards advertised sexual services as imagina-tively and vividly as they advertise computer services, health clubs, or soft drinks. Suppose the sexual partner of your choice could be ordered through a catalog, or through a large brokerage firm that has an 800 number, or at a trade show, or in a local showroom. Suppose the business of recruiting suppliers of sexual services was carried on in the same way as corporate headhunting or training of word-processing operators.

If sex were openly commodified in this way, its commodification would be reflected in everyone's discourse about sex, and in particular about women's sexuality. New terms would emerge for particular grada-tions of sexual market value. New discussions would be heard of partic-ular abilities or qualities in terms of their market value. With this change in discourse, when it became pervasive enough, would come a change in everyone's experience, because experience is discourse dependent. The open market might render an understanding of women (and perhaps everyone) in terms of sexual dollar value impossible to avoid. It might make the ideal of nonmonetized sharing impossible. Thus, the argument for noncommodification of sexuality based on the domino effect, in its strongest form, is that we do not wish to unleash market forces onto the shaping of our discourse regarding sexuality and hence onto our very conception of sexuality and our sexual feelings.

This domino argument assumes that nonmonetized equal-sharing re-lationships are the norm or are at least attainable. That assumption is now contested. Some feminists, notably Catharine MacKinnon, argue that male-female sexual relationships that actually instantiate the ideal of equal sharing are under current social circumstances rare or even impos-sible.[3] According to this view, moreover, women are oppressed by this ideal because they try to understand their relationships with men in light of it, and conceal from themselves the truth about their own condition. They try to understand what they are doing as giving, as equal sharing, while their sexuality is actually being taken from them. If we believe that women are deceived (and deceiving themselves) in this way, attempted noncommodification in the name of the ideal may be futile or even coun-terproductive. Noncommodification under current circumstances is part of the social structure that perpetuates false consciousness about the cur-rent role of the ideal.

Some feminists also argue that many male-female sexual relationships are (unequal) economic bargains, not a context in which equal sharing occurs.[4] If that is true, attempted noncommodification of sexuality means that prostitutes are being singled out for punishment for something per-vasive in women's condition. They are being singled out because their class or race forecloses more socially accepted forms of sexual bargain-ing. This situation returns us to the double bind.

Perhaps the best way to characterize the present situation is to say that women's sexuality is incompletely commodified, perhaps both in the sense that it is a contested concept and in the sense that its meaning is internally plural. Many sexual relationships may have both market and nonmarket aspects: relationships may be entered into and sustained partly for economic reasons and partly for the interpersonal sharing that is part of our ideal of human flourishing. Under current circumstances the ideal misleads us into thinking that unequal relationships are really equal. Yet because the ideal of equal sharing is part of a conception of human personhood to which we remain deeply committed, it seems that the way out of such ideological bondage is not to abandon the ideal, but rather to pursue it in ways that are not harmful under these nonideal circumstances. Market-inalienability (attempted noncommodification) seems harmful as it is practiced in our world. Yet complete commodification, if any credence is given to the feared domino effect, may foreclose our conception of sexuality entirely.

So perhaps the best policy solution, for now, is a regime of regulation expressing incomplete commodification. The issue becomes how to structure an incomplete commodification that takes account of our nonideal world yet does not foreclose progress to a better world of more nearly equal power (and less susceptibility to the domino effect of market rhetoric). In my opinion, we should now decriminalize the sale of sexual services. We should not subject poor women to the degradation and danger of the black market nor force them into other methods of earning money that seem to them less desirable than selling their bodies. At the same time, in order to check the domino effect, I believe we should prohibit the free-market entrepreneurship that would otherwise accompany decriminalization and could operate to create an organized market in sexual services. Such regulation would include, for example, such deviations from laissez-faire as banning brokerage (pimping) and worker training (recruitment).

In structuring a regulatory regime expressing incomplete commodification for sexual activity, an important issue is whether contracts to sell sexual services should be enforced. The usual reason given for precluding specific performance of personal service agreements is that forcing performance smacks of slavery. If sexual service contracts were to be specifically performed, persons would be forced to yield their bodily integrity and freedom. This is commodification of the person. Suppose, then, that we decide to preclude specific performance but allow a damage remedy.

Enforceable contracts might make the "goods" command higher prices. Prostitutes might welcome such an arrangement; it might be on the pro-commodification side of the double bind. The other side is that having to pay damages for deciding not to engage in sex with someone seems very harmful to the ideal of sexuality as integral to personhood. Moreover, it seems that determining the amount of damages due is tantamount to complete commodification. Granting a damage remedy requires an official entity to place a dollar value on the "goods"; commodification is thus officially imposed. *↓ if they are paying it is already comm.*

In this context both specific performance and damages seem to go all the way to complete commodification. Thus, we should continue to make prostitution contracts unenforceable, denying the most important factor of commodification—enforceable free contract. We could either provide for restitution if the woman reneges or let losses lie. If we let losses lie, we preclude any increased domino effect that official governmental (court) pronouncements about commodified sexuality might cause. But letting losses lie would also allow men to take and not pay when women are ignorant or powerless enough to fail to collect in advance. Similar two-edged results are reached by the doctrine of nonenforcement of illegal contracts, under which contracts to render sexual services are currently unenforceable because of the illegality of prostitution.

* * *

Baby-Selling

Just as some women wish to sell their sexual services, some wish to sell their children. Is a regulatory regime expressing incomplete commodification also now warranted for baby-selling? In my opinion, the answer is no, but the issues are very complex.

Let me start with the general issue of selling babies to would-be parents. If our regime were to allow would-be parents to approach a woman of their choice and commission a pregnancy for a fee, with the woman releasing the baby to them at birth, we would no doubt characterize this regime as one in which babies are being produced for sale. I refer to this scenario as "commissioned adoption." A regime allowing commissioned adoption would provide for a full-blown market in babies. The supply of newborn babies for sale would be related primarily to the demand of the would-be parents who wanted to buy them; that is, the quantity of children supplied would depend on the prices would-be parents would pay and how many would be willing to buy children at a given offering price.

If our regime were to allow would-be parents to approach a woman who is already pregnant, or who has already given birth, and for a fee have her release the baby to them, we would also characterize this regime as one in which babies are sold, though not one in which babies are being produced for sale. I refer to this scenario as "paid adoption of 'unwanted' children." This regime would not be a full-blown market in babies, because the supply of newborn babies for sale would not be related primarily to the demand of the would-be parents who wanted to buy them. Instead, supply would probably be related primarily to access to birth control information and education, and to cultural characteristics having to do with sexuality and permissibility of abortion. Of course, this regime could approach a black-market version of a commissioned adoption regime, because some women might conceive babies without any pre-arranged purchaser but hoping to put them up for sale.

As far as I know, no jurisdiction permits paid adoption of "unwanted" children; it is universally prohibited as baby-selling. (Many jurisdictions permit the birth mother to be paid expenses, and this arrangement creates a gray market.) A fortiori, no jurisdiction permits commissioned adoption. Our status quo "official" social regime—and the "official" regime is the one that has the most symbolic cultural significance—bans the exchange of children for money. That cultural significance makes troubling even the market rhetoric I have been using in these paragraphs.

Like relationships of sexual sharing, parent-child relationships are closely connected with personhood, particularly with personal identity and contextuality, and the interest of would-be parents is a strong one. Moreover, poor women caught in the double bind raise the issue of freedom: they may wish to sell a baby on the black market, as they may wish to sell sexual services, perhaps to try to provide adequately for other children or family members. But the double bind is not the only problem of freedom implicated in baby-selling. Under a market regime, prostitutes may be choosing to sell their sexuality, but babies are not choosing for themselves that under current nonideal circumstances they are better off as commodities. If we permit babies to be sold, we commodify not only the mother's (and father's) baby making capacities—which might be analogous to commodifying sexuality—but also the baby herself.

When the baby becomes a commodity, all of her personal attributes—sex, eye color, predicted I.Q., predicted height, and the like—become commodified as well. Hence, as Gary Becker says, there would be "superior" and "inferior" babies, with the market for the latter likened to that for "lemons."[5] As a result, boy babies might be "worth" more than girl babies; white babies might be "worth" more than nonwhite babies. Commodifying babies leads us to conceive of potentially all personal attributes in market rhetoric, not merely those of sexuality. Moreover, to conceive of infants in market rhetoric is likewise to conceive of the people they will become in market rhetoric, and this might well create in those people a commodified self-conception.

Hence, the domino theory has a deep intuitive appeal when we think about the sale of babies. Yet perhaps we are being too pessimistic about our "nature" as market actors if we succumb to it. Maybe the fact that we do not now value babies in monetary terms suggests that we would not do so even if our official regime allowed babies to be sold. Maybe. Perhaps babies could be incompletely commodified, valued by the participants in the interaction in a nonmarket way, even though money changed hands. Perhaps. Although this outcome is theoretically possible it seems risky to commit ourselves to this optimistic view in our nonideal world.

If a free-market baby industry were to come into being, with all of its accompanying paraphernalia, how could any of us, even those who did not produce infants for sale, avoid measuring the dollar value of our children? How could our children avoid being preoccupied with measuring their own dollar value? This measurement makes our discourse about ourselves (when we are children) and about our children (when we are parents) like our discourse about cars.

* * *

I suspect that an intuitive grasp of the injury to personhood involved in commodification of human beings is the reason many people lump baby-selling together with slavery.[6] But this intuition can be misleading. Selling a baby, whose personal development requires caretaking, to people who want to act as the caretakers is not the same thing as selling a baby or an adult to people who want to act only as users of her capacities. Moreover, if the reason for our aversion to baby-selling is that we believe it is like slavery, then it is unclear why we do not prohibit baby-giving (release of a child for adoption) on the ground that enslavement is not permitted even without consideration. Perhaps most important, we might say that respect for persons prohibits slavery but may require adoption. There might be cases in which only adoptive parents will treat the child as a person, or in the manner appropriate to becoming a person.

* * *

Baby-giving is unobjectionable, I think, because we do not fear relinquishment of children unless it is accompanied by—understood in terms of, structured by—market rhetoric. Relinquishing a child may be seen as admirable altruism. Some people who give up children for adoption do so with pain, but with the belief that the child will have a better life with someone else who needs and wants her, and that they are contributing immeasurably to the adoptive parents' lives as well as to the child's. Baby-selling might undermine this belief because if wealth determined who gets a child, we would know that the adoptive parents valued the child as much as a Volvo but not as much as a Mercedes. If an explicit sum of money entered into the birth parent's decision to give the child up, then she would not as readily place the altruistic interpretation on her own motives. Again, however, if babies could be seen as incompletely commodified, in the sense of coexistent commodified and noncommodified internal rhetorical structures, the altruism might coexist with sales.

The objection to market rhetoric as the discursive construction of the relinquishment of a child may be part of a moral prohibition on market treatment of any babies, regardless of whether nonmonetized treatment of other children would remain possible. To the extent that we condemn baby-selling even in the absence of any domino effect, we are saying that this "good" simply should not exist. Conceiving of any child in market rhetoric wrongs personhood. To the extent the objection to baby-selling is not (or is not only) to the very idea of this "good" (marketed children), it stems from a fear that the nonmarket version of human beings themselves will become impossible because of the power of market discourse (the domino effect).

NOTES

1. Reprinted with permission of the publisher from Contested Commodities by Margaret Jane Radin, pp. xi–xiv, 95–96, 102–104, 123–125, 127, 130, 132–140, Cambridge, Mass.: Harvard University Press, Copyright © 1996 by the President and Fellows of Harvard College.

2. I am confining the present discussion to traditional male-female prostitution because I am considering a set of would-be commodities that women would control. Gay male prostitution is an important separate topic requiring an analysis of its own.

3. See, e.g., Catharine MacKinnon, Feminism Unmodified: Discourses on Life and Law (1987).

4. See, e.g., Alison M. Jaggar, Feminist Politics and Human Nature (1983); Patricia A. Roos, Gender and Work 119–154 (1985); Gayle Rubin, *The Traffic in Women: Notes on the 'Political Economy' of Sex, in* Toward an Anthropology of Women 157 (Rayna R. Retier ed., 1975). Reva Siegel, *Home as Work: The First Women's Rights Claims Concerning Wives' Household Labor, 1850–1880,* 103 Yale L. J. 1073 (1994).

5. See Gary S. Becker, A Treatise on the Family 140–141 (enl. ed. 1991).

6. Anita L. Allen, *Surrogacy, Slavery and the Ownership of Life,* 13 Harv. J. L. Pub. Pol. 139, 147–148 (1990).

Moore v. The Regents of the University of California

793 P.2d 479 (Cal. 1990)

Panelli, J.

Introduction

We granted review in this case to determine whether plaintiff has stated a cause of action against his physician and other defendants for using his cells in potentially lucrative medical research without his permission. Plaintiff alleges that his physician failed to disclose preexisting research and economic interests in the cells before obtaining consent to the medical procedures by which they were extracted. We hold that the complaint states a cause of action for breach of the physician's disclosure obligations, but not for conversion.

Facts

* * *

The plaintiff is John Moore (Moore), who underwent treatment for hairy-cell leukemia at the Medical Center of the University of California at Los Angeles (UCLA Medical Center). The five defendants are: (1) Dr. David W. Golde (Golde), a physician who attended Moore at UCLA Medical Center; (2) the Regents of the University of California (Regents), who own and operate the university; (3) Shirley G. Quan, a researcher employed by the Regents; (4) Genetics Institute, Inc. (Genetics Institute);

and (5) Sandoz Pharmaceuticals Corporation and related entities (collectively Sandoz).

Moore first visited UCLA Medical Center on October 5, 1976, shortly after he learned that he had hairy-cell leukemia. After hospitalizing Moore and "withdr[awing] extensive amounts of blood, bone marrow aspirate, and other bodily substances," Golde confirmed that diagnosis. At this time all defendants, including Golde, were aware that "certain blood products and blood components were of great value in a number of commercial and scientific efforts" and that access to a patient whose blood contained these substances would provide "competitive, commercial, and scientific advantages."

On October 8, 1976, Golde recommended that Moore's spleen be removed. Golde informed Moore "that he had reason to fear for his life, and that the proposed splenectomy operation was necessary to slow down the progress of his disease." Based upon Golde's representations, Moore signed a written consent form authorizing the splenectomy.

Before the operation, Golde and Quan "formed the intent and made arrangements to obtain portions of [Moore's] spleen following its removal" and to take them to a separate research unit. Golde gave written instructions to this effect on October 18 and 19, 1976. These research activities "were not intended to have . . . any relation to [Moore's] medical . . . care." However, neither Golde nor Quan informed Moore of their plans to conduct this research or requested his permission. Surgeons at UCLA Medical Center, whom the complaint does not name as defendants, removed Moore's spleen on October 20, 1976.

Moore returned to the UCLA Medical Center several times between November 1976 and September 1983. He did so at Golde's direction and based upon representations "that such visits were necessary and required for his health and well-being, and based upon the trust inherent in and by virtue of the physician-patient relationship." On each of these visits Golde withdrew additional samples of "blood, blood serum, skin, bone marrow aspirate, and sperm." On each occasion Moore travelled to the UCLA Medical Center from his home in Seattle because he had been told that the procedures were to be performed only there and only under Golde's direction.

"In fact, [however,] throughout the period of time that [Moore] was under [Golde's] care and treatment, . . . the defendants were actively involved in a number of activities which they concealed from [Moore]. . . ." Specifically, defendants were conducting research on Moore's cells and planned to "benefit financially and competitively . . . [by exploiting the cells] and [their] exclusive access to [the cells] by virtue of [Golde's] ongoing physician-patient relationship. . . ."

Sometime before August 1979, Golde established a cell line from Moore's T-lymphocytes. On January 30, 1981, the Regents applied for a patent on the cell line, listing Golde and Quan as inventors. "[B]y virtue of an established policy . . . , [the] Regents, Golde, and Quan would share in any royalties or profits . . . arising out of [the] patent." The patent issued on March 20, 1984, naming Golde and Quan as the inventors of the cell line and the Regents as the assignee of the patent.

* * *

With the Regents' assistance, Golde negotiated agreements for commercial development of the cell line and products to be derived from it. Under an agreement with Genetics Institute, Golde "became a paid consultant" and "acquired the rights to 75,000 shares of common stock." Genetics Institute also agreed to pay Golde and the Regents "at least $330,000 over three years, including a pro-rata share of [Golde's] salary and fringe benefits, in exchange for . . . exclusive access to the materials and research performed" on the cell line and products derived from it. On June 4, 1982, Sandoz "was added to the agreement," and compensation payable to Golde and the Regents was increased by $110,000. "[T]hroughout this period, . . . Quan spent as much as 70 [percent] of her time working for [the] Regents on research" related to the cell line.

* * *

Discussion

Breach of Fiduciary Duty and Lack of Informed Consent

Moore repeatedly alleges that Golde failed to disclose the extent of his research and economic interests in Moore's cells before obtaining consent to the medical procedures by which the cells were extracted.

* * *

[A] physician who treats a patient in whom he also has a research interest has potentially conflicting loyalties. This is because medical treatment decisions are made on the basis of proportionality—weighing the benefits *to the patient* against the risks *to the patient*. A physician who adds his own research interests to this balance may be tempted to order a scientifically useful procedure or test that offers marginal, or no, benefits to the patient.

* * *

Accordingly, we hold that a physician who is seeking a patient's consent for a medical procedure must, in order to satisfy his fiduciary duty and to obtain the patient's informed consent, disclose personal interests unrelated to the patient's health, whether research or economic, that may affect his medical judgment.

disclosure is key - if a patient signs that they are aware of + give permission + relinquish claim - No problems

* * *

Conversion

Moore also attempts to characterize the invasion of his rights as a conversion—a tort that protects against interference with possessory and ownership interests in personal property. As a result of the alleged conversion, Moore claims a proprietary interest in each of the products that any of the defendants might ever create from his cells or the patented cell line.

* * *

Moore's Claim under Existing Law

"To establish a conversion, plaintiff must establish an actual interference with his *ownership* or *right of possession*. Where plaintiff neither has title to the property alleged to have been converted, nor possession thereof, he cannot maintain an action for conversion."[1]

* * *

[T]he Court of Appeal in this case concluded that "[a] patient must have the ultimate power to control what becomes of his or her tissues. To hold otherwise would open the door to a massive invasion of human privacy and dignity in the name of medical progress." Yet one may earnestly wish to protect privacy and dignity without accepting the extremely problematic conclusion that interference with those interests amounts to a conversion of personal property. Nor is it necessary to force the round pegs of "privacy" and "dignity" into the square hole of "property" in order to protect the patient, since the fiduciary-duty and informed-consent theories protect these interests directly by requiring full disclosure.

* * *

Should Conversion Liability Be Extended?

* * *

Of the relevant policy considerations [one] is that we not threaten with disabling civil liability innocent parties who are engaged in socially useful activities, such as researchers who have no reason to believe that their use of a particular cell sample is, or may be, against a donor's wishes.

* * *

To expand liability by extending conversion law into this area would have a broad impact. The House Committee on Science and Technology of the United States Congress found that "49 percent of the researchers at medical institutions surveyed used human tissues or cells in their research." Many receive grants from the National Institute of Health for their work. In addition, "there are nearly 350 commercial biotechnology firms in the United States actively engaged in biotechnology research and commercial product development and approximately 25 to 30 percent appear to be engaged in research to develop a human therapeutic or diagnostic reagent."

* * *

[T]he theory of liability that Moore urges us to endorse threatens to destroy the economic incentive to conduct important medical research. If the use of cells in research is a conversion, then with every cell sample a researcher purchases a ticket in a litigation lottery. Because liability for conversion is predicated on a continuing ownership interest, "companies are unlikely to invest heavily in developing, manufacturing, or marketing a product when uncertainty about clear title exists."[2]

* * *

If the scientific users of human cells are to be held liable for failing to investigate the consensual pedigree of their raw materials, we believe the Legislature should make that decision. Complex policy choices affecting all society are involved, and "[l]egislatures, in making such policy decisions, have the ability to gather empirical evidence, solicit the advice of experts, and hold hearings at which all interested parties present evidence and express their views."[3]

* * *

Concurring Opinion

Arabian, J.

* * *

Plaintiff has asked us to recognize and enforce a right to sell one's own body tissue *for profit*. He entreats us to regard the human vessel—the single most venerated and protected subject in any civilized society—as equal with the basest commercial commodity. He urges us to commingle the sacred with the profane. He asks much.

* * *

I share Justice Mosk's sense of outrage, but I cannot follow its path. Does it uplift or degrade the "unique human persona" to treat human tissue as a fungible article of commerce? I do not know the answers to these troubling questions, nor am I willing—like Justice Mosk—to treat them simply as issues of "tort" law, susceptible of *judicial* resolution.

* * *

Where then shall a complete resolution be found? Clearly the Legislature, as the majority opinion suggests, is the proper deliberative forum.

* * *

Mosk, J.
I dissent.

* * *

doesn't this destroy our agency?

The concepts of property and ownership in our law are extremely broad. A leading decision of this court approved the following definition: "'The term "property" is sufficiently comprehensive to include every species of estate, real and personal, and everything which one person can own and transfer to another. It extends to every species of right and interest capable of being enjoyed as such upon which it is practicable to place a money value.'"[4]

Being broad, the concept of property is also abstract: rather than referring directly to a material object the concept of property is often said to refer to a "bundle of rights" that may be exercised with respect to that object—principally the rights to possess the property, to use the property, to exclude others from the property, and to dispose of the property by sale or by gift. But the same bundle of rights does not attach to all forms of property. For a variety of policy reasons, the law limits or even forbids the exercise of certain rights over certain forms of property.

[E]ven if we assume that [California law] limited the use and disposition of his excised tissue in the manner claimed by the majority, Moore at least had *the right to do with his own tissue whatever the defendants did with it*: i.e., he could have contracted with researchers and pharmaceutical companies to develop and exploit the vast commercial potential of his tissue and its products. Defendants certainly believe that *their* right to do the foregoing is not barred by [California law] and is a significant property right, as they have demonstrated by their deliberate concealment from Moore of the true value of his tissue, their efforts to obtain a patent on the Mo cell line, their contractual agreements to exploit this material, their exclusion of Moore from any participation in the profits, and their vigorous defense of this lawsuit. The Court of Appeal summed up the point by observing that "Defendants' position that plaintiff cannot own his tissue, but that they can, is fraught with irony." It is also legally untenable.

The majority's last reason for their conclusion that Moore has no cause of action for conversion under existing law is that "the subject matter of the Regents' patent—the patented cell line and the products derived from it—cannot be Moore's property." The majority then offer a dual explanation: "This is because the patented cell line is both *factually* and *legally* distinct from the cells taken from Moore's body." Neither branch of the explanation withstands analysis.

* * *

[T]he majority assert in effect that Moore cannot have an ownership interest in the Mo cell line because defendants patented it. The majority's point wholly fails to meet Moore's claim that he is entitled to compensation for defendants' unauthorized use of his bodily tissues *before* defendants patented the Mo cell line: defendants undertook such use immediately after the splenectomy on October 20, 1976, and continued to extract and use Moore's cells and tissue at least until September 20, 1983; the patent, however, did not issue until March 20, 1984, more than seven years after the unauthorized use began. Whatever the legal consequences of that event, it did not operate retroactively to immunize defendants from accountability for conduct occurring long before the patent was granted.

Nor did the issuance of the patent in 1984 necessarily have the drastic effect that the majority contend. To be sure, the patent granted defendants the exclusive right to make, use, or sell the invention for a period of 17 years. But Moore does not assert any such right for himself. Rather, he seeks to show that he is entitled, in fairness and equity, to some share in the profits that defendants have made and will make from their commercial exploitation of the Mo cell line. I do not question that the cell line is primarily the product of defendants' inventive effort. Yet likewise no one can question Moore's crucial contribution to the invention—an invention named, ironically, after him: but for the cells of Moore's body taken by defendants, *there would have been no Mo cell line.*

Nevertheless the majority conclude that the patent somehow cut off all Moore's rights—past, present, and future—to share in the proceeds of defendants' commercial exploitation of the cell line derived from his own body tissue. The majority cite no authority for this unfair result, and I cannot believe it is compelled by the general law of patents: a patent is not a license to defraud.

* * *

[T]o the extent that cell cultures and cell lines may still be "freely exchanged," e.g., for purely research purposes, it does not follow that the researcher who obtains such material must necessarily remain ignorant of any limitations on its use: by means of appropriate recordkeeping, the researcher can be assured that the source of the material has consented to his proposed use of it, and hence that such use is not a conversion.

* * *

[E]very individual has a legally protectible property interest in his own body and its products. First, our society acknowledges a profound ethical imperative to respect the human body as the physical and temporal expression of the unique human persona. "The dignity and sanctity with which we regard the human whole, body as well as mind and soul, are absent when we allow researchers to further their own interests without the patient's participation by using a patient's cells as the basis for a marketable product."[5]

A[nother] policy consideration adds notions of equity to those of ethics. Our society values fundamental fairness in dealings between its members, and condemns the unjust enrichment of any member at the expense of another. This is particularly true when, as here, the parties are not in equal bargaining positions. In the case at bar, for example, the complaint alleges that the market for the kinds of proteins produced by the Mo cell line was predicted to exceed $3 billion by 1990. These profits are currently shared exclusively between the biotechnology industry and the universities that support that industry. Thus the complaint alleges that because of his development of the Mo cell line defendant Golde became a paid consultant of defendant Genetics Institute . . . [and] acquired the rights to shares of that firm's stock. . . . Genetics Institute further contracted to pay Golde and the Regents and that defendant Sandoz Pharmaceuticals Corporation subsequently contracted to increase that compensation further.

There is, however, a third party to the biotechnology enterprise—the patient who is the source of the blood or tissue from which all these profits are derived. While he may be a silent partner, his contribution to the venture is absolutely crucial: [B]ut for the cells of Moore's body taken by defendants there would have been no Mo cell line at all. Yet defendants deny that Moore is entitled to any share whatever in the proceeds of this cell line. This is both inequitable and immoral.

* * *

I disagree with the majority's further conclusion that in the present context a nondisclosure cause of action is an adequate—in fact, a superior—substitute for a conversion cause of action. In my view the nondisclosure cause of action falls short on at least three grounds.

* * *

[A major reason] why the nondisclosure cause of action is inadequate for the task that the majority assign to it is that it fails to solve half the problem before us: it gives the patient only the right to *refuse* consent, i.e., the right to prohibit the commercialization of his tissue; it does not give him the right to *grant* consent to that commercialization on the condition that he share in its proceeds. "Even though good reasons exist to support informed consent with tissue commercialization, a disclosure requirement is only the first step toward full recognition of a patient's right to participate fully. Informed consent to commercialization, absent a right to share in the profits from such commercial development, would only give patients a veto over their own exploitation. But recognition that the patient[s] [have] an ownership interest in their own tissues would give patients an affirmative right of participation. Then patients would be able to assume the role of equal partners with their physicians in commercial biotechnology research."[6]

* * *

In sum, the nondisclosure cause of action (1) is unlikely to be successful in most cases, (2) fails to protect patients' rights to share in the proceeds of the commercial exploitation of their tissue, and (3) may allow the true exploiters to escape liability. It is thus not an adequate substitute, in my view, for the conversion cause of action.

* * *

NOTES

1. Moore's novel allegation that he "owns" the biological materials involved in this case is both a contention and a conclusion of law.

2. U.S. Congress, Office of Technology Assessment, New Developments in Biotechnology Ownership of Human Tissues and Cells 27 (1987).

3. Foley v. Interactive Data Corp., 47 Cal.3d 654, 694 (1988).

4. Yuba River Power Co. v. Nevada Irr. Dist. (1929) 207 Cal. 521, 523 [279 P. 128].

5. Mary Taylor Danforth, *Cells, Sales, and Royalties: The Patient's Right to a Portion of the Profits*, 6 Yale L. & Pol'y Rev. 179, 190 fn. omitted.

6. J. J. Howard, Biotechnology, Patients' Rights, and the Moore Case, 44 Food Drug Cosm. L. J. 331, 344 (1989).

D.

Distinguishing between
Exchanges and Gifts

The Gift Relationship
From Human Blood to Social Policy

Richard M. Titmuss[1]

Human Blood and Social Policy

The starting-point of this book is human blood. It investigates by a variety of research methods the characteristics of those who give, supply or sell blood, and analyses in comparative terms blood transfusion and donor systems and national statistics of supply, demand and distribution particularly in Britain and the United States. Criteria of social value, cost efficiency, biological efficacy, safety and purity are applied to public and private markets in blood and to voluntary and commercial systems of meeting steeply rising world demands from medicine for blood and blood products.

The study originated and grew over many years of introspection from a series of value questions. Why should men not contract out of the 'social' and act to their own immediate advantage? Why give to strangers? [W]ho is my stranger in the relatively affluent, acquisitive and divisive societies of the twentieth century?

[W]e came to ask: is medical care analyzed in its many component parts—such as blood transfusion services—a consumption good indistinguishable from other goods and services in the private economic market? What are the consequences, national and international, of treating human blood as a commercial commodity? If blood is morally sanctioned as something to be bought and sold, what ultimately is the justification for not promoting individualistic private markets in other component areas of medical care, and in education, social security, welfare services, child foster care, social work skills, the use of patients and clients for professional training, and other 'social service' institutions and processes?

Blood and the Law of the Marketplace

* * *

All these issues were crystallised and debated in the now famous Kansas City case of 1962.

In 1953 a meeting in Kansas City of doctors, pathologists, hospital administrators and local citizens decided to form a non-profit-making [C]ommunity [B]lood [B]ank. There was a need for more blood which the local hospital blood banks were not fully supplying, and the local branch of the American Red Cross was at the time channelling the blood it collected to the Armed Forces in Korea. Then, in May 1955, a commercial blood bank (calling itself the Midwest Hood Bank and Plasma Center) started operations.

The [commercial] bank was owned and operated by a man and his wife. He had completed grade school, had no medical training, and had previously worked as a banjo teacher, second-hand car salesman and photographer. The blood bank procedures seem to have been actually directed by his wife. She called herself an RN but was not licensed as a nurse in either Kansas or Missouri, and did not show any evidence of experience or training in blood-banking. A medical director was appointed to comply with public health regulations. He was aged 78, a general practitioner with no training in blood-banking. The bank was inspected and licensed by the Federal authority, the National Institutes of Health.

It was situated in a slum area, displayed a sign reading "Cash Paid for Blood," drew blood from donors described as "Skid-Row derelicts" and was said by one witness to have "worms all over the floor." In 1958 another commercial bank, the World Blood Bank Inc., was established in Kansas City and also began operations.

[P]ractically all the large local hospitals entered into blood supply contracts with the Community Bank and ceased operating their own banks. The Community Bank in effect had a virtual monopoly.

The two commercial banks then complained to the Federal Trade Commission alleging restraint of trade. In July 1962, after an investigation lasting several years, the Commission issued a complaint against the Community Blood Bank and [related entities].

* * *

[T]he Commission decided that the Community Blood Bank and the hospitals, doctors and pathologists associated with it were illegally joined together in a conspiracy to restrain commerce in whole human blood.

* * *

Thousands of individuals and professional bodies expressed their opinion, from 1962 onwards, that the Commission's ruling represented a grave threat to the profession of medicine, to scientific standards in blood transfusion, to the survival of nonprofit community blood banks, to the voluntary donor and, ultimately, to the patient. "Consumerism" (as it has come to be called), supported by the State in the form of antitrust powers, would be made sovereign.

* * *

Under the order, professional freedom was seriously restricted. It was illegal to take part in a collective decision (to 'conspire') not to buy commercial blood despite the general weight of evidence that such blood carried a much greater hepatitis risk. Altruism in the form of voluntary blood donations had to be made subservient to the values of the marketplace, even if the consequence of establishing the market was to disable and kill more people.

* * *

We have been concerned to show the connections between the growth of commercial practices in certain sectors of medical care and the increasing application of the laws of the marketplace—of legalised and legitimated doctor-patient hostility. The second is a logical consequence of the first. A private market in blood or clinical laboratory services or hospital treatment or other sectors of medical care will, in the end, require to be supported and controlled by the same laws of restraint and warranty as those that obtain in the buying and selling of consumption goods.

* * *

Though this may be the end of this particular case, the fact that it happened is one illustration among many of the increasing commercialisation of the blood-banking system and of hospital and medical services in general. This trend must logically lead to more and more recourse to the laws and practices of the marketplace. There is no inconsistency in this development. If blood as a living human tissue is increasingly bought and sold as an article of commerce and profit accrues from such transactions, then it follows that the laws of commerce must, in the end, prevail.

* * *

Economic Man: Social Man

[In] *The Price of Blood* by M. H. Cooper and A. J. Culyer the authors, applying 'the simplest tools of economic analysis to the problems of blood supply and demand,' came to the following conclusions: (i) that human blood is an economic good; (ii) that it is possible to attach precise economic meaning to the idea of wastage; (iii) that paying donors for blood would increase supply by encouraging more donors to come forward and by providing an incentive to paid donors to attend sessions more frequently; (iv) that, despite the absence of cost statistics, a commercial market in blood would, if demand continues to rise in the future, provide supplies at a definite cost advantage.

* * *

[W]e must point out that, although attempts have been made to value human life,[2] no money values can be attached to the presence or absence of a spirit of altruism in a society. Altruism in giving to a stranger does not begin and end with blood donations. It may touch every aspect of life and affect the whole fabric of values. Its role in satisfying the biological need to help, particularly in modern societies, is another unmeasurable element. In this book, we have used human blood as an indicator; perhaps the most basic and sensitive indicator of social values and human relationships that could be found for a comparative study. If dollars or pounds exchange for blood, then it may be morally acceptable for a myriad of other human activities and relationships also to exchange for dollars or pounds.

We do not know and could never estimate in economic terms the social costs to American society of the decline in recent years in the voluntary giving of blood. [C]ommercialisation and profit in blood has been driving out the voluntary donor. Moreover, it is likely that a decline in the spirit of altruism in one sphere of human activities will be accompanied by similar changes in attitudes, motives and relationships in other spheres. The ethical issues raised by the use of prisoners for blood product trials and plasmapheresis programs is one example. The growth of profit-making hospitals, geared to short stays, high turnover and 'profitable' patients and which cannot foster a sense of community attachment is another example.

Once man begins to say, as he sees that dollars exchange for blood supplies from Skid Row and a poor and often coloured population of sellers, 'I need no longer experience (or suffer from) a sense of responsibility (or sin) in not giving to my neighbour', then the consequences are likely to be socially pervasive.

* * *

Any adequate cost-benefit analysis would need to take into account (or at least identify) the costs of medical care to the individual and the community; the misuse of scarce resources [including human blood); the costs to the individual and the family in loss of earnings, perhaps for life; the costs of higher mortality rates in terms of implied money values placed on human life and the 'net annual dependency' of other members of the family;[3] the costs of disease and death outside the American economy caused by the commercial export of contaminated plasma products;[4] and the costs, also arising in other countries, of importing from the United States methods and consequences of commercialising blood donor systems, and many other tangible and intangible externalities.[5]

Secondly, no assessment of the costs and benefits of a commercial market in blood would be complete without some appreciation of the market effects on the behaviour of doctors and medical institutions, and the price of restricting professional freedom by legally subjecting medicine to the laws of the marketplace.

A substantial part of the measurable components of some of these costs, and particularly the waste of blood and the costs of administrative chaos, are borne in the United States by the individual. The high costs of malpractice insurance and suits are also largely passed on to and borne by sick people in inflated medical bills. The costs of defensive medical practice in terms of the proliferation of tests, consultations, hospitalisation and other unnecessary interventions are similarly passed on to and borne by the generality of patients. So are the profits in blood, blood products and blood-processing made by commercial blood banks, commercial laboratories and pharmaceutical companies.

NOTES

1. Reprinted with permission from *The Gift Relationship From Human Blood to Social Policy,* by Richard M. Titmuss, 57-58, 230, 232, 260, 263–65 (1997).

2. See, e.g., T. W. Schultz, *Investment in human capital,* Amer. Econ. Rev. 51 (March 1961).

3. J. E. Hayzelden, *The value of human life,* 46 Public Administration 427 (Winter 1968).

4. In 1961, there were two deaths in Israel caused by infected plasma processed and exported by a commercial blood firm in New York (Perlli L., 'Blood banks or blood business?', address delivered at 16th Annual Meeting, American Association of Blood Banks, Detroit (November 1963), p. 6).

5. For an enumeration of the main problems arising out of the general principles of cost-benefit analysis, *see* Prest and Turvey (1966) and M. S. Feldstein, *Cost-benefit analysis and investment in the public sector*, 42 Public Administration, 351 (Winter 1964).

Giving, Trading, Thieving, and Trusting

How and Why Gifts Become Exchanges, and (More Importantly) Vice Versa

Carol M. Rose[1]

Does anybody really ever give anything away? Well, yes and no. Consider our sayings about gifts—what is the most famous one? I think it must be, "Don't look a gift horse in the mouth." This old chestnut suggests that if you get something for nothing, you ought to just be satisfied.

* * *

Another of our famous sayings [warns]: "Beware of Greeks bearing gifts." The Greeks' most famous "gift" was a horse, by the way, and the adage tells you that you would be a fool not to have a close look at that nag.[2] The warning is that what looks like a gift may be a trick, and the old saying suggests that if you are too ready to believe that the other guy is being generous (or maybe foolish), you yourself might just get robbed.

When we come to exchange, we can breathe easier. Exchanges do not make us worry about all these ambiguities. Exchanges are like pure gifts in one way: both are types of transfer, and in both, property goes from somebody to somebody else. But they are very different, too. Though gifts themselves are often the subject of exchanges, generally speaking we think of the pure "gift" as a unilateral transfer—I give you something for nothing. On the other hand, "exchange" entails reciprocal transfers— something goes from me to you, while something else comes back from you to me. Exchanges might not be generous, but at least we can figure out the parties' motives.

Or at least we think we can. [This] essay is about the ways in which the seemingly pure gift and the seemingly pure exchange melt together—patterns in which the unilateral aspects of gift transfers blur into the reciprocal aspects of exchange transfers, and vice versa.

Unfortunately, exchanges are not the only contrasts to gifts. In order to make sense of both gift and exchange, we have to make some room for a third and more scandalous type of transfer—one that also contrasts with gift, but in a different way. What is the third type of transfer? It is the transfer by fraud or force.

* * *

One might plot the relationship between gift, exchange, and larceny as follows:

	Voluntary	*involuntary*
unilateral	gift	larceny
reciprocal	exchange	[?]

The trouble with this chart is that odd blank in the lower right hand corner. On the vertical axis, gift contrasts with exchange in a neat opposition of types of voluntary transfers (unilateral versus reciprocal). On the horizontal axis, gift and larceny make another neat opposition of the types of unilateral transfers (voluntary versus involuntary). But the neat oppositions stop there, because of the emptiness of that lower right hand box. It is hard to think of systematic examples that fit into the lower right category—transfers that are at once reciprocal and involuntary. To be sure, we might think of isolated instances where goods are exchanged reciprocally but against the parties' wills. One example might be a case in which a parent forces two feuding children to restore each others' purloined toys. But such examples are rather hard to concoct.

* * *

This leads back to the opening question: Does anybody really ever give anything away, in the sense of sheer niceness, making the voluntary, unilateral transfer? Anthropologists talk about gift-giving a great deal, and while some anthropological accounts of gifts contrast the sociable spontaneity of gift with the calculating self-interest of exchange, other anthropological accounts might make us pretty skeptical.[3] For example, some explanations of the famous "potlatch," the orgy of giving that periodically overcame the Kwakiutl Indians of the Pacific Northwest, suggest that all this gift-giving was really much closer to trading than to sheer generosity. Some say that the potlatch was a form of insurance—it was a revolving exchange relationship, in which the kin-group with the most successful annual catch gave away wealth in a kind of rough circle of reciprocity, so that all kin-groups were assured that they would not go hungry in a year of bad luck—though in return, they had given away a great deal during their own lucky years.

None of this makes the unilateral gift sound like a very robust category. When we shift to the less exotic subject of our own law, we find that here too, gifts seem to be treated as something of an anomaly. It is not that the law discounts the possibility of unilateral generosity. On the contrary, unilateral generosity is encouraged in our law in a variety of ways, such as the protection of "good Samaritans" who come to the assistance of others who are in need. But gifts as such are certainly not expected as a matter of routine, and are at least slightly mistrusted.[4]

* * *

Gift Leaks into Exchange and Theft; Or, Bad Gifts as Thefts, Good Gifts as Exchanges

Reconsider, for a moment, the quintessential gift. It is an unforced, one-sided transfer, motivated by generosity and a spirit of selfless love without thought of reciprocity. The general attitude of the common law is that this kind of transfer may happen sometimes and should even be encouraged, but that it is not always to be expected and may have to be proved against presumptions to the contrary.

These legal presumptions about gifts contrast with the presumptions in the law of contract. As every first-year law student knows, contracts normally require "consideration" to support the deal—something has to bespeak a reciprocal exchange. However, once consideration is shown, no matter how minuscule, the traditional common law presumes that the deal is a deal—a real and enforceable contract.[5] But gifts are different. As the legal scholar Jane Baron has noted, the enforcement of a promised gift is said to require a special showing of the donor's intent.[6]

Indeed, it is just in these special showings that we can see how the gift category gets swallowed up by exchange on the one hand, and by larceny on the other. The most highly developed portions of the law of gift, or as this legal rubric is more technically known, "donative transfer," probably revolve around wills—the bequests made at the time of death. This in itself only reinforces a certain cultural skepticism about gifts. In the case of transfers at death, the donor is pretty much stuck. She can't take it with her, or get anything for it when she goes, and so the only thing she can do is to give it away. On the other hand, we might think that if the donor could take it with her, she probably would; the only reason she makes a "gift" is because she cannot do anything else. Thus, the element of generosity in wills is at best, shall we say, somewhat forced since death is the ultimate robber.

Moreover, the traditional law of wills is notoriously rigid and suspicious: the will must be in writing, and must be signed, and indeed signed in the right places, and must have two or three witnesses. Otherwise, the whole thing may fall apart. One reason for this rigid stance, of course, is that the donor is not around any more for interrogation, and the only way we can be sure that she intends to make some particular gift is to require her to jump through a number of formalistic hoops while she is still alive. Will formalities are the way that we get her to prove that she seriously intends the gift in the will.

But why are we so anxious about the issue of her intent? Why are we so worried that she might not really have meant it? What we sometimes fear is larceny—that the purported gift really is a theft. The thief here is the person who improperly receives a bequest, and this thief effectively commits a double larceny: he takes both from the testator (since the "gift" violates the testator's wishes) and from alternative recipients of the estate (since they really should have gotten the goodies).

One major example is the will that is contested on grounds of "undue influence"—undue influence exercised on the testator by someone named as a beneficiary in the will. What's the story here? Well, usually some smooth-talking or handsome or beautiful young thing pays extraordinary attention to the befuddled older testator, and just coincidentally talks the testator into changing the will.

Just below this argument is a sub-argument that the smoothie really never did enough for the testator to warrant any bequest at all. Here we see the way gift spills out in the other direction—in the direction of exchange. Consider another way one can contest a will: persons who are not named in a will at all can sometimes take some of the estate's proceeds, on the argument that the testator promised to leave them something in the will. Such a purported promise is viewed with some suspicion by the courts. But in a fairly common claim, the claimant professes to have performed long and devoted service to the deceased, because the deceased promised to make it up to the faithful claimant when the will was read. In other words, the claimant tries to prove the promised gift in the will by showing an element of reciprocity. But this means that the promised "gift" is really a kind of exchange, a payment for services.[7]

* * *

Exchange Leaks into Theft—Or Is It Gift?

At first blush, exchange seems vastly simpler and less opaque than gift. The paradigmatic legal version of exchange is the contract, the promise whose reciprocal character is guaranteed by "consideration." In traditional contract law, any consideration whatever, even the common law's "peppercorn," is sufficient to ground a contractual relation. On that theory, you can give me a peppercorn in exchange for my house, and the law will not inquire into the sufficiency or character of the "consideration" that I receive. Any reciprocity at all will do.

* * *

Even in the common law countries, modern legal developments have made a number of inroads into the older "peppercorn" notion of consideration. We now find a number of doctrines through which the courts do ask more closely about the adequacy of consideration in reciprocal transfers. But the reason is not a fear that the "contract" is a gift; rather, it is the fear that the "contract" is a larceny. Among the most notable of these new developments is an ever-growing doctrine of "unconscionability," particularly in consumer law. Over the last generation, courts have increasingly been called upon to overturn contracts, especially consumer contracts, in which there is some evidence of grossly unequal terms together with what is called "unequal bargaining power" (often meaning lopsided deals between knowledgeable commercial dealers on the one hand, and ignorant consumers on the other).[8]

* * *

Ordinary exchange presents a problem, and it takes the following form: If I trade my tomatoes for your shoes, we are presumably both better off, because I want the shoes more than the tomatoes, and you want the tomatoes more than the shoes. Thus the trade is a "positive sum game," because by engaging in it, we realize gains from trade: both of us gain and neither of us loses. Thus we should both be anxious to cut the deal, right?

Wrong, and here is why. Let us suppose that the total gains from trade amount to a sum of X. We have to decide how this X amount is to be divided between us. There is no set rule for this, and indeed we could conceivably jockey for position to the point that we never cut the deal at all. Thus, inside this positive sum game of exchange, there lurks a zero sum game in which I gain only at your expense, and vice versa.

* * *

The punchline, then, is that there may be an element of giving at the center of quite normal kinds of exchanges, and indeed, if someone does not give, the exchange may never get off the ground. Moreover, this seems to be the case even in roughly equal exchanges, so that exchange seems to have a far more systematic "gift" element than is suggested by the powerfully self-interested rhetoric of contract law.

[*Editors' Note*: Professor Rose observes that the state can also enforce deals through contract law; in fact, contract law fills in that odd fourth-box blank in the chart described earlier, because law forces even an involuntary partner to complete an agreed-upon mutual exchange. The trouble is, law and the state also depend on a kind of gift: someone has to get the ball rolling, do the organizing, call the meetings, and so on, even though most of us would rather sit around and let someone else do the work.]

* * *

If we do not understand gift very well as a matter of economic theory—and I suspect that we do not—then we really do not understand exchange much better, because exchange depends at some deep level on giving. The only thing we really understand is larceny, but appearances to the contrary notwithstanding, larceny does not make the business world go round.

NOTES

1. Reprinted with permission from *Giving, Trading, Thieving, and Trusting: How and Why Gifts Become Exchanges, and (More Importantly) Vice Versa*, by Carol M. Rose, 44 Fla. L. Rev. 295, 296–300, 302–305, 308–311, 316–317 (1992).
2. For the Trojan horse story, *see* The Odyssey Of Homer 132–133 (Ennis Rees trans., 1960).
3. See Marcel Mauss, The Gift: Forms and Functions of Exchange in Archaic

Societies (Ian Cunnison trans., 1967); Arjun Appadurai, *Introduction: Commodities and the Politics of Value, in* The Social Life of Things, 3, 10–12 (1986).

4. See Jane B. Baron, *Gifts, Bargains and Form,* 64 Ind. L.J. 155 (1989).

5. See E. Allan Farnsworth, Contracts 66–69 (1982).

6. Baron, *supra* note 4.

7. See Kennedy v. Bank of Am., 47 Cal. Rptr. 154 (Cal. Ct. App. 1965).

8. See, e.g., Williams v. Walker-Thomas Furniture Co., 350 F.2d 445 (D.C. Cir. 1965).

E.

Commodification
and Community

What Money Can't Buy

The Moral Limits of Markets

Michael J. Sandel[1]

Are there some things that money can't buy? My answer: sadly, fewer and fewer. Today, markets and market-like practices are extending their reach in almost every sphere of life.

* * *

I'd like to argue that this tendency is by and large a bad thing, a development that should be resisted. In explaining why this is so I would like to distinguish two objections to extending the reach of market valuation and exchange. Both figure prominently in arguments about the moral limits of markets. But they are often run together, and it is important to disentangle them.

Two Objections: Coercion and Corruption

The first objection is an argument from coercion. It points to the injustice that can arise when people buy and sell things under conditions of severe inequality or dire economic necessity. According to this objection, market exchanges are not necessarily as voluntary as market enthusiasts suggest. A peasant may agree to sell his kidney or cornea in order to feed his starving family, but his agreement is not truly voluntary. He is coerced, in effect, by the necessities of his situation.

The second objection is an argument from corruption. It points to the degrading effect of market valuation and exchange on certain goods and practices. According to this objection, certain moral and civic goods are diminished or corrupted if bought and sold for money. The argument from corruption cannot be met by establishing fair bargaining conditions. If the sale of human body parts is intrinsically degrading, a violation of the sanctity of the human body, then kidney sales would be wrong for rich and poor alike. The objection would hold even without the coercive effect of crushing poverty.

Each objection draws on a different moral ideal. The argument from coercion draws on the ideal of consent, or more precisely, the ideal of consent carried out under fair background conditions. It is not, strictly speaking, an objection to markets, only to markets that operate against a background of inequality severe enough to create coercive bargaining conditions. The argument from coercion offers no grounds for objecting to the commodification of goods in a society whose background conditions are fair. The argument from corruption is different. It appeals not to consent but to the moral importance of the goods at stake, the ones said to be degraded by market valuation and exchange. The argument from corruption is intrinsic in the sense that it cannot be met by fixing the background conditions within which market exchanges take place. It applies under conditions of equality and inequality alike.

Consider two familiar objections to prostitution. Some object to prostitution on the grounds that it is rarely, if ever, truly voluntary. According to this argument, those who sell their bodies for sex are typically coerced, whether by poverty, drug addiction, or other unfortunate life circumstances. Others object that prostitution is intrinsically degrading, a corruption of the moral worth of human sexuality. The degradation objection does not depend on tainted consent. It would condemn prostitution even in a society without poverty and despair, even in cases of wealthy prostitutes who like the work and freely choose it.

I shall try to argue for the independence of the second objection. I hope also to show that it is more fundamental than the first. Even if it can be shown that a particular good should not be bought or sold, it is a further question whether the sale of that good should be legally prohibited. The moral status of a contested commodity should figure as one consideration among others in determining its legal permissibility.

* * *

Plurality and Commensurability

The argument from corruption has a distinctive feature that holds consequences for the way the debate about commodification should proceed. Unlike the argument from coercion, the argument from corruption will be different in each case. The reason is as follows: The argument from coercion always appeals to the ideal of consent, whereas the argument from corruption appeals to the character of the particular good in question. In the cases of surrogacy, baby-selling, and sperm-selling, the ideals at stake are bound up with the meaning of motherhood, fatherhood, and the nurturing of children. Once we characterize the good at stake, it is always a further question whether, or in what respect, market valuation and exchange diminishes or corrupts the character of that good.

Although the goods at stake will vary, it is nonetheless possible to identify one general feature of arguments from corruption that are leveled against commodification: All call into question an assumption that informs much market-oriented thinking. This is the assumption that all goods are commensurable, that all goods can be translated without loss into a single measure or unit of value[.]

All arguments from corruption against commodification resist this claim. It does not seem to me possible, in general, to prove or refute the thesis of commensurability, which is one of the reasons that arguments by analogy play such an important role in debates about commodification. But it is reasonable to question the idea that all goods can be captured in a single measure of value.

* * *

Republican Citizenship

The case I have in mind [is] military service. I would like to argue that there is reason to limit the role of markets in governing [this] more severely than we are accustomed to do. [A]n excessive role for markets corrupts an ideal the practices properly express and advance—namely, the ideal of citizenship as the republican tradition conceives it.

* * *

Military Service

Rather than draft people and then allow the market to operate, the present-day American all-volunteer army uses market principles from the start. The term "volunteer" is something of a misnomer. Soldiers do not volunteer in the way that people volunteer to work in the local soup kitchen on Thanksgiving—that is, to serve without pay. The volunteer army is a professional army, in which soldiers work for pay. It is voluntary only in the sense that all paid labor is voluntary. No one is conscripted, and the job is performed by those who agree to do so in exchange for money and other benefits.

Compare these three ways of allocating military service—conscription, conscription with a buy-out provision (the Civil War system), and the market system. Which is most desirable? From the standpoint of market reasoning, the Civil War system is preferable to a system of pure conscription because it increases the range of choice. From the standpoint of market reasoning, however, the volunteer army is better still. Like the Civil War system, it enables people to buy their way into or out of military service. But it is preferable to the Civil War system because it places the cost of hiring soldiers on the society as a whole, not just on the unlucky few who happen to be drafted and must therefore serve or hire a substitute to take their place.

* * *

The difference between conscription and the volunteer army is not that one is compulsory, whereas the other is not; it is rather that each employs a different form of compulsion—the state in the first case, economic necessity in the second. Only if people are similarly situated to begin with can it be said that the choice to serve for pay reflects people's preferences, rather than their limited alternatives.

* * *

[E]ven in a society where the choice of work did not reflect deep inequalities in life circumstances, military service should not be allocated by the labor market, as if it were just another job. According to this argument, all citizens have an obligation to serve their country. Whether this obligation is best discharged through military or other national service, it is not the sort of thing that people should be free to buy or sell. To turn such service into a commodity—a job for pay—is to corrupt or degrade the sense of civic virtue that properly attends it.

* * *

In fact, the privatization of war, like the privatization of prisons, is a growing trend. Private corporations that hire mercenary forces play an increasing role in conflicts around the world. Sandline International is a London-based company registered in the Bahamas. It was hired by Papua New Guinea last year to put down a secessionist rebellion. Papua New Guinea's prime minister hired Sandline for $32 million to crush rebels his own army was unable to defeat. "I am sick and tired of our boys coming back in body bags," he said.[2] Sandline, in turn, subcontracted with a South African–based company euphemistically named Executive Outcomes, which supplies and trains the soldiers. "Executive Outcomes has racked up an impressive record of military victories for its customers," reports the *Boston Globe*. "Equipped with Russian attack helicopters, heavy artillery, and battle-hardened veterans recruited from the troops that defended South Africa's former white supremacist government, Executive Outcomes has waged war on behalf of the governments of Angola and Sierra Leone."[3]

In 1989, the United Nations proposed the International Convention against the Recruitment, Use, Financing, and Training of Mercenaries. But only ten nations have signed it, and two of them, Angola and Zaire, have already violated it. The United States did pressure the South African government to restrain the role of Executive Outcomes in Angola. But the American principled position was complicated by the fact that the United States then lobbied the Angolan government to hire a competing U.S. firm, Military Professional Resources Inc., to train the Angolan armed forces.[4]

[*Editors' Note*: Professor Sandel then critiques the commodification of voting and problems concerning the growing gap between rich and poor people that stem from thinking about politics in market terms, arguing that these examples further develop the arguments against commodification based on coercion and corruption.]

My argument in these lectures has been directed primarily against those who think that freedom consists in the voluntary exchanges people make in a market economy, regardless of the background conditions that prevail. Libertarian philosophers and political theorists, rational choice economists, and adherents of the "law and economics" movement are the most obvious targets of my investigation. Also implicated, however, are a group of unindicted co-conspirators. These are the liberal consent theorists who think that the commodification and privatization of public life can be addressed simply by adjusting the background conditions within which markets operate. According to the co-conspirators, there is nothing wrong with commodification that fair terms of social cooperation cannot cure; if only society were arranged so that people's choices to buy and sell things were truly voluntary, rather than tainted by unfair bargaining conditions, the objection to commodification would fall away. What that argument misses are the dimensions of life that lie beyond consent, in the moral and civic goods that markets do not honor and money cannot buy.

NOTES

1. Delivered as a Tanner Lecture on Human Values at Brasenose College, Oxford, 1998. Printed with permission of the Tanner Lectures on Human Values, a Corporation, University of Utah, Salt Lake City, Utah.

2. Colum Lynch, *Soldiers for Hire Tempt War-Weary*, Boston Globe, March 8, 1997, at pp. A1, A12. *See also* Raymond Bonner, *U.S. Reportedly Backed British Mercenary Group in Africa*, N.Y. Times, May 13, 1998; and David Shearer, *Outsourcing War*, Foreign Policy 68 (1998).

3. Lynch, *Soldiers for Hire, supra* note 2.

4. Id.

Community and Conscription

Richard A. Posner[1]

In the theory of the state that John Stuart Mill sketched in *On Liberty*, the government's role is to provide an unobtrusive framework for private activities. Government provides certain goods, such as national defense and (in some versions) education, that private markets will not provide in sufficient quantities. But beyond that it merely protects a handful of entitlements (property rights and some personal liberties) that are necessary to prevent markets from either not working at all or running off the rails, as would happen for example if there were no sanctions for theft. Limited government so conceived—the conception most commonly called "nineteenth-century liberalism," to distinguish it from modern welfare liberalism—has no ideology, no "projects," but is really just an association for mutual protection.

Since the election of Ronald Reagan in 1980, and with scarcely a beat skipped in the presidency of Bill Clinton, the United States has, by such means as widespread privatization and deregulation, welfare reform, and indifference to growing inequalities of income, been experimenting with a partial return to nineteenth-century liberalism. This development is obscured by the fact that the Left believes in personal but not economic liberty, and the Right in economic but not personal liberty, and that the Millian center, which believes in both forms of liberty, has no articulate presence in either of the major political parties. (There is a Libertarian Party, but it is minute and ineffectual.) But as the Left has been notably unsuccessful in restricting economic liberty, and the Right has been largely unsuccessful in restricting personal liberty, what we have in fact, though it rarely is acknowledged, is an approximation, though a very rough one, to a Millian polity.

The most sweeping intellectual challenge to our recrudescent nine-teenth-century liberalism comes not from the dwindling band of social-ists, with their narrow focus on economic issues, or from the rightwingers, with their narrow focus on abortion, homosexuality, reli-gion, and a handful of other purely "social" issues, but from the com-munitarians. These political theorists, who include among others Michael Lind, Robert Putnam, and Michael Sandel, think that liberalism as prac-ticed in the United States today is causing people to lose all sense of com-munal responsibility. They argue that people are becoming self-preoccu-pied and thus indifferent to the claims of the community. As evidence they point to our high rates of crime and divorce and of births out of wedlock, and our declining rates of participation in communal activities such as voting, and even to the prevalence of commuting and of television-watch-ing because these (the first especially) tend to be solitary activities.

For many communitarians, the demon is commodification, the substi-tution of market for nonmarket services. Private prisons, private tutors for four-year-olds applying for admission to $17,000-a-year New York kindergartens, Duke University's sale of freshman places to rich kids, pro-fessional dog walkers, the auction of the electromagnetic spectrum, and surrogate-motherhood contracts are among the gaudier examples. Of greater significance is paid child care, though those communitarians who are liberals in the modern sense do not care to dwell on this point. No longer do mothers feel morally obligated to take care of their children themselves, or grandparents to step in for a busy or absent parent. The purchase of child care is now a legitimate option. The care of the elderly has to a great extent been shucked off to retirement and nursing homes supported by social security. And no longer is military service an obliga-tion of citizenship; there is no draft; the army is a career like any other. Preoccupied with money making and other private projects, many people evade taxes and jury duty, and in most elections fewer than half the eligi-ble voters bother to vote.

* * *

[Communitarianism's] diagnosis of the nation's ills is off center. We know this because, in recent years, at the same time that the ties of community as they are imagined by communitarians have been fraying, the ills to which that fraying was thought to give rise have been abating rather than increasing. Crime rates have fallen, as have abortion, teenage births, and births out of wedlock; welfare dependency has declined; racial tension is less. The causality is complex; but the communitarians owe us an explanation for why their predictions have been falsified. A possible answer that they will not like is that commodification promotes prosperity, and prosperity alleviates social ills. Think of the social and economic implications of abolishing life insurance, which commodifies human life;[2] or reinstituting the draft or imposing other compulsory national service, which would deprive the economy of a significant slice of its productive labor; or ending social security and child-care subsidies in order to strengthen the family. Not that many communitarians would endorse all these measures, but nothing in their theory tells them when to stop turning back the clock.

Michael Sandel in his 1998 Tanner lecture had said that "to turn [military] service into a commodity—a job for pay—is to corrupt or degrade the sense of civic virtue that properly attends it."[3] To Sandel, here following Rousseau, who had said, "I hold enforced labor to be less opposed to liberty than taxes,"[4] the volunteer army is a prime example of rampant and destructive commodification. The suggestion is perverse. Conscription is a form of slavery, and slavery is the ultimate commodification. Conscription treats the persons conscripted as if the state *did* own them.

The volunteer army was not the brainchild of Milton Friedman and other commodifiers. We have had a volunteer army for most of our history, conscription having long been resisted here as in England as a Continental practice associated with Napoleonic militarism. The volunteer army was reinstituted when there was no longer a felt need for a mass of (inevitably sullen) cannon fodder. The criticisms of it by Sandel and Lind are refuted by the public response to it in the recent war with Iraq. Only the Iraqi minister of information described our soldiers as "mercenaries." No American was heard to say that since our soldiers are paid to risk their life, we should regard the death, wounding, or capture of them with the same equanimity with which we regard the occasional death and maiming of race car drivers, lion tamers, and mountain climbers. No American was heard to say, and I doubt that any American thought, that one reason to regret heavy American casualties was that it might force up the wages necessary to attract people to a military career. The armed forces are regarded with unstinted admiration, and the recovery of the handful of captured U.S. soldiers was greeted with national rejoicing. To contend that the voluntary character of the American military degrades the concept of American citizenship would strike virtually all Americans as daft.

It is true, as Sandel has emphasized, that the enlisted men and women in the armed forces (as distinct from the officers) are drawn primarily from the lower middle class and so are not a perfect cross-section of the American population. He regards them as "coerced" by economic necessity to volunteer, just as if they were drafted. This is far-fetched; but in any event the consequence of the demographics of the armed forces—a consequence that communitarian should applaud—is that the nation's admiration for these scions of the lower middle class helps to bind the different income classes together. U.S. military prowess is recognized to be the joint product of the technological and organizational prowess of wealthy corporations, high-paid executives, and highly educated scientists and engineers, on the one hand, and the courage, competence, and high spirits of the young people from the other side of the tracks (to make the point rather too dramatically) who dominate the enlisted ranks. I suspect, by the way, that many television watchers found the privates, noncommissioned officers, and junior officers more impressive than the generals: an egalitarian lesson delivered by—commodification.

A notable omission in the communitarian criticism of the volunteer army is failure to consider that a professional army (a term synonymous with volunteer army) is likely to be much more effective militarily than a conscript army under current conditions of warfare. How much military effectiveness should we give up to promote the communitarian vision? Sandel has not told us. There is a subtler significance of the shift from a conscript to a professional army that he also ignores. As pointed out in a study by David King and Zachary Karabell,[5] one reason for the enhanced esteem of our volunteer military compared to its conscript predecessor is that when labor is hired rather than conscripted the employer must persuade the labor pool that working for him is attractive. When it could no longer rely on the draft to fill its ranks, the military conducted large-scale advertising and marketing campaigns to attract recruits and had great success with its slogan, "Be All You Can Be." Most of the people who saw the ads, however, were not potential recruits, but they were impressed and so the ads helped to change the negative image that the public had of the military as a result of the Vietnam fiasco.[6]

So here was another dividend of commodification, and not an adventitious one either. For one of the differences between allocating resources, human and otherwise, by means of the market (which is all that communitarians mean by "commodification") and using coercion is that the former method fosters cooperation—indeed fosters a form of community. Unable any longer to obtain labor by force, the military was compelled to transform itself into an institution that people would respect and trust.

Bonds of trust replaced bonds forged by fear of punishment. It is what one might have thought communitarians would have wanted.

NOTES

1. From "An Army of the Willing," by Richard A. Posner, *The New Republic,* May 19, 2003. Reprinted with permission of *The New Republic,* © 2003, The New Republic, LLC.

2. See the interesting discussion in Viviana A. Rotman Zelizer, Morals and Markets: The Development of Life Insurance in the United States (1979).

3. Michael Sandel, *What Money Can't Buy: The Moral Limits of Markets,* 21 The Tanner Lectures on Human Values, 87, 112 (Grethe B. Peterson ed. 2000).

4. Id., quoting Jean-Jacques Rousseau, The Social Contract 265 (G. D. H. Cole. Trans. 1973).

5. See David C. King and Zachary Karabell, The Generation of Trust: How the U.S. Military Has Regained the Public's Confidence Since Vietnam (2003).

6. See id., ch. 5.

PART II

New Voices on
Commodification Theory

A.

Commodifying Intellectual and Cultural Property

Culture, Commodification, and Native American Cultural Patrimony

Sarah Harding

Introduction

In 1990 Congress passed the Native American Graves Protection and Repatriation Act[1] ("NAGPRA") requiring federally funded museums to inventory, summarize and then return portions of their Native American collections. In the decade since the passage of NAGPRA Native American tribes have successfully negotiated the return of hundreds of cultural items.[2] While repatriations are often lumped together in the public imagination, NAGPRA does establish different standards for repatriation based on the nature of the item in question. Cultural items are broken down into human remains, "associated funerary objects," "unassociated funerary objects," "sacred objects," and "cultural patrimony." The most intriguing category is "cultural patrimony," defined as objects having "ongoing historical, traditional or cultural importance, central to the Native American group or culture itself," and "considered inalienable by such Native American group at the time the object was separated from such group."[3] This chapter focuses on this category of cultural items.

NAGPRA is merely one manifestation of a growing general concern about the legitimacy of museum control over the cultural objects of indigenous peoples. Concern about the treatment and location of such objects as well as the meaning attributed to them has led to everything from international studies and recommendations[4] to the establishment of private foundations whose primary purpose is to encourage and facilitate repatriations.[5] The repatriation movement is not new,[6] and not limited to the United States, but its visibility and success within the United States have certainly improved since the passage of NAGPRA. The implementation of NAGPRA has not been without its glitches[7] but on the whole it has been a success for Native American tribes.

The response of the museum community to this legal change has been mixed. While many museum curators were part of the initial discussions about NAGPRA and have been active participants in its implementation, others were horrified at the prospect of its passage. In the discussions leading up to the passage of NAGPRA, the museum community argued that it had an ethical obligation to maintain collections, not give them away.[8] While NAGPRA has not led to the dispersion of entire Native American collections, as some museums had feared, tensions linger between museums and Native American communities over NAGPRA. These tensions tend to generate and support a certain bifurcation in our understanding of the meaning and place of cultural patrimony.

On the one hand, we expect Native Americans to value their cultural patrimony as cultural and spiritual entities, intrinsically significant, singular, unique, irreplaceable and thus inalienable. On the other hand a museum may (but not always) know and appreciate an object's original cultural meaning but treat that meaning as secondary to the object's material existence and educational significance. So, for example, while Zuni tradition mandates that Zuni War Gods should neither be publicly displayed nor preserved, such cultural demands are in general anathema to a museum's mission. Indeed, museums would cease to exist if all important cultural objects required similar treatment. Generally, this is not the case even with respect to most Native American artifacts.

These different understandings of cultural patrimony can also be expressed through the language of markets and commodification. Cultural patrimony encompasses a category of objects for which commodification was, in the tribal context, "restricted and hedged."[9] After all, cultural patrimony in NAGPRA is defined as "inalienable." And yet in the context of colonialism important cultural objects were diverted away from their tribal contexts. They were bought and sold, in essence commodified, and more often than not ended up in the museum world where they became objects of fascination and intrigue and where their market value continued to climb. In short one way to view the history of Native American cultural patrimony is to understand it as moving away from culturally specific contexts of valuation to the market/museum world and now back towards culture through NAGPRA's repatriation provisions.

This chapter examines whether the triumph of a purely cultural understanding of value is a reasonable expectation of the repatriation process. In other words, is it meaningful to think of the return of cultural patrimony as a process of decommodification? I particularly want to explore whether, in the context of Native American cultural patrimony, culture and the market really are separate, to take another look at this narrative through the lens of commodification.

I. Return of Cultural Patrimony

The following section details the stories or histories of a small selection of Native American cultural patrimony. These stories represent different paths to repatriation as well as different understandings of the place of repatriated objects. While NAGPRA has not, as was once anticipated and feared, led to the wholesale emptying of museums, there have been many repatriations in the past fourteen years and the stories told here are but a small sampling of the responses to NAGPRA.

A. The Tlingit Beaver

On October 26, 1882, the village of Hoochenoo (Angoon) was destroyed by a U.S. naval ship after what appeared to be a misunderstanding about the response of the Hoochenoo community to the death of a Tlingit shaman. Only one canoe that had been away on a hunt was spared the bombardment and it became the only means of transporting food and provisions to the surviving villagers who had fled into the forest. On the prow of that canoe sat a beaver, handsomely carved and painted red with green markings, its fearsome grin revealing a set of large abalone teeth.[10]

When the canoe was destroyed in a storm many years later, the beaver was removed by the villagers and used only in ceremonies but eventually it disappeared. In 1911 it reappeared in the hands of collector George Emmons and was sold for $45 to the American Museum of Natural History in New York City, where it remained for most of the past century. After a somewhat serendipitous discovery of its whereabouts by representatives of the Tlingit-Haida Central Council, the beaver was returned to the Angoon community. Prior to the discovery the American Museum of Natural History had classified it as "problematic," since the meaning or significance of the beaver was unknown.

For now, the beaver resides in the Alaska State Museum in Juneau, but the Tlingit people hope to construct their own museum in Angoon to house the beaver. While there have been other significant repatriations to the Tlingit, vast stores of Tlingit items remain in museums covered by NAGPRA and tribal members want as much returned as possible. As one member of the community put it, "Our dream is to pull a U-Haul up and take back as much as we can."[11]

B. The Zuni War Gods

For years the Zuni people watched their War Gods, or *Ahayu:da*, disappear. The War Gods are believed to have great powers and serve as protectors of the Zuni people. Each one is carved out of a single piece of cylindrical wood and placed in a series of shrines surrounding the Zuni Pueblo. Their placement in these unprotected shrines make them easy targets for treasure hunters, collectors, and even hikers who are unaware of their significance.

In the 1970s, well before the passage of NAGPRA, Zuni religious leaders began advocating and negotiating for the return of the War Gods. Within a decade they had secured the repatriation of more than twenty. While negotiations for repatriation from the Smithsonian took almost a decade, other institutions, including the private auction house Sotheby's, were quick to respond to the Zuni requests.[12] The passage of NAGPRA hastened the pace and success of the campaign to repatriate the Zuni War Gods and by 1995 a total of eighty War Gods had been returned. The success of the Zuni repatriation effort is partly attributed to their nonconfrontational approach: "The success of the Zuni Tribe in repatriating *Ahayu:da* is due in large measure to its concentrated efforts, its quiet approach which has stressed gentle yet persuasive dialogue . . . and its willingness to explain its concerns to non-Indians."[13]

Once repatriated, the War Gods are not placed in a tribal museum or cultural center, as was requested by many of the museums in the early repatriations. The War Gods are placed back in their shrines, in some cases in newly constructed shrines, exposed to the elements and allowed to deteriorate. It is worth noting that the Zuni tribe has also requested the repatriation of replicas of their War Gods. These images or replicas are believed to "embody knowledge and power that many Zunis consider to be proprietary to Zuni religious organizations," regardless of who has made them. Once repatriated, the replicas are disposed of properly by the appropriate religious authorities.[14]

While the Zuni tribe made an immense effort to repatriate its War Gods, it has not shown equal concern about other items that have been brought to their attention. In fact the effort to repatriate other Zuni objects of cultural patrimony has come mostly from museums. Several factors explain this selective concern for certain sacred objects. First, some sacred material is considered the property of the individual for whom it was made. While transferring such objects outside the tribe is prohibited, the Zuni tribe has been reluctant to repatriate these individually owned religious items. Second, authority and responsibility for repatriations within the Zuni tribe is different for different objects: "religious leaders can only make decisions about things for which they are personally responsible" and "[e]ach societal group must find its own way for dealing with repatriation for items that are its own responsibility."[15] This absence of a single authority or process has made repatriations difficult and often confusing. Finally, while other tribes are eager to repatriate items for extinct branches or societies within their tribe, the Zuni are reluctant to take responsibility for items for which they have not been properly initiated. For all these reasons, the Zuni tribe is not eager to repatriate many sacred items and objects of cultural patrimony, although they do on occasion offer instruction and guidance to museums on the care of these objects.[16]

However, the Zuni tribe has shown some interest in repatriating objects that are not associated with their traditional religious beliefs. A good example is the repatriation of Christian religious art from a Catholic church located in the center of Zuni Pueblo. Even though the icons were Catholic, the Zuni tribe successfully repatriated them on the grounds that the Catholic mission from where they were taken reverted to tribal ownership in the early nineteenth century.[17]

C. The Pueblo of Jemez Repatriations

The Pueblo of Jemez, a relatively small group and one of nineteen remaining Pueblos, has one of the most successful repatriation programs. In October of 1993, the Pueblo of Jemez negotiated the return of 86 ceremonial items from the National Museum of the American Indian. In 1995, they repatriated 138 "prayer feather bundles" from the U.S. Forest Service. Like the Zuni War Gods, these prayer bundles are left in shrines in the mountain and are not to be disturbed. The prayer bundles had been collected by hikers and turned over to the Ranger station. In another repatriation, the Jemez community negotiated the repatriation of the remains of more than 2,000 ancestors, the largest repatriation of human remains under NAGPRA at that time. Many of the larger repatriations carried out by the Jemez have been of sacred items or "unassociated funerary objects" but in many instances, the items in question have also been identified as objects of cultural patrimony.[18]

While this small group seems to emulate the views expressed by some members of the Tlingit tribe in its desire to repatriate as much as possible, the success of the Pueblo of Jemez can be attributed to an approach that in some ways is similar to that taken by the Zuni tribe. According to tribal archaeologist William Whatley, the Pueblo's repatriation program is due in part to its very good rapport with many museums. According to Whatley, the Jemez people "regard . . . museums not as thieves, but as surrogate parents of [ceremonial items]"[19] and treat them as such. Additionally, in accordance with Section 14 of its repatriation policy, the Pueblo has attempted to keep a very low media profile during negotiations, which Whatley believes has contributed to their success.[20]

Perhaps the most interesting aspect of the approach taken by the Pueblo of Jemez is that despite its open and amicable approach with museums, it refuses to provide any information about the final disposition of repatriated items. Section 8 of its Repatriation Policy provides that "[f]inal use, placement or disposition of any object, artifact or item that has been repatriated shall be confidential."[21] The secrecy with which repatriated objects are treated is a distinctive aspect of the Pueblo of Jemez repatriation process, one that is in keeping with their culture.

II. NAGPRA's Narratives

A. Multiple Narratives

These examples of repatriation demonstrate that many different types of cultural objects fall under the definition of "cultural patrimony." In one instance even two British Peace Medals and two Union Jack flags were categorized as cultural patrimony and repatriated to the Minnesota Chippewa tribe.[22] This broad range in cultural patrimony is clearly permissible under the NAGPRA definition, in that it provides that an object's significance can be found in historical, sacred and/or cultural associations. Furthermore, traditional ownership structures can draw even more mundane or everyday items into the definition of cultural patrimony. For example, in traditional Tlingit culture, the primary property-holding unit is the matrilineal clan and ownership of most physical possessions resided in the clan. Consequently, individuals had no right to sell or dispose of most physical possessions.[23] As objects owned by and "central to the Native American group" they are easily swept up into NAGPRA's repatriation scheme.[24]

Thus we see that cultural patrimony is a complex category, encompassing a variety of objects with wide-ranging significance. Responses to NAGPRA from Native American communities are also varied. Some communities seek repatriation sparingly and are content to leave significant objects in distant, nontribal museums with directions for appropriate care and display. While communities such as the Zuni may reject repatriation for cultural and religious reasons, other communities are forced to leave objects in museum care because of the sheer magnitude and cost of a repatriation effort. In contrast to this approach, some communities have taken what one could call the "U-Haul approach," viewing NAGPRA as an opportunity to reacquire as much as possible. This is implicit in the repatriation policies of the Pueblo of Jemez and explicit in the above-quoted statement from a member of the Tlingit community.

Finally, even attitudes toward the uses of NAGPRA seem to vary. The Tlingit and other Northwest Coast tribes view NAGPRA as an opportunity to publicize, one might even say reinvent, their own culture and history. The discovery of the beaver prow, for example, was an opportunity to revisit the terrible destruction of Hoochenoo and renew calls for compensation. Furthermore, rather than sequester objects within the tribe, they appear to recognize and even incorporate the museum-quality aspect of their cultural patrimony into their own understanding of an object's meaning.[25] While cultural objects such as the beaver prow are still spoken of as living spirits, they also become "symbol[s] of survival,"[26] educational tools,[27] and painful reminders of political domination. Michael Harkin has commented that within the Kwakiutl tribe, also of the Northwest Coast, repatriation is sometimes encouraged by younger tribal members "who wish to construct an idealized vision of native culture as a communitarian utopia," a view that conflicts with the views of some elders.[28]

The Pueblo of Jemez, on the other hand, have utilized NAGPRA as a means to draw a shroud of secrecy over their culture. The Jemez approach is most starkly one of retreat, a withdrawal of their culture from the public eye and a private reintegration of cultural patrimony into Pueblo life, that is consistent with traditional Pueblo culture, a culture steeped in secrecy.[29]

B. The Dominant Narrative

What is remarkable about these vastly different approaches is that they almost disappear under the weight of a single overwhelming narrative. NAGPRA's single dominating narrative is a story of unmitigated loss and alienation, of diminished hopes and cultural genocide, and then of cultural revival, reconnection and spiritual peace through repatriation.[30] Regardless of the differences in experience, each loss of a cultural object is, in this narrative, tragic, and each recovery is essential to a rebirth or reconstruction of cultural identity.

This narrative is in one sense unremarkable. It is just one aspect of the larger story of colonization and European settlement.[31] The vast funneling of Native American objects into the hands of museum curators and collectors was bound to bear the impression of both the theft and suppression of Native American cultures and to thus have an homogenizing effect on the meaning of such objects and now their return. In Western museums, historically, culturally, and religiously significant objects, as well as the practical and insignificant, were all subject to the imposition of Western categories of meaning, including the now problematized distinction between art and artifact.[32] Museums thus transformed the meaning of objects, turning the simple material elements of everyday life into marvels and recasting the sacred as aesthetically pleasing educational tools. In this process the history, design, meaning, and spirituality of such objects have been blended into a common message of profound Otherness.

In short, the biographies of a vast array of Native American objects were altered and homogenized not merely by their alienation but also by their classification as collectibles, as museum-quality pieces or, in the language of NAGPRA, as "cultural patrimony."[33] Through the NAGPRA repatriation provisions there is a clear expectation that cultural patrimony will drift back to its culturally distinct modality. Implicit in this expectation is a belief that NAGPRA's repatriation process functions as an alembic, drawing out and crystallizing the pure, culturally distinct element of cultural patrimony.

This narrative of destruction and revival is not unusual. What is extraordinary is that it surfaces in NAGPRA, reflecting the deep politicization of objects that in many cases were freely sold or given[34] and considered by the non-Native American community to be mere trinkets, souvenirs, and exotic collectibles. The contested status of cultural patrimony has indeed become a centripetal force for assertions about the manipulation and representation of cultural identity.[35]

III. The NAGPRA Narrative Revisited: The Role of Commodification

A. Commodification in the Dominant Narrative

What role does commodification play in this narrative and how, if at all, does it help us understand the politics of repatriation and the value of return? Let me begin with two basic points, both taken from Arjun Appadurai's introductory essay in his book *The Social Life of Things*.[36] First is the recognition that commodities are not certain kinds of things, but rather things that at some point in their lives become commodities.[37] All things have the potential to be commodities and commodification is but one stage in the life of an object. This is not to say that all things will experience commodification or that all things have the same potential or "commodity candidacy" but only that commodification is a phase rather than an innate quality.[38]

The second point deals with the nature of the commodity stage. Appadurai defines the commodity situation of a thing as that "in which its exchangeability (past, present, or future) for some other thing is its socially relevant feature."[39] Appadurai then disaggregates the "commodity situation" into (1) the commodity phase; (2) the commodity candidacy; and (3) the commodity context. Whereas the "commodity phase" captures the central insight already mentioned (that things can move "in and out of the commodity state"),[40] the "commodity candidacy" of something refers to the cultural framework or "standards and criteria" that determine exchangeability. The "commodity context" is that "social arena" in which the commodity dimension or "candidacy" is realized.[41]

If we apply these definitions to Native American cultural patrimony and assume that such objects were neither produced for exchange nor intended to be exchanged in a market sense—"inalienable" in the NAG-

PRA definition—then it seems logical to presume that things falling within the category of cultural patrimony were not commodities in their original tribal context. To borrow the words of Appadurai, it is presumed that objects of cultural patrimony existed within a "moral and cosmological framework within which commoditization [was] restricted and hedged."[42] It may be the case that certain items were at one time exchanged for some form of compensation, but through a confluence of events and rituals acquired status and meaning to the exclusion of the market. So while it is unclear what the status of the beaver prow was prior to the destruction of Hoochenoo, that event clearly transformed it into a local icon understood as spiritually significant by the entire community.

How then are we to understand the removal of cultural patrimony from its tribal context? It was not uncommon for cultural patrimony, removed by a member of the tribe or a non-Native American, to make its way through the hands of a few independent collectors before ending up in a major U.S. museum. Each of these transactions involved a commercial exchange including the ultimate purchase by a museum, often with little to no knowledge of the meaning of the object. In short, the removal or alienation of cultural objects from affiliated tribes initiated a distinct phase of commodification.

While in the possession of a major museum it could be argued that cultural patrimony was more or less removed from the open market in Native American artifacts. But in many ways, the market or commodification is never far from the museum experience. First, if we view cultural patrimony as a larger classification rather than looking at the paths of specific objects,[43] the collectibility of cultural patrimony, a status encouraged and enhanced by museum acquisition, tends to generate a market and boost the price for cultural patrimony. So while museums would likely defend themselves against the charge of "merchandising" cultural objects, it is precisely the importance that they bestow on such objects that helps generate and support an active market.[44] Second, it is important for museums to name prices and, for practical reasons such as insurance, to understand the monetary value of their holdings.[45]

Thus while museums serve as a sort of closed sphere where commodification is limited by the establishment of a set of standards and criteria that restrict commercial exchange, these standards exist alongside and in fact inform and encourage a parallel structure of commodification. To return to Appadurai's distinctions, museums arguably enhance the "commodity candidacy" of cultural patrimony while simultaneously fencing it off from a "commodity context."

The removal of cultural patrimony from its tribal context could thus be seen as a "commoditization by diversion, where value . . . is accelerated or enhanced by placing objects and things in unlikely contexts."[46] Within such "unlikely contexts," in this case museums and foreign cultures, shared assumptions of value and meanings are absent. Indeed, most intercultural transfers are, according to Appadurai, likely to result in the breakdown of standards and criteria defining both "commodity candidacy" and "commodity context." Museums may minimize this breakdown, but as key players in the creation of a unique category of cultural commodities they are also active participants in this breakdown or diversion.

What then can be said about the return of cultural patrimony? Is repatriation a process of decommodification, a return of the object to its prior status and context? This seems to be precisely the assumption behind NAGPRA. The value and importance of cultural patrimony is measured by its status prior to alienation as indicated in the reference to the inalienability of the object "at the time the object was separated from [the] group."[47] There is also an assumption of continuity in value and meaning in the choice of the words "*ongoing* historical, traditional or cultural importance."[48] The use of these phrases generates an assumption that cultural patrimony is being reinstated physically into its original cultural milieu and metaphysically into its original context of meaning.

Anthropologist Igor Kopytoff refers to this process as singularization, a process that he argues is the result of a triumph of culture. He states:

[C]ommoditization homogenizes value, while the essence of culture is discrimination. . . . Culture ensures that some things remain unambiguously singular . . . and it sometimes resingularizes what has been commoditized.[49]

Repatriation seems to be a classic case of "resingularization," namely a return of cultural patrimony to its unambiguous and unique cultural status.

If we stopped here we might have an interesting and intuitively appealing understanding of the repatriation process but one that is also striking for its shallowness and excessive in its polarity. While the concept of repatriation contributes to this polarity (museums versus Native Americans; market versus culture; science versus religion; commodification versus decommodification), arguably this is not a realistic understanding of repatriation. It could be argued that once commodified, the commodity potential of a repatriated object of cultural patrimony is always present. In short, the value and meaning of an object is not solely the product of the last transaction, or in this case repatriation, but rather a reflection of its cumulative history.

B. Culture, Commodification, and NAGPRA

The vast removal of cultural patrimony and its subsequent commodification was indeed a tragedy of immense proportion. The magnitude of that wrong, however, does not make it possible to undo or erase that commodification. Indeed that history is embedded in the object and in some cases part of the stories told about it. Furthermore, the commodification of cultural patrimony is one of the things that makes its repatriation so valuable to Native American tribes. It's not that Native Americans wish to cash in on that value (I am not aware of any cases where repatriated cultural patrimony has been resold), but market value is one of the features that makes repatriation difficult for museums and thus all the more significant for Native Americans. The fact that Native American cultural objects sell for significant sums in the major auction houses[50] is not lost on Native American tribes. In short, the significance of cultural patrimony to the museum community, including its exchange value, is one reason that such objects become important sites of political struggle and thus why the diversion of cultural patrimony itself becomes central to understanding its value and significance.[51]

Kopytoff makes a similar point when he suggests that a diversion, described above as a process of "resingularization," makes sense only in relation to the path from which the object is diverted. In a discussion of "priceless" art, he writes, "[S]ingularity, in brief, is confirmed not by the object's structural position in an exchange system, but by intermittent forays into the commodity sphere, quickly followed by reentries into the closed sphere of singular 'art.'"[52] But there is an expectation in dealing with art that conditions of commodification will arise, that it will indeed return to the market, if only intermittently. The expectation with respect to repatriation, whether accurate or not, is that returning an object to its culturally affiliated tribe will permanently remove the object in question from market conditions. A good example of this is the placement of repatriated Zuni War Gods in their mountain shrines. However, even if we assume this to be true—that returned cultural patrimony will not reappear on the market—knowledge of the object's place within a system of exchange is implicit in repatriation and integral to an understanding of the object's value, even if resale is not intended.[53]

The significance of the diversion itself is most evident in the U-Haul approach discussed above. It reveals a tendency to deal with cultural patrimony as a homogenous category, a large undifferentiated class of valuables. While the cultural affiliation of this undifferentiated class is still of primary significance, a close second is sheer entitlement. It is the privilege and possibility of repatriation that is significant, not just the specific objects. In this instance cultural patrimony seems to be neither completely homogenous and commodified nor heterogeneous and decommodified. Instead it sits somewhere between these two poles, a "contact zone"[54] where the homogenizing forces of a larger, complex society, pushing toward commodification meet the heterogeneous, singularizing tendencies of smaller cultural groups.

This does not mean that those who hold the U-Haul perspective are disingenuous or unworthy beneficiaries of the repatriation process. To the contrary, it would be disingenuous on the part of the museum community to criticize an approach that is both a direct and indirect product of their domination. Directly, resingularization occurs only when a tight and complex understanding of an object's value is shared by the relevant community.[55] But such conditions typically depend on access to the object. The long period of separation of cultural patrimony from tribal contexts inevitably led to a deterioration of knowledge about specific objects. What connection remained was typically the product of stories and/or the occasional picture.[56] A greater appreciation of cultural patrimony as singular and unique will in some cases require a period of acculturation.

Indirectly, the U-Haul perspective is a manifestation of the expectations of assimilation and the confluence of conflicting cultural orders. As anthropologist Elizabeth Povinelli writes in the context of Australian Aborigines, it shouldn't be "surprising" to us "that the embodiment of 'culture' reflects the variations, slippages, dispersions, and ambivalences of discursive and moral formations across the variegated terrain of indigenous and nonindigenous social life."[57] Whether the product of concerns about survival or mere opportunism, these "slippages," as we might describe the U-Haul approach, are social facts that must be considered as stark cultural realities and political necessities, rather than as evidence of cultural dilution or even betrayal. In short, the U-Haul approach, stemming more from commercial culture than from purportedly traditional culture is, for all its inconsistencies, entirely appropriate.

The role or relevance of commodification when dealing with something like the Zuni War Gods is a little more remote. More so than other objects of cultural patrimony, Zuni War Gods really are reinstated in their former place within the community and so the argument set out above is less applicable. But the brief foray of these carved fetishes into non-Zuni society does bear some ongoing significance. The commodification of Zuni War Gods is in many ways a clear negation of their existence. In a strange sort of reversal, preservation is their destruction, display a concealment of their powers, and exchange an abrupt denial of their value. Under these circumstances it is harder to argue that such objects are "contact zones," or that their commodification continues to be relevant after repatriation, since one context of valuation seems to operate to the exclusion of the other.

However it could be argued that the strength of the Zuni War God repatriation movement is at least partially a product of this oppositional construction—mediated of course by the openness of the Zuni tribe. The sharp contrast generated by the incongruity of a museum context highlights the unique cultural identity of the War Gods. To be more explicit, it is, as Michael Harkin has pointed out, "a characteristic intellectual habit of Western civilization to assume that people outside it represent marvelous inversions of their own social and cultural form."[58] Regardless of the correctness of this assumption, it is reinforced when we are confronted with something as unique as a Zuni War God. From a museum perspective, the very uniqueness of the War Gods and the negation of their value in a museum context fit our assumptions about Native American cultures and generate a clear case for repatriation.

From the Native American perspective, dialogue concerning the appropriate disposition of the War Gods provides a perfect avenue for the articulation and assertion of this cultural difference, which, again whether accurate or inaccurate, is important in the struggle over the representation of cultural identity.[59] In short, the fact that Zuni War Gods can be understood as representing the very inversion of a commodity is itself an important aspect of the political dimension of the repatriation process. The secrecy of the Pueblo of Jemez with respect to the disposition of repatriated objects can also be understood as a reflection of this oppositional tendency.

This argument requires more thought and energy than the time and space remaining. For now, I wish only to suggest that whether we are speaking of the repatriation of a Zuni War God, a Jemez prayer bundle, or the Tlingit beaver prow, it is not possible to erase a history of commodification nor is that history insignificant in understanding the current value of such objects. To the contrary, commodification is a part of the biographies of these objects and can serve a vital political function.

Contrary to the expectations embedded in NAGPRA, commodification and culture are not mutually exclusive categories but, instead, overlap and are, in some instances, even mutually dependent. Western fascination with Native American culture was the catalyst for the creation of a market in cultural patrimony. Repatriation is not a reversal of this process but rather an example of Native American ingenuity in capitalizing on the significance of this market and in the process gaining a foothold in the battle over the representation of Native American identity.

Kopytoff writes that valuation in "small-scale societies in the past resulted in a relative consonance of economic, cultural and private valuations."[60] Once cultural patrimony was removed from such contexts and placed in larger more complex social environments, commodification was inevitable. What I have tried to stress in this chapter is that a return to the closed sphere of a Native American tribe will result in some form of decommodification, or as Kopytoff states an "upward conversion," but will not erase the complex biography of cultural patrimony. Cultural patrimony cannot be valued as it was before. As Douglas Cole remarks in the context of Northwest Coast cultural heritage, "[T]he objects remain the same bit of wood or stone but their meanings and their values are shifting, multiple, transitory, mutable, invented, even reinvented."[61] The commodity potential is part of this reinvention and will continue to be present and part of the constant interplay between two different cultural and social contexts.

To view repatriation in any other way would be to ignore the role of present-day Native Americans in refining and reinterpreting the meaning of their cultures. Viewing repatriation as nothing more than return and decommodification evokes an image of Native Americans as mere passive recipients of their cultural identity, beholden to their ancestors and the museum community for the re-creation of their cultures. It is an understanding of repatriation that objectifies Native American cultures and fixes cultural identity to a point in the distant past. As such, it is a racialized understanding of the repatriation process and a product of the total-izing nature of the structures of thinking generated by colonialism. While objects of cultural patrimony do indeed function as cultural reminders or placeholders, the repatriation of Christian art or the construction of tribal museums to house and display returned items are powerful reminders of the extent to which Native Americans are active participants in the cre-ation of new cultural identities, a process inevitably intertwined with commodification.

NOTES

I am grateful for the wonderful conversations generated by the Commodification Futures conference, for the excellent comments from Jan Hoffman French, and the fine research assistance of Joel Tobin.

1. 25 U.S.C. §§ 3001–3013 (1994) ("NAGPRA").

2. *See* http://www.cr.nps.gov/nagpra.

3. NAGPRA § 3001(3)(D).

4. *See* Erica-Irene Daes, Protection of the Heritage of Indigenous People (Of-fice of the High Commissioner for Human Rights, United Nations) 1997.

5. *See* American Indian Ritual Object Repatriation Foundation. http://www.repatriationfoundation.org.

6. For example, members of the Zuni community were actively engaged in ne-gotiations for the return of their War Gods long before the passage of NAGPRA. *See* T. J. Ferguson, Roger Anyon, and Edmund J. Ladd, *Repatriation at the Pueblo of Zuni, reprinted in* Repatriation Reader 239 (Devon A. Mihesuah, 2000).

7. The most significant dispute to date is probably the battle over the Ken-newick Man, the 9,000-year-old skeletal remains found in the Columbia River Basin. Recently the Ninth Circuit found that the remains do not fall within NAGPRA because they are too old to have any clear connection to a present-day Native American group. Bonnichsen v. United States, 357 F.3d 962 (2004).

8. *See, e.g.*, H.R. Rep. No. 101-877, at 13 (1990) ("Testimony from the mu-seum community stressed the responsibilities which museums have to maintain their collections and concern for liability surrounding repatriation."); *Hearing on S. 1021 and S. 1980 Before the Senate Select Committee on Indian Affairs,* 101st Cong., 61–64 (1990) (Statement of Tom Livesay, Director, Museum of New Mex-ico, on behalf of the American Association of Museums, arguing that housing Native American cultural property in museums serves an educational purpose).

9. Arjun Appadurai, *Introduction: Commodities and the Politics of Value, in* The Social Life of Things: Commodities in Cultural Perspective 23 (1986).

10. An abbreviated retelling of the destruction of Hoochenoo appeared in

Stephen Kinzer, *Museums and Tribes: A Tricky Truce,* N.Y. Times, Dec. 24, 2000, Arts and Leisure 37. See also the official notice of repatriation, Fed. Reg. vol. 64, no. 132, p. 37567, and http://www.alaska.net/~pepper/Beaver_Prow .html.

11. David Whitney, *Old Photographs Were Key to Return,* http://www.tlin-git-haida.org/what'shap/objects.html (July 19, 2000) (on file with author).

12. Surprisingly, Sothebys in New York City was the first organization to repatriate a War God. Ferguson, Anyon, and Ladd, *Repatriation at the Pueblo of Zuni, reprinted in* Repatriation Reader, 239, 241 (Devon Mihesuah, 2000).

13. *Id.* at 246.

14. *Id.* at 254. *See also* Russell Thornton, *Who Owns the Past? in* Studying Native America 385, 405 (Russell Thornton ed. 1998) (further discussion of repatriating images or reproductions).

15. *Id.* at 251.

16. *Id.* at 251–253.

17. *Id.* at 256. This repatriation took place in the late 1980s, just prior to the passage of NAGPRA.

18. *See, e.g.,* 68(31) Fed. Reg. 41009–41010 (2003) (notice of repatriation of 44 items of cultural property to the Pueblo of Jemez).

19. *News and Notes,* 2(2) American Indian Ritual Object Repatriation Foundation News and Notes (1995–96). (Available at www.repatriationfoundation .org/V2i2.html.) This view also appears in section 2 of the Pueblo of Jemez Repatriation Policy that can be found at the Pueblo of Jemez Department of Resource Protection NAGPRA/Cultural Preservation Resource Page at http:// www.nmia.com/~quasho/nagpra.htm.

20. Pueblo of Jemez Repatriation Policy, *supra* note 19.

21. *Id.*

22. 65 (184) Fed. Reg. 57208–57209 (2000).

23. Thornton, *supra* note 14 at 404.

24. NAGPRA § 3001(3)(D).

25. For a discussion of Native American museums within the Northwest Coast tribes *See* James Clifford, *Four Northwest Coast Museums: Travel Reflections, in* Exhibiting Cultures: The Poetics and Politics of Museums Display 212 (Ivan Karp and Steven D. Lavine eds. 1990).

26. http://www.alaska.net/~pepper/Beaver_Prow.html.

27. Whitney, *supra* note 11. ("Our main goal is to teach our children the stories behind them. . . . It means a lot to the people, the children and the history of the Tlingit people." Quoting Dennis Starr, a Tlingit representative.)

28. Michael Harkin, *Privacy, Ownership, and the Repatriation of Cultural Properties: An Ethnographic Perspective from the Northwest Coast* 5 (2001) (paper presented at Categories, Culture and Property, Chicago-Kent College of Law, September 28, 2001, on file with the author).

29. *See, e.g.,* Elizabeth Brandt, *On Secrecy and the Control of Knowledge: Taos Pueblo, in* Secrecy: A Cross-Cultural Perspective 123 (Stanton Teftt ed. 1980).

30. *See* Reuben Snake, *Reculturalization of Sacred Objects,* 4(4) Akwe:kon Journal 14 (1992) ("So it becomes imperative for us to reclaim these things and (*sic*) in order to renew our spiritual life, our spirituality. . . . The term reculturalization means regaining what our grandfathers and grandmothers used to know so well. We need to bring that back into the culture of our people."); NAGPRA Review Committee Report 2 (1999) ("These repatriations have helped restore a sense of spiritual and cultural integrity to participating Native American people.").

31. Susan Stewart, On Longing: Narrative of the Miniature, the Gigantic, the Souvenir, the Collection 153 (1984) (arguing that collecting, ordering, displaying, and so on help establish control over our environment and thus are common under conditions of pioneering and settlement). *See also* Curtis M. Hinsley Jr., *Digging for Identity: Reflections on the Cultural Background of Collecting, in* Repatriation Reader, *supra* note 6 at 37, 47–52 (discussing the use of archeology and collecting as a means to establish an embedded identity and rightful claims to settlement and stewardship).

32. James Clifford, The Predicament of Culture 228 (1988).

33. Appadurai, *supra* note 9 at 34 (discussing the shift in meaning of specific objects generated by the imposition of larger classifications).

34. Douglas Cole, Captured Heritage xi (1995) (many Northwest Coast Indians "entered the art and artifact market freely—exploiting it for their own use").

35. The centrality of the repatriation project to Native American assertions of sovereignty is evident in the fact that looting is a much more serious threat to Native American cultural objects and yet the Native American community broadly speaking has chosen to focus its efforts on repatriation. *See* Robert Mallouf, *Unraveling Rope, in* Repatriation Reader, *supra* note 6 at 59, 67.

36. Appadurai, *supra* note 9 at 13.

37. *See also* Igor Kopytoff, *Cultural Biography of Things, in* The Social Life of Things, *supra* note 9 at 64. ("Commoditization, then, is best looked upon as a process of becoming rather than as an all-or-none state of being.")

38. Appadurai, *supra* note 9 at 13.

39. *Id.*

40. *Id.*

41. *Id.* at 14.

42. *Id.* at 23.

43. *Id.* at 34 ("a particular relic may have a specific biography, but whole types of relic, and indeed the class of things called "relic" itself, may have a

larger historical ebb and flow, in the course of which its meaning may shift significantly.").

44. Kopytoff, *supra* note 37 at 82–83.

45. *Id.* at 83.

46. Appadurai, *supra* note 9 at 28.

47. NAGPRA § 3001(3)(D).

48. *Id.*

49. Kopytoff, *supra* note 37 at 73.

50. A quick visit to the American Indian Art department of Sotheby's at http://search.sothebys.com/jsps/live/dept/DeptGlobal.jsp?dept_id=5 provides ample evidence of the market value of Native American objects.

51. Writing about the circulation of medieval relics, Patrick Geary writes, "[T]he account of the relics' translation had to itself become part of the myth of production—the story of how they had come to their community was itself part of the explanation of who they were and what their power was." *Sacred Commodities: The Circulation of Medieval Relics, in* The Social Life of Things, *supra* note 9 at 169, 186.

52. Kopytoff, *supra* note 37 at 82–83.

53. *Id.* at 76. In this sense, cultural patrimony is like some luxury goods—oriental rugs or art—that when purchased are not intended for resale but knowledge of resale value contributes greatly to a confirmation of their worth. *Id.* at 75; *see also* Brian Spooner, *Weavers and Dealers: The Authenticity of an Oriental Carpet, in* The Social Life of Things, *supra* note 9 at 195.

54. Michael Harkin, *From Totems to Derrida: Postmodernism and Northwest Coast Ethnology* 46 (4) Ethnohistory 818, 818 (1999).

55. Appadurai, *supra* note 9 at 23 (a process referred to as "enclaving").

56. Stories and pictures were key to the discovery of the Tlingit beaver prow. *See* David Whitney, *A Culture Comes Home* Sept. 24, 1999, at http://nativenet.uthscsa.edu/archive/nn-dialogue/9909/0004.html.

57. Elizabeth A. Povinelli, The Cunning of Recognition: Indigenous Alterities and the Making of Australian Multiculturalism 3 (2002).

58. Harkin, Privacy and Ownership, *supra* note 28 at 3.

59. Nicholas Thomas, Entangled Objects: Exchange, Material Culture, and Colonialism in the Pacific 29 (1991).

60. Kopytoff, *supra* note 37 at 88.

61. Cole, Captured Heritage, *supra* note 34 at xiv.

U.S. vs. Corrow

119 F.3d 796 (10th Cir. 1997)

John C. Porfilio, Circuit Judge.

This appeal raises issues of first impression in this Circuit under the Native American Graves Protection and Repatriation Act, 25 U.S.C. §§ 3001–3013 (NAGPRA); and the Migratory Bird Treaty Act, 16 U.S.C. §§ 701–712 (MBTA). Richard Nelson Corrow challenges the constitutionality of 25 U.S.C. § 3001(3)(D) of NAGPRA which defines "cultural patrimony," the basis for his conviction of trafficking in protected Native American cultural items in violation of 18 U.S.C. § 1170(b). First, he contends the definition is unconstitutionally vague, an argument the district court rejected in denying his motion to dismiss that count of the indictment and to reverse his conviction. Second, he invites us to read a scienter requirement into § 703 of the MBTA to vitiate the government's proof he possessed protected bird feathers. Failing these propositions, he attacks the sufficiency of the evidence supporting his two counts of conviction. We affirm.

Background

Until his death in 1991, Ray Winnie was a *hataali*, a Navajo religious singer. For more than twenty-five years Mr. Winnie chanted the Nightway and other Navajo ceremonies wearing Yei B'Chei originally owned by Hosteen Hataali Walker. Yei B'Chei or Yei B'Chei *jish* are ceremonial adornments, Native American artifacts whose English label, "masks," fails to connote the Navajo perception these cultural items embody living gods. Traditionally, a *hataali* passes the Yei B'Chei to a family or clan member who has studied the ceremonies or loans the Yei B'Chei to another Navajo clan, Mr. Winnie having acquired his Yei B'Chei from a different clan during his *hataali* apprenticeship. When Mr. Winnie died, he left no provision for the disposition of his Yei B'Chei, and no family or clan member requested them.

Richard Corrow, the owner of Artifacts Display Stands in Scottsdale, Arizona, is an aficionado of Navajo culture and religion, having, on occasion, participated in Navajo religious ceremonies. Some time after Mr. Winnie's death, Mr. Corrow traveled to Lukachukai, Arizona, to visit Mrs. Fannie Winnie, Mr. Winnie's 81-year-old widow, chatting with her; her granddaughter, Rose Bia; and other family members: a great granddaughter, Harriette Keyonnie; and a son-in-law. During one visit, Mrs. Winnie displayed some Navajo screens and robes, and Mr. Corrow inquired about the Yei B'Chei. By his third visit in August 1993, the Winnie family revealed the Yei B'Chei, twenty-two ceremonial masks, and permitted Mr. Corrow to photograph them. Mr. Corrow told Mrs. Winnie he wanted to buy them, suggesting he planned to deliver the Yei B'Chei to a young Navajo chanter in Utah to keep them sacred. Although Mr. Corrow initially offered $5,000, he readily agreed to the family's price of $10,000 for the Yei B'Chei, five headdresses, and other artifacts. Mr. Corrow drafted a receipt, and Mrs. Winnie, who spoke no English, placed her thumbprint on the document after Ms. Bia read it to her in Navajo.

In November 1994, the owners of the East-West Trading Company in Santa Fe, New Mexico, contacted Mr. Corrow telling him that a wealthy Chicago surgeon was interested in purchasing a set of Yei B'Chei. In fact, the purported buyer was James Tanner, a National Park Service ranger operating undercover on information he had received about questionable trade at East-West. When Agent Tanner visited the business, its owners showed him photographs of seventeen of the twenty-two Yei B'Chei that Mr. Corrow purchased from Mrs. Winnie. In the photos, he noticed eagle and owl feathers in several of the large headdresses and ceremonial sticks bundled with small eagle feathers. After negotiations, Agent Tanner agreed to a purchase price of $70,000 for the Yei B'Chei, $50,000 for Mr. Corrow and a $20,000 commission to East-West's co-owners.

* * *

The government subsequently charged Mr. Corrow [with] trafficking in Native American cultural items in violation of 18 U.S.C. §1170, 25 U.S.C. §§3001(3)(D), 3002(c), and 18 U.S.C. §2; and [with] selling

Golden Eagle, Great Horned Owl, and Buteoine Hawk feathers protected by the MBTA in violation of 16 U.S.C. §703, 16 U.S.C. §707(b)(2), and 18 U.S.C. §2. The jury convicted Mr. Corrow of illegal trafficking in cultural items [and] possession of protected feathers.

In this challenge, Mr. Corrow asserts the court erred in failing to dismiss on the ground the NAGPRA definition of cultural patrimony is unconstitutionally vague, trapping the unwary in its multitude of meanings and creating easy prey for the untrammeled discretion of law enforcement. Were NAGPRA's definitional bounds nevertheless discernible, Mr. Corrow then urges the evidence was insufficient to support his conviction on either count.

NAGPRA

Congress enacted NAGPRA in 1990 to achieve two principal objectives: to protect Native American human remains, funerary objects, sacred objects and objects of cultural patrimony presently on Federal or tribal lands; and to repatriate Native American human remains, associated funerary objects, sacred objects, and objects of cultural patrimony currently held or controlled by Federal agencies and museums. The legislation and subsequent regulations provide a methodology for identifying objects; determining the rights of lineal descendants, Indian tribes and Native Hawaiian organizations; and retrieving and repatriating that property to Native American owners. NAGPRA's reach in protecting against further desecration of burial sites and restoring countless ancestral remains and cultural and sacred items to their tribal homes warrants its aspirational characterization as "human rights legislation."[1]

Nonetheless to give teeth to this statutory mission, 18 U.S.C. § 1170 penalizes trafficking in Native American human remains and cultural items and creates a felony offense for a second or subsequent violation. Subsection 1170(b), the basis for prosecution here, states:

> Whoever knowingly sells, purchases, uses for profit, or transports for sale or profit any Native American cultural items obtained in violation of the Native American Grave Protection and Repatriation Act shall be fined in accordance with this title, imprisoned not more than one year, or both, and in the case of a second or subsequent violation, be fined in accordance with this title, imprisoned not more than 5 years, or both.

One must look to NAGPRA for the definition of "cultural item." Section 3001(3) states:

> "cultural items" means human remains and—(D) "cultural patrimony" which shall mean an object having ongoing historical, traditional, or cultural importance central to the Native American group or culture itself, rather than property owned by an individual Native American, and which, therefore, cannot be alienated, appropriated, or conveyed by any individual regardless of whether or not the individual is a member of the Indian tribe or Native Hawaiian organization and such object shall have been considered inalienable by such Native American group at the time the object was separated from such group.

Thus, to be judged "cultural patrimony" the object must have (1) ongoing historical, cultural or traditional importance; and (2) be considered inalienable by the tribe by virtue of the object's centrality in tribal culture. That is, the cultural item's essential function within the life and history of the tribe engenders its inalienability such that the property cannot constitute the personal property of an individual tribal member. "The key aspect of this definition is whether the property was of such central importance to the tribe or group that it was owned communally. . . ."[2]

In this prosecution, then, the definition of cultural patrimony divided into its three component parts required the government prove Mr. Corrow trafficked in an object that (1) was not owned by an individual Native American; (2) that could not be alienated, appropriated, or conveyed by an individual; and (3) had an ongoing historical, traditional, or cultural importance central to the Native American group. Mr. Corrow contends the first and second elements are unintelligible. Thus, he argues the definition does not comport with the due process clause of the Fourteenth Amendment because it fails to give ordinary people fair notice about what conduct is prohibited in such a manner that discourages arbitrary and discriminatory law enforcement.

In support, Mr. Corrow arrays the conflicting expert testimony, characterized as a conflict between orthodox and moderate Navajo religious views. For the government, Alfred Yazzie, an ordained *hataali* and Navajo Nation Historic Preservation representative, testified the Yei B'Chei must remain within the four sacred mountains of the Navajo for they represented the "heartbeat" of the Navajo people. Also for the government, Harry Walters, a Navajo anthropologist, stated there is "no such thing as ownership of medicine bundles and that these are viewed as living entities." He equated ownership with use, knowing the rituals, but acknowledged often cultural items are sold because of economic pressures. For Mr. Corrow, Jackson Gillis, a medicine man from Monument Valley, testified that if no claim is made by a clan relative or other singer, the *jish* pass to the widow who must care for them. If the widow feels uncomfortable keeping the *jish*, Mr. Gillis stated she has the right to sell them. Harrison Begay, another of Mr. Corrow's expert witnesses, agreed, explaining that because the masks themselves are "alive," a widow, uneasy about their remaining unused, may sell them. Billy Yellow, another *hataali* testifying for Mr. Corrow, reiterated the traditional disposition of a *hataali*'s Yei B'Chei to a spouse, the children, and grandchildren, although he stated nobody really owns the *jish* because they are living gods.

Given these conflicting views on the alienability of the Yei B'Chei, Mr. Corrow asks how an individual, even one educated in Navajo culture can "ascertain ownership when the group itself cannot agree on that point?" Mr. Corrow's invocation of void-for-vagueness review, however, obfuscates both its doctrinal reach and its application to the facts of this case.

"[T]he void-for-vagueness doctrine requires that a penal statute define the criminal offense with sufficient definiteness that ordinary people can understand what conduct is prohibited and in a manner that does not encourage arbitrary and discriminatory enforcement. . . ." [G]iven the limitations of language and syntax, a statute must convey to those individuals within its purview what it purports to prohibit and how it will punish an infraction. While the Court equates that requirement roughly with a notion of "fairness," it swathes it with the constitutional guarantees of the Fifth Amendment.

* * *

However, the Court has made equally clear our analysis is not global. [I]n a facial challenge the complainant "must demonstrate that the law is impermissibly vague in *all* of its applications."

Mr. Corrow cannot meet that burden. First, deciding whether the statute gave him fair notice, the district court found, after reviewing all of the expert testimony, Mr. Corrow is knowledgeable about Navajo traditions and culture and "would have been aware that various tribal members viewed ownership of property differently." The court cited the testimony of Ms. Charlotte Frisbie, author of *Navajo Medicine Bundles or Jish: Acquisition, Transmission and Disposition in the Past and Present* (1987). Ms. Frisbie related several calls from Mr. Corrow inquiring about the prices of certain Navajo artifacts. Although she stated he did not specifically ask her about these Yei B'Chei, she expressed her objection to dealers and commercial handlers selling Native American cultural objects in the open market. Ms. Frisbie also reminded him both of the Navajo Nation's implementing procedures to return cultural items and of the enactment of NAGPRA. Most damning, Ms. Bia, Mrs. Winnie's granddaughter, recounted Mr. Corrow's representation that he wanted to buy the Yei B'Chei to pass on to another young chanter in Utah. Reasonably, a jury could infer from that representation that Mr. Corrow appreciated some dimension of the Yei B'Chei's inherent inalienability in Navajo culture. Although Mrs. Winnie stated she believed the Yei B'Chei belonged to her, she testified, "[t]here was another man that knew the ways and he had asked of [the Yei B'Chei] but I was the one that was stalling and ended up selling it." Although this man trained with her husband, he had not offered her any money. This is not a case of an unsuspecting tourist happening upon Mrs. Winnie's hogan and innocently purchasing the set of Yei B'Chei.

Surely, this evidence establishes Mr. Corrow had some notice the Yei B'Chei he purchased were powerfully connected to Navajo religion and culture. While it may be true that even the experts in that culture differed in their views on alienability, *no* expert testified it was acceptable to sell Yei B'Chei to non-Navajos who planned to resell them for a profit, the very conduct § 1170(b) penalizes. All experts testified the Yei B'Chei resided within the Four Corners of the Navajo people and acknowledged the ritual cleansing and restoration required were the Yei B'Chei to be defiled in any way. Thus, while the parameters of the designation "cultural patrimony" might be unclear in some of its applications and at its edges, there is no doubt, in this case as applied to Mr. Corrow, the Yei B'Chei were cultural items which could not be purchased for a quick $40,000 turn of profit.

Consequently, we believe Mr. Corrow had fair notice—if not of the precise words of NAGPRA—of their meaning that Native American objects "having ongoing historical, traditional, or cultural importance central to the Native American group . . . rather than property owned by an individual Native American" could not be bought and sold absent criminal consequences.

* * *

Our analysis of the fairness issue infuses our disposition of the second vagueness concern, the potential for arbitrary and discriminatory enforcement. Here, the Department of the Interior National Park Service officer, Mr. Young, examined a photograph of the Yei B'Chei and discussed their significance with other knowledgeable Park Service officers and representatives of the Navajo Nation before deciding the items constituted cultural patrimony. Mr. Young testified he participated in other NAGPRA investigations and was aware that law enforcement officers must first consult with tribal representatives to determine whether an item has ongoing historical, cultural, or traditional importance. We conclude, therefore, as applied to Mr. Corrow, § 1170(b) provides sufficient guidance to law enforcement to dispel the fear of subjective enforcement. We affirm.

* * *

MBTA

Under 16 U.S.C. §703, it is "unlawful at any time, by any means or in any manner to . . . possess, offer for sale, sell . . . any migratory bird, any part . . . or any product, which consists, or is composed in whole or in part, of any such bird or any part . . . included in the terms of the conventions between the United States and Great Britain for the protection of migratory birds."

Since its enactment, the majority of courts considering misdemeanor violations under § 703 of the MBTA have treated these offenses as strict liability crimes, eliminating proof of scienter from the government's case. Although we have not previously so held, we now join those Circuits which hold misdemeanor violations under § 703 are strict liability crimes. Simply stated, then, "it is not necessary to prove that a defendant violated the Migratory Bird Treaty Act with specific intent or guilty knowledge."[3]

* * *

Here, in fact, the district court instructed the jury it must find Mr. Corrow knowingly possessed Golden Eagle and Great-Horned Owl feathers. [T]he district court pointed to the photographs of the Yei B'Chei Mr. Corrow gave to East-West, the feathers found in his suitcase, and testimony of an F.B.I. agent indicating Mr. Corrow's awareness of the illegal trade in protected feathers. Under our announced position, this evidence abundantly satisfied § 703.

We therefore AFFIRM the judgment of the district court.

NOTES

1. Jack F. Trope & Walter R. Echo-Hawk, *The Native American Graves Protection and Repatriation Act: Background and Legislative History*, 24 Ariz. St. L.J. 35, 37 (1992).

2. Francis P. McManamon & Larry V. Nordby, *Implementing the Native American Graves Protection and Repatriation Act*, 24 Ariz. St. L.J. 217, 233–34 (1992).

43 C.F.R. § 10.2(d)(4) states: *Objects of cultural patrimony* means items having ongoing historical, traditional, or cultural importance central to the Indian tribe or Native Hawaiian organization itself, rather than property owned by an individual tribal or organization member. These objects are of such central importance that they may not be alienated, appropriated, or conveyed by any individual tribal or organization member. Such objects must have been considered inalienable by the culturally affiliated Indian tribe or Native Hawaiian organization at the time the object was separated from the group. Objects of cultural patrimony include items such as Zuni War Gods, the Confederacy Wampum Belts of the Iroquois, and other objects of similar character and significance to the Indian tribe or Native Hawaiian organization as a whole.

3. United States v. Manning, 787 F.2d 431, 435 n. 4 (8th Cir.1986).

Property in Personhood

Madhavi Sunder

With her groundbreaking articles "Property and Personhood"[1] and "Market-Inalienability,"[2] legal theorist Margaret Jane Radin helped a generation that came of age during the halcyon days of law and economics to reconsider that movement's moral and philosophical underpinnings. Inspiring voluminous debate and dialogue including, indeed, this very anthology, Radin's prescient work is often cited today for its incisive *critique* of commodification. Radin powerfully revealed how commodification can undermine personhood. For many then, Radin stands for all that is *wrong* with commodification.

But in fact, Radin's rich body of work is much more nuanced. Far from offering a single-minded assault on commodification, Radin is a "philosophical pragmatist" who acknowledges that economic and cultural inequalities mandate that sometimes even very private things may be bought and sold, but only under carefully regulated circumstances. Radin is concerned that in the nonideal world in which we live, real people may lose out if markets are completely closed off to them. A central insight of what Radin calls the "double bind" is that "both commodification and noncommodification may be harmful."[3] Thus, Radin rejects the polar extremes of either a "pure market domain" where everything is commodifiable or a "pure nonmarket domain" where certain things may never be sold.[4] A pragmatist must decide commodification questions through a nuanced, case-by-case approach that acknowledges the need, in some instances, for partial commodification.[5] Radin urges that markets in what she calls "contested commodities"—"sex, children, body parts, and other things"—might not be categorically prohibited, but they ought to be regulated to protect against undue harm to one's person-

164

hood.[6] Thus, Radin opened the door to thinking about *managing* commodification.

These insights are helpful in guiding our understanding of an increasingly important twenty-first century phenomenon: the rise of property *in* personhood. At the turn of the century, three important and powerful forces are converging: identity politics, intellectual property, and the Internet Protocol.[7] As scholars such as Charles Taylor have described, during the past decade we have witnessed a rise in claims by traditionally disempowered groups to a right to recognition by the state as a separate and distinct cultural group—a phenomenon that has come to be known as "identity politics."[8] At the heart of recognition claims lies a desire to control how cultural groups are *represented* to the world. Today cultural groups seek to be able to contest others' depictions of them (or lack thereof) with rights to self-representation.[9] Simultaneous to the rise of identity politics has been an explosive growth of intellectual property rights, in the United States and around the world. To be sure, the development of digital technologies and the Internet have been primary catalysts for this recent intellectual property expansion.[10]

These phenomena have been separately chronicled; their convergence has been less examined. In fact, more and more identity groups today are turning toward intellectual property and other property laws as a means to protect themselves against cultural imperialism, cultural appropriation, and digital appropriation. Fears that globalization, the Internet, and heightened cultural traffic will lead to homogenization, unequal distribution of cultural power, and the loss of culture have led scholars and activists increasingly to turn to property and intellectual property law to regain control over cultural traditions, knowledge, symbols, and artifacts. In particular, subordinated groups, from Native North Americans to African and Asian Americans and third world peoples, perceive intellectual property as a powerful means of exercising exclusive control over intangible cultural resources, such as folklore and stories (through copyright), agricultural knowledge (through patent), and religious symbols (through trademark).

Take a few examples. Some traditional communities have sought to patent their indigenous knowledge and oppose multinational corporations' claims to patent their plants and medicinal remedies.[11] Native Americans similarly have contested trademarks held by professional football teams and businesses, which consist of demeaning images of Indians.[12] A small New Mexican Indian tribe has sued the state government for using a spiritual symbol on the state flag without the tribe's permission.[13] Australian aboriginal communities have sought collective copyrights in their artwork,[14] just as indigenous peoples in Canada have sought copyrights in traditional stories, which reflect the history and spirituality of their communities.[15] Native Americans are considering a "right of publicity" to prohibit the use of Crazy Horse's image to sell malt liquor.[16]

To be sure, significant doctrinal and policy impediments hamper the realization of many such claims.[17] Many of these claims are not recognized under traditional intellectual property laws because:

- there is no recognized individual author, or creator of the works;
- the works have historically been shared communally rather than used exclusively;
- our common cultural heritage is perceived as belonging in the public domain;
- folklore and other intellectual resources are dynamic and not "fixed" in a tangible form of expression as required by traditional intellectual property law; and
- naturally occurring phenomenon (such as one's DNA or plants) are considered raw materials that are not transformed into private property by their mere existence.

Despite these legal and policy barriers, cultural groups continue to advocate significant changes in traditional intellectual property laws and in the distribution of rights over cultural resources. These new claims for intellectual property challenge claims to exclusive rights to intangible resources historically controlled by powerful corporations and individuals. Today, disempowered groups argue for exclusive rights of their own to control their cultural resources and meet the material, intellectual, and spiritual needs of their people.[18]

The new indigenous peoples' claims for intellectual property are significant. There is an increasing awareness that much of the world's biogenetic and intellectual resources are found in the global South.[19] Indigenous peoples increasingly seek to capitalize on this wealth for themselves.[20] They assert an equal right to hold property along with their Western and Northern counterparts and to share in the surpluses these resources create.

At the same time, there is also an evolution in the way peoples conceive of themselves, their relationship to community, and ultimately, their relationship to property.[21] In an important book, Professor of Law Thomas Franck describes the rise of individualism and the emergence, worldwide, of an "empowered self."[22] Increasingly, people the world over are asserting themselves as *individuals,* Franck argues, and affirm a belief in *universal values* such as freedom and equality.[23] But, as I have argued elsewhere, today individuals—and groups—are appropriating these concepts in revolutionary ways, in some cases turning original understandings on their head.[24] The global campaign for "indigenous intellectual property" is an example.[25] This campaign conceives intellectual property rights as human rights—specifically, as human rights to protect cultural integrity and self-determination. This conception of intellectual property stands in stark contrast to the economic/utilitarian understanding of rights as incentives for creation that has been the predominant theory of intellectual property in the United States.[26] At the same time, indigenous intellectual property claims challenge the traditional focus of human rights law on civil and political rights, turning instead to distributive justice claims and social and economic rights. Thus, indigenous intellectual property campaigns merge traditional property and human rights understandings to create novel conceptions of both property and human rights. This campaign highlights the relationship between property and personhood. As one Australian human rights expert describes the essence of the global campaign for "indigenous intellectual property":

> The elements of a people's cultural heritage which are contained within the notions of "indigenous intellectual property" cannot be artificially segregated or excised from their other rights. It is therefore inappropriate to see a people's rights in relation to the exercise and integrity of their culture as somehow separate from their right to self-determination, or their land and territorial rights.[27]

Despite the cogence of this analysis, current trends in academic thinking do not bode well for these new claims for property in personhood. Traditional commodification scholars would bemoan the propertization of indigenous culture, arguing that culture should be common property accessible to all. More significantly, early commodification theory warns that because of current inequalities, the commodification of indigenous culture is more likely to lead to alienation, rather than preservation, of indigenous culture.[28] Recent developments in anthropology also might render one skeptical of indigenous intellectual property. Scholars in this discipline argue that property rights threaten to make dynamic cultures static.[29] Still other scholars view these claims as the first step on a slippery slope toward slavery.[30]

Finally, there are the critiques from intellectual property. As we witness what scholars have labeled "the new enclosure movement"[31] and lament what appears to be an inexorable march toward the intellectual propertization of "every thing, every word, and every idea,"[32] more and more intellectual property scholars are warning that our common cultural heritage and the free circulation of ideas are massively threatened.[33] Indeed, protecting the public domain of ideas and information has quickly shot up to the top of intellectual property scholars' agenda.

I am sympathetic to these projects.[34] But I am also concerned that these progressive, ideal theories elide nonideal constraints and important new claims for justice being made through the language of intellectual property rights. Critiquing each and every new claim for property rights may support current power relations by legitimating the current distribution of intellectual property rights. Revealing the relationship between intellectual property and progressive, ideal theories about commodification, culture, and the public domain helps us understand how, despite the best of intentions, the postmodern lawyer, collaborating with the postmodern anthropologist, might inadvertently leave minority cultures at the mercy of the forces of commerce and neocolonialism.[35]

To be sure, there are many reasons for concern about these new claims for property. But at the heart of the claims lies a challenge to current intellectual property definitions, theoretical justifications, and distributions. These challenges cannot be dismissed easily. They require us to carefully consider how these new property claims are already transforming intellectual property law and how law ought to respond to shifts in global social relations.

Articulating who is seeking greater property rights and why they seek them is a complex task. Far from being a simple story of intellectual property rights expanding into the public domain, the new claims for property rights are struggles over the right to create one's identity and to control cultural meanings. Indigenous and other subordinated peoples who have historically not owned property—to the contrary, under traditional property law, their cultural products have been characterized as a commons

and thus free for the taking for others to create property from their resources—are challenging this traditional relationship. They are asserting
their right to be the subjects, not the objects, of property.

As the concept of identity undergoes such a profound change, it is not
surprising that the property concept is morphing with it. Assertions of
power over one's own identity necessarily lead to assertions of property
ownership. As Radin has taught us, property is an essential part of what
it means to be fully human.[36] Property enables us to have control over our
external surroundings. Seen in this light, it is not enough to see all claims
for more property simply as intrusions into the public domain and violations of free speech. Instead, we may begin to see them as assertions of
personhood.

Outright rejection of indigenous claims for property in their knowledge effectively suppresses their challenge to current social relations and
turns a blind eye to new assertions by individuals to exercise authorship
over their lives. Rather than simply regressively clamp down on each and
every new claim for intellectual property rights, we need to examine the
context and ask what new descriptive possibilities for cultural formation
rights talk enables, and which emerging normative values about property
and personhood law should recognize.

Property rights are useful to the extent that they can transform the intangible harms of cultural imperialism and the loss of local knowledge,
ideas, and dignity into tangible, legally recognizable harms capable of remedy. The idea is that like land, culture and identity can be stolen, appropriated, and expropriated. By viewing culture, like property, along a spectrum from fungible to inalienable, the property concept can help us to understand culture in a more complex way, namely, as both ethereal and real.

The property concept alone will not do all the work of helping us to
recognize the complex nature of culture, but we need not throw out the
baby with the bathwater. If what concerns critics most is that property
rights in personhood or culture would restrict the free flow of information and ideas within and between cultures, this concern does not rule out
the possibility of tailoring law to narrowly address the problem of im-
balances of cultural power. Recall Radin: when ideal theory does not
work, we may respond with nonideal theory that takes ideals and reality
into account. Operationally, we might at times allow a market but control its dangers through regulation.

In the context of property in personhood, this might mean recognizing
new claims for property in personhood while protecting against their ex-

cesses. I would suggest here that the problem of property in personhood may not be the confluence of property and identity per se. Rather, the problem is that current claims often represent a confluence of bad identity politics and bad intellectual property. The main problem with current claims for property in personhood might not be the inherent impropriety of the claims themselves, but rather that they are too often premised upon an outmoded, essentialized view of identity, culture, or property.

Current claims for property in personhood often see culture as static, bounded, homogeneous and—at all costs—to be protected against external influence and interaction.[37] In fact, cultures are not homogeneous groups with singular points of view that are threatened by contact with the outside world and in need of legal protection but, rather, are dynamic, open, and evolving normative communities that are internally diverse, even teeming with dissent.[38] Intellectual property rights in culture could insulate cultures from interaction with other communities, creating ossified and static cultures that reinforce traditions through law. Such a rigid notion of cultural meanings has particularly pernicious consequences for individuals within cultural communities, such as women or sexual subordinates, who espouse nontraditional viewpoints that are cast as foreign and external to the group, or as potentially diluting.[39]

Often, new claims for property in personhood are also premised on an outmoded, essentialized view of property. Claimants conceive of property rights in absolute terms: property accords, in William Blackstone's words, "sole and despotic" dominion over resources.[40] In the view of the new intellectual property claimants, then, property is the absolute right to control, to exclude, and to transfer. But in fact, this absolute thing-ownership conception of property has disintegrated.[41] Today, property has been reconceived not in the static terms of absolute ownership but, rather, as a "web of social relations."[42] Modern property is conceived as a complex and dynamic set of legal rights and responsibilities among various social actors.[43] Property as social relations views resources as shared and examines the *effects* that the allocation of property rights has on others, as well as on social relationships. Normatively, this approach argues that judges and legislators should take these effects into account when creating and distributing property rights.[44] This regulatory approach stands in contrast to the free market model of property.[45]

Both property and culture are concepts that potentially are as oppressive as they are liberating. Exclusive rights to cultural identity threaten to freeze power differences within cultures and impede information and culture flows between cultures. In short, we can legitimately fear that the intellectual propertization of identity politics threatens to transform dialogical processes of identity formation into monological processes. To the extent that property in personhood claims are premised upon essentialized, outmoded understandings of either property or culture (or both), these claims threaten to take us backward, and, most significantly, may be counterproductive for the groups that are claiming them and for society as a whole. In this sense, scholars have been properly wary of such claims.

But the good news is that there may, in fact, be some room for property in personhood claims if they are grounded on more modern understandings of both culture and property. The good news about the deconstruction of these concepts is that both have, by and large, been resuscitated for contemporary analysis. Both culture and property have "disintegrated," but they have not been destroyed.[46] To the contrary, both concepts remain viable and strong precisely because they increasingly recognize heterogeneity, contingency, and the need for flexibility.

The concept of culture, for example, although no longer understood as static, bounded, and homogeneous, still acknowledges the existence of communities of meaning and shared norms. Modern cultures do not have rigid borders. Cultural information, people, and capital flow more freely across borders than ever before. Thus the interaction between cultures is a complex process of negotiation. New ideas are confronted, contested, integrated, and rejected sometimes, always within particular historical and cultural contexts. The new intellectual property claimants might meet with a warmer reception if they adopt a modern view of culture as needing some special protections in light of the disparate impact of a free market on traditionally subordinated groups, while recognizing cultures as subject to change in light of modernity and interaction among and within groups. The new intellectual property claims also should address problems of heterogeneity and hierarchy within cultures. Any approach to protecting identity groups through intellectual property would have to consider the need to provide access to cultural resources to all members of a culture, not just to the most powerful or traditional members of a group. Finally, we must be wary of the poorest cultures being coerced into alienating their resources and, indeed, their identities. These are clearly difficult balances to strike.

I end with the suggestion that the very conceptualization of contemporary property law as the regulation of social relations may, indeed, make it quite well suited to resolving the problem of property in person-hood. Contemporary property law recognizes that property relations are dialogical—that the exercise of one person's property rights invariably has effects on others. Contemporary property law attempts to negotiate relationships among competing parties with overlapping property inter-ests. Far from advocating absolute rights, current property law attempts to negotiate

- relations among neighbors;[47]
- the competing interests of present owners (who seek perpetual rights to control) and future owners (who seek freedom and changed conditions) of the same property;[48]
- individual rights versus those of a community;[49] and
- private interests in incentives and rewards versus rights of access for the public.[50]

In each of these cases, property law recognizes that social relations are complex negotiations between intergenerational equity and liberty, indi-viduals' desire for freedom and community, the right to exclude and the desire for access, and tradition and modernity.

To the extent that contemporary property law offers a balanced, com-plex, and dialogical view of social relations—or identity itself—the pos-sibilities for property rights in identity are not entirely bleak. Indeed, where scholars increasingly criticize identity politics for relying on a monologic, not dialogic, understanding of identity, property could be just what identity politics needs. In other words, while current claims for property in personhood tend toward essentialized views of both property and culture, they need not do so. Far more sophisticated understandings of both property and culture exist. If properly appropriated, intellectual property could be used to highlight the problems of culture loss, fashion creative remedies to the problems of unequal distribution in the power to make and control cultural meaning, and to rethink identity politics it-self.

We should not categorically fear the rise of new property rights. Rather, there is much to be gained from articulating competing descrip-tive and normative visions of intellectual property, particularly those that challenge the historically dominant paradigms. Rather than default into a suspicion of new identity-based claims to intellectual property, we might better spend our time thinking creatively about creating just property regimes[51] and paying more heed to the changing substantive needs and desires of individuals and communities.

NOTES

1. Margaret Jane Radin, *Property and Personhood,* 34 Stan. L. Rev. 957 (1982).

2. Margaret Jane Radin, *Market-inalienability,* 100 Harv. L. Rev. 1849 (1987).

3. Id. at 127.

4. Id. at 46.

5. Id. at 102–122.

6. See generally id.

7. Elsewhere I refer to this convergence by the meme "IP^3." See Madhavi Sunder, *IP^3* (draft 2004) (on file with author).

8. See Charles Taylor, *The Politics of Recognition, in Multiculturalism* 25, 25–73 (Amy Gutmann ed., 1992).

9. Id. at 25.

10. See generally Lawrence Lessig, The Future of Ideas: The Fate of the Commons in a Connected World (2001).

11. See Lakshmi Sarma, *Biopiracy: Twentieth-Century Imperialism in the Form of International Agreements,* 13 Temp. Int'l & Comp. L.J. 107 (1999); Lester I. Yano, *Protection of the Ethnobiological Knowledge of Indigenous Peoples,* 41 UCLA L. Rev. 443 (1993); Michael M. Phillips, *Bitter Remedies: The Search for Plants that Heal Generates International Feuding,* Wall St. J., June 7, 2001, at A1; Doris Estelle Long, *The Impact of Foreign Investment on Indigenous Culture: An Intellectual Property Perspective,* 23 N.C.J. Int'l Law & Com. Reg. 229 (1998).

12. Hornell Brewing Co., Inc. v. Brady, 819 F.Supp. 1227 (1993); Harjo v. Pro-Football, 30 U.S.P.Q.2d 1828 (Trademark Trial and Appeal Board, 1999).

13. See Phil Patton, *In New Mexico, a Battle Over a Familiar Symbol,* N.Y. Times, Jan. 13, 2000.

14. See Milpurruru v. Indofurm (1994) 30 I.P.R. 209; Yumbulul v. Reserve Bank of Australia (1991) 21 I.P.R. 481.

15. See Lenore Keeshig-Tobias, *Stop Stealing Native Stories,* Globe and Mail, Jan. 26, 1990, at A7.

16. See Nell Jessup Newton, *Memory and Misrepresentation: Representing Crazy Horse in Tribunal Court, in* Borrowed Power: Essays on Cultural Appropriation (1997).

17. See Bellagio Declaration, Mar. 11, 1993, *reprinted in* International Intellectual Property Anthology 107 (Anthony D'Amato & Doris Estelle Long eds.,

1996); Christine Haight Farley, *Protecting Folklore of Indigenous Peoples: Is Intellectual Property the Answer?*, 30 Conn. L. Rev. 1 (1997); Terence Dougherty, *Group Rights to Cultural Survival: Intellectual Property Rights in Native American Cultural Symbols*, 29 Colum. Human Rights L. Rev. 355 (1998).

18. See Rebecca Tsosie, *Reclaiming Native Stories: An Essay on Cultural Appropriation and Cultural Rights*, 34 Ariz. St. L.J. 299 (2002); Susan Scafidi, *Intellectual Property and Cultural Products*, 81 B.U. L. Rev. 793 (2001); Rosemary Coombe, *The Properties of Culture and the Politics of Possessing Identity: Native Claims in the Cultural Appropriation Controversy*, 6 Canadian J.L. & Juris. 249, 268 (1993).

19. See Inger Sjorslev, *Copyrighting Culture: Indigenous Peoples and Intellectual Rights, in* Legal Cultures and Human Rights: The Challenge of Diversity 43 (Kirsten Hastrup ed. 2001).

20. See id.

21. Cf. Marilyn Strathern, Property, Substance, and Effect: Anthropological Essays on Persons and Things (1999).

22. See Thomas M. Franck, The Empowered Self: Law and Society in the Age of Individualism 74–75 (1999).

23. See id.

24. See Madhavi Sunder, *Piercing the Veil*, 112 Yale L. J. 1399 (2003); Madhavi Sunder, *Cultural Dissent*, 54 Stan. L. Rev. 495 (2001).

25. Sjorslev, *supra* note 19, at 59.

26. See William Fisher, *Theories of Intellectual Property, in* New Essays in the Legal and Political Theory of Property 168, 169 (Stephen R. Munzer, ed. 2001).

27. See Sjorslev, *supra* note 19, at 59.

28. Here I echo an argument I have made earlier. See Madhavi Sunder, Comment *on* Stuart Kirsch, *Lost Worlds: Environmental Disaster, 'Culture Loss,' and the Law, in* 42 Current Anthropology 189 (April 2001).

29. See, *e.g.*, Michael Brown, Who Owns Native Culture? (2003); Elizabeth A. Povinelli, The Cunning of Recognition 4 (2002).

30. See Jane M. Gaines, *The Absurdity of Property in Person*, 10 Yale J. L. & Human. 537, 546 (1998).

31. James Boyle, *The Second Enclosure Movement and the Construction of the Public Domain*, 66 L. & Contemp. Probs. 33 (2002); Yochai Benkler, *Free as the Air to Common Use: First Amendment Constraints on Enclosure of the Public Domain*, 74 N.Y.U. L. Rev. 354, 364–386 (1999).

32. Mark A. Lemley, *The Modern Lanham Act and the Death of Common Sense*, 108 Yale L. J. 1687, 1715 (1999).

33. See, *e.g.*, Lessig, *supra* note 10; Brown, *supra* note 29.

34. See Sunder, *Piercing the Veil*, *supra* note 24; Sunder, *Cultural Dissent*, *supra* note 24; Madhavi Sunder, *Intellectual Property and Identity Politics—*

Playing With Fire, 4 Iowa J. Gender, Race, & Justice 69 (2000); Madhavi Sunder, *Authorship and Autonomy as Rites of Exclusion: The Intellectual Propertization of Free Speech in Hurley v. Irish-American Gay, Lesbian and Bisexual Group of Boston,* 49 Stan L. Rev. 143 (1996).

35. I borrow here from language I have used elsewhere. *See* Sunder, Comment on Stuart Kirsch, *supra* note 28, at 189.

36. Margaret Jane Radin, Reinterpreting Property (1993). To be sure, Hegel's—and perhaps Radin's—personality or personhood theory of property may be characterized as culturally specific. Many cultures would undoubtedly disagree with Hegel that "[a] person must translate his freedom into an external sphere in order to exist as Idea." See Hegel, Philosophy of Right 40 (trans. T. M. Knox 1962).

37. For an incisive critique of the excesses of the politics of recognition, see Povinelli, *supra* note 29, at 17. See generally Mary Ann Glendon, Rights Talk 76–108 (1991).

38. See Sunder, *Cultural Dissent, supra* note 24.

39. See id.

40. William Blackstone, Commentaries on the Laws of England (2004).

41. Thomas C. Grey, *The Disintegration of Property,* in XXII NOMOS: Property 69 (J. Roland Pennock & John W. Chapman eds., 1980) (describing evolving conception of property from view of property as "thing" to "disintegrated" view of property as "web of social relations.").

42. See Stephen R. Munzer, *Property as Social Relations, in* New Essays in the Legal and Political Theory of Property 36–75 (Stephen R. Munzer, ed. 2001).

43. See id.

44. See id. at 62–63 (citations omitted).

45. Id. at 60 (citations omitted).

46. See Grey, *supra* note 41, at 74–75; Sunder, *Cultural Dissent,* supra note 24 at 513–516.

47. See Joseph William Singer, Property Law: Rules, Policies, and Practices (3d ed.) 197–552 (2002) (describing contemporary balancing or standards approaches in cases involving border disputes, adverse possession, and nuisance claims between neighboring landowners).

48. See id. at 622–627 (discussing present interest owner's obligation not to "waste" the property so as to unreasonably deprive future interest holders of their property right); see id. at 467–473 (applying doctrine of changed conditions to find that beach resort town could allow restaurants to serve alcohol despite covenant by earlier settlers to ban such sales in order to maintain quiet, religious community).

49. See id. at 483–487 (discussing tensions between individuals and the condominium associations and cooperatives to which they belong); see id. at

639–704 (chronicling property disputes between cotenants, husbands, and wives, and unmarried partners).

50. See generally Fisher, *supra* note 26.

51. For examples of such a nuanced approach see Carol M. Rose, *Romans, Roads, and Romantic Creators: Traditions of Public Property in the Information Age*, 66 L. & Contemp. Probs. 89 (2003); Carol M. Rose, *Expanding the Choices for the Global Commons: Comparing Newfangled Tradable Allowance Schemes to Old-Fashioned Common Property Regimes*, 10 Duke Env. L. & Pol. Forum 45 (1999); Carol M. Rose, *The Several Futures of Property: Of Cyberspace and Folk Tales, Emission Trades and Ecosystems*, 83 Minn. L. Rev. 129, 139 (1998).

B.

Commodifying Identities

Kwanzaa and the
Commodification of Black Culture

Regina Austin[1]

A people expresses its personhood collectively through its culture. Sometimes that culture is made tangible in the form of a thing, as with the music (rap or hip hop), dance (breakdancing), poetry ("spoken word"), street art (graffiti), and styles of dress (urban) that are part and parcel of the collective way of life and meaning making of contemporary black and brown urban youth. When an aspect of black culture is turned into a commodity or a thing that can be bought and sold in markets accessible to, and more importantly controlled by, whites, it generally provokes fierce debate among blacks. White rapper Eminem is the latest target of accusations that whites are ripping off black people's cultural stuff.[2] Before him, there was, of course, rock 'n' roll legend Elvis Presley; and before Elvis, there was jazz clarinetist Benny Goodman.

In the view of the critics, commodifying black culture is the equivalent of pickling a luscious fruit or vegetable and plopping it in a jar or plucking a flower in full bloom and pressing it in a scrapbook. Commodification, in other words, is like embalming or mummifying a living thing. Black culture similarly loses its organic edge, its authenticity, its purity, its originality, its spontaneity, its vibrancy, and most importantly its rootedness when it is commodified.[3]

Furthermore, commodification portends the dilution of black culture because it is often accompanied by an effort to increase the commodified thing's appeal to consumers in the white-dominated mainstream. Dilution carries with it the implication that black culture is inferior and does not operate according to its own uncompromising standards of excellence. Commodification, especially if it is in accord with hegemonic white tastes, may destroy the very qualities that gave blacks gratification and enjoyment in the thing and its accompanying rites and performances. When it comes to judging the merits of cultural productions, blacks tend to privilege the spontaneous, the impromptu, and the improvised over the premeditated, the guarded, the scored, and the scripted (all of the latter being characteristics that facilitate commodification.) Black cultural production is often a reaction to the relative social isolation and material deprivation that blacks have suffered, and still suffer. Many blacks accordingly resent commodification because it allows nonblacks to experience the pleasure of blacks' outsider or rebellious culture without having to endure any of the pain that produced it. Thus, an homogenized, calcified black cultural commodity that others freely buy loses its power to resist oppression, to unsettle the status quo, and to shake things up.

In addition, crossing over or selling out opens the way for the appropriation of black cultural forms by nonblacks and for the economic exploitation of its black creators and innovators. Whites stand ever ready to separate a black cultural artifact from its black producers, repackage it with a white face on it, and sell it to a white audience that is both attracted and repelled by things black. Before blacks know it, what they once sold to themselves and others is being sold back to them.

Thus, for blacks, *commodification* (which turns some aspect of a person or a people into a sellable thing) is inextricably linked with *commercialization* (which turns the thing into a commodity that is bought or sold in markets on a large scale and for a substantial profit) and *co-optation* (which turns the commodity away from and against its creators or innovators in a way that gives little or no credit to them). Appropriation by white producers siphons off respect, recognition, and revenue that blacks would otherwise reap. The lack of acknowledgment of blacks' creative genius and intelligence is particularly galling given that blacks are still struggling to prove their innate equality and their collective and individual complexity. Moreover, as social historian Robin Kelley puts it, whites tend to *appropriate* black culture without *embracing* it. If they were to embrace black culture, whites would have "to embrace the people who created it and to fully embrace their liberation; it was never simply a matter of consumption."[4]

Thus, with a price on its head (or its side or its bottom), black culture commodified becomes disconnected from its source, out there, frozen in time and space, unbeholden to the people and the socioeconomic conditions that gave it vitality, like an ungrateful child. Alienated from blacks, the thing becomes a major source of black alienation.

Although all or part of the critique of commodification outlined here will elicit an "amen" from a broad spectrum of black people, there are counter concerns that grow out of the concrete circumstances confronting many black people today. First, the violence and social chaos afflicting many black neighborhoods have left some folks feeling as if blacks have collectively lost their way. Many of those feeling bereft of hope believe that blacks must consciously work to create or re-create traditions and rituals that will provide mechanisms for self-validation and accountability to self and to others. They are looking backward in search of cultural forms that were lost as long ago as slavery. But the need to establish new cultural traditions and to reformulate and disseminate the values around which a rich community life can be built seems to require some amount of commodification of black culture because, through their use, transfer, and interpretation, commodities become embedded in social relations and help social relations to grow and solidify.

Second, it is becoming increasingly clear that the economic advancement of black people depends upon their creating markets and audiences for the products of their labor. This goal cannot be met without promoting increased consumption of the sort that fuels production which in turn creates jobs. From this perspective, commodities might be considered devices for packaging people's needs and desires in ways that create employment and material gains. Blacks are perhaps uniquely situated to gain from the production and sale of the things that can be made of black culture, provided, of course, they compete with whites and prevent whites from achieving market dominance with regard to those things. To the extent that the critique of commodification is anti-market, however, it poses an obstacle here too.

The critique of commodification and its counters are not totally irreconcilable. In particular, some of the alienation commodification produces might be ameliorated if there were a greater link between commercialized black cultural production and consumption. Moreover, consumption linked to production might be an effective form of resistance if black folks had something tangible to show for their market activity, *i.e.*, if it generated new institutions and cultural practices, as well as new sources of wealth, that are sufficient to support the production and reproduction of the good life for blacks. To secure the benefits of a nonalienated consumption by aligning it with more cooperative production and ownership, blacks will need not only alternative structures but also an alternative rhetoric to market capitalism's with its emphasis on individualized, self-interested wealth maximization.

There are any number of strategies that blacks have employed in an attempt to be mindful of both the critique of commodification and its counters. This is the point where the law enters the picture. Blacks intent on commodifying black culture largely for the benefit of blacks or on resisting the efforts of others to commodify black culture for their own gain have relied on intellectual property law as both a weapon and shield. Though there is little or no protection for collectively or communally generated work,[5] individual producers of black cultural artifacts or commodities have invoked the copyright laws to prevent appropriation of their work. For example, Faith Ringgold is a black feminist visual artist who, over a long career, has fought both black male artists and the white art establishment to gain recognition. She brought suit against Black Entertainment Television after set designers for the television sitcom "Roc" used as a background prop a $20 poster of Ringgold's "Church Picnic" from the High Museum in Atlanta.[6] The poster was "cropped . . . before framing . . . so as to omit the legend identifying the poster with the High Museum." The set designer evidently "wanted the viewers to believe that the set was decorated with an original painting, rather than a poster reproduction." Ringgold did not sue on the ground that the defendants were co-opting her art, turning it against its creator, and employing it for a purpose to which she was diametrically opposed. Rather, she claimed that the appropriators were using her art for the very purpose for which she had created it—as decorative art! The bold colors, the theme of the work, the race of the figures of the poster decorated the mise en scene. It embellished the set the way the poster was supposed to embellish the home or office or space of any purchaser of the poster. The court granted that the work may have been created to fulfill other goals like "illuminating human understanding, providing inspiration, or provoking thought," but for the purposes of the litigation its most salient feature was its "decorative purpose." By accepting the commodification of her art, Ringgold prevented its alienation.

Blacks may also be able to avoid commodification by inventing or creating things that whites cannot or will not rip off. Afrocentricity, which puts some notion of Africa or African America at the center of the universe, has produced cultural creations that do not invite whites to share in its framing of a vision of the black good life. Afrocentric artifacts, however, are not immune from being lawfully appropriated or alienated by efforts either to critique or to parody Afrocentricity. For example, posters depicting African rites of passage for young men and women by Michigan artist Earl Jackson were used without his permission in the Whoopi Goldberg/Ted Danson movie *Made in America* that involved an interracial relationship. Jackson sued, but, unlike Ringgold, lost. Jackson objected to the use made of his work on the ground that it was antithetical to the Afrocentric political or social vision he expressed in his art. The posters were used in a scene in which the couple kissed so vehemently that one of the posters was knocked askew. The court labeled this parody and concluded that it constituted fair use of Jackson's art.[7]

Alternatively, blacks might take something the dominant white culture holds dear, transform it, and see how whites like it. *The Wind Done Gone*, "an unauthorized parody" of *Gone with the Wind* illustrates this approach.[8] It survived a copyright challenge brought by the trustee of the estate of Margaret Mitchell.[9] Another option available to blacks resisting commodification would be to create something expressly for consumption by the white-dominated mainstream, sell it as an authentic black cultural artifact, and laugh all the way to the bank.

As these strategies suggest, cultural appropriation is a two-way street. With regard to some cultural commodities, it is futile to try to separate what is "ours" from what is "theirs." Blacks have historically absorbed the commingled stuff of white and black culture (with more than a dollop of Native American, Latin, and Asian culture too) and turned it into something fresh and flavorful, with the view to combating blacks' political and material subordination and advancing their social and material liberation. Every group has its conceits. Cultural appropriation should be understood as a weapon in a continuing contest between blacks, whites, and others in which blacks are attempting to prove that not only are they more creative than other people, they are also more moral, both politically and economically.[10]

Hip-hop culture comes close to avoiding the things that the espousers of the commodification critique say should be avoided and doing the things that promoters of commodification say should be pursued. Many younger black people are less fearful of markets and commodification than their elders. As black culture critic Greg Tate opines, "The way that hip-hop collapsed art, commerce, and interactive technology into one mutant animal from its inception seems to have almost predicted the forms culture would have to take to prosper in the digital age."[11] Hip-hop samples or borrows from and parodies white masters (and black ones too). It invites whites to enjoy its beats or its style as long as they include in their embrace the minority producers of the music and fashions. For a long time, hip-hop music defied appropriation by white imitators. The real problem with hip-hop culture is that, with its misogyny, homophobia, and crass materialism, it does not take seriously black claims to moral leadership in politics and economics. It sacrifices women, gays, and black community for the sake of individual success. The explicit, self-congratulatory emphasis on money making and conspicuous consumption in the music (the "bling, bling" as they say in the vernacular) bespeaks the alienation of its black producers from their product, which enjoys an amazingly large young white paying audience.

The African American holiday of Kwanzaa is a better example of an attempt to work out the tensions between the critique of commodification and its counter arguments. Kwanzaa was created in 1966 by black nationalist Ron, now Maulana, Karenga.[12] Kwanzaa was not entirely created out of whole cloth. Rather, it represents a cultural synthesis or rescue and reconstruction that draws elements from African harvest festivals, as well as Christmas, Hanukkah, and the rituals of New Year's Eve.[13] Celebrated between December 26th and January 1st, Kwanzaa's timing coincides with that of harvest celebrations on the African continent and the year-end celebrations of mainstream America.[14] Kwanzaa, however, allows black Americans to participate in the festive season with a culturally specific holiday of their own.[15]

More than that, Kwanzaa also (intentionally) comes at the end of the Christmas shopping season. Kwanzaa was supposed to challenge the crass commercialism associated with the Christmas holiday.[16] Its creator emphasized that Kwanzaa represents a cultural choice, not a religious one. It gives blacks "a spiritual alternative to the commercialization of Christmas," which Karenga associates with "the European cultural accretions of Santa Claus, reindeer, mistletoe, frantic shopping, alienated gift-giving, etc."[17]

The values of Kwanzaa are embodied in the seven principles known as the Nguzo Saba. They include unity (umoja), self-determination (kujichagulia), collective work and responsibility (ujima), cooperative economics (ujamma), purpose (nia), creativity (kuumba), and faith (imani).[18] For our purposes, ujamma or the principle of cooperative economics is the most important.[19] Cooperative economics entails blacks' "build[ing] [their] own businesses, control[ling] the economics of [their] own community, and shar[ing] in all its work and wealth." Blacks "must harness [their] resources and put them to the best possible use in the service of the community." There must be "respect for the dignity and obligation of work," but of course it is understood that work has more worth when it is not exploitative and is engaged in "cooperatively for the common good of the community." Ujamma also encourages the sharing of wealth as an antidote to "exploitation, oppression, and inequality."

Kwanzaa has its own symbols and rituals. The symbols are to be placed on a kind of altar around which a nightly ritual is to be performed. Included among the symbols are corn (to represent the children), a candle holder called a kinara, seven candles (1 black, 3 red, and 3 green), a unity cup (for drinking and pouring libations for the ancestors), gifts, and a mat on which to place them all.[20] Each succeeding night of Kwanzaa involves the lighting of one additional candle and an exploration of one of the seven principles. On the last day there is a feast and gifts are exchanged.

Kwanzaa involves some gift giving, but it is supposed to be limited so as to avoid the alienation that arises when presents are given "to impress or punish rather than to please or to share."[21] The gifts are primarily for children and they are given directly by the family members whose sacrifice made them possible. There is no elf, jolly fat man, or hired stranger who acts as an intermediary. The gifts are to be purchased after Christmas "to take advantage of the after-Christmas sales and to escape the exorbitant prices established for the season." Moreover, the gifts are given to recognize commitments made and kept and are not to be mandatory or excessive. Finally, the gifts are supposed to include a book and an item associated with black heritage.

Kwanzaa has changed over time.[22] The holiday spread by word of mouth and by the efforts of individual activists and community organizers. Local and national black media also aided the popularization of the holiday. There are any number of books, for both adults and children, that serve as manuals for the observance of the holiday.[23] Kwanzaa creates an opening for African Americans to experiment with "Africanized" culture and traditions, including dress, food, dance, and music, as a positive source of enjoyment and merriment. As more and more blacks have embraced the holiday, it has become more mainstream and more bourgeois.[24] Schools, public libraries, churches, and community centers have become substantial promoters of the holiday in an effort to include African Americans in the year-end multicultural holiday mix. Kwanzaa joins Hanukkah, Christmas, the Winter Solstice, and Three Kings Day as the focus of assemblies, programs, and pageants celebrated at the end of the calendar year. (Eid Al Fitr, which marks the end of the Muslim observance of Ramadan, has not yet been added to the list, although some school districts with substantial Muslim enrollments give students time off.) Broad inclusiveness of various nonreligious year-end ethnic holidays like Kwanzaa helps to squelch the First Amendment-Establishment Clause challenges that celebration of Christmas (with its trees and crèches) and Hanukkah (with its menorahs) alone or together provokes.[25] Thus, Kwanzaa achieves inclusion by parallelism and as cultural cover gives as good as it gets. The secular nature of the holiday, however, may stifle its adoption in locales where blacks emphasize the sacred aspects of Christmas.

Over time Kwanzaa has become more commercial. There are countless books about Kwanzaa, as well as videos and audio recordings. Kwanzaa is promoted at fairs and expos held throughout the country. Not all of the commercialism has been in keeping with the principle of ujamma or cooperative economics. For example, during the past decade, Kwanzaa Holiday Expos have been held in metropolitan cities with substantial black populations. Among the exhibitors have been the usual small-scale black vendors of Afrocentric goods (clothes, books, art work, jewelry, and music), but also large corporations (banks, life insurance companies, and cosmetics manufacturers) that are hardly black-owned. Similarly, large retailers, distillers, and greeting card manufacturers have used Kwanzaa as a marketing device,[26] and the U.S. Postal Service has even issued a Kwanzaa stamp.

The commercialism has increased participation in and the celebration of the holiday. It has also given the holiday legitimacy and respectability, and stimulated a demand for the wares of African American producers and sellers. But commercialism has also provoked critical responses from roughly two different camps within the African-American community, both of which draw on various aspects of the critique of commodification outlined above. In one camp, there are the American traditionalists. They dismiss Kwanzaa as a made-up holiday, a figment of the imagination of a single, rather far-out radical black nationalist or separatist. They consider Kwanzaa to be artificial, in bad taste, foreign to black American culture, and inconsistent with black Christianity. They doubt that Kwanzaa resonates at some deep level with values to which black people are emotionally attached or which are associated with their religious faith. Estimates of the number of celebrants of the holiday, they say, are overblown. The traditionalists maintain that Kwanzaa simply cannot compete with Christmas because it is essentially anti-materialist. It would get more play if it were celebrated in February during Black History/Heritage Month.

The second camp of critics consists of the Kwanzaa purists. They are interested in preserving the virtues of Kwanzaa. They emphasize its allegedly ancient roots and fear that it will be lost as a tool of resistance and redemption if it is not saved from commercial contamination. They want to preserve the centrality of cooperative economics to the holiday and are prepared to dissuade (via threats of boycotts) white-controlled corporations and multinationals that dare to capitalize on Kwanzaa.[27] At the same time, they are distressed that interest in the holiday as an event to be celebrated privately by black families in their homes may have plateaued.

To a certain extent, both camps have a rather stilted, static view of culture that is inconsistent with the vibrant holiday Kwanzaa is or has the potential of being. Kwanzaa takes advantage of the dynamic nature of history and culture. It proclaims its vulgarity, its appeal to and affinity with ordinary people, particularly women and children, schoolteachers and their pupils. It recognizes that there is old in the new and new in the old. So what if Kwanzaa is a made-up holiday. What holiday is not made-up or invented? It does not matter that Kwanzaa is a touch derivative and just a little pat, beginning as it does right after Christmas and culminating in a feast on New Year's Eve. It may indeed be too political for and more than a little threatening to many people, but so too were other holidays at their origin. Celebrants of Kwanzaa have every right, consciously, even self-consciously, to create history and deliberately make social and material space for themselves and their children.

It is true that Kwanzaa creates a community of consumers. Skeptics of commodification often object to communities based on consumption, where the only link between people is their common acquisition and possession of commodities. In such cases, the commodities are more important than the values with which the commodities are associated. Moreover, it is charged that the resistance of communities based on consumption never amounts to much. But the community of Kwanzaa celebrants does not entirely fall prey to these criticisms. Kwanzaa fills a void by recognizing that it is not enough for blacks to achieve social and political integration. With its embrace of both family values and economic self-determination, Kwanzaa does something that Black History Month and

Martin Luther King's Birthday do not do. Kwanzaa is not about heroes or heroines. It addresses everything from violence and the breakdown of the black family to what constitutes a good time. It is a medicine for all sorts of ills. Kwanzaa responds to many blacks' needs for rituals and rites that give them the responsibility and security that go with defined roles that will keep them and their children safe.

Beyond that, Kwanzaa is a mechanism for creating among the peoples of the African Diaspora the structures of feeling and the material conditions that promote cooperative economics and the internal production of jobs and wealth. Kwanzaa does this by directly addressing blacks' economic marginalization. It accepts the market as a site of conflict and recognizes that if blacks do not compete and consume, they will die. Kwanzaa is respectful of the critique of the commodification of black culture, but it takes the chance of falling into the pitfalls the critique identifies because of the belief that black people must risk competing if they are to break the economic and social bonds of white supremacy. And so Kwanzaa takes on Christmas—the commercial Christmas, not the Christmas rooted in traditional Christianity. Kwanzaa thereby subverts capitalism by creating its own space within capitalism, and by redeploying the tools of capitalism with African elements for the benefit of Africans in America. It does this by structuring economic activity on the ground. Kwanzaa does not confront the market with negativism or pessimism. It responds to the market with a competing theory and a positive plan. It acknowledges the relevance of the market and marketing to the black good life. It represents inclusion for those who equate consumption with equality.

That said, Kwanzaa does not totally conform to its blueprint. Kwanzaa is swathed in ironies.[28] It was invented for the black masses, but black middle-class families and educators have turned out to be its chief proponents and adherents. It was nationalist or separatist in origin, but now it is celebrated by public institutions as a mechanism for incorporating and integrating African and African American culture into their programs. Though black nationalism is associated with patriarchy, black females and children find the holiday empowering. It is supposed to be reflective of blacks' African heritage but adherents recognize that it is a uniquely African-American take on Africa. It nonetheless provides the occasion for a formal and sustained engagement with authentic African or African-diasporic culture. African Americans are increasingly immigrants from Africa, the Caribbean, and Central and South America and worshipers of Islam as opposed to Christianity. Kwanzaa is a more inclusive holiday than Christmas for an ethnically diverse black community. Kwanzaa is part of the lasting legacy of the black nationalist movement of the '60s and a prediction of the direction in which the black community will evolve in the twenty-first century. Finally, Kwanzaa was anti-capitalist in conception, but it has spread through commercialization, which has helped to sustain a market for Afrocentric commodities manufactured and distributed by black-owned concerns. Indeed, Kwanzaa recognizes blacks' need to compete on equal terms with the white mainstream culturally, socially, and economically.

It is possible to draw some general conclusions about the contemporary salience of the critique of the commodification of black culture and the countervailing concerns from the success of Kwanzaa. Black people still have reasons to be concerned about white society's tendency to alienate things from their black creators and innovators. Commodification per se is not the problem though; the real struggle is over the meaning that is embedded in the things to which blacks' creativity and intellect have contributed and in the social interactions from which and by which that meaning flows. In this view, meaning and money are generated in markets that are essentially occasions for social interaction. Moreover, competition is to be embraced, not feared or avoided. Black people should not allow themselves to be alienated from their things without a struggle. The commodities that are produced by or through black culture represent an extension of their collective selves. As the discussion of hip hop and Kwanzaa reveals, black people cannot be reduced to commodities but they cannot survive without commodification either.

NOTES

I wish to thank Manthia Diawara and Gera Peoples for their helpful comments and Arthur Luk, Palisa Kelley, and Baye Nelson for their research assistance.

1. Reprinted with permission from *Black Renaissance* (Sept. 2004).

2. See Carl Hancock Rux, *Eminem: The New White Negro, in* Everything but the Burden: What White People Are Taking from Black Culture (Greg Tate ed., 2003) [hereinafter Everything but the Burden]. Eminem is the star of the surprisingly successful movie *8 Mile* and he won Grammies for his album. Unlike his predecessors, Eminem is aware of the fact that he is making more money selling black culture to whites than blacks would make doing the same thing. He acknowledges his indebtedness to blacks. Dr. Dre, a black rapper and Eminem's music producer, is also getting paid.

3. Consider, for example, artist and cinematographer Arthur Jafa's account of the sources of black musical expressivity. Arthur Jafa, *My Black Death, in* Everything but the Burden, *supra* note 2, at 244, 248–49. Black music achieved a mobility forbidden to the black body. Not only did it weather the Middle Passage, but "free of the class strictures of its natal context . . . and unconstrained by a need to speak the experiences of a ruling class, [it] evolved new forms with which to embody new experiences. A black music evolved equal to the unprecedented existential drama and complexity of the circumstances in which black people (Africans) found themselves."

4. Robin Kelley, *Reds, Whites, and Blues People, in* Everything but the Burden, *supra* note 2, at 44, 67.

5. See Susan Scafidi, *Intellectual Property and Cultural Products,* 81 B.U. L. Rev. 793 (2001).

6. See Ringgold v. Black Entertainment Television, 126 F.3d 70 (2d Cir. 1997).

7. See Jackson v. Warner Brothers, 993 F. Supp. 585 (E.D. Mich. 1997).

8. Alice Randall, The Wind Done Gone (2001). The title page contains the following disclaimer: "This novel is the author's critique of and reaction to the world described in Margaret Mitchell's *Gone with the Wind.* It is not authorized by the Stephens Mitchell Trusts, and no sponsorship or endorsement by the Mitchell Trusts is implied."

9. See Suntrust Bank v. Houghton Mifflin Co., 268 F.3d 1257 (11th Cir. 2001) (concluding that the publication of *The Wind Done Gone* could not be enjoined because of the strength of its author's fair use defense).

10. See, e.g., Robin Kelley, *supra* note 4, at 46, 61 (arguing that white American socialists were enamored with black culture because it was the product of the theoretical insights of black Americans; the former appropriated black culture for use "in the service of emancipating the world"); Michaela Angela Davis, *The Beautiful Ones, in* Everything but the Burden, *supra* note 2, at 124, 131–32, 132 (describing blacks as having an irresistible impulse to create" as compared with whites' "ability to infiltrate"; moreover, "white people need black people to create [*sic*] define and validate American style" for which "America always had to love black people" while black people could do without the love and were "more beautiful" without white people).

11. Greg Tate, *Introduction: Nigs R Us, or How Blackfolk Became Fetish Objects, in* Everything but the Burden, *supra* note 2, at 1, 7.

12. Maulana Karenga, The African American Holiday of Kwanzaa: A Celebration of Family, Community & Culture 27 (1989).

13. Id. at 15, 69.

14. Id. at 32.

15. Id. at 33.

16. Id. at 32–33.

17. Id. at 33–34.

18. Id. at 35–72.

19. Id. at 61–64.

20. Id. at 75–93.

21. Id. at 85.

22. See generally, Elizabeth Pleck, *Kwanzaa: The Making of a Black Nationalist Tradition, 1966–1990,* J. Am. Ethnic Hist., Summer 2001, at 3.

23. The books explain the rituals and symbols of the holiday; offer recipes and menus for the nightly meals; suggest inspirational readings (stories, essays, proverbs, and poems); detail arts and crafts projects for making gifts and the accouterments for the nightly ceremonies; provide programs for more elaborate, formal observances; and list the names of booksellers, apparel vendors, gift shops and art galleries selling wares compatible with the Afrocentric nature of the holiday. See, e.g., Eric v. Copage, Kwanzaa: An African-American Celebration of Culture and Cooking (1991); Ida Gamble-Gumbs & Bob Gumbs, How to Plan a Kwanzaa Celebration: Ideas for Family, Community and Public Events (1998); Cedric McClester, Kwanzaa: Everything You Always Wanted to Know but Didn't Know Where to Ask (rev. ed. 1994); Marcia Odle McNair, Kwanzaa Crafts: Gifts and Decorations for a Meaningful and Festive Celebration (1998); Dorothy Winbush Riley: The Complete Kwanzaa: Celebrating Our Cultural Harvest (1995); Linda Robertson, The Complete Kwanzaa Celebration Book (1993). The children's books include, in addition to an explanation of the holiday, brief summaries of African American history, biographies of great black Americans, and an introduction to words in the Swahili language. See, e.g., Martin Hintz and Kate Hintz, Kwanzaa: Why We Celebrate It the Way We Do (1996); David F. Marx, Kwanzaa (Rookie read-about holiday series) (2000); Dana Meachen Rau, Kwanzaa (A True Book) (2000); Lola M. Schaefer, Kwanzaa (Holidays and celebrations series) (2001).

24. See generally Anna Day Wilde, *Mainstreaming Kwanzaa,* Public Interest, Spring 1995, at 68.

25. See ACLU of New Jersey v. Schundler, 168 F.3d 92 (3rd Cir. 1999); Sechler v. State College Area School District, 121 F. Supp.2d 439 (M.D. Pa. 2000).

26. The chairman of Kwanzaa Holiday Expo was quoted as saying that his company had "been working to repackage and remarket Kwanzaa. Corporate America seems a lot more comfortable in associating with it." Douglas Martin, *The Marketing of Kwanzaa,* N.Y. Times, Dec. 20, 1993, at B1.

27. See, e.g., Mary A. Johnson, *Preserving a Black Tradition; Celebrants Warn of Commercialism,* Chicago Sun-Times, Dec. 26, 1993, at 7; Conrad Worrill, *Kwanzaa Belongs to Us, Don't Let Them Commercialize It,* Phila. Trib., Jan. 1, 1994, at 7A.

28. See Pleck, *supra* note 22.

Eating the Other
Desire and Resistance

bell hooks[1]

The Oppositional Imagination

Within current debates about race and difference, mass culture is the contemporary location that both publicly declares and perpetuates the idea that there is pleasure to be found in the acknowledgment and enjoyment of racial difference. The commodification of Otherness has been so successful because it is offered as a new delight, more intense, more satisfying than normal ways of doing and feeling. Within commodity culture, ethnicity becomes spice, seasoning that can liven up the dull dish that is mainstream white culture. Cultural taboos around sexuality and desire are transgressed and made explicit as the media bombards folks with a message of difference no longer based on the white supremacist assumption that "blondes have more fun." The "real fun" is to be had by bringing to the surface all those "nasty" unconscious fantasies and longings about contact with the Other embedded in the secret (not so secret) deep structure of white supremacy. In many ways it is a contemporary revival of interest in the "primitive," with a distinctly postmodern slant. As Marianna Torgovnick argues in *Gone Primitive: Savage Intellects, Modern Lives*:

> What is clear now is that the West's fascination with the primitive has to do with its own crises in identity, with its own need to clearly demarcate subject and object even while flirting with other ways of experiencing the universe.

Certainly from the standpoint of white supremacist capitalist patriarchy, the hope is that desires for the "primitive" or fantasies about the Other can be continually exploited, and that such exploitation will occur in a manner that reinscribes and maintains the *status quo*. Whether or not desire for contact with the Other, for connection rooted in the longing for pleasure, can act as a critical intervention challenging and subverting racist domination, inviting and enabling critical resistance, is an unrealized political possibility. Exploring how desire for the Other is expressed, manipulated, and transformed by encounters with difference and the different is a critical terrain that can indicate whether these potentially revolutionary longings are ever fulfilled.

Contemporary working-class British slang playfully converges the discourse of desire, sexuality, and the Other, evoking the phrase getting "a bit of the Other" as a way to speak about sexual encounter. Fucking is the Other. Displacing the notion of Otherness from race, ethnicity, skin-color, the body emerges as a site of contestation where sexuality is the metaphoric Other that threatens to take over, consume, transform via the experience of pleasure. Desired and sought after sexual pleasure alters the consenting subject, deconstructing notions of will, control, coercive domination. Commodity culture in the United States exploits conventional thinking about race, gender, and sexual desire by "working" both the idea that racial difference marks one as Other and the assumption that sexual agency expressed within the context of racialized sexual encounter is a conversion experience that alters one's place and participation in contemporary cultural politics. The seductive promise of this encounter is that it will counter the terrorizing force of the *status quo* that makes identity fixed, static, a condition of containment and death. And that it is this willingness to transgress racial boundaries within the realm of the sexual that eradicates the fear that one must always conform to the norm to remain "safe." Difference can seduce precisely because the mainstream imposition of sameness is a provocation that terrorizes. And as Jean Baudrillard suggests in *Fatal Strategies*:

> Provocation—unlike seduction, which allows things to come into play and appear in secret, dual and ambiguous—does not leave you free to be; it calls on you to reveal yourself as you are. It is always blackmail by identity (and thus a symbolic murder, since you are never that, except precisely by being condemned to it).

To make one's self vulnerable to the seduction of difference, to seek an encounter with the Other, does not require that one relinquish forever one's mainstream positionality. When race and ethnicity become commodified as resources for pleasure, the culture of specific groups, as well as the bodies of individuals, can be seen as constituting an alternative playground where members of dominating races, genders, sexual practices affirm their power-over in intimate relations with the Other. While teaching at Yale, I walked one bright spring day in the downtown area of New Haven, which is close to campus and invariably brings one into contact with many of the poor black people who live nearby, and found myself walking behind a group of very blond, very white, jock type boys. Seemingly unaware of my presence, these young men talked about their plans to fuck as many girls from other racial/ethnic groups as they could "catch" before graduation. They "ran" it down. Black girls were high on the list, Native American girls hard to find, Asian girls (all lumped into the same category), deemed easier to entice, were considered "prime targets."

* * *

The current wave of "imperialist nostalgia" (defined by Renato Rosaldo in *Culture and Truth* as "nostalgia, often found under imperialism, where people mourn the passing of what they themselves have transformed" or as "a process of yearning for what one has destroyed that is a form of mystification") often obscures contemporary cultural strategies deployed not to mourn but to celebrate the sense of a continuum of "primitivism." In mass culture, imperialist nostalgia takes the form of reenacting and reritualizing in different ways the imperialist, colonizing journey as narrative fantasy of power and desire, of seduction by the Other. This longing is rooted in the atavistic belief that the spirit of the "primitive" resides in the bodies of dark Others whose cultures, traditions, and lifestyles may indeed be irrevocably changed by imperialism, colonization, and racist domination. The desire to make contact with those bodies deemed Other, with no apparent will to dominate, assuages the guilt of the past, even takes the form of a defiant gesture where one denies accountability and historical connection. Most importantly, it establishes a contemporary narrative where the suffering imposed by structures of domination on those designated Other is deflected by an emphasis on seduction and longing where the desire is not to make the Other over in one's image but to become the Other.

* * *

Should youth of any other color not know how to move closer to the Other, or how to get in touch with the "primitive," consumer culture promises to show the way. It is within the commercial realm of advertising that the drama of Otherness finds expression. Encounters with Otherness are clearly marked as more exciting, more intense, and more threatening. The lure is the combination of pleasure and danger. In the cultural marketplace the Other is coded as having the capacity to be more alive, as holding the secret that will allow those who venture and dare to break with the cultural anhedonia (defined in Sam Keen's *The Passionate Life* as "the insensitivity to pleasure, the incapacity for experiencing happiness") and experience sensual and spiritual renewal. Before his untimely death, Michel Foucault, the quintessential transgressive thinker in the West, confessed that he had real difficulties experiencing pleasure:

> I think that pleasure is a very difficult behavior. It's not as simple as that to enjoy one's self. And I must say that's my dream. I would like and I hope I die of an overdose of pleasure of any kind. Because I think it's really difficult and I always have the feeling that I do not feel *the* pleasure, the complete total pleasure and, for me, it's related to death. Because I think that the kind of pleasure I would consider as *the* real pleasure, would be so deep, so intense, so overwhelming that I couldn't survive it. I would die.

Though speaking from the standpoint of his individual experience, Foucault voices a dilemma felt by many in the West. It is precisely that longing for *the* pleasure that has led the white West to sustain a romantic fantasy of the "primitive" and the concrete search for a real primitive paradise, whether that location be a country or a body, a dark continent or dark flesh, perceived as the perfect embodiment of that possibility.

* * *

Mutual recognition of racism, its impact both on those who are dominated and those who dominate, is the only standpoint that makes possible an encounter between races that is not based on denial and fantasy. For it is the ever present reality of racist domination, of white supremacy, that renders problematic the desire of white people to have contact with the Other. Often it is this reality that is most masked when representations of contact between white and non-white, white and black, appear in mass culture. One area where the politics of diversity and its concomitant insistence on inclusive representation have had serious impact is advertising. Now that sophisticated market surveys reveal the extent to which poor and materially underprivileged people of all races/ethnicities consume products, sometimes in a quantity disproportionate to income, it has become more evident that these markets can be appealed to with advertising. Market surveys revealed that black people buy more Pepsi than other soft drinks and suddenly we see more Pepsi commercials with black people in them.

The world of fashion has also come to understand that selling products is heightened by the exploitation of Otherness. The success of Benneton ads, which with their racially diverse images have become a model for various advertising strategies, epitomize this trend. Many ads that focus on Otherness make no explicit comments, or rely solely on visual messages, but the recent fall *Tweeds* catalogue provides an excellent example of the way contemporary culture exploits notions of Otherness with both visual images and text. The catalogue cover shows a map of Egypt. Inserted into the heart of the country, so to speak, is a photo of a white male (an *Out of Africa* type) holding an Egyptian child in his arms. Behind them is not the scenery of Egypt as modern city, but rather shadowy silhouettes resembling huts and palm trees. Inside, the copy quotes Gustave Flaubert's comments from *Flaubert in Egypt*. For seventy-five pages Egypt becomes a landscape of dreams, and its darker-skinned people background, scenery to highlight whiteness, and the longing of whites to inhabit, if only for a time, the world of the Other. The front page copy declares:

> We did not want our journey to be filled with snapshots of an antique land. Instead, we wanted to rediscover our clothing in the context of a different culture. Was it possible, we wondered, to express our style in an unaccustomed way, surrounded by Egyptian colors, Egyptian textures, even bathed in an ancient Egyptian light?

Is this not imperialist nostalgia at its best—potent expression of longing for the "primitive"? One desires "a bit of the Other" to enhance the blank landscape of whiteness. Nothing is said in the text about Egyptian people, yet their images are spread throughout its pages. Often their faces are blurred by the camera, a strategy which ensures that readers will not become more enthralled by the images of Otherness than those of whiteness. The point of this photographic attempt at defamiliarization is to distance us from whiteness, so that we will return to it more intently.

In most of the "snapshots," all carefully selected and posed, there is no mutual looking. One desires contact with the Other even as one wishes boundaries to remain intact. When bodies contact one another, touch, it almost always a white hand doing the touching, white hands that rest on the bodies of colored people, unless the Other is a child. One snapshot of "intimate" contact shows two women with their arms linked, the way close friends might link arms. One is an Egyptian woman identified by a caption that reads "with her husband and baby, Ahmedio A'bass, 22, leads a gypsy's life"; the second woman is a white-skinned model. The linked hands suggest that these two women share something, have a basis of contact and indeed they do, they resemble one another, look more alike than different. The message again is that "primitivism," though more apparent in the Other, also resides in the white self. It is not the world of Egypt, of "gypsy" life, that is affirmed by this snapshot, but the ability of white people to roam the world, making contact. Wearing pants while standing next to her dark "sister" who wears a traditional skirt, the white woman appears to be cross-dressing (an ongoing theme in Tweeds). Visually the image suggests that she and first world white women like her are liberated, have greater freedom to roam than darker women who live peripatetic lifestyles.

* * *

Resurgence of black nationalism as an expression of black people's desire to guard against white cultural appropriation indicates the extent to which the commodification of blackness (including the nationalist agenda) has been reinscribed and marketed with an atavistic narrative, a fantasy of Otherness that reduces protest to spectacle and stimulates even greater longing for the "primitive." Given this cultural context, black nationalism is more a gesture of powerlessness than a sign of critical resistance. Who can take seriously Public Enemy's insistence that the dominated and their allies "fight the power" when that declaration is in no way linked to a collective organized struggle. When young black people mouth 1960s' black nationalist rhetoric, don Kente cloth, gold medallions, dread their hair, and diss the white folks they hang out with, they expose the way meaningless commodification strips these signs of political integrity and meaning, denying the possibility that they can serve as a catalyst for concrete political action. As signs, their power to ignite critical consciousness is diffused when they are commodified. Communities of resistance are replaced by communities of consumption. As Stuart and Elizabeth Ewen emphasize in Channels of Desire:

> The politics of consumption must be understood as something more than what to buy, or even what to boycott. Consumption is a social rela-

tionship, the dominant relationship in our society—one that makes it harder and harder for people to hold together, to create community. At a time when for many of us the possibility of meaningful change seems to elude our grasp, it is a question of immense social and political proportions. To establish popular initiative, consumerism must be transcended —a difficult but central task facing all people who still seek a better way of life.

Work by black artists that is overtly political and radical is rarely linked to an oppositional political culture. When commodified it is easy for consumers to ignore political messages. And even though a product like rap articulates narratives of coming to critical political consciousness, it also exploits stereotypes and essentialist notions of blackness (like black people have natural rhythm and are more sexual).

Regarded fetishistically in the psycho-sexual racial imagination of youth culture, the real bodies of young black men are daily viciously assaulted by white racist violence, black on black violence, the violence of overwork, and the violence of addiction and disease. In her introduction to *The Body in Pain,* Elaine Scarry states that "there is ordinarily no language for pain," that "physical pain is difficult to express; and that this inexpressibility has political consequences." This is certainly true of black male pain. Black males are unable to fully articulate and acknowledge the pain in their lives. They do not have a public discourse or audience within racist society that enables them to give their pain a hearing. Sadly, black men often evoke racist rhetoric that identifies the black male as animal, speaking of themselves as "endangered species," as "primitive," in their bid to gain recognition of their suffering.

When young black men acquire a powerful public voice and presence *via* cultural production, as has happened with the explosion of rap music, it does not mean that they have a vehicle that will enable them to articulate that pain. Providing narratives that are mainly about power and pleasure, that advocate resistance to racism yet support phallocentrism, rap denies this pain. True, it was conditions of suffering and survival, of poverty, deprivation, and lack that characterized the marginal locations from which breakdancing and rap emerged. Described as "rituals" by participants in the poor urban non-white communities where they first took place, these practices offered individuals a means to gain public recognition and voice. Much of the psychic pain that black people experience daily in a white supremacist context is caused by dehumanizing oppressive forces, forces that render us invisible and deny us recognition. Michael H. (commenting on style in Stuart Ewen's book *All Consuming Images*) also talks about this desire for attention, stating that breakdancing and rap are a way to say "listen to my story, about myself, life, and romance." Rap music provides a public voice for young black men who are usually silenced and overlooked. It emerged in the streets—outside the confines of a domesticity shaped and informed by poverty, outside enclosed spaces where young males['] bod[ies] had to be contained and controlled.

* * *

When I began thinking and doing research for this piece, I talked to folks from various locations about whether they thought the focus on race, Otherness, and difference in mass culture was challenging racism. There was overall agreement that the message that acknowledgment and exploration of racial difference can be pleasurable represents a breakthrough, a challenge to white supremacy, to various systems of domination. The over-riding fear is that cultural, ethnic, and racial differences will be continually commodified and offered up as new dishes to enhance the white palate—that the Other will be eaten, consumed, and forgotten. After weeks of debating with one another about the distinction between cultural appropriation and cultural appreciation, students in my introductory course on black literature were convinced that something radical was happening, that these issues were "coming out in the open." Within a context where desire for contact with those who are different or deemed Other is not considered bad, politically incorrect, or wrong-minded, we can begin to conceptualize and identify ways that desire informs our political choices and affiliations. Acknowledging ways the desire for pleasure, and that includes erotic longings, informs our politics, our understanding of difference, we may know better how desire disrupts, subverts, and makes resistance possible. We cannot, however, accept these new images uncritically.

NOTE

1. Reprinted by permission from *Black Looks: Race and Representation* (South End Press, 1992) by bell hooks.

Cities and Queer Space
Staking a Claim to
Global Cosmopolitanism

Dereka Rushbrook

Queer Sustainability: Commodification and Gay Space

Queerness is today an object of consumption, both for queers seeking to constitute their identities through the accumulation of the appropriate combination of objects and for nonqueers asserting a certain display of cosmopolitan chic. This consumption goes beyond the purchase of material objects to include the acquisition of queer spaces and experiences, as evidenced in the rise of the gay tourism industry[1] and the increased popularity of gay clubs and entertainment among nonqueers. This essay explores the implications of the growth in straight-identified visitors to this space for the future of the space itself.

Historically, the struggle for gay and lesbian visibility in public spaces and the existence of gay and lesbian spaces have played an important role in the evolution of a gay community in the United States. The growth of the gay and lesbian movement relied upon access to public space, at the same time that gay and lesbian lives and activisms shaped the availability of such spaces. Gay public space has long existed in less obviously visible forms,[2] and activist groups such as Queer Nation, the Lesbian Avengers and ACT UP have worked to queer the everyday space of the street that has been naturalized as heterosexual.[3] The formation of gay and lesbian communities, however, historically has been linked to the existence of more permanent and bounded spaces such as meeting places, bars, and neighborhoods, locations that are central to a gay imaginary and that offer a site of entry to a gay community. Here, I argue that while gay and lesbian public space in the urban West often appears more permanent and

199

stable than it might have only decades ago, its ongoing commodification raises questions about its very nature.

The ability to acquire or resist political power is often linked with the successful construction of place.[4] In some cities, gays—primarily white, middle-class males—have translated the economic power associated with gay gentrification into group-based political power at the local level.[5] Access to the social meeting places of bars was critical to the birth of political movements that demanded public recognition and acceptance.[6] While police harassment meant that these bars were not necessarily "safe" places, it also encouraged a solidarity that contributed to the growth of a grass-roots civil rights movement that fought for access to public space.[7] Indeed, although gay and lesbian political organizations already existed, it is the 1969 police raid on the Stonewall Inn in New York City that is generally credited as the event that gave rise to today's gay and lesbian rights movement. While gay and lesbian spaces were critical to the individual social lives and identity formation of many gays and lesbians, they were also fundamental to the growth of a visible community and rights movements.

The success of that movement, however, has been accompanied by a transformation in the nature of gay and lesbian spaces, which have become more clearly marked and open, if not necessarily more safe, over time. Mass-audience tourist guides and Web sites often list at least a few token gay and lesbian establishments or tours of gay districts; neighborhoods, stores, and bars are frequently marked by rainbow flags; and pride events draw mainstream media coverage and large, non-queer-identified crowds. This transformation, closely associated with the commodification of gay and lesbian identity, raises questions about the sustainability of gay and lesbian spaces and the extent to which they can persist as sites of community formation and political activism. These sites have proven fragile, vulnerable not only to local politics but also to secondary waves of gentrification that push out gays and lesbians who can no longer afford the rising rents, as they themselves pushed out earlier neighborhood residents, often people of color. Here, however, I am concerned with those spaces that persist as gay and lesbian, at least nominally, while becoming sites of tourism for straight-acting spectators.

Although these spaces have been important historically, I do not wish to portray them, or the notion of gay and lesbian community, as unproblematic or utopian. Such spaces have long been exclusionary and segmented along lines of race, class, and sexuality. The notion of community itself is premised on "various forms of exclusion and constructions of Otherness."[8] Moreover, the deployment of the term "community" has been critiqued for its ability to deflect attention away from politics, conflicts of interest and the structure of capitalism itself, while maintaining existing social relations, masking state power and transferring costs onto the (local) community—usually women.[9] Here, then, I use the term "gay and lesbian community" loosely to refer to a group sharing a common, differentiating characteristic, recognizing that this formation simultaneously excludes other individuals and groups that are nonheteronormative. But perhaps the difficulty of challenging heteronormativity has paradoxically facilitated both the successes of mainstream gay and lesbian politics and the commodification of a gay and lesbian identity. The latter process now threatens the sustainability of the very spaces that initially enabled the formation of gay and lesbian identities, working to engender a new homonormativity that precludes undesirable forms of sexual expression.[10]

The Transformation of Gay Space

In the 1990s, gay and lesbian issues gained a new prominence in the mainstream U.S. media, which variously turned its attention to the issue of gay marriage, gays in the military, hate crimes, the sexuality of Hollywood stars, antidiscrimination legislation, and a host of similar issues. A thriving niche market continued to develop, offering an infinite array of rainbow- and pink triangle–adorned merchandise. While independent gay and lesbian bookstores closed down around the country, consumers could find (a narrower range of) gay and lesbian magazines and literature in corporate chains such as Borders and Barnes & Noble. At the same time, television shows such as *Will and Grace* and *Queer as Folk* and movies such as *Boys Don't Cry, In and Out,* and *Philadelphia* found widespread popularity among audiences far beyond the gay and lesbian niche market.

These changes were reflected in the increasing visibility of gay and lesbian residential and commercial zones in cities across North America and Europe. This visibility was accompanied by the consumption of these spaces by both gay and straight tourists. The product of earlier processes of gentrification by primarily white, middle- or upper-class gay men and originally commodified for gay consumption, these districts were in-

202 | B. *Commodifying Identities*

creasingly normalized as cities enforced zoning laws restricting the use of
public space.[11] Once liminal areas in decline, they move from zones of gay
recreation into the "fashionable mainstream."[12] As community celebrations such as Pride parades became increasingly commercialized, gay and
lesbian communities started to police themselves, voicing "law-and-
order, 'gays-are-respectable-too'" approaches that sometimes went beyond official efforts in their regulation of behavior at public events.[13]
These respectable gay neighborhoods and appropriately contained gay
spectacles would become significant components of city marketing campaigns designed to promote images of cosmopolitan diversity. Marketed
as equivalent to ethnic neighborhoods, queer space functioned as an indicator of the diversity and cosmopolitanism sought by cities positioning
themselves as appropriate sites for the global economy's footloose, high-
tech industries.[14]

In one instance of these marketing efforts, the Toronto Tourism
Board's Web site highlighted the city's Greektown, Italian, and China-
town neighborhoods, and the opportunity for tourists to visit the "pul-
sating heart of the gay community" where they could see "gay men and
women chatting in the eclectic mixture of cafes and restaurants or holding hands as they walk[ed] down the busy streets, giv[ing] an indication
of the relaxed and open-minded attitude Torontonians have towards the
gay and lesbian community." Seattle's tourism board similarly touts the
city's multiple forms of marketable diversity, including sexuality and ethnicity, if not class, as commodifiable axes of difference. Moreover, gays
have been increasingly targeted as consumers in response to marketing
studies that purported to show a demographic group with above-average
discretionary income.[15] The visibility of a gay niche market, with adver-
tisements and products that directly or indirectly targeted gays, was her-
alded as a sign of success within mainstream gay and lesbian movements.
At the same time, gays and gay space were also becoming commodities
themselves, marketed directly or indirectly by cities seeking to establish
their reputations as cosmopolitan centers.

While the marketers' recognition of gays as an important demographic
group was initially celebrated as a sign of growing tolerance and acceptance, numerous writers have pointed to the ways in which the rise of the
gay niche market and a commodified gay identity has privileged some
gays over others and been associated with a mainstreaming of gay politics that has reduced the pressure for social change and coalition building
with other disenfranchised groups.[16] Others have pointed to the ways in

which gay gentrification—typically white, male, and middle- or upper-middle class—has negatively impacted communities of color, working-class communities, sex workers, or other segments of the gay community who previously inhabited that space.[17] For example, scholars have critiqued the rise of lesbian chic in the early 1990s mass media for the ways in which depictions of lesbians reinforced sexist and heterosexist norms, and also for the ways they erased race and class differences within the lesbian community.[18] The chic lesbian who sells as a commodity, inside and outside the gay community, is typically one who is privileged and white and who fits a slim model of feminine style that is suited for mainstream consumption.[19]

Less attention, however, has been given to the question of how gay lifestyles and gay space have been commodified for straight consumption and how this commodification might impact the queer community. The "tourist gaze" seeks out difference, and the objects of the gaze must embody this out-of-the-ordinary nature, clearly marked as Other.[20] These boundaries between a normative heterosexuality and the queer are further reinscribed when gay space becomes the site for the consumption of the Other in the quest for cosmopolitanism. "Shopping in a cultural supermarket" with a global reach,[21] the cosmopolitan citizen is one who displays an openness and interest in engaging with the Other as well as competence in maneuvering within different systems.[22] Cultural capital consists in part of an ability to effortlessly move through multiple milieus and exotic surroundings.[23] Queer space, reinforced by the cachet of "cool," has become one of those places in which to negotiate and play with multiple, shifting identities. While certain forms of cosmopolitan knowledge can be performed through the acquisition of material objects alone—familiarity with exotic menus, an extensive world music collection, appropriately marked T-shirts—demonstrating a familiarity and ease with queerness almost always requires the authenticating presence of queer bodies. In a *New York Times* article on the European club scene, for example, Roger Cohen writes that Berlin's Greenwich club offers a "cooler note," where

> cowhide adorns the padded walls and a certain animal intensity is definitely in the air as couples, heterosexual and homosexual, admire each other. . . . This establishment, full of Asian-Germans and African-Germans, gives a real sense of the new Berlin, a city whose population is an exotic mix.[24]

Here, the cosmopolitan traveler who can afford to do so is invited to partake in a sophisticated, and explicitly exotic, blend of racial and sexual diversity.[25] This is a tourism that extends beyond the lesbian and gay heritage walking tours, offered by tourism operators alongside an array of ethnic neighborhood options, in cities such as New York and San Francisco.

The Consumption of Queer Space[26]

Queer spaces—whether neighborhoods, temporary spectacles such as gay pride parades, or queer bodies themselves—are increasingly consumed by a broader public in ways that shape the nature of those spaces. These tourists disrupt the assumed homogeneity of queer space when sexuality is presumed to be the operative axis of difference. At the same time, the designation of neighborhoods as queer *or* ethnic in opposition to a normative white straightness produces a hierarchy of mutually exclusive zones of difference in which the queer is normalized as white. These zones operate as sites of a highly commercialized tourism industry, deployed by cities as part of their strategies designed to attract cosmopolitan workers and mobile capital in the financial, information, and high-tech industries.

Local governments have long been boosters of economic growth, a role that has been enhanced by the increasing mobility of capital and technological innovations.[27] Cities have become increasingly entrepreneurial, "selling place" to attract flows of capital and white-collar worker-consumers.[28] To market themselves as postindustrial, postmodern sites appropriate for the new millennium's leading industries, secondary cities such as Sydney, Chicago, and Manchester, England, promote a cosmopolitan image in a spatial competition for resources in which the cities themselves are the commodities.

The new urban centers of innovation and growth depend not only upon the supply of adequate infrastructures and an educated labor force, but also, and more importantly, upon the presence of the "creative class," the educated and highly mobile workers employed in the knowledge-based growth engine of the new economy.[29] This group of highly paid professionals is drawn by the existence of a tolerant environment and diverse cultural base, measured by a "bohemian index." In this world, gays are the "canary in the new-economy coal mine," a signal to the high-skilled population critical to growth; cities that have a gay-friendly image have a competitive edge. One magazine aimed at local government offi-cials used its cover to draw attention to such image-shaping efforts around the country, subtitling its "Chasing the Rainbow" led with the question "Is a Gay Population an Engine of Urban Renwal?"[30]

While this form of marketing is new, the gay spaces themselves are not, although their relationship with local governments, which now promote rather than repress commercial establishments and events that serve gays, has changed. The commercial neighborhoods associated with—and per-haps exploited by—such promotional campaigns are often sanitized ver-sions of earlier sexually transgressive landscapes that serve to heighten existing forms of marginalization and exclusion, while opening new con-sumption opportunities for those who can afford them.[31] Serving the needs of some segments of the gay community, they may simultaneously foreclose opportunities for political alliances within and across the gay— and queer—community. The very success of rights movements that were nurtured within these communities fragments and undermines the politi-cal potential of those spaces.

Two different arenas exemplify the says in which queer space is con-sumed: gay and lesbian clubs and pride parades. This discussion centers on gay rather than lesbian spaces because lesbian geographies have tended to be less commodified and territorialized, often described as "in-visible" or "imperceptible."[32]

Gay Clubs and Pride Events

> Now we know we can come too, I think we make it more cosmopolitan, more stylish.   —Jane[33]

Jane's statement that "now we know we can come" is typical of new (straight-identified) patrons of gay bars. The increasing openness of gay space has contributed to a greater willingness of straight-acting visitors, often accompanied by a gay friend, to frequent gay establishments. While due in part to a greater acceptance of a wide diversity of lifestyles, this consumption also reflects a variety of other motives, often based on a per-ception that gay bars are likely to offer better music, more attractive men, less "trouble" for women, and a "better" atmosphere. At the same time, however, it is not only the atmosphere that is consumed; the bars' gay pa-trons are themselves objects of consumption. In the same *Guardian* article, other women visiting Manchester's Canal Street, the gay zone made famous by a series of television shows, expressed a very different set of motivations for their presence, analogous to visiting a freak show before heading elsewhere for the bulk of the evening: "We've had a dabble in the gay bit, and had a look at the funny business. . . . It was a laugh here."[34]

In addition to objectification by the straight gaze, gays and lesbians point to the misunderstandings that arise:

> "They don't know the rules!" complains a gay clubber in Spirit. "Like, they get really offended when you go into the women's toilets. They just don't understand how gay bars work—they get really shocked."[35]

Moreover, at the simplest level, straight-identified (but not necessarily straight-acting) tourists in gay bars complicate the dating scene. In "Sex 2K: The Gay Cruise," one protagonist proclaims that gay men had a more difficult time finding a partner than did straight people, as "straights are everywhere" but that gays had a difficult time identifying potential dates and therefore were restricted to gay bars in the search for a mate. At the same time, the presence of straight-identified individuals may both undermine and facilitate the central role that gay bars historically played in the coming out narratives of gays and lesbians, discouraging entry by individuals who fear running into straight friends or acquaintances while they are exploring their identities, but encouraging others who no longer feel that mere entry into a bar constitutes a declaration of their sexuality. In some cases, the arrival of a heterosexual crowd leads to the disappearance of gay bars, as gays abandon the spaces that are no longer their own.

This sort of tourism is by no means new, and it has long been both reinforced and in part constructed by entrepreneurs seeking to profit from a "bourgeois voyeurism." As Stallybrass and White note, middle-class identity is dependent upon the existence of an Other that is both rejected and desired, excluded but necessary.[36] The literature on tourism takes into account both the surface nature of tourists' quests and their search for authenticity. The cosmopolitan tourist insists upon the "right to travel anywhere and to consume at least initially all environments."[37] This quest is dependent upon the presence of the appropriate bodies that authenticate the site, and, for the more adventurous tourist, relies upon the absence of fellow travelers.[38] In many instances, however, tourists are put at ease by the construction of boundaries that police the bodies they gaze upon.

In the Harlem clubs of the 1920s, first visited by bohemians and homosexuals in search of the exotic and of a more tolerant atmosphere, increased accessibility to mainstream visitors resulted in the commodification of a subculture's "spectacles," which became a performance for white tourists,[39] and crowding out the establishments' original black patrons, forcing them to find new spaces.[40] The Other was contained in a way that allowed for the entertainment of whites; boundaries were differentially porous, as whites were able to visit the exotic spaces of black Harlem to consume entertainment and culture, while Harlem's residents found travel outside the neighborhood restricted to labor opportunities. White homosexuals in particular celebrated the tolerant, open atmosphere that seemed to pervade Harlem's nightlife, finding a haven unavailable elsewhere in the city. Black Harlem was perhaps more ambivalent toward homosexuality than many whites would have liked to believe, but its reliance on tourism led to clubs using drag performances and balls as one more exotic drawing card that created at least an illusion of wide open sexuality.[41]

A similar ambivalence and differential mobility surrounding sexuality exists today. While many straight-identified tourists are comfortable in gay clubs and drag performances, often feeling free to perform their heterosexuality (at times far in "excess" of any performance that would be undertaken in an everyday "normal" space), gay men are unlikely to feel free to undertake similar performances of their sexuality in straight clubs. Thus, while the entry of straight tourists into gay spaces could be celebrated as a sign of acceptance, as a breaking down of boundaries, as a move toward a truly queer space, and may in fact have some progressive impact on individual politics, the question remains as to why they choose gay space.[42] Were the rights movements aimed at opening public space to gays and lesbians more successful in commodifying gay and lesbian spaces than in changing the heteronormative nature of "the street"?

In some instances, gay and lesbian bars that are already marked themselves by their playlists and the age and sex of their clientele find that entertainment guides further note the perceived percentage of their clientele that is gay, and patron comments on visitor Web sites note the presence of "too many straight girls."[43] This perceived "watering down" of gay space has led other clubs to develop membership and admission policies, asking customers to declare their sexuality or noting that while "straight friendly," they don't allow "just anyone" entry in order to maintain a "true safe gay space" or a "strict policy of majority Gay and Lesbian customers."[44]

Organizers of gay pride events have faced similar challenges; the Sydney Mardi Gras markets some secondary events as "exclusively gay and lesbian" in an effort to prevent the dilution of the celebration's queerness.[45] Gay pride parades frequently have a primarily self-identified heterosexual audience.[46] While this has generally been true, the political meaning of the parade has changed. Originally designed to raise straights' awareness of the existence of gays and lesbians in their midst, or to draw attention to the state regulation of queer desire or the AIDS crisis, gay pride parades have become increasingly commodified in recent years, often turning into weeklong festivals. Cities that once put up regulatory barriers to discourage such events now regularly promote them as tourist events, recognizing their contribution to the local economy. In Toronto, Montreal, and Sydney, parades that attracted a few thousand spectators two decades ago are now weeklong affairs that bring millions of dollars and hundreds of thousands of visitors.

Gay spectacles are envisioned as "well performed and *risqué,*" thus constructing the heterosexual as normal and the queer as deviant, a deviance that must be reflected in a visual display.[47] Straight-identified spectators at gay pride parades "combine fascination in, with revulsion against, queer bodies."[48] In short, presence should not be assumed to indicate acceptance.

Conclusion

Over the past decade, the successes of the gay rights movements have significantly reduced the marginalization of gay communities, contributing to the increased visibility of both gay individuals and of commercialized gay space.[49] While governmental neglect facilitated gay gentrification of central-city districts, intervention by those same governments to market gay neighborhoods now serves to promote these areas to a wider range of consumers and tourists. Intertwined with a search for an ever-elusive authenticity, this restructuring promotes a logic of assimilationist sexual citizenship.[50]

It would be foolish to seek a return to the lesbian and gay spaces of the past if the community and political activism were made possible only by repression by the state and the larger heteronormative world. Indeed, such a quest would erase the dynamism of these continually changing spaces and posit a utopia that never existed. The closed nature of those spaces elicited an identity politics that tended to foreground sexuality and erase exclusions and hierarchies within a broader gay and lesbian community. The very successes of gay and lesbian rights movements—at least for appropriately normalized and domesticated queers—destabilized the form of those putatively homogenous mainstream gay and lesbian spaces at the same time that it reinforced the marginalization of the less desirable queer. In some cases this has happened quite literally, as the popularity of particular gay bars among straight-identified consumers has transformed those spaces into "straight" clubs, abandoned by the gays who initially inhabited them, sometimes seeking out newly hidden gay spaces. Those urban spaces that appear to have become more inclusive—regardless of sexuality and ethnicity, if not class—should be further investigated.[51] As the increased visibility and porosity of gay spaces has changed their nature, other spaces are less likely to require that gays and lesbians check their sexuality at the door. It is here, perhaps, that some hope for progressive political action and a more sustainable, less exclusive community might be found, as gays and lesbians participate in labor organizations, immigrant rights networks, antisweatshop and prison-abolition coalitions, and other grassroots movements, opening the space for a sustained coalitional politics.

NOTES

1. Jasbir Kaur Puar, *Circuits of Queer Mobility: Tourism, Travel, and Globalization* 8 GLQ: A Journal of Lesbian and Gay Studies 101 (2003).

2. *See, e.g.,* George Chauncey, Gay New York: Gender, Urban Culture, and the Making of the Gay Male World, 1890–1940 (1994); Queer Sites: Gay Urban Histories Since 1600 (David Higgs, ed., 1999).

3. *See, e.g.,* Gill Valentine, *(Re)negotiating the 'Heterosexual Street': Lesbian Productions of Space, in* Body Space (Nancy Duncan, ed., 1996).

4. David Harvey, Justice, Nature, and the Geography of Difference 321 (1996).

5. Lawrence Knopp, *Sexuality and Urban Space: A Framework for Analysis, in* Mapping Desire: Geographies of Sexuality (David Bell & Gill Valentine, eds., 1998).

6. Elizabeth Lapvosky Kennedy & Madeline D. Davis, Boots of Leather, Slippers of Gold: The History of a Lesbian Community (1993).

7. Patricia A. Cain, Rainbow Rights: The Role of Lawyers and Courts in the Lesbian and Gay Civil Rights Movement 89 (2000).

8. Culture, Power, Place: Explorations in Critical Anthropology 13 (Akhil Gupta & James Ferguson, eds., 1997).

9. Lois Bryson & Ian Mowbray, *Community: The Spray-On Solution?* 16 Aust. J. Soc. Issues 255, 255–267 (1981).

10. Lisa Duggan, *The New Homonormativity: The Sexual Politics of Neoliberalism, in* Materializing Democracy: Toward a Revitalized Cultural Politics (Russ Castronovo & Dana Nelson, eds., 2002).

11. Queer Sites: Gay Urban Histories Since 1600 (David Higgs, ed., 1999).

12. Alan Collins, *Sexual Dissidence, Enterprise and Assimilation: Bedfellows in Urban Regeneration* 41 Urban Studies 1803, 1789–1806 (2004).

13. Mariana Valverde & Miomir Cirak, *Governing Bodies, Creating Gay Spaces: Policing and Security Issues in 'Gay' Downtown Toronto* 43 Brit. J. Criminology 102, 102–121 (2003).

14. While relying on parallels between the consumption of queer space and the consumption of racialized or ethnic spaces, I do not want to claim that the experiences are by any means identical. For analyses of the relationship between commodification, racialization, and community, particularly the creation of a "commodity identity" associated with low-wage labor, *see, e.g.,* Carlos G. Velez-Ibanez, Border Visions: Mexican Cultures of the Southwest United States (1996); and Robert E. Birt, The Quest for Community and Identity: Critical Essays in Africana Social Philosophy (2002).

15. Gay marketing organizations produced numerous studies boasting of the desirable demographic characteristics of the gay niche market, contributing to the construction of the gay community as white, high-income, and male in the popular imagination. This image contributed to the political right wing's ability to portray gays as an advantaged special interest group and erased gender, racial, and class differences within the gay community. *See e.g.,* Homo Economics: Capitalism, Community, and Lesbian and Gay Life (Amy Gluckman & Betsy Reed, eds., 1997). Badgett argues that these findings result from biased samples. *See* M. V. Lee Badgett, *Beyond Biased Samples, in* Homo Economics 66.

16. *See, e.g.,* Gluckman & Reed, *supra* note 15; Urvashi Vaid, Virtual Equality: The Mainstreaming of Gay and Lesbian Liberation (1995); Alexandra Chasin, Selling Out: The Gay and Lesbian Movement Goes to Market (2000).

17. *See* Queer Sites, *supra* note 11.

18. Margaret Moritz, *Lesbian Chic: Our Fifteen Minutes of Celebrity? in* Feminism, Multiculturalism and the Media: Global Diversities (Angharad N. Valdivia, ed., 2002).

19. *See* Victoria A. Brownworth, Too Queer: Essays from a Radical Life

(1997), for a discussion of the impact of lesbian chic on "fat politics" and body image within the lesbian community.

20. John Urry, Consuming Places (1995).

21. Gordon Mathews, Global Culture/Individual Identity: Searching for Home in the Cultural Supermarket (2000).

22. Ulf Hannerz, *Cosmopolitans and Locals in World Culture, in* 7 Theory, Culture & Soc. 237, 237–251 (1990). There are of course other meanings attached to the term "cosmopolitan." *See, e.g.,* Bruce Robbins, Feeling Global: Internationalism in Distress (1999); *See also* Cosmopolitics: Thinking and Feeling Beyond the Nation (Pheng Cheah & Bruce Robbins, eds., 1998).

23. Pierre Bourdieu, Distinction: A Social Critique of the Judgment of Taste (1984).

24. Roger Cohen, *Night Moves of All Kinds: Berlin,* New York Times, travel section 11 (September 17, 2000).

25. In this description, Asian and African are offered as other, presumably in opposition to whiteness, while homosexual is offered as the other of heterosexual, implicitly erasing queers of color (whether as consumers or commodities) from the discourse of cosmopolitanism and globalization.

26. *See* Dereka Rushbrook, *Cities, Queer Space and the Cosmopolitan Tourist* 8 GLQ 183–206 (2002) for a more extended discussion.

27. *See* Harvey, *supra* note 4; *see also* Culture, Power, Place, *supra* note 8.

28. Sharon Zukin, The Cultures of Cities (1995); Tim Hall & Phil Hubbard, *The Entrepreneurial City: New Urban Politics, New Urban Geographies* 20 Progress in Human Geography 1 (1996).

29. Richard Florida, The Rise of the Creative Class: And How It's Transforming Work, Leisure, Community and Everyday Life (2002).

30. *Governing: The Magazine of States and Localities,* October 2003, http://governing.com/articles/10gays.htm (last visited August 8, 2004).

31. Stephen Whittle, *Consuming Differences: The Collaboration of the Gay Body with the Cultural State, in* The Margins of the City: Gay Men's Urban Lives (Stephen Whittle, ed., 1994); Stephen Quilley, *Constructing Manchester's 'New Urban Village': Gay Space in the Entrepreneurial City, in* Queers in Space: Communities | Public Places | Sites of Resistance (Gordon Brent Ingram et al., eds., 1997); Knopp, *supra* note 5.

32. Anne-Marie Bouithillette, *Queer and Gendered Housing: A Tale of Two Neighbourhoods in Vancouver, in* Queers in Space, *supra* note 31; Tamar Rothenberg, *'And She Told Two Friends': Lesbians Creating Urban Social Space, in* Mapping Desire: Geographies of Sexuality (David Bell & Gill Valentine, eds., 1995); Gill Valentine, *Out and About: Geographies of Lesbian Landscapes* 19 Int'l J. Urb. & Regional Res. 96, 96–111 (1995).

33. Decca Aitkenhead, *Village People,* The Guardian, Oct. 23, 2001.

34. Id.

35. Id.

36. Peter Stallybrass & Allon White, The Politics and Poetics of Transgression (1986).

37. Urry, *supra* note 20.

38. Jane Desmond, Staging Tourism: Bodies on Display from Waikiki to Sea World (1999).

39. Kevin Mumford, Interzones: Black/White Sex Districts in Chicago and New York in the Early Twentieth Century (1997).

40. Lewis A. Erenberg, Steppin' Out: New York Nightlife and the Transformation of American Culture, 1890–1930 (1981).

41. Lillian Faderman, *Lesbian Chic: Experimentation and Repression in the 1920s, in* The Gender and Consumer Culture Reader (Jennifer Scanlon, ed., 2000).

42. Leila Rupp & Verta Taylor, Drag Queens at the 801 Cabaret (2003).

43. http://www.bbc.co.uk/leeds/nightlife/bars/fibre.shtml (last visited August 5, 2004).

44. www.cruz101.com; www.napoleons.co.uk; www.essentialmanchester.com (last visited August 5, 2004).

45. Knopp, *supra* note 5.

46. Lynda Johnston, *Borderline Bodies, in* Subjectivities, Knowledges, and Feminist Geographies (Liz Bondi et al., eds., 2001).

47. Id.

48. Id.

49. This has, to some extent, made gay and lesbian space more secure, its persistence seemingly a function of the marketplace rather than the goodwill of the state. To accept this, however, is to erase the complicity of the state with capital. Mitchell argues that although the city "is the place where difference lives," the bourgeois city is one where "spaces . . . are being produced *for* us rather than *by* us"; it is less a site of participation than of expropriation by dominant economic interests. Don Mitchell, The Right to the City: Social Justice and the Fight for Public Space 18 (2003).

50. David Bell and Jon Binnie, *Authenticating Queer Space: Citizenship, Urbanism and Governance* 41 Urban Studies 1818, 1807–1820 (2004).

51. *See* Alan Latham, *Urbanity, Lifestyle, and Making Sense of the New Urban Cultural Economy: Notes from Auckland, New Zealand* 40 Urban Studies 1699–1724 (2003).

Selling Out

The Gay and Lesbian Movement Goes to Market

Alexandra Chasin[1]

The 1990s have seen the rise of the production, distribution, and consumption of commodities aimed at a gay and lesbian market. In the same decade, gay and lesbian issues entered the public arena in unprecedented ways; gays in the military, gay marriage, and gay adoption were debated in courts, in legislatures, and in the media. A social movement whose origin many date to the Stonewall Rebellion is largely responsible for formulating these issues. What, then, is the relation between the recent growth of gay and lesbian market activity, on the one hand, and a continuing political and social movement, on the other? In the last three decades of the twentieth century, in which the market became dramatically hypersegmented, hyperspecialized, and globalized, gay men and lesbians in the United States saw the emergence of a liberation movement with our name on it and the growth of gay and lesbian institutions of all kinds. It has been demonstrated that a sense of community is established through participation in institutions, so that gay community, in particular, or the belief in it, would be established through participation in gay institutions.[2] For decades that participation took such forms as attending house parties, drag balls, bathhouses, or bars, buying physique magazines, and/or reading certain literature such as *The Well of Loneliness* or *Death in Venice*. More recently, opportunities for participation have proliferated and have become more and more public; they now include attending gay-themed and/or gay-authored Broadway productions and movies, joining any number of support groups, working in or utilizing any of thousands of service organizations, logging on to queer email groups, and attending demonstrations in Washington. Note that all of these acts constitute or imply some form of consumption; each one is imbricated in consumer culture.

All of this market activity naturally multiplies opportunities for identity-based consumption for gay men and lesbians. Of course, people engaged in same-sex sexual behavior have consumed commodities for as long as there have been commodities; what is new is the constitution and consolidation of a social identity in the marketplace. Advertising is one of the central agents of that constitution and consolidation. Indeed, gay and lesbian identity and community were effectively consolidated through the market; in the 1990s, market mechanisms became perhaps the most accessible and the most effective means of individual identity formation and of entrance into identity-group affiliation for many gay people. When consolidated this way, group identity can form the basis of a political movement for rights equal to those of other citizens; capitalism has, as it has had for centuries in the West, liberal and liberalizing effects. In other words, capitalism enables a political struggle for rights. More specifically, group-based activity in the marketplace is dependent on, and essential to, political organizing for legal rights and protections based in identity. That's what identity politics is. The same economic forces, however, or maybe capitalists in particular, tend to favor the displacement of that struggle back onto the market. The corollary effect is that consumption becomes a form of political participation, perhaps supplanting other, more direct, models of participation. What are the consequences of defining an individual act of private consumption as a mode of political participation?

* * *

Caveat Emptor, or Buyer Beware!

The Gay and Lesbian Niche Market of the 1990's

* * *

Between 1991 and 1993, *American Demographics* was joined by the *Wall Street Journal*, the *New York Times, Advertising Age,* and other mainstream publications in featuring news of a gay niche market.[3] By 1995 Grant Lukenbill had published his book-length plea to mainstream marketers: *Untold Millions: Positioning Your Business for the Gay and Lesbian Consumer Revolution.* Lesbian and gay business expos began cropping up in cities around the country. Professional gay associations such as the National Lesbian and Gay Journalists Association, and business associations such as the Greater Boston Business Council proliferated, while gay and lesbian employee groups organized in workplaces. Thus, throughout the 1990s, there was an explosion of discourse about the gay market.

* * *

This discourse exploded as a result of many factors, but perhaps the most significant was the market research conducted and distributed by a handful of gay marketing firms. Of these, Simmons Market Research Bureau and a small firm called Overlooked Opinions probably had the most widespread, as well as the most notoriously destructive, effects. Simmons' earlier surveys had less dramatic impact; then, in 1991, Overlooked Opinions announced that gay men had an average annual income of $42,889, while lesbians earned, on the average, $36,072.[4] These figures exceed average income figures for men and women in general, largely because they are based on a nonrandom sample; Overlooked Opinions' sample comes from periodical readers, as well as lists compiled at events and bookstores. [T]hese figures portray gay economic status very inaccurately, based as they are on a disproportionately white, affluent, male, and educated sample.

By contrast, a 1994 study produced by the Yankelovich firm produced figures for annual income that were significantly lower than Overlooked Opinions' figures, reflecting an average annual income for gay men of $21,500 ($1,000 *less* than men in the overall population) and $13,000 for lesbians (negligibly greater than women in the overall population).[5] Slowly, some marketers became more careful to qualify their claims about the gay market, relying more and more on the Yankelovich data, except when referring narrowly to readers of gay magazines, and then usually attaching asterisks or fine print that acknowledged Overlooked Opinions as the source. Facts were extremely hard to come by in this arena. Hype was not.

* * *

It's Not about Politics, It's about Money

* * *

A less cynical interpretation held that the visibility of gay men and lesbians in mainstream advertising, on the one hand, and mainstream ads in gay and lesbian media, on the other, signals or generates tolerance by, and inclusion in, mainstream culture. But that is an equation with a political basis, and thus is incompatible with a distinction between politics and business. It was not uncommon to find contradictory claims: the gay and lesbian niche market is not a matter of politics, *and* it's a matter of good politics.

It's about Money and Politics

Plenty of people argued that gay and lesbian commerce *was* political. From this perspective, if the historical economic disregard for gay men and lesbians was governed by homophobia, then the new acknowledgment of a gay market demonstrated a new attitude, and the *Wall Street Journal* was right when it announced that "Overcoming a Deep-Rooted Reluctance, More Firms Advertise to Gay Community."[6] Again, opportunities for identity-based consumption for gay men and lesbians seemed, to many, to signal an invitation into mainstream culture, the turning of the tides of homophobia to enfranchisement. This interpretation of target marketing to gays allows that the market has moral agency. It also allows for the argument that homophobia is bad for business. Thus, profitable and ethical business practices would equally suggest targeting the gay market.

* * *

In terms of realizing one's social or political vision, socially responsible shopping is sometimes effective and almost always more successful than shopping without one's values in mind. I am not saying it is wrong or retrogressive to take consumption seriously as a tool for registering preferences in a field of limited choice. I am saying that I think it is worth speculating on the effects of reducing politics to symbolic and economic phenomena.

It Is about Politics—Bad Politics

As should be clear by now, most of the media reports of gay wealth in the 1990s, like the claims for the viability of a gay niche market, were celebratory. They celebrated the idea that gay entrepreneurs and mainstream corporations alike could make money while making the gay community as a whole more politically powerful. What's not to celebrate? The fact is that while a very few gay people might make money from this market, there is no reason to think that their financial profit amounts to either economic or political betterment for the whole identity group. Indeed, the optimistic claims and reports were not just misleading or inaccurate, they were also embedded in the logic of identity politics; they assumed or insisted that all gay people share political purposes. In a small independent 'zine, an alternative voice decried the commodification of queer things and queer people represented by the merchandise displayed by Rainbow Pride. The writer in *Rude Girl* emphasized both the falsity of, and the investment in, the *appearance* of unity.

> Not surprisingly, Rainbow Pride abounds in the new and wretched incarnations. A Pride jacket, pride soap (with optional "Lufa" sponge), pride T-shirts, flags, shorts, windsocks, headbands, hats, camera straps, towels, bathrobes ($139.95! Hubris!), suncatchers, necklaces, and a lamp which prismatically projects a rainbow onto the wall. If the gay community ever held hopes of any real unifying symbolism or reverence with this Rainbow Flag, I believe they have blown it.[7]

As the exclamation points above suggest, the cost of enfranchisement, the property requirement, prices some consumers out of citizenship. In this manner, gay-identity marketers, in their assumption of group unity on the basis of sexuality, cover over class differences in the gay and lesbian community. From the oppositional point of view expressed in *Rude Girl*, the political aims symbolized by the Rainbow Flag are undermined by class difference and/or the indifference of marketers to those aims. On the one hand, a gay community with symbols of its own status as a nation (flags, military pins with gay rights insignia, currency) presents the appearance of unity. On the other hand, that appearance is conveyed in commodity form, so that its ownership is not equally available to poorer gay men and lesbians.

* * *

"I'm Going to Disneyland"

The recurring themes and issues in all the talk about the gay and lesbian niche market in the 1990's were dramatized in a television show watched by an estimated 43 million viewers. The *Ellen* "Coming-Out Episode," broadcast on April 30, 1997, set its heroine's coming-out in economic metaphors and expressions, as well as locating it, literally, in a market.

The show opens with Ellen's date with an old male friend, at the end of which Ellen rebuffs his romantic overtures and leaves his hotel room. Within minutes of being "read" as a lesbian by his female colleague, however, Ellen rushes back to her date's room, desperate to prove her heterosexuality. As she reenters his room, she pursues him physically and verbally. "Show me the money" are her words, which simultaneously constitute a plea for a disclosure of body parts and of sexuality, and (especially) for a confirmation of her heterosexuality. But the deal is never consummated; Ellen's heterosexuality is left unconfirmed, and no "money" is shown or exchanged. Ellen is left to negotiate her sexuality on her own.

Later that night, at the very moment of coming to gay consciousness, Ellen dreams of making a trip to the grocery store. The store is the precise site of Ellen's psychic reassessment of her sexual identity. [T]he express check-out counter opens to consumers with "10 lesbians or less." In this distortion of familiar check-out counter terms, a direct correspondence is made between lesbian and commodity. And the conflation continues. As her groceries are rung up, Ellen mishears the total she must pay, thinking she owes "A lesbian twenty-nine," as though she must tender lesbians to the cashier.

At one point, the show refers outside itself, to its host network and sponsor. After Ellen comes out in therapy, her therapist asks, "What are you going to do now?" Ellen's response is automatic: "I'm going to Disneyland!" The irony is that Ellen is already in Disneyland. For one, she emerges into gay consciousness and identity through commodity consumption in a world in which Disney stands as the premiere symbol of commodification. Yet on another, more literal, level, Ellen—the character, if not the actor—owes her very life to her broadcast by ABC, which is owned by Disney. For the coming-out episode, *Ellen* was mostly sponsored by ads for Disney movies. Clearly, Disney stepped in to subsidize the show following a great deal of controversy about its sponsorship in the preceding weeks. The right-wing American Family Association had launched a campaign urging people to lobby Disney to not to air the show and scheduled sponsors not to buy time during it. In opposition, gay men, lesbians, and their allies had organized support for Disney in its decision to broadcast. Chrysler pulled its ad and opened a phone line for viewers to register their opinion about its withdrawal. (General Motors and Johnson & Johnson were also on the original roster of advertisers.)

The connections between that market and the gay and lesbian political movement are embodied in one particular character on *Ellen*. Susan, the object of Ellen's affection, has been in a same-sex relationship for nine years and stands as the authentic lesbian in this episode. Playing on the stereotype of gays as recruiting straights, Susan jokes that Ellen's denial of her lesbianism will have to be reported as the failure of Susan's recruitment effort. "I'll have to call headquarters and tell them I lost you," quips Susan. Here, Susan implies that she is aligned with some political movement offstage, perhaps the movement represented in the commercial break—Human Rights Campaign sponsored an ad about employment discrimination that aired during Ellen's coming-out episode. In any case, Susan's membership in the gay movement is implicit, but her prize from headquarters, when she does finally make the recruit, is quite material—it is a toaster oven. At the broadest level, everyone is invested in Ellen's sexuality—even her friends attempt to cash in on it by betting on it. Ellen's entrance into gay identity is thus measured by the commerce that enables it. The representation of Ellen's sexuality stands at the intersection between a gay and lesbian movement that has prized affirmation along with civil rights, and a community whose very visibility was, in the 1990s, a function of its status as a niche market. The movement implied but not seen on *Ellen* is a large bureaucracy recruiting consumers for the cause, and in this way it is not so different, after all, from so many American institutions. Of this, viewers gay and straight could rest assured.

NOTES

1. Reprinted from *Selling Out: The Gay and Lesbian Movement Goes to Market,* by Alexandra Chasin, 23–24, 34–36, 38, 41–44, 53–56 (Palgrave Macmillan 2000).

2. Miranda Joseph, *The Performance of Production and Consumption,* 54 Social Text 25 (1998).

3. Joan E. Rigdon, *Overcoming a Deep-Rooted Reluctance. More Firms Advertise to Gay Community,* Wall Street Journal 18 July 1991, B1–B2; Joe Schwartz, *Gay Consumers Come Out Spending,* American Demographics April 1992, 10–11; *Special Report: Marketing to Gays and Lesbians,* Advertising Age, Jan. 18, 1993, 29–37; Tammerlin Drummond, *Not in Kansas Anymore: With*

Other Tourists Shying Away, Miami Beach Woos the Nation's $17 Billion Gay and Lesbian Travel Market, Time Sept. 25, 1995, 54–56.

4. These and the following figures and studies are presented and reviewed in Amy Gluckman and Betsy Reed, *Lost in the Gay Marketing Moment: Leaving Diversity in the Dust*, in Dollars and Sense Nov.–Dec. 1993, 16. They are reviewed again by Lee Badgett in a report that offers more accurate demographic data: M. V. Lee Badgett, *Income Inflation: The Myth of Affluence Among Gay, Lesbian, and Bisexual Americans* (NGLTF Policy Institute, 1998).

5. These data from the Yankelovich study are graphed in Badgett, *supra* note 4, at 12.

6. Rigdon, *supra* note 3 at B1–B2.

7. Alison Wonderland, *Shocking Gray, Part 2*, Best Plus Rude Girl 1–14, 16.

C.

Commodifying Intimacies

1. COMMODIFYING SEX

"Sex in the [Foreign] City"

Commodification and the Female Sex Tourist

Tanya Katerí Hernández[1]

We must not think that by saying yes to sex, one says no to power.[2]

Introduction to the Sex Tourism Context

Toward the end of the last century a number of countries including the United States instituted legislation to sanction tourists going to foreign lands to engage sexually with minors.[3] Sex tourism generally refers to the growing phenomenon in this era of globalization of travel to other countries for the direct or indirect purpose of having sexual relations with exotic natives in exchange for money, luxury items, clothing, or plane tickets.[4] The term "sex tourism" is widely associated with organized sex tours, often conjuring up images of groups of middle-aged businessmen being shepherded into state-sanctioned brothels in South Korea or go-go bars in the Philippines and Thailand. However, if "sex tourism" is used as a broad term to describe the activities of individuals who, whether or not they set out with this intention, use their economic power to attain powers of sexual command over local women, men, and/or children while traveling for leisure purposes, it refers to a much wider range of people, sexual practices and geographical locations.[5]

While male heterosexual participation in sex tourism is certainly more pervasive and well known than that of female heterosexuals, social scientists have begun to examine the conduct of female tourists who have sexual encounters with "native men" while on vacation. Thus far, the social science literature about these female travelers divides into two per-spectives. The first perspective views the behavior of female tourists as the equivalent of male tourists and thus labels the women "female sex tourists." Female sex tourists are thought to resemble male sex tourists inasmuch as they "use their greater economic power to initiate, control, and terminate sexual relationships with the partner(s) of their choice, and use the same kind of exoticizing racisms to delude themselves that the men/boys concerned are genuinely sexually attracted to them and are not *really* prostitutes."[6] In contrast, the second perspective views the women as engaging in an entirely distinct interaction from male sex tourism, one that is more accurately termed "romance tourism" because it is rooted in a discourse of romance that masks and mutes the economic aspects of the relationships.[7]

Rather than entering the debate as to which term most appropriately characterizes the behavior of female tourists, this chapter seeks to ex-plore the significance of the conduct regardless of which term is used. In-deed, my main concern is the very ambiguity entangled in the sexual in-teractions of female tourists who are invested in the discourse of ro-mance. Thus for ease of linguistic contrast to male sex tourists I will use the term "female sex tourist" to analyze the conduct of the female par-ticipants, regardless of whether they are cognizant of the economic as-pects of their conduct. But in point of fact, this analysis embraces both perspectives on female sex tourism to assess the commodifying charac-teristics that exist in the broad range of conduct known generically as fe-male sex tourism. My principal aim is to interrogate the premise in some of the social science literature that female sex tourism "provides an arena for change [by providing the opportunity] to explore new avenues for negotiating femaleness and maleness."[8] My focus then is an explo-ration of the premise that female tourists' transgressive male-like behav-ior in the sex tourism context is a potential path to gender equality and thus in keeping with human flourishing. I ask two principal questions: first, whether female sex tourism commodifies sexual intimacy, and, sec-ond, whether any commodifying aspects of the interaction could sub-stantially interfere with human flourishing so that lawmakers should consider regulating it like child sex tourism. I conclude that because fe-male sex tourism is embedded in the intersecting inequalities of gender, race, and class, it is better addressed as a part of the larger struggle against societal inequality than through a legal ban or continued societal disregard.

Is Female Sex Tourism Commodification, Romance, or Both?

In examining sex tourism, I employ Margaret Jane Radin's theory of human flourishing, which proposes a nonideal pragmatic evaluation of market-inalienabilities based on a conception of personhood or human flourishing rather than classical liberalism as evidenced in much economic discourse.[9] Radin defines human flourishing as, among other things, "being able to live one's own life in one's very own surroundings and context."[10] She goes on to say that "in this conception of human flourishing separation does not connote the idea of alienability of all the self's attributes and possessions, but rather something like its opposite."[11] Her theory of human flourishing engages the pragmatic concern of sellers' poverty, and how poor people might be harmed by a policy forbidding them to sell, say, sex, even though the policy was intended to protect them from the harm of that sale.[12] This is the problem of the "double bind."[13] Radin's analysis of the double bind is particularly attractive here because sex tourism is a site where neocolonial politics of power, wealth, race, gender, and sexuality interact, and her analysis of human flourishing accounts for the many overlapping double binds.

While an organized prostitution industry facilitates male sex tourism in some host countries,[14] a growing number of sex tourist destinations are characterized by the informal nature of the market. Indeed, a fair number of sex tourists prefer the informality of interacting outside what is viewed as the formal prostitution market. To be specific, sex tourism is often appealing to both providers of sexual services and their clients of both genders because of the way in which it can allow the commercial nature of the intimate interaction to be muted.

In a number of concrete ways "the market" is seemingly less present in the sex tourism context than in domestic prostitution. Sex tourists, for example, often do not openly negotiate a set fee for a predetermined amount of sexual intimacy. Instead, the sex tourist interaction is informal and looks like dating. The commercial exchange for sex is manifested in payments for things like meals, clothing, entertainment and tickets abroad.

In what way then does sex tourism differ from dating (or alternatively, how does dating differ from sex tourism)? In heterosexual male sex tourism the White[15] men who make up the bulk of sex tourists consciously seem to understand their transactions to be market-based and their female partners to be fungible commodities. For instance, one sex tourist proudly boasted, "Some of them have slept with me for just a price of a bar of soap."[16] Male sex tourism then commodifies female natives.[17] But is commodification also part of the conscious and unconscious instrumental intimate interactions female tourists have with "native" men abroad?

Answering the question can be tricky because female sex tourists for the most part speak in the discourse of romance. In contrast, their male companions express market concerns. In fact, social scientists have noted that "economic gain is the primary motive of both male and female sex providers"[18] engaged in sex tourism.

One piece of evidence supporting this view is that sex providers shun tourists with limited economic means. For instance, the men in Indonesia who seek out female tourists state that they want women "who would pay for everything."[19] Similarly, in Barbados male hosts of female sex tourists explain:

> I like to get involved with executive ladies, with women with class, women with cash. Technically speaking I love women who have money. I can tell the ones who got money.
>
> As a matter of interests if you meet someone, and they say they like you they will return shortly, like next week. That's how you find out if they have a lot of zeros behind the point. Not many people can do that if you save for the vacation.[20]

Thus, while the female sex tourists may describe their experiences as "holiday romances," the men who participate in the romances with them are very clear about their monetary interests in the relationships.

Both male and female native hosts commonly reject the prostitute identity, a rejection made possible by the interaction's informality and its muted economic exchange. Yet male hosts and even their families have great clarity about the commercial nature of the tourist relationship. For instance, one Kenyan "beach boy/gigolo" makes a practice of entertaining his German patron in his home while his wife sleeps in another room without protest because she sees few other economic choices for the family to survive.[21] Another way in which the instrumental nature of the relationship reveals itself is in the lack of any interest the tourists have in establishing a long-term association. In addition, those native "boyfriends" who articulate an interest in a longer-term association with female sex tourists do so expressly in the interest of garnering greater economic opportunities and security.

Despite the lack of organized sex tours for female sex tourists that would overtly smack of sexual commodification, the female tourists can still be characterized as consumers who view the native men as fungible.[22] For instance, one German female sex tourist interviewed by sociologist Julia O'Connell Davidson detailed how in the first week of her vacation in the Dominican Republic she had sexual relations with three Dominican men, "for whom she had bought meals, drinks, and gifts," interactions that sound more like prostitution than her view of them as "holiday romances."[23] Further evidence of fungibility is that when Swedish female sex tourists provide their male hosts in the Gambia with plane tickets to visit Sweden, one Gambian male is not uncommonly substituted for a "boyfriend" who has become tiresome.[24]

"As their homes become the playgrounds of the foreigners, some people learn to become playthings themselves."[25] But it may not necessarily follow that the commodification of female sex tourism in our nonideal world harms human flourishing in such a way that lawmakers should seek to ban the market as has been done in the context of child sex tourism.[26]

Is Female Sex Tourism an Act of Commodification That Harms Human Flourishing?

Like male sex tourism, female sex tourism follows a particular demographic pattern in which predominantly White heterosexual patrons from industrialized nations travel to economically strained countries for sexual intimacy with much younger opposite sex partners of a different race.[27] It is thus logical to ask whether when interracial intimacy is sought by White female heterosexual tourists[28] it is also accompanied by many of the same troublesome aspects of "racialized commodification"[29] that are present when White heterosexual men act as sex tourists.

At first blush the male hosts seem to occupy an objectified status of sexual object parallel to that of native women who engage male sex tourists. In particular, as in the male sex tourism context, the natives' race plays a significant role. To be specific, sex tourists seek out native men to indulge particularized racialized fantasies. For instance, researchers who have studied the female sex tourism dynamic in Jamaica note that most of their subjects emphasized how Black Jamaican men possessed bodies of great sexual value. To quote one study, "Black bodies become commodities."[30] In response, Jamaican men who engage the female sex tourists often elaborate a Rastafarian identity to appeal to tourist women. One author described these men's instrumental choices to lock their hair and speak in the Rastafarian dialect as a "staged authenticity," constructed to attract tourist women who associate Blackness with presumed sexual prowess[31]—hence the common the term "rent-a-dred." Commentators have noted the intertwining of "the exotic and the erotic."[32]

The presumed sexual potency of Jamaican men as quintessential sexual objects is not restricted to Jamaica. Native men of Indonesia are said to play up their exotic appeal for female tourists by walking around tourist haunts barechested with their long hair flowing, "swaying seductively to reggae tunes.[33] Similarly, men in locations as disparate as the Gambia in West Africa,[34] and Belize and Costa Rica[35] in Latin America adopt the appearance and language of the Rastafarian movement to attract female tourists. In Kenya warriors from the Masai and Samburu tribes hold a parallel allure as authentically African.[36] Similarly, studies of female sex tourism in Otavalo in Ecuador,[37] and Barbados in the Caribbean,[38] all consistently report the correlation between male participants' racial appearance and female tourists' sexual interest.

Thus the social science literature suggests that female sex tourists are often motivated in large part to interact intimately with native men by their own racialized sexual fantasies about men of another race and ethnicity. Do those race-based motivations in and of themselves compromise the human flourishing of the men in the host countries? These men are not physically coerced into interacting with the female tourists (unlike many female sex workers). In fact, more often than not men from the host countries actively position themselves to become acquainted with female tourists. But while the women may not physically coerce them, the crushing poverty of the host country does to a great extent motivate the men. In fact, the male participants affirmatively state that they do not engage female tourists who are unable or unwilling to shower them with gifts, money, dinners, clothes, and the highly valued prize of transport to an industrialized nation where greater economic opportunities await them.[39] Furthermore, when the men discover they have expended their sexual energy on tourists who are not as moneyed as they had imagined, the men report feeling deceived and duped. Clearly, the sex alone is neither a consolation nor the ultimate goal of the relationship when economic profit is missing. As one sociologist observes, "Tourists are resources to deploy strategically for making money and improving their networks."[40] This pattern helps to explain why, even though the men do not perceive of themselves as sex workers, they are viewed as such by many of their compatriots in the host countries.[41]

While the male participants have been described in the sex tourism literature as being feminized by their financial dependence upon older female patrons, the male participants themselves articulate a hyper-masculinized perspective on their activities. For example, in Indonesia the men who host female tourists insist that Western women come to Bali to conceive children with the local men, believing that they dispense "better seed" than Western men.[42] In Barbados, one man stated, "Dem girls does come down here specially for fun and games. Dem girls does boast to their friends back home of the sweet foopin' we guys does give dem. Then you find their friends does want to come down too to taste some of de action."[43] What is unclear is whether the men actually view their conduct as a mechanism for performing masculinity or whether they simply utilize the rhetoric of masculinity in order to combat what they experience as the feminizing forces of sex tourism. For instance, in the men's conversations with field researchers and among their peers, they routinely describe themselves as sexual predators, which seems to be validated by the sociological observations of their behavior.

Indeed, every account of female sex tourism details the sexual initiative of the men and their obsessive pursuit of White female tourists. For example, in the Gambia, young men "hang around the airport and the hotels trying to find a 'friend.'"[44] In Indonesia, the men linger at beach resort bars and restaurants and approach female tourists saying, "Excuse me Miss, where you stay? Are you married? Have boy-friend? Want boy-friend? Me your boy-friend. Have many girlfriends from Europe, America, all very happy."[45] In Otavalo, Ecuador men greet White female tourists by stating that they want a relationship with a "gringa" and a "gringo" baby.[46] An anthropological study of Arab men in Israel similarly reported how one man described how tourist women were "ecstatic about the size of his 'Palestinian cock' and his technique, and were carried to the heights of sexual fulfillment," and then stated, "I figure I got a good deal with the profit and the fuck thrown in."[47]

These statements by the Palestinian interviewee suggest that the telling of the tale to other men is a significant factor in how sex tourism can be understood as bolstering masculinity for the male hosts in addition to being a discursive attempt to recast their activities within a masculine narrative. The anthropologist studying Palestinian men observed:

> As I have suggested above sexual tales relate how the structurally "fucked"—the victims of a market and of a map—become the "fuckers"; they tell, in other words, of the way a group of persons "feminized" by their economic and political positions are able, through sexually dominating the women of the dominators, to retake a "masculine" position both in relation to the women and, through a triangular struggle in which they prove more masculine then the women's men, in relation to those men as well. Thus in a domain which I can only refer to as mythological, the slaves become the masters of those who, in the real world, appeared in positions of dominance.[48]

The role of sex as a means of domination for the native men is significant not only for those Palestinian men in Israel who otherwise feel disempowered by their political situation and their low economic status vis-à-vis tourists but also for the vast majority of male hosts in many other locations. Sociologists studying sex tourism in Barbados noted that "conquest of the white female is perceived in terms of acceptance and integration into the society she represents."[49] Native men sexually pursue the female tourists while maintaining their own fantasies of sexual domination, getting a sense of empowerment that they achieve by presuming to dominate not only women but moneyed White women in particular. The men therefore both contest and validate the same racial hierarchy that subordinates them.

Furthermore, sex tourism can also be a vehicle for the men to react against native women's demands for respect and support, in much the same way that White male sex tourists often use sex tourism to discipline people they consider troublesome "women libbers" in their home countries.[50] For instance, in a study of native male participation in sex tourism in Barbados, a number of the subjects echoed the statements of one informant: "Bajan women is too much trouble, you gotta feed she she carr' she out, and buy things for she to eat and drink, but a white girl you just gotta tell she ooh you look brown today, and she would gi' you it just like that." Another said, "I think fellas just getting fed up, trying to ask a woman out, and just walking with her face in the air. Tourist women are not like that."[51] Thus, as some native men see it, sex tourism validates their masculinity by allowing them to exercise power over White women and rejecting the native women who they envision as emasculating with their demands for mutual respect and financial responsibility, demands that often exceed the men's economic abilities.

In short, the narratives that the men construct and retell about their instrumental interactions with White female tourists psychologically empower the men, allowing them to maintain a traditional gender script as sexual predators while also engaging in the feminized role of sexually servicing others for payment. Thus, while the men may not perceive themselves as victims, both their discourse and actions appear to compromise human flourishing. Specifically, the men's actions have them actively engaged in packaging themselves as sexual products to be sold in the market of female tourists while simultaneously viewing the women as fungible economic and sexual opportunities rather than persons. Their subordinating discourse psychologically empowers them at the expense of the societal ideal of gender equality and racial equality.

In a similar vein, it is important to assess both the actions and the discourse of the White female tourists engaged in sex tourism. What in the nature of sex tourism leads some scholars to conclude that the female tourists are following an alternative path to sex equality by rewriting the gender script?[52] First, leisure travel itself is one imbued with the potential for "escape from the bonds of everyday social structure."[53] While away from one's home base and community obligations, one can also feel on vacation from the community norms that otherwise influence behavior. Thus being on vacation from one's own patriarchal society, which the tourist knows and feels constrained by, may permit the women to experience a greater sense of freedom and gender equality.

But why should travel to third world countries no less patriarchal in many ways from the United States and the European Union provide the women with greater gender equality? Race becomes key. While being a transient in the host country may partially explain why the tourists are not subjected to the host country's patriarchal norms, a more powerful explanatory factor is the enhanced status that the women's Whiteness and capital accord them. The women occupy a space of greater permissiveness because the men and the host country need the women to support the economy. The host countries heavily depend upon the patronage of White North American and European travelers in a manner that parallels the dependent relationships many of the host countries historically experienced as European colonies. Indeed, many commentators view tourism as a neocolonial experience for the host countries and visitors alike, in which tourists discover Natives and use their economic global power and capital to purchase them.[54] Just as colonialism educated the colonized people to value Whiteness itself as a form of status, neocolonial tourism does the same. Franz Fanon's classic observations about the effects of colonialism on colonized people resonate greatly in the contemporary sex tourism context.

> Out of the blackest part of my soul, across the zebra striping of my mind, surges the desire to be suddenly white. I wish to be acknowledged not as a black but as white. . . . Who but a white woman can do this for me? By loving me she proves that I am worthy of white love. I am loved like a white man. I am a white man.[55]

Therefore, while sex tourism may empower female tourists to express their sexuality and have greater control over those intimate relationships, the source of their empowerment is their Whiteness and their wealth.[56] Only the narrowest conception of human flourishing would laud the ability of White women to have the same access to race privilege as colonizing White men.

Furthermore, rather than bolstering their role as empowered sexual subjects, the validation that the women receive as sex tourists situates them in the very traditional role of adored sex object.

> Western women are also taught that "femininity" means being glamorous and beautiful, and, because female sex tourists are flattered, charmed, wooed and indulged by local men and boys, their sex tourism gives them the illusion that they are esteemed as "truly feminine."[57]

As one White female traveler in Ecuador enthused, "I don't get this much attention at home."[58] Because female sex tourists tend to be older women marginalized in the youth-worshipping cultures of their countries of origin, the attention they receive as tourists allows them to receive the validation as sexual objects they are denied back home. "[W]omen who consider themselves too fat or otherwise unattractive suddenly discover that they are considered beauties, and the experience is heady."[59] In fact, native hosts complain that female clients are more taxing than male clients because they demand a prolonged performance of adoration and romance before providing the men with any financial compensation. Thus, while mass tourism has facilitated the ability of Western women to enter the masculine domain of travel and to reap the status advantages as White travelers with proportionally more money than their native companions, it has not worked to undermine any of the traditional gender norms that otherwise trap women.

In fact the pursuit of the traditional dichotomy between masculinity and femininity in the female sex tourist interaction may very well facilitate male domination of women generally inasmuch as it parallels Catharine MacKinnon's classic distillation of male dominance in which she states: "[F]emaleness means femininity, which means attractiveness to men, which means sexual attractiveness, which means sexual availability on male terms."[60] While the female tourists are not physically harmed or coerced or economically subjugated in the manner MacKinnon's gender dominance theory directly speaks to, the men who host them often view the female tourists as objects for pursuit who lack human subjectivity, thereby dehumanizing women as a class and reinforcing a sexist ideology that produces a second-class status for women generally. The sex can be viewed as being on "male terms" to the extent that the men service only those whom they pursue as masculinized sexual predators, for a monetary exchange the men deem worthy. It is also sex on male terms to the degree that the femininity the women wish to experience cannot be self-actualized but instead can be provided only through the male gaze of the native host.[61]

At the same time, the female sex tourist context also embodies elements of female agency not present in contexts like rape, sexual harassment, pornography or the formal prostitution context, which counsels against a wholesale application of dominance theory to sex tourism. Though they are actively pursued by the men, it is the female tourists who choose which men to get involved with, the duration of the relationship and the frequency of the interaction. In this manner the women set the terms for their sexual pleasure in the way critics of dominance theory describe women as doing in other contexts.[62] But while it is true that the female tourists report enjoying both the sex and their sexuality through their relationships with native hosts, their enjoyment is seemingly enhanced by the traditional gender script of romance with which the native hosts pursue them. Thus, while the women are not coerced into sex in the paradigmatic dominance theory manner, their decision "to say yes to sex" is not the complete exercise in feminist empowerment that scholar Katherine Franke might envision.[63] What is debatable is whether the romance narrative of female sex tourism is a less benign form of the "dope for dupes," as Germaine Greer described romance.[64] The gender role reversal in the economics of female sex tourism precludes women from being financially dependent upon native hosts but simultaneously reinforces their dependence upon male adoration for fulfillment. This need is a dangerous one, as Simone de Beauvoir pointed out, because in this context patriarchy obtains women's acquiescence to their own subordination.[65]

Thus, the disaggregation of women's emotional dependence upon men from their material dependence upon men in the female sex tourism context does not necessarily eviscerate the connection between romance and gender subordination. Instead, the danger of the female sex tourism romance narrative may lie in its reinforcement of the Harlequin-romance paradigm that centers men in many women's lives.[66] While the female tourists may not be economically dependent upon their male hosts, they return to their countries of origin with visions of a gendered-romance that facilitate the continued connection between emotional dependence and material dependence. In other words, the "holiday romance" leaves unchallenged the gendered norms the women return home to. And like the escapism of a Harlequin romance, the escapism of a sex tourism adventure may diminish the inclination to question the patriarchy of the romance narrative.[67]

Perhaps then female sex tourism is yet another context in which women retain partial agency to enjoy their sexuality in the midst of choices compromised by continued gender inequality.[68] But the exercise of that partial agency is not necessarily something for a feminist to celebrate, as sex tourism seems to be "settling for the best inequality has to offer" rather than reflecting a true political transformation for women.[69] Particularly disturbing is the fact that sex tourism provides access to the role of sexual subject through the performance of Whiteness and femininity.[70] Sex tourists simultaneously perform their Whiteness[71] and femininity as sources of power by taking on the feminine role of a passive object of beauty waiting to be pursued by native hosts. In turn the native hosts adore their White beauty[72] but are controlled by the women's financial status. The female sex tourist may be acting as a sexual subject but does so within a realm that provides a compromised path to that goal.

Accordingly, on balance, female sex tourism does not seem to have the potential to enhance human flourishing. Some commentators are hopeful that the experience of having male-like control in a relationship while on vacation might encourage those women to be more assertive in relationships back at home. But the lesson taught while on vacation is not necessarily in keeping with human flourishing since what the women learn is the benefit of controlling others with the power of wealth.[73] In addition, the sex tourism interaction also furthers the use of racial stereotyping because the male companions in the quest for economic profit do all they can to make the women's racialized sexual fantasies a reality. In fact, the female sex tourists often perceive themselves as racially progressive because they have financially assisted men of color in need.[74] In this way, the globalization of sex tourism can serve to further entrench the existing racial hierarchy and the exploitation of economic disparity, all in the service of a traditional and gendered expression of sexuality.

What Should Be Done?

Inasmuch as there are ways in which female sex tourism is both empowering to the participants in differing ways and collusive with racial, class, and gender hierarchies, it can be viewed as being subject to what Radin terms "the double bind," in which the binary choices of market inalienability and complete commodification each have ways of oppressing those who are already oppressed. Radin suggests that double binds in nonideal worlds may sometimes be best addressed by a partial commodification approach rather than complete market inalienability or complete commodification, so as to further a nonmarket conception of personhood and community.[75] As she explains, "[A]n incomplete commodification can sometimes substitute for a complete noncommodification that might accord with our ideals but cause too much harm in our nonideal world."[76]

Yet what is principally troublesome about the female sex tourism context is its very nature as a venue for partial commodification. In other words, the way in which each participant has instrumental motivations that can be veiled by the discourse of romance and the economic disparities of the parties, is insidious because it facilitates the maintenance of gender hierarchy, racial stereotypes and race hierarchy in such a covert manner that it is hard to identify, let alone challenge. Overt commodification as exists in some formal prostitution markets would have the ironic benefit of clarifying the instrumental nature of the interaction but would be accompanied with all the same dangers to human flourishing. The alternative of complete market inalienability would be impossible to enforce because of the ways in which the participants often deceive themselves into thinking the interaction is of a romantic nature rather than an economic one.

Indeed, it is sex tourism's close parallels with traditional "strategic dating" that make it least prone to regulation and ultimately most disturbing. Commentators note that in postfeminist culture, the materialism manifest in strategic dating "can be an expression of healthy self-assertion, of a woman's 'being able to seek that which she desires.'"[77] Thus the empowered woman of today can openly use her sexuality to marry a rich man or alternatively use her money to validate her sexuality. Sex tourism suggests to women that they can have access to gender equality by using their power as consumers. In fact, the mantra of feminist as consumer is being widely disseminated in popular culture. For instance, in the theme song to the popular film *Charlie's Angels* the female singers proudly state:

> The shoes on my feet, I bought them
> The clothes I'm wearing, I bought them
> The rock I'm rockin', I bought it
> Cause I depend on me.[78]

To conclude, what is in great part disturbing about sex tourism is the way in which market rhetoric is present in much the same way it is present in many relationships, historic and contemporary. But in the sex tourism context there exists a tremendous asymmetry in economic power and status of the parties by virtue of their country affiliation in the capitalistic world order. Thus what is disquieting about sex tourism is what is disquieting about the existence of gender and race hierarchy and the conception of consumption as human fulfillment. These are not dilemmas readily resolved by partial commodification, complete market inalienability or wholesale commodification. Legally banning sex tourism is not only unsatisfying because the very informal nature of the commercial exchange would make such a law impracticable but also because the existence of gender inequality might expose women to biased enforcement as a patriarchal punishment for their transgression of gender norms as female purchasers of male sexuality and interracial intimacy. Similarly, the continued existence of racism might lead to the biased enforcement of a legal ban against people of color who supply the sex, rather than the White purchasers. In addition, people of color would be excluded from yet another source of needed income.

In order to resolve what is disturbing about the commodification of sex tourism, we would first need to dismantle racism, sexism, and the cultural predisposition toward viewing consumption as fulfillment. Because sex tourism is at the crossroads of racial hierarchy, gender subordination, and neocolonial wealth inequality, any legal prophylactic narrowly focused on sex tourism would be ineffective. Instead, the concerns with sex tourism would be better addressed as part of the larger struggle against societal inequality. As Margaret Jane Radin states,

> If neither commodification nor noncommodification can put to rest our disquiet about harm to personhood in conjunction with certain specific kinds of transactions—if neither commodification nor noncommodification can satisfy our aspirations for a society exhibiting equal respect for persons—then we must rethink the larger social context in which this dilemma is embedded. We must think about wealth and power redistribution.[79]

In short, it is the very pervasiveness of commodification within gender and racial subordination that makes crafting a legal solution to female sex tourism problematic. For as long as poverty in the third world continues to exist, those nations will be motivated to promote a tourism of exotic racial difference for the consumption of White travelers. As long as racialized sex stereotypes continue to exist moneyed travelers will be interested in indulging their racial fantasies by purchasing them abroad. And as long as women continue to be fed the notion that their value is reflected in the male pursuit of their beauty, female travelers will continue to engage in sex tourism. What is needed is not legal reform but social change.

NOTES

1. Funding for this research project was provided by the Dean's Research Fund of Rutgers University School of Law–Newark.

2. Michel Foucault, The History of Sexuality, Vol. I, 157 (Robert Hurley, trans., 1978)

3. See, e.g., Margaret A. Healy, Prosecuting Child Sex Tourists at Home: Do Laws in Sweden, Australia, and the United States Safeguard the Rights of Chil-

dren as Mandated by International Law?, 18 Fordham Int'l L.J. 1852, 1857–1858, 1871 (1995) (noting the existence of the 1994 Child Sexual Abuse Prevention Act, which makes it illegal to travel interstate or to a foreign country to engage in sexual activities with minors, and further that the Act is underenforced because doing so might hamper the lucrative tourist industry).

4. Kamala Kempadoo, *Continuities and Change: Five Centuries of Prostitution in the Caribbean, in* Sun, Sex, and Gold: Tourism and Sex Work in the Caribbean 3, 4 (Kamala Kempadoo, ed., 1999).

5. Julia O'Connell Davidson, Prostitution, Power and Freedom 75 (1998).

6. *Id.* at 181.

7. Deborah Pruitt & Suzanne LaFont, *For Love and Money: Romance Tourism in Jamaica*, 22 Annals of Tourism Research 422 (1995).

8. Pruitt & LaFont, *supra* note 7, at 423.

9. Margaret Jane Radin, *Market-Inalienability*, 100 Harv. L. Rev. 1849, 1851 (1987).

10. Margaret Jane Radin, Contested Commodities 76 (1996).

11. *Id.*

12. Radin, *supra* note 9, at 1910.

13. Radin, *supra* note 10, at 130 ("The double bind is a series of dilemmas in which both alternatives are, or can be, losers for the oppressed.").

14. In fact, for male sex tourists the enterprise is a highly organized commercial activity in that "sex tour packages" are commonly promoted and touted and multiple publications and Web sites exist to assist the male traveler identify locations for "cheap dates." *See generally* The Erotic Traveler (newsletter dedicated to identifying travel locations that facilitate sexual fantasies); Bruce Cassirer, Travel and the Single Male: The World's Best Destinations for the Single Male (1992); Wade T. Wilson et al., Fantasy Islands: A Man's Guide to Exotic Women and International Travel (1998). *See also* http://www.tsmtravel.com (Travel and the Single Male Web site); http://www.worldsexarchives.com (World Sex Archives "dedicated to providing information about sex tourism"); http://www.adult-travel.net (adult travel guide to "great sex tourism destinations"); http://travelsexguide.tv (Travel Sex Guide to "adult sex traveler").

15. In this chapter, the words Black and White appear capitalized when they refer to persons whose race is Black or White to denote the political meaning of race and the social significance of being White or Black as something more than just skin color. Victor F. Caldwell, Book Note, 96 Colum. L. Rev. 1363, 1369 (1996).

16. Julia O'Connell Davidson, *Sex Tourism in Cuba*, 38 Race & Class 39, 44 (1996).

17. *See* Tanya Katerí Hernández, *Sexual Harassment and Racial Disparity: The Mutual Construction of Gender and Race*, 4 U. Iowa J. Gender, Race & Justice 183, 200–209 (2001) (describing the marketing and use of women of color as a sexual commodity for tourism in many foreign countries).

18. Martin Oppermann, *Sex Tourism,* 26 Annals of Tourism Research 251, 257 (1999).

19. Heidi Dahles & Karin Bras, *Entrepreneurs in Romance: Tourism in Indonesia,* 26 Annals of Tourism Research 267, 281 (1999).

20. Joan L. Phillips, *Tourist-Oriented Prostitution in Barbados, in* Sun, Sex, and Gold: Tourism and Sex Work in the Caribbean 183, 188 (Kemala Kempadoo, ed., 1999).

21. Otto Pohl, *Kenya Cracking Down on 'Beach Boys,' Gigolos Serving Tourists,* N.Y. Times, Feb. 14, 2002, at A12.

22. Pruitt & LaFont, *supra* note 7, at 426.

23. Davidson, *supra* note 5, at 183.

24. Ulla Wagner & Bawa Yamba, *Going North and Getting Attached: The Case of the Gambians,* 51 Ethnos 199, 213 (1986).

25. Yapady Wolf, *The World of the Kuta Cowboy,* Inside Indonesia (June 1993).

26. *See* Healy, *supra* note 3.

27. Hernández, *supra* note 17, at 204–206 (detailing the demographic pattern of male sex tourist locations and parallels with the racial disparity in sex harassment victimization).

28. The complete absence of literature regarding the sexual activities of women of color who travel abroad precludes an analysis of any of the distinctions and parallels that may exist across race. *See, e.g.,* Michele Wallace, *A Black Feminist's Search for Sisterhood, in* All the Women are White, All the Blacks Men, But Some of Us Are Brave 5, 11 (Gloria T. Hull et al., eds., 1982) (describing the 1978 formation of the National Black Feminist Organization in response to the distinct position of Black women as women subject to racism and classism in feminism); *see also* Mary C. Lugones & Elizabeth V. Spelman, *Have We Got a Theory for You! Feminist Theory, Cultural Imperialism and the Demand for 'The Woman's Voice,'* 6 Women's Stud. Int. Forum 573, 580–581 (1983) (urging that White women and others engage in the work of considering the particularities of Latina, Black and other women of color rather than continuing the abstraction of "woman"). Once the empirical work about women of color tourists becomes available, it will be interesting to examine whether the perceived scarcity of "marriageable" men of color in the United States makes the sexual intimacy with men of color abroad more meaningful. Specifically, does the perceived scarcity of men in the United States make women of color's intimate relations with native men abroad less instrumental and thus less subject to commodification critiques? *See, e.g.,* Robert Staples, The World of Black Singles 42 (1981) (noting that because of the surplus of Black women it is a buyer's market in the marital arena for Black men). Alternatively, women of color may also engage in instrumental interactions as an antidote to the historical and pervasive societal depiction of women of color and in particular Black women as unattrac-

tive in comparison to White women. *See* bell hooks, Ain't I a Woman: Black Women and Feminism 48–86 (1981) (detailing the historic and continued systematic devaluation of black womanhood). With their enhanced economic status vis-à-vis the native men, women of color tourists may very well be able to purchase the experience of being adored and respected. It is unknown how many women of color tourists seem predisposed to consider marrying let alone prolonging their relationships with the native men—notwithstanding film and fiction depictions like "How Stella Got Her Groove Back." Terry McMillan, How Stella Got Her Groove Back (1996).

29. "Racialized commodification" is a term I have used to reflect the ways in which commodification is itself implicated in the constructions of Whiteness, femininity, and thus gender. Hernández, *supra* note 17, at 208–209.

30. Jacqueline Sanchez Taylor, *Sex Tourism in the Caribbean, in* Tourism, Travel and Sex (Stephen Clift & Simon Carter, eds., 1999).

31. Pruitt & LaFont, *supra* note 7, at 431.

32. *Id.*

33. Wolf, *supra* note 25.

34. Naomi Brown, *Beachboys as Culture Brokers in Bakau Town, The Gambia,* 27 Community Development Journal 361, 364 (1992); Wagner & Yamba, *supra* note 24, at 199.

35. Heidi Dahles, *Gigolos and Rastamen: Globalisation, Tourism and Changing Gender Identities,* in Gender/Tourism, Fun?: International Conference 45, 52 (1997).

36. Pohl, *supra* note 21, at A12 (describing the "mystique" of the Masai and Samburu for female European tourists).

37. Lynn A. Meisch, *Gringas and Otavalenos: Changing Tourist Relations,* 22 Annals of Tourism Research 441 (1995).

38. Cecilia A. Karch & G. H. S. Dann, *Close Encounters of the Third World,* 34 Human Relations 249 (1981).

39. Dahles, *supra* note 35, at 50 ("'ticket to a better life' is a recurring theme in the analysis of men's motivations to forge a relationship with foreign women"); Dahles & Bras, *supra* note 19, at 287 (the men "will only invest time when the guest is worth the effort. They are pragmatic in their contacts with tourists. As long as the tourist will yield the expected amount of money or provide access to other sources of income," then the men will pursue a relationship.).

40. Dahles & Bras, *supra* note 19, at 274.

41. Dahles, *supra* note 35, at 56.

42. Dahles & Bras, *supra* note 19, at 281.

43. Karch & Dann, *supra* note 38, at 252.

44. Ulla Wagner, *Out of Time and Place—Mass Tourism and Charter Trips,* 42 Ethnos 38, 43 (1977).

45. Dahles & Bras, *supra* note 19, at 267.

46. Meisch, *supra* note 37, at 454.

47. Glenn Bowman, *Fucking Tourists: Sexual Relations and Tourism in Jerusalem's Old City,* 9 Critique of Anthropology 77, 86 (1989).

48. *Id.* at 88.

49. Karch & Dann, *supra* note 38, at 257.

50. Equality Now, Sex Tourism: "Real Sex With Real Girls, All for Real Cheap" (Dec. 1996) at http://www.equalitynow.org/english/navigation/hub_ph01 _en.html (describing U.S. sex tour brochure for men that states, "Had enough of the American bitches who won't give you the time of day and are only interested in your bank account? In Asia you'll meet 'girls' who will treat you with respect and appreciation, unlike their American counterparts.").

51. Phillips, *supra* note 20, at 192.

52. Pruitt & LaFont, *supra* note 7, at 436.

53. Wagner, *supra* note 44, at 45.

54. Martin Oppermann, *Who Exploits Whom and Who Benefits?, in* Sex Tourism and Prostitution: Aspects of Leisure, Recreation, and Work 154 (Martin Oppermann et al., eds., 1998) (describing the work of scholars who link colonialism with tourism).

55. Frantz Fanon, Black Skin, White Masks 63 (1970).

56. bell hooks's description of the power dynamics of White heterosexual males' searches for interracial intimacy resonates greatly with the White heterosexual female attraction to sex tourism. *See* bell hooks, Black Looks: Race and Representation 23 (1992) ("When race and ethnicity become commodified as resources for pleasure, the culture of specific groups, as well as the bodies of individuals, can be seen as constituting an alternative playground where members of dominating races, genders, sexual practices affirm their power-over in intimate relations with the Other.")

57. O'Connell Davidson, *supra* note 5, at 182.

58. Meisch, *supra* note 37, at 451.

59. *Id.*

60. Catharine A. MacKinnon, *Feminism, Marxism, Method, and the State: An Agenda for Theory,* 7 Signs: J. of Women in Culture & Soc'y 515, 530–531 (1982).

61. *See* Catharine A. MacKinnon, *A Feminist/Political Approach "Pleasure under Patriarchy," in* Theories of Human Sexuality 65, 80 (James H. Geer & William T. O'Donohue, eds., 1987) ("Men's power over women means that the way men see women defines who women can be.").

62. *See* Gayle Rubin, *Thinking Sex: Notes for Radical Theory of the Politics of Sexuality, in* Pleasure and Danger: Exploring Female Sexuality 267, 302 (Carol Vance, ed., 1984); Drucilla Cornell, *Sexual Difference, The Feminine, and Equivalency: A Critique of MacKinnon's Toward a Feminist Theory of the State,*

100 Yale L.J. 2247, 2248 (1991) (Book Review); Nan Hunter & Sylvia A. Law, *Brief Amici Curiae of Feminist Anti-Censorship Taskforce et al., in American Booksellers Association v. Hudnut,* 21 U. Mich. J.L. Ref. 69, 125–131 (Fall 1987–Winter 1988); Robin West, *Fifteenth Anniversary Celebration: The Difference in Women's Hedonic Lives: A Phenomenological Critique of Feminist Legal Theory,* 15 Wisc. Women's L.J. 149 (2000).

63. Katherine M. Franke, *Theorizing Yes: An Essay on Feminism, Law and Desire,* 101 Colum. L. Rev. 181, 198 (2001). The sex tourism context demonstrates that even consensual sex can be accompanied by dangers to feminism.

64. *See* Germaine Greer, The Female Eunuch 192–212 (2001) (opposing the false consciousness of romantic love as a cheap ideology that oppresses women and keeps them dependent upon men).

65. Simone de Beauvoir, The Second Sex 799 (1974).

66. *See* Ann Snitow, *Mass Market Romance: Pornography for Women Is Different,* 20 Radical Hist. Rev. 141 (1979), *reprinted in* Women and Romance: A Reader 307, 313 (Susan Ostrov Weisser, ed., 2001) ("When women try to picture excitement, the society offers them one vision, romance. When women try to imagine companionship, the society offers them one vision, male, sexual companionship. When women try to fantasize about success, mastery, the society offers them one vision, the power to attract a man.").

67. Janice A. Radway, *Women Read the Romance: The Interaction of Text and Context,* 9 Feminist Stud. 53 (1983), *reprinted in* Women and Romance, *supra* note 66, at 323, 337 ("[W]omen materially express their discontent with their restricted social world by indulging in a fantasy that vicariously supplies the pleasure and attention they need, and thereby effectively staves off the necessity of presenting those needs as demands in the real world").

68. *See* Kathryn Abrams, *Sex Wars Redux: Agency and Coercion in Feminist Legal Theory,* 95 Colum. L. Rev. 304, 376 (1995) (urging a more complex view of women as living under conditions that constrain their agency but still permit them to exercise self-will). *But see* Jennifer Baumgardner & Amy Richards, Manifesta: Young Women, Feminism and the Future 136 (2000) (describing some third wave feminists reared in the wake of the feminist movement of the 1970s as embracing feminine enculturation without the threat of patriarchy—"We, and others, call this interaction of culture and feminism 'Girlie.' Girlie says we're not broken, and our desires aren't simply booby traps set by the patriarchy. Girlie encompasses the tabooed symbols of women's feminine enculturation—Barbie dolls, make-up, fashion magazines, high heels—and says using them isn't shorthand for 'we've been duped.'"

69. MacKinnon, *supra* note 61, at 90. Stated differently, when "the object is allowed to desire, if she desires to be an object," gender equality has not been achieved. Andrea Dworkin, Pornography: Men Possessing Women 109 (1981).

70. In other words, sex tourism allows White heterosexual women to "affirm

'white power' when they flirt with having contact with the Other." hooks, *supra* note 56, at 36.

71. "Performing whiteness" is a concept that some commentators have used to describe the social construction of race and its perpetuation through the performance of particular normative scripts that indicate a racial identity. John Tehranian, Note, *Performing Whiteness: Naturalization Litigation and the Construction of Racial Identity in America,* 109 Yale L.J. 817, 828 (2000). It is a concept that was developed from Judith Butler's performativity analysis of gender constructs and identity. *See* Judith Butler, Gender Trouble: Feminism and the Subversion of Identity 25 (1990) (arguing that gender is a social construct promulgated through public drama).

72. Beauty itself has been constructed to mean Whiteness, and thus in relishing the role of adored beauty, the female sex tourist performs her Whiteness. *See* Angela P. Harris, *Race and Essentialism in Feminist Legal Theory,* 42 Stan. L. Rev. 581, 597 (1990) ("Beauty is itself white").

73. Consider the perversity of such a lesson for human flourishing in a capitalist context in which a spouse can openly state in dinner conversation "[o]f course, it's a given that the one who does the supporting holds the one being supported in contempt." Vivian Gornick, *The End of the Novel of Love,* Chronicle of Higher Education, Aug. 15, 1997, at B4.

74. In fact, some women may also feel that they have furthered the cause of racial equality by engaging in cross-racial sex. Yet over the entire course of the history of cross-racial sexual encounters, the cause of racial equality has rarely been advanced. See Adrienne D. Davis, *Slavery and the Roots of Sexual Harassment, in* Directions in Sexual Harassment Law 457 (Catharine A. MacKinnon & Reva B. Siegel, eds., 2004).

75. Margaret Jane Radin, *Justice and Market Domain, in* Markets and Justice, Nomos XXXI 177 (John W. Chapman & J. Roland Pennock, eds., 1989) ("Complete removal from the market—is not the only alternative to complete commodification. Incomplete commodification describes a situation in which things are sold but the interaction between the participants in the transaction cannot be fully or perspicuously described as sale of things.").

76. Radin, supra note 10, at 104.

77. Ruth La Ferla, *They Want to Marry a Millionaire,* N.Y. Times, Mar. 4, 2001, § 9 at 1 ("The gold digger is alive and well, thriving in a bottom line, postfeminist culture, where marrying for money is no longer something that many women feel compelled to hide.").

78. "Independent Women," Ann Wilson et al., *Charlie's Angels* film theme song 2000.

79. Radin, *supra* note 75, at 187.

Taking Money for Bodily Services

Martha C. Nussbaum[1]

All of us, with the exception of the independently wealthy and the unemployed, take money for the use of our body. Professors, factory workers, lawyers, opera singers, prostitutes, doctors, legislators—we all do things with parts of our bodies, for which we receive a wage in return. Some people get good wages and some do not; some have a relatively high degree of control over their working conditions and some have little control; some have many employment options and some have very few. And some are socially stigmatized and some are not.

* * *

It will therefore be my conclusion that the most urgent issue raised by prostitution is that of employment opportunities for working women and their control over the conditions of their employment. The legalization of prostitution, far from promoting the demise of love, is likely to make things a little better for women who have too few options to begin with.

* * *

[Three Types of Bodily Services]

* * *

It will be illuminating to consider the prostitute by situating her in relation to several other women who take money for bodily services:

- A factory worker in the Perdue chicken factory, who plucks feathers from nearly frozen chickens. . . .

243

- A professor of philosophy, who gets paid for lecturing and writing. [and]
- A person whom I'll call the "colonoscopy artist": She gets paid for having her colon examined with the latest instruments, in order to test out their range and capability.

By considering similarities and differences between the prostitute and these other bodily actors, we will make progress in identifying the distinctive features of prostitution as a form of bodily service.

* * *

The Prostitute and the Factory Worker

Both prostitution and factory work are usually low-paid jobs, but, in many instances, a woman faced with the choice can (at least over the short haul) make more money in prostitution than in this sort of factory work. Both face health risks, but the health risk in prostitution can be very much reduced by legalization and regulation. The prostitute may well have better working hours and conditions than the factory worker; especially in a legalized regime, she may have much more control over her working conditions. She has a degree of choice about which clients she accepts and what activities she performs, whereas the factory worker has no choices but must perform the same motions again and again for years. The prostitute also performs a service that requires skill and responsiveness to new situations, whereas the factory worker's repetitive motion exercises relatively little human skill and contains no variety.

The factory worker however is unlikely to be the target of violence, whereas the prostitute needs—and does not always get—protection against violent customers. (Again, this situation can be improved by legalization: Prostitutes in the Netherlands have a call button wired up to the police.) This factory worker's occupation, moreover, has no clear connection with stereotypes of gender. The prostitute's activity does derive some of its attraction from stereotypes of women as sluttish and immoral, and it may in turn perpetuate such stereotypes. The factory worker suffers no invasion of her internal private space, whereas the prostitute's activity involves such (consensual) invasion. Finally, the prostitute suffers from social stigma, whereas the factory worker does not—at least among people of her own social class.

* * *

The Prostitute and the Professor of Philosophy

These two figures have a very interesting similarity: Both provide bodily services in areas that are generally thought to be especially intimate and definitive of selfhood. Just as the prostitute takes money for sex, which is commonly thought to be an area of intimate self-expression, so the professor takes money for thinking and writing about what she thinks—about morality, emotion, the nature of knowledge, whatever—all parts of a human being's intimate search for understanding of the world and self-understanding. It was precisely for this reason that the medieval thinkers I have mentioned saw such a moral problem about philosophizing for money.

[There are other similarities:] In both cases, the performance involves interaction with others, and the form of the interaction is not altogether controlled by the person. It may appear at first that the intimate bodily space of the professor is not invaded—but we should ask about this. When someone's unanticipated argument goes into one's mind, is this not both intimate and bodily? (And far less consensual, often, than the penetration of prostitute by customer?) Both performances involve skill. It might plausibly be argued that the professor's involves a more developed skill, or at least a more expensive training—but we should be cautious here. Our culture is all too ready to think that sex involves no skill and is simply "natural," a view that is surely false and is not even seriously entertained by many cultures.[2]

Finally, the professor of philosophy, if a female, both enjoys reasonably high respect in the community and also might be thought to bring credit to all women in that she succeeds at an activity commonly thought to be the preserve only of males. She thus subverts traditional gender hierarchy, whereas the prostitute, while suffering stigma herself, may be thought to perpetuate gender hierarchy.

* * *

The Prostitute and the Colonoscopy Artist

I have included this hypothetical occupation for a reason that should by now be evident: it involves the consensual invasion of one's bodily space. (The example is not so hypothetical, either: Medical students need models when they are learning to perform internal exams, and young actors do earn a living playing such roles.)[3] The colonoscopy artist uses her skill at tolerating the fiber-optic probe without anesthesia to make a living. In the process, she permits an aperture of her body to be penetrated by another person's activity—and, we might add, far more deeply penetrated than is generally the case in sex. She runs some bodily risk, since she is being used to test untested instruments, and she will probably have to fast and empty her colon regularly enough to incur some malnutrition and some damage to her excretory function. [I]t may also involve some stigma, given that people are inclined to be disgusted by the thought of intestines.

And yet, on the whole, we do not think that this is a base trade or one that makes the woman who does it a fallen woman. We might want to ban or regulate it if we thought it was too dangerous, but we would not be moved to ban it for moral reasons. Why not? Some people would point to the fact that it does not either reflect or perpetuate gender hierarchy, and this is certainly true. But surely a far greater part of the difference is made by the fact that most people do not think anal penetration by a doctor in the context of a medical procedure is immoral, whereas lots of people do think that vaginal or anal penetration in the context of sexual relations is (except under very special circumstances) immoral and that a woman who goes in for that is therefore an immoral and base woman.
* * *

[Truly Human Functioning]

The stigma traditionally attached to prostitution is based on a collage of beliefs, most of which are not rationally defensible. [T]he correct response to this problem seems to be to work to enhance the economic autonomy and the personal dignity of members of that class, not to rule off-limits an option that may be the only livelihood for many poor women and to further stigmatize women who already make their living this way.

In grappling further with these issues, we should begin from the realization there is nothing per se wrong with taking money for the use of one's body. That's the way most of us live, and formal recognition of that fact through contract is usually a good thing for people, protecting their security and their employment conditions. What seems wrong is that relatively few people in the world have the option to use their body, in their work, in what Marx would call a "truly human" manner of functioning, by which he meant (among other things) having some choices about the work to be performed, some reasonable measure of control over its conditions and outcome, and also the chance to use thought and skill rather than just to function as a cog in a machine. Women in many parts of the world are especially likely to be stuck at a low level of mechanical functioning, whether as agricultural laborers, factory workers, or prostitutes. The real question to be faced is how to expand the options and opportunities such workers face, how to increase the humanity inherent in their work, and how to guarantee that workers of all sorts are treated with dignity.

NOTES

1. Reprinted by permission from Sex and Social Justice (1999), by Martha C. Nussbaum. Copyright 1999 by Oxford University Press. All rights reserved.

2. Thus the *Kama Sutra,* with its detailed instructions for elaborately skilled performances, strikes most Western readers as slightly comic since the prevailing romantic ideal of "natural" sex makes such contrivance seem quite unsexy.

3. See Terri Kapsalis, Public Privates: Performing Gynecology from Both Ends of the Speculum (1997); and Terri Kapsalis, *In Print: Backstage at the Pelvic Theater,* Chi. Reader, April 18, 1997, 46. While a graduate student in performance studies at Northwestern, Kapsalis made a living as a "gynecology teaching associate," serving as the model patient for medical students learning to perform pelvic and breast examinations.

The Currency of Sex
Prostitution, Law, and Commodification

Ann Lucas

Introduction

According to one study, "[m]oney is *the* reason for prostitution. [N]o woman . . . prostitutes herself for any [other] reason. . . . Without the money prostitution would cease to exist."[1] While accurate, this observation is banal, if not tautological: absent money, prostitution is simply sex. Put another way, prostitution is commodified sexuality, and, not surprisingly, most objections to prostitution are commodification-based. Some argue, for example, that exchanging sex for money degrades a human attribute, sexuality, the debasement of which impedes human flourishing. This argument poses a serious challenge to advocates of prostitution's decriminalization (removal of criminal penalties) or legalization (replacement of criminal penalties with regulations like zoning rules). Commodification concerns suggest that eliminating criminal sanctions for prostitution could be so detrimental to human interaction that prostitution must continue to be prohibited or severely restricted.

One of the most thoughtful, articulate critics of commodification is Margaret Jane Radin.[2] Taking her views as representing the primary commodification-based objections to prostitution, this chapter argues that there is no necessary correspondence between noncommodification and flourishing, and that laws prohibiting prostitution actually inhibit the flourishing of prostitutes, their customers, and others. This chapter also explains why decriminalizing (completely commodifying) prostitution need not be feared. Finally, because legalizing prostitution is the more likely alternative to criminalization,[3] this analysis advocates a different approach to legalization than that proffered by commodification critics.

The Dangers of Socially Accepted Prostitution

Radin believes that commodifying essential aspects of personhood in-
hibits human flourishing. Things integral to personhood include work,
sexuality, wisdom, character, and bodily integrity, in her view.[4] Putting
such personal attributes and attachments on the market converts them
into possessions, "fungible objects" considered separable from the individual, when in fact to detach them degrades or harms the person.[5] Thus,
prostitution—commodified sexuality—is detrimental to humanity because sexuality is integral to personhood and should be neither traded on
the market nor analyzed in market rhetoric.

As a result, perhaps sex should be "market-inalienable." Market-inalienability prohibits the "separation of something—an entitlement,
right, or attribute—from its holder"[6] when this separation (alienation) is
accomplished by sale. Other transfers, such as gifts, may be allowed.
Some things must be kept out of the market because market valuation and
rhetoric change our understanding and experience: "a world in which
human interactions are conceived of as market trades is different from one
in which they are not. Rhetoric is not just shaped by, but shapes, reality."[7]

On this basis, Radin rejects the argument that inalienability rules are
paternalistic. Inalienability rules would be unnecessary if we always recognized our best interests because in that case we would never attempt to
transfer personal goods or services when harm could result. In such situations, inalienability rules would paternalistically restrain individual liberty. However, Radin argues, inalienability rules are not paternalistic if
they foster "proper self-development."[8] Where proper self-development
is necessary for liberty to be meaningful, then inalienability rules that promote self-development also promote rather than restrain liberty. Radin
concludes that inalienability rules are, in some cases, morally justified.

Radin's social concerns reinforce her position on inalienability. Commodification of personal attributes might harm not just the individual but
society as a whole. Indeed, this is one of Radin's main concerns about the
use of market rhetoric: once one person's attributes are considered fungible, it becomes more likely that everyone will think of such attributes
(their own and others') in market terms. This threat of unchecked commodification begets the "domino theory":

> The domino theory assumes that for some things, the noncommodified
> version is morally preferable; it also assumes that the commodified and

noncommodified versions of some interactions cannot coexist. To commodify some things is simply to preclude their noncommodified analogues from existing. Under this theory, the existence of some commodified sexual interactions will contaminate or infiltrate everyone's sexuality so that all sexual relationships will become commodified. If it is morally required that noncommodified sex be possible, market-inalienability of sexuality would be justified.[9]

Radin therefore believes that, ideally, prostitution would be prohibited (sex would be market-inalienable) because this rule would best promote human flourishing. However, recognizing that our world is not ideal, she evaluates market-inalienability within a social context of unequal power and resources.

In our nonideal world, Radin sees prostitution as one practice that should be commodified incompletely (regulated) rather than prohibited entirely. Radin is motivated by concern for women who sell sexual services because they lack better alternatives; for example, she observes that it is more humane to let a woman sell sex than to require that her children starve.[10] Similarly, in nonideal circumstances, prohibiting prostitution for the benefit of women in general or society as a whole may not be effective, because noncommodification may simply solidify preexisting gender inequality.[11] Thus Radin concludes that, under current conditions, some criminal penalties for prostitution should be eliminated. To prevent the domino effect of "an organized market in sexual services,"[12] however, she advocates measures such as prohibiting brokering/pimping, recruitment, training, advertising, and contract enforcement.[13] In essence, then, she favors one form of legalization—stringent regulation of prostitution —in a nonideal world such as ours.

A more considered analysis of commodification's real-world effects, as well as closer attention to those whose flourishing is most debilitated under current conditions, indicate that there is good reason to allow commodification in the prostitution context. However, because the best approach, decriminalization (complete commodification), is unlikely, I argue that regulation should prioritize prostitute welfare and empowerment, not antiproliferation.

Gifts, Sales, and Other Exchanges

Several aspects of commodification require greater scrutiny in order to assess its consequences accurately. One such subject is the distinction between sales and other transfers (such as gifts), which some commentators overstate. Radin, for example, argues,

> To relinquish something to someone else by gift is to give of yourself. Such a gift takes place within a personal relationship with the recipient, or else it creates one. Commodification stresses separateness . . . between ourselves and other people. To postulate personal interrelationship and communion requires us to postulate people who can yield personal things to other people and not have them instantly become fungible. Seen this way, gifts diminish separateness. This is why . . . people say that sex bought and paid for is not the same "thing" as sex freely shared. Commodified sex leaves the parties as separate individuals and perhaps reinforces their separateness; they only engage in it if each individual considers it worthwhile. Noncommodified sex ideally diminishes separateness; it is conceived of as a union because it is ideally a sharing of selves.[14]

This stark distinction between gifts and sales cannot account for anonymous gifts, which may neither create nor further personal relationships, nor for gifts that reinforce separation or hierarchy, such as tips to a doorman.[15] It ignores the fact that many gifts are instrumental and obligatory in nature, not altruistic,[16] as well as the way that sales between friends often occur precisely because of, and indeed may strengthen, a preexisting relationship. Finally, it fails to recognize that sales between friends often involve a *combination* of gift (the reduction in price, the "great deal") and sale (the exchange of money for goods or services).

Anonymous charitable contributions, self-interested gifts to political parties, low-interest loans from parents to children, and myriad other examples demonstrate that commodification does not always involve profit-seeking and selfishness, nor does gift-giving invariably entail interpersonal sharing and altruism. As such, it appears *un*necessary "to postulate people who can yield personal things to other people and not have them instantly become fungible" in order to ensure "interrelationship and communion."[17] For example, in the spirit of friendship I may yield my labor, a personal thing, to another in helping to paint her kitchen. I might also sell my labor as a professional home-painter. The fact that my labor is somewhat fungible need not diminish the significance or quality of my gift. Similarly, I may develop a lifelong, intimate friendship with a person I first met in an economic context. In short, self-interest and altruism are not always polar opposites. Instead, self-interested exchange can coexist with or even contribute to relationship and intimacy.[18]

Moreover, just as rhetoric shapes reality, so does reality shape our understanding and use of rhetoric, including economic rhetoric. Viviana Zelizer explains, "noneconomic factors . . . constrain, limit, and shape money and the market. . . . The process of rationalization and commodification of the modern world has its limits, as money and the market are transformed by social, moral, and sacred values."[19] Money itself "is neither culturally neutral nor socially anonymous. It may well 'corrupt' values and convert social ties into numbers, but values and social relations reciprocally transmute money by investing it with meaning and social patterns."[20] Zelizer's work demonstrates that the power of market arrangements and vocabulary are frequently exaggerated. She also shows that commodification involves not just one economic rhetoric, but many.[21]

These considerations apply to a comparison of commodified and non-commodified sex. While Radin argues that noncommodified sex ideally involves sharing, in the nonideal world there is plenty of noncommercial sex that neither involves much sharing (in the sense Radin means) nor diminishes separateness. Less obviously, perhaps, commercial sex sometimes does involve sharing and diminish separateness. Clients sometimes patronize prostitutes precisely for the human connection afforded, using sex simply as the means to or the pretext for closeness.[22] Commodified sex can also be altruistic. Just as an overworked physician might see an extra patient for benevolent, nonmonetary reasons, but still charge the patient, so might a prostitute see a client when she preferred not to, as a favor to him, and still accept payment. Prostitutes report doing this, especially for favorite clients.[23] Indeed, the facts that prostitutes have repeat business and favorite clients themselves indicate that interpersonal relationships are sometimes established through commodified sex,[24] just as they may be established in other commodified exchanges.

In short, the line between gifts and sales frequently is not a bright one. Some sales have gift-like characteristics or consequences, and some gifts have sale-like attributes or results. As for interpersonal relations, commodified transactions do not always reinforce separation, and gift-giving does not always promote closeness. If the two categories are not always easily distinguished, even in regard to sexual exchanges, then this objection to commodified sex is flawed.

Sexuality and Flourishing

There is other evidence that commodified and noncommodified sex may comfortably coexist. Some "radical sex" advocates,[25] queer theorists, and sex workers, among others, argue that a variety of consensual sexual activities can enhance interpersonal communion, such as fantasy and role-playing, or dominance and submission. While such practices do not interest all sexually active adults, for those who engage in them, or in commercial sex, can we confidently say they should be restricted to so-called "vanilla sex"? In other words, can we be confident that flourishing is promoted by restricting unorthodox sexual expression between consenting adults? Or would we be more confident in calling these restrictions paternalistic and heterosexist?[26] Although many people develop strong interpersonal bonds through monogamous, conventional sexual expression, others forge equally deep connections via different sexual routes. Because these variations seem to coexist successfully,[27] commodification-based objections to prostitution appear mistaken.

Moreover, the ideal of sexuality as interpersonal sharing likely also reflects a mistaken belief that "mere" physical, sexual gratification is base and unimportant. In reality, physical pleasure probably promotes flourishing. Most of us would agree that some physical pleasures—such as physical exertion, adrenaline, taste, comfort, health, fitness, or nonsexual touch—at least in moderation, and whether commodified or not, should be available to all as part of a rich conception of human flourishing. The experience of consensual sexual gratification, even without interpersonal sharing, likely also belongs in this list.[28]

In addition, in our nonideal world some individuals may be limited to a choice between commodified sex and involuntary celibacy.[29] Prostitution and other commodified sexual exchanges offer such individuals options many of them feel are much better than the alternative.[30] For others, commodified pleasure offers a respite from drudgery and pain. Just as capitalist commodification may enhance freedom in comparison to serfdom—a peasant allowed to pay a levy in money instead of specific goods had some choice of livelihood,[31] even if his flourishing remained limited in other ways—so too may commodified sexual pleasure represent an advance over noncommodified nonpleasure. If our analysis seeks to examine the real world and to foreground commodification's effects on society's marginal or disadvantaged members, then the possibility that commodification may improve their lot is extremely important. Unless we are entirely confident that unwanted celibacy or unsatisfying noncommercial sex promotes flourishing more than commodified sex does, we should keep these people in mind when analyzing the proper sociolegal response to prostitution.

Sexuality and/as Work

The possibility that commodified and noncommodified sex may comfortably coexist is bolstered by the coexisting economic and noneconomic aspects of work. Like sex, work is integral to personhood, yet work is incompletely commodified. (That is, although we receive money for it, work is regulated rather than entirely free of legal restraints.)[32] Radin suggests that this incomplete commodification represents social recognition that work has personal significance apart from its economic value to us. She proposes that things like "collective bargaining, minimum wage requirements, maximum hour limitations, health and safety requirements, unemployment insurance, retirement benefits, prohibition of child labor, and antidiscrimination requirements"[33] be understood as measures designed to respect "workers' . . . personhood, to recognize and foster the nonmarket significance of their work. . . ."[34]

By promoting safety and providing security for hard times, such regulations do recognize workers' essential humanity. However, it is doubtful that the regulations intend to advance or succeed in advancing work's "nonmarket significance." In fact, some regulations, such as minimum wage laws, may apply mainly to jobs that have little personal significance for workers.[35] If the regulations are not related to human flourishing in the way Radin imagines, then it is hard to maintain that work is less commodified than other things. After all, goods and services are also extensively regulated. Consider food and product safety laws or informed consent requirements: like workplace regulations, these provisions certainly protect basic health, safety, and dignity. But it is improbable that toasters, for example, are incompletely commodified "to recognize and foster [their] nonmarket significance" to their users.

Examining protectionist laws reinforces this argument. Protectionist labor legislation seeks to shield those who are incapable of fully protecting themselves from workplace injury, exploitation, and other harms. Restrictions on child labor are one example. Despite Radin's claim, such laws are not meant to promote work's "nonmarket significance" for children since, in general, children are not supposed to work. Rather, these laws simply minimize harm. Another example is the set of protectionist laws passed in the nineteenth and early twentieth centuries that, among other things, excluded women from some occupations and limited their hours in others. Despite claims of protection, these laws actually functioned more to subordinate and restrict women by depicting them as vulnerable, dependent, and maternal.[36] At best, these laws evince an extremely cabined view of women's flourishing. Designed primarily to protect women's reproductive and nurturing capacities to ensure the physical, intellectual, and emotional health of the next generation, these laws did not "enhance work's non-market significance" for women, but instead sought to reinforce sociolegal norms about women's proper social and familial roles. These examples demonstrate that the incomplete commodification of work, by itself, reveals little about the conditions necessary for flourishing.

Yet often work does have nonmarket significance, as Radin observes.[37] Thus, the earlier comparison of work and consumer goods is not an argument that work has or should have no more personal significance than toasters. Rather, the comparison demonstrates that work is nearly as commodified as toasters are but has personal significance that appliances generally do not.

What does this observation imply for prostitution? Prostitution is, for most prostitutes, also work, not recreation. If some work can be partially commodified and still have personal significance, why not prostitution? Some would answer that prostitution is different because selling sex involves something much more personal than selling the ability to type, for example. Yet wisdom is an important personal attribute along with work and sexuality,[38] and many people "sell" their wisdom in performing their jobs, such as consultants, physicians, and professors.[39] If one personal attribute can be safely "sold" *as work* for most people, so might another. Even thinking of prostitution as primarily sex, not work, the analogy still holds. If work is important to personhood and can be incompletely commodified, so might sexuality. In sum, commodification apparently does not shape our world to the extent commodification critics fear. Market rhetoric coexists with other rhetorics, commodified transactions are gift-like in some circumstances, work is nearly as commodified as toasters, and we are able to tell the difference between them. Thus, commodified sexuality need not imperil noncommodified sexuality.[40]

Fungibility, Loss, and Empowerment: Diversity Revisited

Recognizing that sexuality and wisdom are personal attributes used in paid work raises another question about common definitions of commodification. Radin argues,

> To understand [things integral to personhood] as monetizable or completely detachable from the person—to think, for example, that the value of one person's moral commitments is commensurate or fungible with those of another, or that the "same" person remains when her moral commitments are subtracted—is to do violence to our deepest understanding of what it is to be human.[41]

This definition begs the question whether things such as sexuality and wisdom are really lost, subtracted, or detached when they are sold. Tangible items like cars, homes, and toasters generally are detached when sold. However, attributes like wisdom and sexuality are different sorts of commodities. What is sold by an expert witness, for example, is a package of services involving wisdom, analysis, and testimony. Her wisdom itself is shared, not lost. Indeed, it may even be amplified by being applied to a new fact situation during this sale. Thus, not everything that is nominally "for sale" is really lost to its original owner when it is traded on the market.

Sexuality is also shared rather than transferred when money changes hands. The prostitute sells sexual services, not the whole of her sexuality. (Otherwise she could profitably engage in prostitution only once.) Certainly, the person selling wisdom or sex may be changed by the experience, since experience changes us. But certainly the experience of sharing wisdom may enhance the seller's life, even if, or perhaps because, she was paid to do so. The same is true for sex. Although some prostitutes report negative consequences for their self-development from their experiences in prostitution, others report feelings of empowerment, self-awareness, and autonomy.[42] Thus, it is simply not true that all sales of wisdom or sexuality involve a loss of something integral to self.

The experiences of male prostitutes underscore this point. Although often overlooked, male prostitution is clearly germane to an evaluation of commodified sexuality. While prostitutes' job satisfaction is difficult to quantify, some evidence indicates that many male prostitutes—particularly those who self-identify as gay—find their senses of self enhanced in prostitution, not diminished.[43] In other words, many male prostitutes do not experience prostitution as involving a loss of something integral to self. (As just noted, many female prostitutes make the same claim. However, men's claims that they are not exploited are usually accepted more readily than similar claims by women.)[44] Moreover, for men or women whose flourishing is *not* enhanced through prostitution, it remains unclear whether selling sexual services is the culprit,[45] or whether prostitution's *illegality* is responsible for their plight.[46] In sum, it depends on the person and her/his circumstances and experiences whether selling sex involves a loss of anything, or whether it fosters self-development.

The issue of loss of something integral to self is problematic for another reason. While commodifying personal attributes may be dangerous, it is also dangerous to categorize them as essential to personhood. If certain things are essential to personhood, are people without those attributes less human? Are rape victims less human, or people with cognitive disabilities? Most people (including Radin) would answer in the negative.[47] If, then, a rape survivor or a person with severe dementia is no less human than others, are things like bodily integrity and character always essential to personhood? Some might say that if a person has such things she/he should not trade them on the market, but that if a person lacks them, loses them involuntarily, or altruistically gives them up, she/he is still fully human. A better response is that what is integral to personhood varies somewhat from person to person, and often over time in the same person. What is integral to personhood also varies by culture.[48] Thus, the equation between sex and self, work and self, or bodily integrity and self appear ethnocentric and essentialist,[49] giving us cause to distrust any rigid schema of items integral to personhood. We can conclude that trading sex for money does not invariably mean a person's self-development has been or will be impaired.

If we concede that it depends on the person whether sexuality is integral to her personhood, are we capitulating to a view that life for some is inevitably nasty, brutish, and short? Many (possibly including Radin) would suggest that in a better world, every adult would experience sexuality as communion and interpersonal sharing. If this is correct, then those who do not now experience sexuality in this way have been deprived of something that enriches human life. The question is whether this position is informed by a valid conception of flourishing or is instead paternalistic. Consider those who are voluntarily celibate, for religious or secular reasons. In this case, it does seem paternalistic for outsiders to decide that interpersonal sexual sharing is essential to everyone. That being the case, where and how do we draw the line? What about sexually active people who do not consider sexuality vital to their selfhood?

Unless we are completely certain that an enumerated list of things integral to personhood is accurate, respect for cultural variation, individual autonomy, and diverse (though perhaps not unbounded) conceptions of human flourishing dictate allowing the individual some room to decide for herself what is most important to her. If sexuality is not one of those things, then she may not be harmed by its commodification. Others may not be harmed by her commodified sexuality, either. Where what is integral to self varies, and where most people recognize that fact, all-or-nothing concerns are much less salient. In this situation, the commodification of some sexual acts is not likely to contaminate all sexual relations, mitigating the market rhetoric problem of commodification. That is, the domino theory need not apply to sexuality.

Is the Domino Effect Really a House of Cards?

Discussing her concerns that commodified sex could produce a domino effect, Radin speculates,

> What if sex were fully and openly commodified? Suppose newspapers, radio, TV, and billboards advertised sexual services as imaginatively and vividly as they advertise . . . soft drinks. Suppose the sexual partner of your choice could be ordered through a catalog. . . . Suppose the business of recruiting suppliers of sexual services was carried on in the same way as corporate headhunting. . . .
>
> If sex were openly commodified in this way, its commodification would be reflected in everyone's discourse about sex, and in particular about women's sexuality. New terms would emerge for particular grada-

tions of market value. . . . With this change in discourse, when it became pervasive enough, would come a change in everyone's experience, because experience is discourse[-]dependent. The open market might render an understanding of women (and perhaps everyone) in sexual dollar value impossible to avoid. It might make the ideal of nonmonetized sexual sharing impossible.[50]

She concludes, "complete commodification . . . may foreclose our conception of sexuality entirely."[51]

These concerns are misplaced. At least three considerations undermine the threat of contaminated sexuality foretold by the domino theory.

Commodification Contained

First, we have evidence that preexisting commodified versions of things have not foreclosed the development of noncommodified versions. For example, historically marriage was mainly an economic exchange between families and communities, as evidenced by things like dowries, bride-price, and inheritance laws. This view of marriage now competes with the companionate marriage ideal, with the latter prevailing in much of the world. A similar process occurred in the United States (and elsewhere) in regard to children: in the late nineteenth century, children began to be valued in "sacred" and "sentimental" terms rather than in the explicit economic terms of an earlier period.[52] These two examples illustrate that even as capitalism and commodity markets have expanded and entrenched, economic rhetoric and thinking have neither wholly replaced noneconomic valuations, nor prevented the ascendance of competing ideologies.[53] Put more simply, the existence of a more-commodified form of something has not precluded the genesis or spread of less-commodified forms.[54]

As for commodified sexuality, despite the parade of horribles such as ordering sexual partners through catalogs, it is hard to imagine sexuality becoming much more commodified than it already is.[55] Sex is currently commodified, fully or partially, through legal products and services including film, Internet, and print pornography, strip clubs and peep shows, telephone sex services, sex therapy and sexual surrogacy, bathhouses, sex clubs, and sexuality workshops. Prostitution, although illegal and stigmatized, is widespread. Yet noneconomic rhetoric and ideals about sexuality persist. It thus is doubtful that legal prostitution would have profoundly negative effects on human sexuality. Indeed, there is little evidence that male sexuality, gay or straight, has been tainted even slightly by male prostitution, despite its long history.[56] Moreover, because we already live in a consumer culture involving pervasive commodification, trying to protect people from having commodified senses of self by prohibiting commodification in specific instances (such as those involving sexual services) may be futile.[57]

Commodified and noncommodified sexuality can coexist in part because most people recognize the existence of "commodity contexts."[58] That is, things often do not possess permanent identities as commodities, but exist in multiple settings, both commercial and noncommercial. The legitimation of prostitution thus might simply promote greater social appreciation of the diversity of sexual experiences and options, by clarifying that prostitution represents a commodity context for sex, which exists alongside other contexts, both economic and noneconomic, for sexual expression. The domino theory posits a simple, linear world. Our world is more complex, characterized by both-and, not either-or.

Prostitute Agency

The second challenge to the domino theory rests in human agency. That is, even if prostitutes were obtained through catalogs, customers would still interact sexually with a real person, not with an idealized, mute, pornographic image. Just as men who marry mail-order brides are often surprised by their new wives' independence—far from bride catalogs' imagery of subservience and docility—so too are some customers surprised when prostitutes control the sexual transaction. Those who patronized prostitutes, even through catalogs, would often be quickly disabused of the image of prostitutes as willing sex slaves. Sex is not truly fungible when it is sold in prostitution because of prostitutes' individuality and agency.[59] The domino effect, therefore, is less likely to materialize under complete or partial commodification (decriminalization or legalization) than some fear.

Benefits of Commodification

Third, the domino theory overlooks potential positive social changes from commodification. One important benefit of commodification could be a reduction in forced prostitution. While the size of this problem is disputed,[60] even a single instance of forced prostitution (or any forced labor) constitutes involuntary servitude or slavery, and thus severely diminishes victims' flourishing.

The criminalization of prostitution in most of the world greatly contributes to involuntary prostitution and trafficking. Although not all would-be voluntary prostitutes are deterred by criminal sanctions, criminalization does limit the number of prostitution practitioners. Indeed, deterrence is a primary justification for criminalization, even if it works imperfectly, and the domino theory is predicated in part on deterrence (the theory posits that absent legal restriction, supply of and demand for prostitutes would surge). However, due to patterns of prostitution law enforcement that are nearly worldwide—enforcement is overwhelmingly concentrated on female prostitutes, not on customers, managers, or male prostitutes[61]—criminalization has unequal deterrent effects.

At present, those who coerce, trick, or force others into prostitution can earn great profits. Were prostitution legal, the likelihood of market saturation by willing providers—since providers are the majority of those deterred by existing laws and enforcement patterns—and the concomitant price competition would reduce, and possibly remove, the profit motive for procurers to victimize others.[62] In addition, where prostitution is illegal, victims of coercion often cannot obtain help. In most places, including international trafficking destinations, prostitutes are considered bad, immoral women, to be arrested rather than assisted, regardless of how they entered the trade.[63] Full or partial commodification could lessen such stigma and promote recognition of involuntary prostitutes as victims of forced labor.[64]

Another benefit of commodification would be that if prostitution were legal, prostitutes could openly discuss their work, describe its pros and cons, demand that abuses cease, seek employment benefits, obtain police protection, and improve working conditions.[65] Customers could frankly discuss their experiences, both in the crass, economic way that commodification critics fear but also in honest terms about what benefits they receive, what risks they take, what needs they seek to fill.[66] Given the secrecy and reticence surrounding sexuality in many cultures, societies could benefit from more open discussion.

Considering prostitution in light of activism surrounding the devaluation of women's unpaid household and family labor also indicates commodification's benefits. Numerous proposals have been made to remunerate women for this work.[67] The fact that compensation is proposed as a way to acknowledge the importance of this work indicates that commodification sometimes *raises* the status of certain human activities.[68] Thus, "corporate headhunting"[69] for sex workers might help everyone appreciate the labor involved in prostitution, both because headhunting indicates social significance, and because headhunters would likely seek *skilled* workers, not just attractive ones. As Radin says, the rhetoric we use helps shape our reality. The rhetoric we now use degrades, marginalizes, and devalues prostitutes (and occasionally their clients). Market rhetoric itself might be only a small improvement, but by displacing the rhetoric of degradation it could open a path to much more significant changes in our thinking.

This, then, is the flip side of commodification. Full or partial commodification of sex (decriminalizing or legalizing prostitution) could vastly improve the lives of prostitutes and also benefit society. By reducing the stigma, isolation, secrecy, danger, and abuses associated with prostitution, commodification could enhance prostitutes' full human flourishing. Moreover, we have strong reason to doubt that prostitution law reform will initiate a cascade of falling dominoes that spell doom for existing ideals about sexuality. While prostitution's increased visibility and legitimacy could change discourse, and thus experience, these changes would be much more complex and contradictory than the domino theory predicts. The domino theory's simple cause-and-effect logic appears particularly specious when we remember the *mutually* constitutive relationship between rhetoric and experience, the existence of multiple discourses of commodification, the diversity of human understanding and experience, the human capacity for resistance to power, and the potential for law reform to empower subjugated groups. The decriminalization or legalization of prostitution would be valuable for everyone, if indeed many of commodification's adverse effects are already with us, and the positive ones have yet to be realized. Prostitutes' lives would be significantly improved, while society would experience at most a negligible increase in commodified sexual images and rhetoric along with many improvements in other social relations.

Prostitution Law Reform

To prevent the domino effect, Radin advocates the incomplete commodification (legal regulation) of prostitution, specifically, the prohibition of brokering/pimping, recruitment, training, advertising, and contract enforcement. These proposals reflect incomplete analyses of both commodification generally, and prostitution specifically.

Prostitutes report that this kind of incomplete commodification, as practiced in Canada, Great Britain, New Zealand, and elsewhere, is not much better than complete criminalization.[70] Almost everything that facilitates the practice of prostitution is prohibited, so although the actual exchange of sex for money is legal, prostitution remains "illegal in all but name"[71] and engenders nearly the same level of abuse of prostitutes as under full criminalization. Radin's antiproliferation regulations thus would perpetuate prostitutes' marginalization and inhibit their flourishing. Yet Radin proposes incomplete commodification precisely to *improve* the lot of the most vulnerable prostitutes in the real world; in an ideal world, she would prohibit prostitution entirely. Sadly, her regulations cannot satisfy her real-world objective.

Legal regulation informed by a fuller appreciation of commodification and prostitution in the real world would look very different than Radin's version. Instead of trying to limit prostitution's proliferation, the law could regulate prostitution like other work. For example, prostitutes could be protected by OSHA regulations, allowed to organize, and made eligible for employment-related benefits.[72] Such changes could have far-reaching symbolic, as well as material, consequences—but not those feared by commodification critics. Like social and market rhetoric, legal rhetoric helps shape our thinking.[73] Existing criminal laws against prostitution reinforce stigma, whether that criminalization is complete (sex is market-inalienable) or partial (sex is incompletely commodified). Legal recognition of prostitutes as workers with shared interests in safety, benefits, and professionalism could go far in reshaping current conceptions,[74] without harming the larger society.[75]

Conclusion: The Centrality of Empirical Data and Heterogeneity

Many analyses of commodified sex are inadequate because they are insufficiently informed by actual lived experience, and by variation in lived experience. In seeking the best rules governing prostitution, analysis should account for the experiences of prostitutes, both female and male, and their clients.[76] This is not to suggest that prostitutes alone be allowed to make the rules, nor that our own judgment as prostitution outsiders (if we are such) be suspended. Instead, this is an argument that more comprehensive investigation of possibilities and experiences enhances everyone's judgment.

As we have seen, commodification critics are concerned not just about how selling sex affects prostitutes' senses of self but about the social effect—the effect on the rest of us—when anyone's sexuality is commodified. Their reasoning would be more persuasive if supported by actual experience: Where prostitution is legal, is sexuality discussed in market rhetoric? If not, why not? Is the status of women in such countries lower than it is where prostitution is illegal? Although we lack definitive answers, the experience so far in those European and Australian jurisdictions with legal prostitution suggests that it has neither diminished women's social status, nor made market valuations of sexuality any more common than they are, for example, in the U.S.[77]

Similarly, have commodified love, sexuality, marriages, family relationships, or personhood resulted from practices like awarding money damages for pain and suffering, loss of consortium, and wrongful death, or compensating women upon divorce for unpaid household and family labor?[78] Inquiries like these would assist us in evaluating the domino theory. For example, there is little evidence that child wrongful-death awards have made even a significant minority of parents (or nonparents) think about children as commodities.[79] Similarly, while the availability of life insurance likely helps commodify human life, most people appear not to think about their spouses primarily in terms of "what is she/he worth to me dead?" (Indeed, we prosecute, punish, and denounce those few individuals who kill to collect insurance proceeds.)

Both reasoning and evidence indicate that commodified and noncommodified sexuality and rhetoric coexist without diminishing human flourishing. Indeed, this diversity and coexistence may actually *enhance* flourishing in other areas of life. Regarding one prostitution law reform proposal, Laurie Shrage suggests,

> In arguing for socialist and feminist regulationism in regard to prostitution, perhaps we provide a model for pressing for socialist and feminist regulation of other industries as well. If we no longer treat sex com-

merce as an evil produced by capitalism and patriarchy, but see the evil in the way sex commerce is produced and shaped in a classist, sexist, and racist society, then we should develop social policies that attempt to reshape it in anti-classist, anti-sexist, and anti-racist ways. . . . In short, perhaps in the future we can offer a more humane, feminist and socialist sex industry as a model for other kinds of labor reform.[80]

In regard to prostitution, embracing commodification and legitimation have more merit than fearing them, restricting them, and disempowering people.[81] Excessive caution about commodification does not do justice to the complexity, variety, and resilience of societies and individuals, and overlooks commodification's potential for positive social transformation. Moreover, unwarranted fear of commodification may contribute to the reification of concepts like the madonna/whore dichotomy, to the benefit of none and the detriment of all—especially prostitutes, promiscuous women, and other sexual "deviants" on the disfavored side of the line.

NOTES

I thank Kristin Luker, Marjorie Shultz, Reva Siegel, Christine Littleton, Brooke Bedrick, Mark Harris, Laura Beth Nielsen, Kaaryn Gustafson, KT Albiston, Bronwen Morgan, Amy Toro, Tom Scanlon, Brad Roth, Tom Ginsburg, the late Noah Baum, Rob Hennig, Sue Ochi, Rob Katsura, Valerie Margolis, Joe Quirk, Alfonso Morales, Patricia Ewick, Martha Nussbaum, Barbara Sullivan, Carolyn Patty Blum, participants in the Feminism and Critical Race Theory seminar at Boalt Hall, and participants in the Commodification Futures conference in Denver for comments and sources; conference organizers Joan Williams, Martha Ertman, and Adrienne Davis; Martha Ertman for thoughtful editing; and Georgina Romero, Nancy Flores, and Georgie Unwin for research assistance.

1. Cecilie Høigård & Liv Finstad, Backstreets: Prostitution, Money and Love 40 (Katherine Hanson et al. trans., 1992).

2. Margaret Jane Radin, *Market-Inalienability,* 100 Harv. L. Rev. 1849 (1987) [hereinafter Radin, *Market-Inalienability*]; Margaret Jane Radin, Contested Commodities: The Trouble with Trade in Sex, Children, Body Parts, and Other Things (1996) [hereinafter Radin, Contested Commodities]. I refer to Radin and like scholars as "commodification critics."

3. Sylvia A. Law, *Commercial Sex: Beyond Decriminalization,* 73 S. Cal. L. Rev. 523, 554 (2000).

4. Radin, Contested Commodities, *supra* note 2, at 56, 87–88.

5. *Id.* at 88.

6. *Id.* at 16.

7. Radin, *Market Inalienability, supra* note 2, at 1870.

8. *Id.* at 1899.

9. Radin, Contested Commodities, *supra* note 2, at 95. However, Radin recognizes that *some* sexual relationships have both economic and noneconomic aspects. *Id.* at 134.

10. Radin, *Market Inalienability, supra* note 2, at 1910–11.

11. *Id.* at 1916.

12. *Id.* at 1924.

13. Radin, Contested Commodities, *supra* note 2, at 135–36.

14. Radin, *Market Inalienability, supra* note 2, at 1907–8 (citations omitted).

15. Viviana Zelizer, The Social Meaning of Money 78 (1997).

16. Marcel Mauss, The Gift (W. D. Halls trans., 1990) (1950).

17. Radin, Contested Commodities, *supra* note 2, at 94.

18. Marjorie Maguire Shultz, *Contractual Ordering of Marriage: A New Model for State Policy,* 70 Cal. L. Rev. 204, 263–64 (1982).

19. Viviana Zelizer, Pricing the Priceless Child: The Changing Social Value of Children 211–12 (1985).

20. Zelizer, *supra* note 15, at 18. Cultural meanings attached to money and exchange vary greatly. *See, e.g.,* Money and the Morality of Exchange (Maurice Bloch & Jonathan Parry eds., 1989); The Social Life of Things: Commodities in Cultural Perspective (Arjun Appadurai ed., 1986). On sex commerce transforming meaning, *see* Laurie Shrage, Moral Dilemmas of Feminism: Prostitution, Adultery and Abortion 110–11, 147 (1994).

21. Zelizer, *supra* note 15, *passim. See also* Maurice Bloch & Jonathan Parry, *Introduction: Money and the Morality of Exchange, in* Money and the Morality of Exchange, *supra* note 20, at 1, 22–23; Stephen J. Schnably, *Property and Pragmatism: A Critique of Radin's Theory of Property and Personhood,* 45 Stan. L. Rev. 347, 385 (1993).

22. *See, e.g.,* Dolores French, Working: My Life as a Prostitute 29 (1988); Carol Queen, *Toward a Taxonomy of Tricks: A Whore Considers the Age-Old Question, "What Do Clients Want?," in* Tricks and Treats: Sex Workers Write about Their Clients 105, 112–13 (Matt Bernstein Sycamore ed., 2000); Ann M. Lucas, The Dis(-)ease of Being a Woman: Rethinking Prostitution and Subordination 305–8 (1998) (unpublished Ph.D. dissertation, University of California, Berkeley); Sallie Tisdale, Talk Dirty to Me: An Intimate Philosophy of Sex 187 (1994); Janet Lever & Deanne Dolnick, *Clients and Call Girls: Seeking Sex and Intimacy, in* Sex for Sale: Prostitution, Pornography, and the Sex Industry 85 (Ronald Weitzer ed., 2000); Alexa Albert, Brothel: Mustang Ranch and Its Women 100, 105 (2001). *See also* Martin A. Monto, *Why Men Seek Out Prostitutes, in* Sex for Sale, *supra,* at 67, 77–81.

23. *See generally* French, *supra* note 22, at 72; Albert, *supra* note 22, at 100–105; Lever & Dolnick, *supra* note 22, at 97–100.

24. *See, e.g.,* Sunny Carter, *A Most Useful Tool, in* Sex Work: Writings by Women in the Sex Industry 159, 164 (Frédérique Delacoste & Priscilla Alexander eds., 2d ed. 1998); Carolyn Sleighthholme & Indrani Sinha, Guilty Without Trial: Women in the Sex Trade in Calcutta 115–16 (1996); Lucas, *supra* note 22, at 311–15.

25. Pat Califia, Public Sex: The Culture of Radical Sex (1994).

26. They are heterosexist if they presume "good" sexuality mirrors serially monogamous heterosexuality; stable, committed gay male relationships often accept casual or anonymous sex as an important form of sexual expression. *Cf.* Margaret Davies & Ngaire Naffine, Are Persons Property? Legal Debates About Property and Personality 8 (2001); Shrage, *supra* note 20, at 51; Shultz, *supra* note 18, at 247; Marjorie Maguire Shultz, *Reproductive Technology and Intent-Based Parenthood: An Opportunity for Gender Neutrality,* 1990 Wis. L. Rev. 297, 348.

27. *See* Shrage, *supra* note 20, at 79.

28. *See generally* Martha Nussbaum, Sex & Social Justice 292 (1999).

29. *See, e.g.,* Hugh Gene Loebner, *Being a John, in* Prostitution: On Whores, Hustlers, and Johns 221, 221 (James E. Elias et al. eds., 1998).

30. *See, e.g., id.*; Janet Radcliffe Richards, The Sceptical Feminist 200 (1980), *quoted in* Shrage, *supra* note 20, at 96; Califia, *supra* note 25, at 245.

31. Bloch & Parry, *supra* note 21, at 5.

32. Radin, Contested Commodities, *supra* note 2, at 104–9.

33. *Id.* at 108.

34. *Id.* at 109.

35. Radin recognizes that some work lacks personal significance for the worker. *Id.* at 106.

36. *See, e.g.,* Judith Baer, The Chains of Protection: The Judicial Response to Women's Labor Legislation (1978); Ronnie Steinberg Ratner, *The Paradox of Protection: Maximum Hours Legislation in the United States,* 119 Int'l Lab. Rev. 185 (1980); Mary E. Becker, *From* Muller v. Oregon *to Fetal Vulnerability Policies,* 53 U. Chi. L. Rev. 1219, 1221–25 (1986).

37. Radin, Contested Commodities, *supra* note 2, at 104–6.

38. *Id.* at 56, 87–88.

39. Lucas, *supra* note 22, at 71; Nussbaum, *supra* note 28, at 283–84, 291–92.

40. Using different reasoning, Schnably also reaches this conclusion. Schnably, *supra* note 21, at 353, 379, 392–97.

41. Radin, Contested Commodities, *supra* note 2, at 56.

42. *See, e.g.,* Lucas, *supra* note 22, at 290–94, 298–99; French, *supra* note 22, at 16-17, 38, 147, 179, 276.

43. *See, e.g.*, Julian Marlowe, *It's Different for Boys, in* Whores and Other Feminists 141, 142 (Jill Nagle ed., 1997); Ann M. Lucas, *Hustling for Money: Male Prostitutes' Experiences of Social Control, in* For the Common Good: A Critical Examination of Law and Social Control 188, 198–202 (R. Robin Miller & Sandra Lee Browning eds., 2004).

44. Marlowe, *supra* note 43, at 142.

45. *See* Debra Satz, *Markets in Women's Sexual Labor,* 106 Ethics 63, 78, 81 (1995).

46. *See, e.g.*, Duncan Kennedy, *Sexual Abuse, Sexy Dressing, and the Eroticization of Domination, in* Sexy Dressing Etc. 126, 137 (1993); Richards, *supra* note 30, at 199, *quoted in* Shrage, *supra* note 20, at 97.

47. Radin analyzes rape extensively. Radin, Contested Commodities, *supra* note 2, at 88.

48. *See* Barbara Sullivan, *Rethinking Prostitution, in* Transitions: New Australian Feminisms 184 (Barbara Caine & Rosemary Pringle eds., 1995). *Cf.* Nussbaum, *supra* note 28, at 278–80; Schnably, *supra* note 21, at 362–75.

49. Sullivan, *supra* note 48. *Cf.* Shrage, *supra* note 20, at 79, 168; Satz, *supra* note 45, at 71; Califia, *supra* note 25.

50. Radin, Contested Commodities, *supra* note 2, at 133.

51. *Id.* at 134.

52. Zelizer, *supra* note 19.

53. *Id.*

54. *See* The Social Life of Things, *supra* note 20; C. Toren, *Drinking Cash: The Purification of Money through Ceremonial Exchange in Fiji, in* Money and the Morality of Exchange, *supra* note 20, at 142, 150. Radin notes that commodified and noncommodified versions of some things coexist, see Radin, *Market Inalienability, supra* note 2, at 1923 n.260, but says commodified and noncommodified sex cannot.

55. *See, e.g.*, Schnably, *supra* note 21, at 385 & n.181, 390–91.

56. Marlowe, *supra* note 43, at 142.

57. *Cf.* Schnably, *supra* note 21, at 392.

58. Arjun Appadurai, *Introduction: Commodities and the Politics of Value, in* The Social Life of Things, *supra* note 20, at 3, 13–16.

59. *Cf.* Nussbaum, *supra* note 28, at 292.

60. *See, e.g.*, Alison Murray, *Debt-Bondage and Trafficking: Don't Believe the Hype, in* Global Sex Workers: Rights, Resistance, and Redefinition 51 (Kamala Kempadoo & Jo Doezema eds., 1998).

61. *See, e.g.*, Priscilla Alexander, *Prostitution: Still a Difficult Issue for Feminists, in* Sex Work, *supra* note 24, at 184, 205; Deborah L. Rhode, Justice and Gender: Sex Discrimination and the Law 261 (1989); Robert Gemme, *Legal and Sexological Aspects of Adult Street Prostitution: A Case for Sexual Pluralism, in* Prostitution, *supra* note 29, at 474; Marjan Wijers, *Women, Labor and Migra-*

tion: The Position of Trafficked Women and Strategies for Support, in Global
Sex Workers, *supra* note 60, at 69, 73; Sullivan, *supra* note 48, at 194.

62. Child prostitution and trafficking might not diminish, as child prostitution would properly remain criminalized.

63. *See* Wijers, *supra* note 61, at 72; Ann Lucas, *Women and Prostitution, in* Women and International Human Rights Law 683, 694 & n.52 (Kelly D. Askin & Dorean M. Koenig eds., 1999); Nussbaum, *supra* note 28, at 289.

64. *Cf.* Jo Bindman, *An International Perspective on Slavery in the Sex Industry, in* Global Sex Workers, *supra* note 60, at 65.

65. *See* Shrage, *supra* note 20, at 160–61.

66. *See, e.g.,* Jim Korn, *My Sexual Encounters with Sex Workers: The Effects on a Consumer, in* Prostitution, *supra* note 29, at 204; Loebner, *supra* note 29.

67. *See, e.g.,* Reva B. Siegel, *Home as Work: The First Woman's Rights Claims Concerning Wives' Household Labor, 1850–1880,* 103 Yale L.J. 1073 (1994); Katharine Silbaugh, *Commodification and Women's Household Labor,* 9 Yale J.L. & Feminism 81 (1997); Martha M. Ertman, *Commercializing Marriage: A Proposal for Valuing Women's Work Through Premarital Security Agreements,* 77 Tex. L. Rev. 17 (1998); Joan Williams, *Un*bending Gender: Why Family and Work Conflict and What to Do about It 114–41 (2000).

68. *See* Shultz, *supra* note 18, at 221; Shultz, *supra* note 26, at 336–37, 380.

69. Radin, Contested Commodities, *supra* note 2, at 133.

70. *See, e.g.,* Jody Freeman, *The Feminist Debate over Prostitution Reform: Prostitutes' Rights Groups, Radical Feminists, and the (Im)possibility of Consent,* 5 Berkeley Women's L.J. 75, 81–82 (1989–90) (Canada); Neil McKeganey & Marina Barnard, Sex Work on the Streets: Prostitutes and Their Clients 102 (1996) (Britain); Belinda Cooper, *Prostitution: A Feminist Analysis,* 11 Women's Rts. L. Rep. 99, 101 n.8 (1989) (England); Nickie Roberts, Whores in History: Prostitution in Western Society 285 (1992) (France); Gabriela Silva Leite, *Women of the Life, We Must Speak, in* A Vindication of the Rights of Whores 288, 291 (Gail Pheterson ed., 1989) (Brazil). *See generally* Lucas, *supra* note 63, at 702–8; Tisdale, *supra* note 22, at 189–91.

71. McKeganey & Barnard, *supra* note 70, at 102.

72. *Cf.* Priscilla Alexander, *Sex Work and Health: A Question of Safety in the Workplace,* 53 J. Am. Med. Women's Ass'n 77 (1998); Tracy M. Clements, *Prostitution and the American Health Care System: Denying Access to a Group of Women in Need,* 11 Berkeley Women's L.J. 49 (1996). German, Brazilian, Dutch, and Australian prostitutes receive some employment benefits. *See, e.g.,* Erik Schelzig, *Perks for the Oldest Profession; German Law Offers Prostitutes Union Rights, Profit Sharing,* Wash. Post, May 12, 2002, at A13; *Prostitutes Can Draw Social Security in Brazil,* Associated Press, Nov. 22, 2000, *available in* LEXIS; Suzanne Daley, *New Rights for Dutch Prostitutes, But No Gain,* N.Y.

Times, Aug. 12, 2001, at 1; Lainie Barnes, *Red Light Burning Bright,* Advertiser (Adelaide, South Australia), July 27, 2000, at 19, *available in* LEXIS.

73. Radin, Contested Commodities, *supra* note 2, at 202.

74. *Cf.* Shultz, *supra* note 26, at 344.

75. *See* Nussbaum, *supra* note 28, at 288.

76. *See* Shrage, *supra* note 20, at xi.

77. *Cf.* Nussbaum, *supra* note 28, at 290; Schnably, *supra* note 21, at 394–95.

78. Radin explores torts philosophically but not empirically. Radin, Contested Commodities, *supra* note 2, at 184–205.

79. Zelizer, *supra* note 19, at 163, 167, 212; Zelizer, *supra* note 15, at 29. *See generally* Shultz, *supra* note 26, at 336.

80. Shrage, *supra* note 20, at 161.

81. Schnably, *supra* note 21, at 397.

2. COMMODIFYING CARE

For Love nor Money
The Commodification of Care

Deborah Stone

American politics has long engaged a lively debate about whether care can and should be commodified. The debate starts with rather more narrow economic questions: Is care a commodity and can it be produced and distributed like one? Should people who do informal, voluntary caregiving be paid for their efforts as they would be for other kinds of work? Should people who need or want caretaking have to purchase it like any other service? The term "commodification" usually refers to this economic sense. But the debate moves swiftly into the realm of politics: Is care a *political good,* and should it be organized like one?

In the political sense, commodification engages three issues. First, should society pay families for caregiving? That is, is it ever proper or necessary to pay parents and grandparents for raising their children, pay spouses for caring for each other, or pay adult children and grandchildren for caring for their elders?

Second, should caregiving count toward meeting the obligations of citizenship? This would mean that in the public economy, personal caregiving could be exchanged for public protection, in the same way that in the private market, personal paid labor can be exchanged for private and public protections. Should public income support programs such as public assistance, Social Security, and health insurance, credit caregiving in the same way they now credit paid work toward eligibility for membership in these collective social safety nets?

Third, is care itself a basic human need, like income, food, and shelter, that ought to be collectively guaranteed to citizens at some minimum level? Is the assurance of adequate care one of the purposes of government? Should government be in the business of provision, production, and distribution of care?

Meanwhile, despite the apparent tentativeness and openness of the debate, much care has already been commodified in both the political and economic senses. To some extent, modern states have answered all three of these political questions in the affirmative. And care has been an economic commodity for a long, long time. We have paid child care, health care, disability care, and elder care in a plethora of forms. A few public programs even pay relatives to take care of their own.

So a puzzle arises: why are we so reluctant to bring care even more into the political economy? Why, as citizens, do we resist paying relatives for home health care, giving allowances to single mothers who care for their kids, giving pensions to women who raise families and iron shirts, and insuring elders for long-term care? These debates are animated by lots of unexamined fears and assumptions. My purpose here is not to address the policy questions but, rather, to skulk around the political and philosophical underground of these care debates to understand the sources of our inchoate collective resistance to commodifying care.

In thinking about these issues, I treat care in a broad sense. I include ordinary child care, elder care, and care for the sick and the disabled. I include care for relatives, friends, and strangers, although, as I will insist, caregiving quickly makes intimates of strangers. For policy planning, it often makes sense to distinguish these different kinds of care, but for understanding what care means to people both psychologically and culturally, I think it is important to look for the commonalities across all kinds of care.

How Is Care Political?

Care is prepolitical. It is the ancient human activity of nurturing children, spouses, friends, parents, the sick and disabled, the elderly, the lonely, the poor, the miserable.[1] To ask about care is to descend below the macrolevel of political systems, below the intermediate level of political institutions, below the microlevel of civil society and social capital, on down to the molecular level of political sentiments, down to loyalty. Loyalty is that most elemental of political sentiments, for politics is all about alliances as well as conflicts.[2] And care is where the seeds of loyalty germinate. People come to develop attachments and bonds in the act of caring for and being cared for. The parents who nurture their infant are no less bonded to it, driven by *its* needs, than the infant is bonded to them, dependent on them for its survival.

We could say care is the basic molecule of social capital. If social capital consists of "social networks and the norms of reciprocity and trustworthiness that arise from them" (as Robert Putnam defines it in *Bowling Alone*),[3] care relationships are where trust, reciprocity, and mutual respect first grow. And it is precisely here, at the place where our deepest yet least understood connections to one another take hold, that the fears and fictions of policy debates begin to form. This is where we need to look to understand what's going on above ground.

The reciprocity of care is not obvious at first; indeed, the word "giving" in "caregiving" suggests a one-way affair. It seems as if the caregiver ministers to physical and emotional needs, and perhaps even decides exactly what help the cared-for person needs before ministering. What, then, does the cared-for person give? Care is reciprocal in a different way than is "tit for tat" exchange. Joan Tronto includes "care-receiving" as a crucial ingredient of care: "The object of care will respond to the care it receives."[4] Put less abstractly, the cared-for person gives to the caregiver a sense of being needed and appreciated, and of making a difference—not a trivial gift. This kind of reciprocity may not be the calculated, premeditated exchange of markets, but care, conceived this way, is reciprocal nonetheless.

And caregivers do perceive this reciprocity. One aide in a nursing home explained to anthropologist Nancy Foner why she gets pleasure from her work: "You're working here. You're saving someone's life. They can't feed themselves, can't dress themselves. I feel I'm helping them."[5] A day care provider told Margaret Nelson, "Cassie [a child] left the other day and told me she loved me. Things like that are the reward. What can you have more than a child who loves you?"[6] One of my neighbors, a retired engineer who, among his many other volunteer activities drives a woman to dialysis once a week, an hour each way, once told me. "I get so much more from her than I give to her. I'm really just selfish." The perception of rewards from caregiving is remarkably common. In Robert Wuthnow's study of helping and caring, 91 percent of survey respondents agreed that "[w]hen you help someone in need, you get as much from it as they do."[7] The common formulation—"I get more than I give"—raises fascinating questions (why, for example, do people define themselves as selfish when they are being their most altruistic selves?), but one thing it surely indicates is the common perception among people who care for others that caregiving is a reciprocal activity.

Care is a realm of touch, tears, frustration, love, anger, fear. We associate caregiving with maternal instinct of the natural world; with families and neighborhoods and face-to-face relations; with intimacy and the feeling of security that comes with intimacy; with spontaneous response to need and suffering, unmediated by rules and rationales. Although much care has already been formalized, both economically and politically, care is still the last bastion of this prepolitical social life, the part that has only relatively recently been hit by "-ization": industrialization, marketization, rationalization, bureaucratization. Thus, caregiving is to the contemporary American psyche what the wilderness and the frontier were to the late nineteenth-century American psyche, and as we see this frontier disappearing, we, too, are gripped with angst.

One set of fears has to do with nostalgia, with what we are losing and have lost—namely, all that is precious about care and that, like wilderness, nurtures us against the noise and policies of modernity. Another set of fears is dystopic and full of dread—dread of all the ways we are capable of neglecting and exploiting on another, just as we have done to our wilderness.

So what *are* the fears? And are they real?

The Fear That Money Will Extinguish Love

Feminist theorists—and others—worry that money will change the very essence of care. Commodifying care might change the relationship between caregiver and cared-for because it would add economic relations to a prior noneconomic relationship. And since the essence of care *is* the relationship, commodification might also change the nature and quality of the care itself. After all, as theorist Elizabeth Anderson writes, market transactions "leave the parties free to switch trading partners at any time," hardly the kind of loyalty one expects in a caregiving relationship. Perhaps more frightening, in market relations, "Each party is expected to take care of herself," for the market assumes self-interested behavior.[8]

If care is brought into the market economy and caregiving is recast as wage labor, the motivation of caregivers might change. They might possibly do it for money instead of for love. If care is motivated by altruism,[9] by a concern for the welfare of the other (and culturally, we certainly wish it that way, even if scientifically we understand that care is sometimes motivated by guilt, necessity, or darker motives still), commodification, we fear, would introduce the motive of self-interest. Caregivers might put their own financial aspirations above the needs of the people they care for. Worse, they might downright abuse their charges, who are now the raw material of their income-producing activity. Writing in the *Wall Street Journal* about a trend toward paying adult children for elder care, Sue Schallenbarber warns, "But there's a vast dark side to this trend. Paid caregiving setups underlie a good chunk of the financial abuse suffered by the elderly. In California, where many aged and disabled people are allowed to pay family caregivers, it's surprisingly common for relatives to take the money and fail to provide the care."[10] The fear here is that in markets, money drives out other more honest and virtuous motivations. People will take the money and run. Markets, we fear, suppress our best natures and evoke our worst.

Experience with care markets demonstrates something extraordinary: Even when people get paid a pittance for taking care of utter strangers in the most physically and emotionally demanding jobs, love creeps in. Study after study of nursing home aides, home health aides, child care workers, nannies and *au pairs,* even domestic workers finds the most amazing alchemy. People who care for strangers, no matter what the pay, commonly fall in love with the people they care for and come to consider them family. They say they love their clients. Even though they have been trained by their teachers and warned by their supervisors and their friends to keep their emotional distance, they inevitably get close to clients and they say things like "You get attached to them," and "You can't help it."[11]

Paid caregivers often come to regard their charges as kin, and commonly say they feel as if the person they take care of is their own mother, sister, brother, child.[12] A family day care provider described her relationship with the children she cares for: "And these children, they are so close to you. You're like a second mom to them. And you being there when they come home after school—you listen to the different little things they want to talk with you about. It becomes a personal thing, where, you know, they can't get to mom right away. But they can get to you."[13] Family day care providers (women who take children into their own homes for pay) might be expected to portray themselves as professional, yet in fact the vast majority see their work as being "like a mother" to the children in their care. They describe their relationships in mother-child terms: "They are my part-time kids"; "I'm like a second mom"; "I think of them as extended members of my family"; "These guys are like my own kids."[14] One nanny told Cameron Macdonald, "I felt those kids were mine."[15] Another nanny, a Filipina working in Washington, D.C., told the *Wall Street Journal* that she calls her American family's child "my baby," and that "I give [her] what I can't give to my children. . . . She makes me feel like a mother."[16] Clients and their families often come to feel the same way about hired caregivers. When I first told the chair of my political science department, Sidney Milkis, about my research on home health care, I expected him to ask me about its connection to political science. Instead, he told me a story. He said his mother had had a home health aide for a long time before she died. At his mother's funeral, he insisted that the aide ride in the limousine with the family. "She was my mother's best friend, the most important person to her, and I wanted her to have a place of honor." When researchers Emily Abel and Margaret Nelson had to decide where to locate their father as he was dying—close to his children, or in his own home with a paid caregiver who had been caring for him for years—they chose to leave him with the person whose relationship at that point in his life was far closer to him than their own.[17] One employer of a domestic told Judith Rollins why she kept employing a woman who routinely came late and didn't clean very well. "It's worth much more to me to have her loyalty and her trust. And know if I'm sick, she'll come and take care of me, know I can count on her being there."[18]

If anything, caregivers resist letting money affect their relations with the people they care for, and even try to deny that money is part of the relationship. They want to pretend money isn't there. In my study of home health care, a retired public health nurse, who was still consulting for a home health agency and was very aware of the current state of the field, told me that when she was in practice, nurses would never discuss money with clients, and never had to. She thought that one of the most difficult features of home health nursing today was that even on the first visit, and often on subsequent ones, nurses are forced into discussing just "how much" care they will be able to provide. They have to go over the patient's insurance and talk about what is covered, for how long, and more painfully, what *isn't* covered, and how quickly the care might terminate. From the get-go, they have to discuss withholding care. Almost every nurse and therapist I interviewed said she hated having to discuss eligibility and time limits with patients. They hate having to puncture the pretense that their caring is unlimited.

Paid caregivers, even the most lowly paid, don't just talk the language of love. They often sacrifice their economic self-interest for the sake of the people they take care of. In my research on home health care, many aides —earning in the neighborhood of $7–10 an hour—told me about purchasing food or other necessities for their poverty-stricken clients, and of visiting and helping clients after hours, on their own time, without pay. Family day care providers often continue to care for children whose parents can't or don't pay because they love the children and can't abandon them.[19] Nannies and *au pairs* sometimes stay in jobs they loathe, accept poor pay and working conditions, and decline to confront their employers because they love "their children."[20] Domestics sometimes continue in financially nonsensical jobs out of attachment to their employer. One Chicana domestic explained to Mary Romero why she continued working for an elderly woman despite low wages and a long commute: "I guess you can say she needs companionship. I feel sorry for her, you know. . . . I go once a month to her house. I like to go early so I can sit and talk to her."[21]

The point is not that all paid caregiving relationships are rosy and loving but that many of them are. These stories are legion, and they suggest that experience contradicts some of the mythology about how market motivation displaces other motivations. Money may distort some caregiving relationships in some ways, but it doesn't have to. Much of the time, despite the fact of pay, people take care of their clients exactly the way they take care of their relatives. And they love them, too. Maybe not exactly the same way, but so often they say they love their clients as if they were "my own."

To be sure, paid caregivers remain acutely aware that they are *not* family. Their relationship with the people they care for could be severed at any time. They do not have claim to ties with their fictive kin in the same way people can usually claim ties to real kin. In her study of family day care providers, Nelson found that many providers develop an attitude of "detached attachment" to protect themselves from the pain of separation and loss when a child is removed from their care. "I reserve something, knowing that they're not mine"; "I hold back a little"; "I don't want to get too attached."[22] And yet, despite this self-conscious reserve among people who care for pay—what Nelson calls "the emotional labor of creating a distance"[23]—what's striking is not the holding back itself but *what* caregivers feel they must hold back. They don't feel they have to check their avarice; they feel they have to check their love.

The Fear That Love Will Trump Self-Interest

This triumph of love over money leads to another feminist fear, one that is paradoxically precisely the opposite: that money *won't* extinguish love. Put another way, altruism will triumph over self-interest and become self-sacrifice. According to law professor Robin West, women's classically nurturing, altruistic, care-taking personalities are a fearful response to patriarchal oppression; women care because they don't feel they have other choices, and in their altruism, they betray their autonomous selves.[24] In this view, the "care ethic" celebrated by Carol Gilligan and the "different voice" tradition[25] are really the manifestation of repressed ambition.

Robin West's is an extreme view, but much of the feminist writing on child care and health care workers notes that women care workers "don't feel right" about asking for more money or treating their work as a job, so they allow themselves to be exploited. Although they need their wages, they accept the cultural norm that women are supposed to care "out of love," and they fear that asking for more money will lead others to think worse of them. Raising issues of pay or working conditions makes the economic aspect of the work visible and brings it to the forefront.

Child care researcher Marcy Whitebrook found that most paid child care providers were unwilling to advocate for pay increases for themselves; however, when told that pay increases would reduce staff turnover and create higher quality care for the children, they were willing to join the political fight.[26] In other words, when the issue was cast as fighting for their won self-interest, they demurred; when it was cast as altruism, they joined. Since care workers' job is to care for people in both the psychic and practical senses, they fear that if they allow themselves to be seen as economic actors, their image as caregivers will be tarnished. Indeed, love undermines money, not vice versa.

Mary Romero and other scholars of domestics, nannies, and low-wage caregivers emphasize how employers can exploit these intense emotional connections to extract labor without paying its true worth. The feminist fear that women in paid caregiving are easily exploited is a real concern. But the mere fact of payment is not the cause of exploitation, nor does paying for caregiving necessarily lead to *under*paying for it. Unions and other forms of collective organization are one answer to this problem. When care is acknowledged as paid work, real work, the new framework actually enables workers to feel legitimate about asking for decent pay and benefits. The goal of the Service Employees International Union (which organizes home care workers among many others), the Worthy Wages campaign for childcare workers, and the Domestic Workers' Association in Los Angeles is to create the culture change that enables workers to resist exploitation, and to create the political bargaining power to back up their demands.[27] And these organizations do in fact succeed in raising wages and sometimes in getting benefits.[28]

The Fear That Care Will Stifle Real Work

A standard feminist complaint is that care work is regarded as lowly work, and for a long time, the standard feminist answer has been to recast care work to reveal its essence as highly skilled labor.[29] This revisionist literature on the "invisibility" of women's work is based on the premise that if social scientists show how much skill and complex knowledge go into caregiving, society will recognize the value of care work and pay up. For example, here is the sort of claim meant to convince that caregiving is skilled work: "Attending to others involves not only abstract learning and reasoning but relational intelligence, social learning and skilled knowledge."[30] This literature assumes that care work is devalued in part because women are devalued in general, and in part because the men and few women who hold the power to value work don't appreciate the difficulty and complexity of care work.

There's another, perhaps more potent reason markets and politics don't value care work: Care is so full of love, and anything that involves love can't be real work. All the warm, fuzzy, personal, relationship "heart stuff" is recreation, not work. It is fun, not virtue. Real work is hard, exhausting, depleting, and disciplining. It is physical and mental but not emotional or spiritual. There's a Calvinist bent to our conception of work —you save your soul in the future by punishing and depriving yourself now.

Care challenges this notion of work. It is everything that work is not supposed to be. Just as conservatives have always feared that helping people on the basis of need might undermine their motivation to work,[31] indulging the desire to care seems to threaten the work ethic. Care, as Suzanne Gordon says, often necessitates "being with another human being, not necessarily doing for him or her. But in our culture, we value doing, not being."[32] If people had the choice, we fear, they might sit around caring all the time, basking in feelings instead of doing something harder and more productive. Current debates are suffused with fear that care is shirking real work.

Nowhere is this fear more evident than in TANF (Transitional Assistance for Needy Families) rules about child care. Assistance programs will assist women who take care of other people's children for pay, but not those who would take care of their own instead of working for pay. Consider the case of Regla Belette, a client of the New York Department of Human Services.[33] She and her partner, Angel Martinez, have three children. They could not make ends met, to say the least. To qualify for assistance, Ms. Belette had to be working for money, so instead of taking care of her own children, she was assigned by New York City to take care of her sister's three children, and paid to do so, while her sister worked in *her* workfare assignment. How, you might wonder, did Ms. Belette and Mr. Martinez care for their own children? Presumably, they had to pay someone else to look after their children while Ms. Belette looked after her sister's; or they had to get a relative to do it for free; or maybe New York City paid another workfare recipient to mind the Belette-Martinez kids; or perhaps they reluctantly just let their children hang out on their own. Ponder for a minute what a convoluted way the state assures care of children, just to avoid counting care of one's own kids as honest work.

Caregiving of every kind entails many ways of being that don't easily fit our instrumental notion of "doing." Care workers consciously seek to build trust at the start of their relationship with clients, deliberately sacrificing more instrumental goals. Home health aides, for example, are often supposed to help clients bathe, but most clients are reluctant to let someone help them with bathing. So the aides don't even try to give a bath in the first few weeks; they spend their time instead talking, listening, and building up the comfort level while doing other, less intimate tasks. They spend time doing things that look like waste to efficiency-minded managers, things like chatting, fooling around, hanging out, sitting and gabbing.

Once care becomes a market commodity, purchasers begin to think in terms of getting their money's worth. Several employers of domestics told Mary Romero that their maids were like therapists. But one white woman candidly acknowledged that she couldn't see paying black maids for that kind of skilled labor: "It got where what they [two domestics] could produce for $3.39 an hour wasn't worth it. I just couldn't afford to have a black—I called them my black psychiatrists. They were 'my black people who came,' and we chatted and had a good time. I couldn't afford to pay them for that."[34] Purchasers of care also think they have to discipline caregivers, making sure they don't slack off "doing" for the pleasures of "being with." While working as a nurse's aide in a nursing home, sociologist Timothy Diamond stopped to sit and talk with a patient he'd found crying in her bed; before he could find out why she was crying, the supervisor come by and reprimanded him for not doing his work, which at the moment was supposed to be taking vital signs, not getting intimate with a patient.[35]

In many care occupations, caregivers believe that their relationship with clients *is* the service they provide, or at least, the most important thing they give, above whatever instrumental tasks they are paid to provide. They believe intimacy, closeness, friendship, company, trust, security, and love are what the clients really need, never mind what supervisors prescribe or payers authorize. They redefine their jobs, sometimes consciously, sometimes less so, elevating the relationship to the foremost goal. Family day care providers, according to Margaret Nelson, tend to think that intellectual stimulation and learning activities are secondary goals and emphasize instead building a certain kind of relationship with the children in their care, such as giving the children "a sense of family" or "offering closeness and security—my own motherhood."[36] Physical therapists are trained and paid to provide physical therapy, but, as several of them told me, "sometimes the client just needs someone to talk to." One physical therapist explained how the requirement to document her services in fifteen-minute increments interfered with her work: "I let [someone] cry on my shoulder for fifteen minutes because things aren't going as well as she wished they were . . . or she has some concerns . . . or she's worried about whether her husband's going to be able to take care of her and can she stay here [at home]." This kind of care, the physical therapist conceded, "may be social work [i.e., NOT physical therapy and therefore not reimbursable], but right now *I'm* there, and she needs *me* to listen."[37]

No wonder, then, we fear treating care as a political and economic commodity. I have been using "we" in a deliberately ambiguous way, for the complexity of "we" is a major reason why commodification of care is an issue. People who care for a living, no less than those who care without pay, have their own definition of the work, and it is one that is deeply at odds with what "we"—when we're not caring ourselves—deem work and how we regulate it in the rest of our economic lives. As caregivers ourselves, we fear having an alien conception of care imposed on us. As purchasers of care and as taxpayers, we fear being forced to pay for that infinitely combustible mixture of human need and compassionate response.

The Fear That Bureaucracy Will Extinguish Care

In my study of home health care, it became obvious that money—the fact of getting paid for caregiving—wasn't the great transformer of caregiving. Rather, *the political and managerial control of money* is what restrained and changed the way nurses, therapists, and aides cared for their patients. In the private sector, once patients (or children or clients or anybody else) become the raw material out of which profits are made, the entrepreneur is dedicated to keeping costs down. In an economic sense, the cost of care is almost all in the labor, so keeping costs down means suppressing care. When care is a market good, its essence—the human component, the relationship—has to be minimized because it is an input, and efficiency requires getting the most output for the least input.

There's a similar dynamic in the public sector. Once citizens become the users of publicly financed services as patients, children, clients, or any other type of beneficiary, they also become budget expenditures. Government, as a payer itself and as the representative of taxpayers' interests, quickly gets dedicated to keeping down expenditures, and hence care. That is the paradox of public services (or one of them): while the political mandate and intent is to *provide* services, there is a simultaneous political imperative to *minimize* them.

Whether care is a market commodity or a public good, the impact is the same. Private producers need to minimize care because every provision eats a little bit more profit, and with it, investors' goodwill. Public providers need to minimize care because every provision eats a little more budget, and with it, taxpayer-voter support. Thus, when we commodify care, money enters care relationships not through the caregiver's purse. Money walks into the relationship because third parties—payers—force their way in. They enter the care relationship by trying to count it, monitor it, define it, and limit it. These managerial processes are the same whether conducted by private entrepreneurs or public payers.

How, then, does commodification change the nature of care? First, once care becomes a commodity, there is pressure to reduce it to its most mundane, physical, countable elements. If care is to be managed (and I don't mean HMOs here), managers need to transform it into something they can measure. They must extract observable, countable tasks out of inherently invisible and fluid relationships. In health care, that tends to mean reducing care to the physical, "hands-on" tasks—giving medicines, taking vital signs, changing bandages, assisting people with eating, bathing, moving, and dressing. Care plans for home health aides typically include a menu of about fifty things an aide might be asked by the supervising nurse to do for a client. Not one of them is "talking" or "listening."[38] As Timothy Diamond wrote about the time he was reprimanded for taking time to console a crying patient, her blood pressure was probably high that day because she was upset. But, he noted acerbically, "[T]here was a place [in the chart] to record her high numbers, but not her crying."[39]

Home care aides, when asked what is the most important thing they do, usually say something like "I make her smile," or "I give him something to live for," or "making them happy," or "making them feel good." Both aides and clients would say that the chitchat surrounding the physical tasks is what gives care its value. In the talking and listening, clients get to express who they are and to preserve their identities as something other than sick, declining persons. Aides get to give clients their lives back and to make a difference—which is far more important to them than, say, giving a bath or a meal.[40] None of these things is what home care planners and payers measure (or pay for). What caregivers aim to do and what people who receive care value are not the same things that managers count as outputs.

Second, once care is a commodity, caregivers have to be accountable. Accountability means showing results. Results, in our culture, mean progress, increases, growth. Caregivers come under enormous pressure to demonstrate progress and good results. Under Medicare's rules for home health services, clients are no longer eligible if they cease making progress or are incapable of making further progress. In the realm of caring for very sick, disabled, or frail elderly people, progress is hard to come by, so care providers have to devise clever strategies to appear *as if* they are producing progress. (Being happy or feeling better doesn't count as progress.)

One strategy is to accept as clients only those people who are very likely to make progress in the first place, which means, of course, to withhold care from those who most need it. Another strategy is to define objectives down or divide them into baby steps that look like progress. For example, a sample care plan developed by a management consulting firm for home health agencies offers some achievable "outcomes" for patients whose "prognosis is death": "Long-term criteria: anxiety reduced, as evidenced by avoidance of anxiety-producing situations; client verbalizes fears and concerns."[41] Yet another strategy is to document predictions of progress in lieu of the real thing. For example, when home health nurses visit patients with skin wounds, they are required to write down a date by which they believe the wounds will have healed.[42] Thus do pressures for accountability in bureaucratized care lead to a well-known phenomenon in human services. Instead of measuring real results, evaluators specify process standards. Service providers then hustle to document that they have leapt through all the procedural hoops.

Even in child care, where individual progress is the normal course of things, there are pressures to translate care into educational progress.[43] In their political quest to make child care a public commodity, child care advocates recast child care in terms of progress. They specify developmental goals, describe day care in terms of learning activities, and document children's progress toward goals (which sometimes means simply writing down that children have "participated in a learning activity"). As Lucie White notes, "Child care is now referred to in policy circles as EEC— early education and care; the effort to make child care a politically palatable public issue takes the form of transforming care into education."[44] Mere care isn't good enough.

Third, if society is going to underwrite care, to guarantee it as a legal right and accept it as a collective financial responsibility, the vague, undefined, and ambiguous relation of care has to be made well-defined, concrete, and limited. It has to be rendered into a contractual relationship because contracts are the essence of legal relationships. Yet, few people, when raising a child or caring for their ailing spouse or parent would conceive of their relationship as a well-defined set of tasks, planned in advance: "Okay, I'm going to do this, this and this for you, no more, no less." Instead, people care by responding to another person's requests, to their own assessment of the person's needs at the moment, and to their vision of what it *means to be* a parent, a child, a spouse, or a friend. Contracts tend to prohibit that kind of flexibility and responsiveness, or at least discourage it. To be sure, most contracts for professional services leave a great deal of room for the professional to use her or his judgment, and legal scholars have elaborated a notion of "relational contracts" that are designed to permit flexibility. However, entrepreneurs and governments seek to minimize flexibility, for they are acutely conscious of the downside risk—that the consultant will advise greater expenditures.

Once care is commodified, it has to become contractual, in spirit if not in law. Contracts are the legal expression of limited relationships, the exact opposite of familial and love relationships. Once caregivers have contracts with payers, the substance of care must be rendered into a contractual language. Caregivers' relationships to the people they care for then have to be squeezed to fit into the caregivers' relationship to the payer. For example, several physical therapists told me they try to help patients accomplish their own personal mobility goals. However, Medicare's rules permit them to work with a client who has lost walking ability only until the client can safely exit the house in an emergency and walk twenty-five yards. One therapist said this rule prevented her from helping a woman walk to the corner bus stop, which would have enabled her to visit her husband in a nursing home; another said the rule prevented her from helping a man learn to walk downstairs to his basement workshop. Thus, the care relationship has to mirror the contractual relationship. Much of the fluidity, responsiveness, and flexibility are lost, not to mention dialogue and mutual influence in deciding what care shall be given. Perhaps, too, the bureaucratic impulse to define relationships contractually is why policy makers want to separate parents from their own children before paying them for child care. Policy makers are human enough to know that parents are unlikely to observe the bounds of a contract in their relationship to their children.

Last, and perhaps the most important consequence of bureaucratization of care, is the transfer of power from inside to outside of care relationships. Payers, as third-party overseers of care, remove the power to decide what to do from the caregiver. *The payer's power over the caregiver, far more than money's influence on the caregiver's motives, changes the way a caregiver cares.* This is one way to interpret the struggles over health insurance and managed care. Payers, whether private or public insurers, fear the budgetary impact of unrestrained compassion. Payers know all too well how caregivers, at the bedside, often wish to do everything possible for their patients. They can't stop, they can't let go, they can't say "enough is enough." Payers try to contain compassion by setting caps on reimbursement. The prospective pay systems introduced first into the hospital sector, then into outpatient care, nursing homes, and home health care, are all designed to stem the outpouring of uncontrollable compassion that caring for sick and dying people unleashes.[45] This new third-party relationship is the source of the classic caregiver lament: "I wish I could do that for you, but I can't. Insurance, Medicare, The Department (take your pick) won't let me." Read: how I care for you is not my decision to make. When care is paid for by third parties instead of by care recipients themselves, the *recipients* also cede power to the payers. They lose the power to define and shape the care they receive. In all the goal-setting and rule-making by payers, recipients' goals count for little.

Thus, bureaucratization, it seems to me, is the most serious concern about commodifying care. The transfer of power from the caregiver-recipient dyad to some third party, be it a business, a government agency, or a legislature, is the real threat to care and care relationships. Corruption of motives by the influence of money, exploitation of women and low-wage workers, and loss of productivity are certainly genuine concerns, worth worrying about, but they are not the crux of the issue.

Experience with bureaucratic care makes us wary, and for good reason.[46] As people who are vulnerable, we fear that when we need care, we won't get all that we need. As caregivers, we have learned the pain of having to curb our compassion and the helplessness of losing our autonomy. Suddenly, we are thrust into the same condition as the dependent people who need our help.

In the novel *Talk Before Sleep,* Elizabeth Berg writes about four women taking care of a friend dying of breast cancer. These women, the friends as well as the sick one, are fighting a battle. Not a military battle or a political battle but a battle against death, despair, and the loss of meaning. This is the big one, and it seems impossible to win. But salvation, Berg writes in her preface, is "to be found in caretaking, whatever form that caring takes."

This, finally, is why care is political, even if it never becomes a political issue. Care is a way of fighting. It is how we fight when we are so powerless that defeat is certain, when fighting is the only thing that will preserve hope, and preserving hope is the only possible victory. It is the way we do whatever we can to make life better for the people we love, for the world, and for ourselves. Caring is what we do when our self-interest and our concern for others merge. Caring is the essential political act.

And here is perhaps the source of our deepest fear about making care into an economic and political commodity. Caring labor is sacred labor. When we treat it like productive labor, we might destroy its transcendent power and its power to give us hope.

NOTES

For helpful comments and discussions, I would like to thank Larry Jacobs, Margaret Nelson, Mark Schlesinger, Joan Tronto, and Viviana Zelizer, as well as participants in seminars at Yale University, University of Michigan, and Hunter College.

1. Caregiving could just as well be applied to the way we tend pets, animals, gardens, crops, forests, and the natural environment, but I'll stick to the human-to-human domain. That's enough for one paper.

2. As E. E. Schattschneider so brilliantly observed, every conflict creates alliances at the same time as it creates divisions. E. E. Schattschneider, The Semi-Sovereign People (1970).

3. Robert Putnam, Bowling Alone: The Collapse and Revival of American Community 19 (2000).

4. Joan Tronto, Moral Boundaries: A Political Argument for an Ethic of Care 107–8 (1992).

5. Nancy Foner, The Caregiving Dilemma: Work in an American Nursing Home 49(1994).

6. Margaret Nelson, *Mothering Others' Children, in* Circles of Care: Work and Identity in Women's Lives 210, 215 (Emily K. Abel and Margaret K. Nelson, eds., 1990).

7. Robert Wuthnow, Acts of Compassion: Caring for Others and Helping Ourselves 56 (1991).

8. Elizabeth Anderson, Value in Ethics and Economics 145 (1993).

9. There is much debate about this, and a large literature that says even care of others is ultimately beneficial to the self, and probably motivated by self-interest, or at least determined by genetic self-interest at a nonconscious level. *See* Deborah Stone, Help: The Good Samaritan Ethic in American Public Life (forthcoming 2005).

10. Sue Schallenbarger, *Wanted: Caregiver for Elder Woman; Only Family Members Need Apply,* Wall Street Journal, June 20, 2002, p. B1.

11. See Deborah Stone, *Caring by the Book, in* Care Work: Gender, Labor and the Welfare State 89–111 and 315–17 (Madonna Harrington Meyer, ed., 2000).

12. Social scientists call this phenomenon "fictive kin," a term that comes from Carol Stack's study of helping networks in a black ghetto, All Our Kin

(1974). Tracy Karner applied it to the relations of home health care workers and their clients in *Professional Caring: Homecare Workers as Fictive Kin*, 12 J. Aging Studies 69 (1998). In my research with home care nurses and aides, "love" was a frequent part of their vocabulary. Stone, *Caring by the Book*, *supra* note 11.

13. Mary Tuominen, The *Conflicts of Caring*, *in* Care Work, *supra* note 11, at 112–35, 119, 317–20.

14. Quotations are from Nelson, *Mothering Others' Children*, *in* Circles of Care, *supra* note 6, at 210–32, quotations on 215.

15. Cameron Macdonald, *Shadow Mothers: Nannies, Au Pairs, and Invisible Work*, *in* Working in the Service Society 244–63, quote on 255 (Cameron Lynne Macdonald and Carmen Sirianni, eds., 1996).

16. Quotations are from Robert Frank, *High-Paying Nanny Positions Puncture Fabric of Family Life in Developing Nations*, Wall St. J. Dec. 18, 2001, A1, and cited in Arlie Hochschild, *Love and Gold*, *in* The Commercialization of Intimate Life: Notes from Home and Work 185–97 quote on 185 (2003). As Hochschild notes, a terrible sadness accompanies this devotion of immigrant nannies to American children, for if they have left children of their own in their home country, their love for their American charges is in large part displaced love, thwarted love.

17. Emily K. Abel and Margaret K. Nelson, *Intimate Care for Hire*, American Prospect, May 21, 2001, pp. 26–29.

18. Judith Rollins, Between Women: Domestics and Their Employers 120 (1985).

19. Mary Tuominen, *Exploitation or Opportunity? The Contradictions of Child Care Policy in the United States*, 18 Women and Politics, 53 (1997); Mary Tuominen, *The Hidden Organization of Labor: Gender, Race/Ethnicity and Child Care Work in Formal and Informal Settings*, 37 Soc. Perspectives, 229 (1994); and Margaret Nelson, Negotiated Care: The Experience of Family Day Care Providers (1990).

20. Macdonald, *Shadow Mothers*, *supra* note 15, at 253–4.

21. Mary Romero, Maid in the U.S.A. 107 (1992).

22. Nelson, *Mothering Others' Children*, supra note 14 at 219–21, quotations on p. 220.

23. *Id.* at 221.

24. Robin West, Caring for Justice, 109–27 (1997); *Id.* at 120 ("What I wish to propose is that the giving self constituted through duressed private altruism becomes in a literal sense *incapable* of the self-regarding acts that are constitutive of the liberal self—and that *is* the harm that these acts occasion.").

25. Carol Gilligan, In a Different Voice (1982).

26. Marcy Whitebook, Executive Director, Center for the Child Care Work-

force, Washington, D.C., personal interview, October 25, 1999; and Center for the Child Care Workforce, National Childcare Staffing Study (1989).

27. The video *Invisible No More: Home Care* produced by the Service Employees International Union (S.E.I.U.) (2000) documents this political consciousness of unionized home care workers. See also Deborah Stone, *Why We Need a Care Movement*, Nation 13–15 (March 13, 2000). On the Domestic Workers Association in Los Angeles, a part of the Coalition for Humane Immigrant Rights of Los Angeles, see Pierrette Hondagnu-Sotelo, *Sin Organizacion No Hay Solucion: Latina Domestic Workers and Non-traditional Labor Organizing*, 8 Labor Stud. J. 54–81 (1997).

28. Stu Schneider, *Victories for Home Care Workers*, Dollars and Sense 25 (Sept./Oct. 2003).

29. See, for a tiny sample of this genre, Arlene Kaplan Daniels, *Invisible Work*, 34 Social Problems, 403 (1987) (for women's work generally); Paula England, Comparable Worth: Theories and Evidence (1992); Patricia Benner, From Novice to Expert: Excellence and Power in Clinical Nursing Practice (1984) (for nursing); Marjorie DeVault, Feeding the Family: The Social Organization of Caring as Gendered Work (1991) (for grocery shopping, menu planning, and food preparation and meal orchestration); Ronnie Steinberg, *Emotional Labor in Job Evaluation: Redesigning Compensation Practices*, 561 Annals of the Am. Acad. Pol. & Soc. Sci. 143 (1999) (for client-oriented municipal work and nursing).

30. Suzanne Gordon, *Feminism and Caregiving*, American Prospect, Summer 1992, pp. 119–27, quotation on p. 120.

31. See Deborah Stone, The Disabled State (1984).

32. Gordon, *Feminism and Caregiving, supra* note 30, at 121.

33. Nina Bernstein, *As Deadline Looms, Answers Don't Seem So Easy*, N.Y. Times, June 25, 2001, p. A1.

34. Romero, Maid in the U.S.A., *supra* note 21, at 106.

35. Timothy Diamond, *Nursing Homes as Trouble, in* Circles of Care, *supra* note 6, at 176 (from Timothy Diamond, Making Gray Gold (1992).

36. Margaret Nelson, *Family Day Care as Mothering, in* Qualitative Research in Early Childhood Settings 23–24, quotes on pp. 28–29 (J. Amos Hatch ed., 1995).

37. See Stone, *Caring by the Book, supra* note 11, at 99.

38. Deborah Stone, Reframing Home Health Care Policy 8 (2000).

39. Diamond, *Nursing Homes as Trouble, supra* note 35, at 177.

40. See Stone, *Caring by the Book, supra* note 11.

41. This language is taken from a care plan package designed by a home care consulting firm and offered for sale to home health agencies for their use in managing their care provision.

42. In interviews, nurses told me that Medicare requires this prognostication

as some kind of assurance that patients were indeed progressing. Nurses felt such predictions were pure guesswork.

43. I thank Professor Lucie White for this insight. Personal communication, August 21, 1998.

44. *Id.*

45. See Deborah Stone, *Rationing Compassion,* American Prospect, May 2000, 16–18.

46. As Francesca Cancian argues, "[M]arket relations and bureaucracy need not undermine emotional caregiving." Francesca M. Cancian, *Paid Emotional Care, in* Care Work, *supra* note 11, at 136–48, quotation on p. 136. She and others find stories of hope in institutional settings where caregivers have devised ways to provide nurturing care in spite of market and bureaucratic pressures. But the larger point remains: we have good reason to fear.

*Un*bending Gender
Why Family and Work Conflict and What to Do about It

Joan C. Williams[1]

The gendered structure of market work is the crucible in which the dominant family ecology is forged. Under the current definition, the ideal worker is away from home nine to twelve hours a day, so that an ideal-worker parent with preschool children typically sees them awake for only an hour or two a day. When the children reach school age, the issues shift: who will pick them up from school, help with homework, and take time off for medical appointments, illnesses, or the school play? An ideal worker needs to delegate all, or virtually all, of this care in the manner of the typical father. Typically he delegates it to the child's mother, who either drops out of the workforce to provide this flow of family work or remains a market participant but is marginalized by her inability to perform as an ideal worker. The family work of a full- or part-time homemaker allows her husband to concentrate his efforts on market work. Once family work is acknowledged as *work,* a new rationale emerges for income sharing after divorce: An asset produced by two people should be jointly owned by them. The only reason to award the fruits of the dominant domestic ecology one-sidedly to the husband is an unacknowledged continuation of coverture. The alternative is joint ownership.

* * *

In the degree cases, wives' lawyers [generally rely] on human capital theory. The proponents of human capital theory rely on commercial analogies that seem jarring and out of place when applied to family relations. Joan Krauskopf, in an early application of human capital theory to post-divorce entitlements, characterized the family as "a firm seeking to maximize its total welfare" and the wife as someone seeking "a fair return on her investment." Ira Ellman pursues a long analogy of the wife to a company that supplies specialized parts to IBM and argues that both the wife and the parts supplier make "investments a self-interested bargainer would make only in return for a long-term commitment." Cynthia Starnes speaks of the "income generating marital enterprise" in which "a dissociated spouse should receive a buyout of her investment."

Human capital theorists' highly commercialized language weakens wives' claims in two ways. First, this language reinforces the sense that such theorists are flailing around for inherently unconvincing rationales. Second, it sends the message that granting wives an entitlement threatens intimate relations with undesirable commodification. Human capital theory triggers fears of a world in which all human relations assume a market model of commercialized self-seeking. Its commercial analogies and its focus on wives' "return on investment" imply that the only alternative to a one-sided allocation of the ownership of the family wage to the husband is the specter of a family life corroded by strategic behavior.

Courts' negative response to human capital theory reflects not only commodification anxiety but also their rejection of the relief wives typically demand in degree cases. In conclusion, courts' rejection of wives' claims in the degree cases is in response to the rhetoric used and the specific entitlement demanded. The joint-property proposal avoids both language that signals an unhealthy commodification of family life and the demand for a permanent entitlement for ex-wives from the earnings of their former husbands.

NOTE

1. Reprinted with permission from Un*bending Gender: Why Family and Work Conflict and What to Do about It,* by Joan C. Williams, 124–25, 135–36 (Oxford University Press, 2000).

Minnesota v. Bachmann

521 N.W. 2d 886 (Minn. Ct. App. 1994)

Schumacher, Judge.

Appellant Suzanne Margie Bachmann claims that the district court erred by denying her motion for postconviction relief on the basis that she was not eligible for work release privileges. We affirm.

Facts

In November 1993, Bachmann pleaded guilty to one count of burglary in the second degree and one count of check forgery. As part of her sentence, she was ordered to spend 90 days in the county jail.

Following her sentencing, Bachmann requested that she be granted work-release privileges while serving her 90-day jail term. Bachmann is not presently employed outside the home. Instead, she wished to be released from jail on weekdays in order to care for her four children and perform other homemaking services for her husband and children, for which her husband agreed to pay her $1.50 per hour. The district court concluded that Bachmann was not eligible for work-release and denied her motion.

* * *

Analysis

A district court's denial of work-release privileges typically will be reversed only in the rare instance where the court has abused its discretion. In this case, however, the issue is not whether the particular facts of Bachmann's case justify work-release. Rather, it is whether Bachmann's status as a homemaker by itself renders her eligible for work-release privileges. As this is a question of statutory interpretation, our review is de novo.

Minn. Stat. § 631.425, subd. 3 (1992) provides:

> If the person committed under [the work-release statute] has been regularly employed, the sheriff shall arrange for a continuation of the employment insofar as possible without interruption. If the person is not employed, the court may designate a suitable person or agency to make reasonable efforts to secure some suitable employment for that person. An inmate employed under this section must be paid a fair and reasonable wage for work performed and must work at fair and reasonable hours per day and per week.

Bachmann argues that homemaking is employment within the meaning of this statutory language. We disagree.

Bachmann's homemaking services clearly have economic value.[1] Nevertheless, homemaking is generally not considered employment. For example, in the context of workers' compensation:

> The upkeep and care of a home for one's self and family are not in the category of a trade, business, profession or occupation, as generally understood. A home is not established and maintained in the expectation of pecuniary gain. Such a venture is solely an expense.

Persons engage in a trade, business, profession or occupation for profit, or as a means to gain a livelihood, but not so in establishing and maintaining a home.

But we think a housewife is not an occupation within the meaning of the compensation act, since that work pertains exclusively to the management of the home. Furthermore, in the maintenance of the home the husband and wife are one. The one acts for the other. No matter who is the legal owner of the home, the running thereof is not an industry nor a business, trade, profession or occupation within the purview of the Workmen's Compensation Act.[2]

Similarly, in holding that a domestic servant could not picket the home in which he had been employed, the supreme court reasoned:

> The validity of defendant's argument depends upon whether a home, exclusively used as such, may be said to be a place for the carrying on of an

industrial or a business enterprise. Obviously the home cannot be so classified.

"The home is an institution, not an industry."[3]

And the same result was reached in *Anderson v. Ueland,*[4] where we said: "the home is a sacred place for people to go and be quiet and at rest and not be bothered with the turmoil of industry," and that as such it is "a sanctuary of the individual and should not be interfered with by industrial disputes." We think [this] conception of "home" as "a sanctuary of the individual" is sound. The word is defined as, "the abiding place of the affections, esp. domestic affections"; as "the social unit formed by a family residing together in one dwelling," and as "an organized center of family life."[5] The fact that Bachmann's husband has offered to pay an hourly wage to her does not change our conclusion. First, Bachmann has an obligation to care for her children regardless of whether she is paid to do so.[6] Second, income received by Bachmann is marital property.[7] Thus, Bachmann's husband has a common ownership interest in her income.[8] The Bachmanns have not shown that their proposed wage agreement results in either gain or loss to either person; unlike the typical employment relationship, the economic exchange between the Bachmanns would be purely illusory.

Finally, we note by way of analogy that the legislature has provided that a homemaker whose driver's license has been suspended or revoked may be eligible for a limited license under certain conditions.[9] In doing so, it explicitly included homemakers in the list of persons eligible for a limited license, a step it has not taken in regard to the work-release statute. Moreover, the fact that within this statutory scheme homemakers are a class distinct from drivers who need a license for their livelihood further suggests that the legislature generally considers homemaking to be distinct from employment.[10] We therefore conclude that homemaking is not employment as contemplated by Minn. Stat. § 631.425 (1992).

Decision

The district court properly concluded that Bachmann was not eligible for work-release to perform homemaking responsibilities for her family. Affirmed.

NOTES

1. *See Rindahl v. National Farmers Union Ins.*, 373 N.W.2d 294, 297 (Minn. 1985) (under Minnesota No-Fault Act, injury to person who performs most of household duties "most definitely results in an economic loss to the family unit").

2. *Eichholz v. Shaft*, 166 Minn. 339, 343–44, 208 N.W. 18, 19–20 (1926).

3. *Barres v. Watterson Hotel Co.*, 196 Ky. 100, 102, 103, 244 S.W. 308, 309, 310 (Ky. App. 1922).

4. 197 Minn. 518, 521, 267 N.W. 517, 518, 927 (1936).

5. *State v. Cooper*, 205 Minn. 333, 335–36, 285 N.W. 903, 904–05 (1939) (citations omitted).

6. *See, e.g.*, Minn. Stat. § 609.378, subd. 1 (1994) (failure to provide child with necessities is a crime).

7. *Swick v. Swick*, 467 N.W.2d 328, 330 (Minn. App. 1991), *pet. for rev. denied* (Minn. May 16, 1991).

8. Minn. Stat. § 518.54, subd. 5 (1992).

9. Minn. Stat. § 171.30, subd. 1(2) (1992).

10. *See* Minn. Stat. § 171.30, subd. 1(1) (1992) (driver may be eligible for limited license if necessary for livelihood).

Commodification and Women's Household Labor

Katharine Silbaugh[1]

Plural Meaning

The most important response to the commodification critique, and one that Radin herself embraces, is the notion of what she calls "plural meanings": multiple understandings of a single activity that can co-exist.[2]

> The way to a less commodified society is to see and foster the non-market aspect of much of what we buy and sell, to honor our internally plural understandings, rather than to erect a wall to keep a certain few things completely off the market and abandon everything else to market rationality.[3]

While Radin's insight into the possibility of plural meaning is useful, it is impossible not to notice her hierarchy among models. She seeks a less commodified society, not plural conceptions of human activity. Radin gives little encouragement for us to bring out the market aspects of non-market activity such as home labor. Her claim falls short of being for a richness of understanding that includes economics as itself one creative force in personality. I hope to make the claim for that possibility by bringing forward some of the negative aspects of non-market understandings. I wish to do this while maintaining the notion that neither an economic nor an emotional understanding of non-market activities is intrinsic to the activities themselves. This latter point saves room for Radin's desire to promote plural meaning, but it rests less on an implicit trajectory toward an ideal of a singular, and for her non-market, conception.

* * *

Radin asks if we can both know the price of something and simultaneously know that it is priceless.[4] I believe the answer is yes. An important illustration of this point can be found in Viviana Rotman Zeliz[e]r's historical examination of the life insurance industry.[5] In the first half of the nineteenth century there was tremendous public resistance to the sale of life insurance in the United States because the public took offense at the suggestion that a life could be valued in monetary terms. [But t]oday's life insurance market does not offend most people on commodification grounds, despite its known actuarial focus. Life insurance is considered a kind and responsible purchase for family members, who do not thereby come to view the insured loved one as bearing a price. Students of insurance would argue that it is not about pricing life at all but about subjectively chosen levels of risk. Thus, a "price" does not unseat the understanding of pricelessness. It instead serves a limited purpose that is unrelated to real value.

* * *

The Limited Influence of Talk in Legal Discourse: Plural Meaning as the Norm

Does talking about home labor as productive mean commodifying it? It becomes important to think about what is meant by commodification. To assume that there is no important difference between analyzing the economics of something and creating an unregulated market for that same thing is terribly damaging to intellectual discourse. "Wages for housework" is not the only possible outcome of this exercise.

We routinely ask questions about value in legal practice as if a market exists where one does not. Consider the wrongful death suit or any tort suit that includes a claim for pain and suffering damages. The value of these claims is obviously not established by a real market. Moreover, it is not difficult for most people to accept that there should not ever be a real market in these things. Nonetheless, in a tort action, we allow money to change hands as if a market value were placed on these things. Cass Sunstein identifies this as "as if" reasoning. We think of damages "as if" they could be marketized, but at the same time we know that they cannot.[6] This is a clear practical example of the existence of what Radin calls plural meanings.

Monetization of things for which there is no market and no push for a market for the purpose of providing a remedy within the law is an illustration of the resilience of non-market conceptions. While legal academics may fret about the message we are sending by placing a value on the loss of an arm, the non-legal world does not appear to have been influenced into believing that arms are worth an x sum of money, despite the many years that a monetary remedy has been provided for the loss of an arm. Loss of consortium damages are an even better example of this phenomenon. This routine fact of legal discourse should deflate somewhat the worry over the domino effect if we decide to analyze legal policies affecting home labor using economic understandings. Law's pragmatic focus on remedies has not had an enormous spillover effect into social understandings in non-legal discourse.

* * *

Women as Noncommodifiable: Questioning the Origins of an Idea

Does concern about the comparison between wage labor and home labor commodification grow out of an implicit assumption that there is something intrinsically different about home labor? We might want to ask whether it is coincidental [that reluctance to recognize an economic dimension to labor follows] gender lines: women's work [is often viewed as] essentially non-marketable. Consider the problems with assuming that women are inclined to make gifts of attributes of their personalities. Women serve, men sell. It is a familiar notion about which many feminists have been skeptical.[7]

The Gender Line: Cashless Women

At a practical level, women should at least be wary of anti-commodification arguments, because these arguments arise when women receive money for something, not when women are paying money for something. The argument is used most frequently in legal discourse when talking about women receiving money for surrogate parenting and sexual contact, and herein for household labor. One might respond that the emphasis of the anticommodification argument is that some aspect of women's personhood is going to be sold, not that women are about to receive money. It is the sale that is objectionable, not that women may end up with cash. Consider, though, that it is not uncommon to find people who approve of altruistic transfer in these same areas, for example, human egg donation and surrogacy. In fact, the current fee caps in both of these fields reflect that ideal in practice: donors are not supposed to be too motivated by money, so fees are held down to ensure that there is a partially altruistic motivation for donating.[8] In these cases, it seems arguable that the difference that a woman experiences may simply be whether money comes to her, and how much, as compared to other wage labor that she might similarly perform from partially altruistic motivation.[9] This difference occurs in the name of non-commodification. [C]oncern about exploitation due to the commodification of women's reproductive capacity might just as easily turn into exploitation from non-commodification, not just in a "nonideal" world. Here the mixed motivations of women are exploited by highlighting the altruistic aspects of those motives in a discriminatory fashion. Only women's mixed motives relating to feminine activities are highlighted and offered as justification for leaving women without cash. Mixed motivations in the labor force at large do not require regulatory practices aimed at keeping wages down.

Social practices also exist where the characterization of the problem as "withholding money from women" seems even more apt at the practical level than "preventing the sale of women," given the particular form that current decommodification takes. Prostitutes and pimps have a relationship that results where prohibition on sale ensures that although a female attribute is being sold, a woman is not getting most of the money.

We do not usually see the anticommodification argument raised as forcefully when things typically associated with male personhood are being sold. While it may be that women's personhood is more at risk for being inappropriately objectified and commercialized, we should at least consider an alternative understanding of why commodification concerns focus on women's issues. It may have as much to do with notions of femininity and a desire to elevate a romantic essentialism about femininity as it does with a desire to protect women's integrity. Consider [Elizabeth] Anderson's argument that women's reproductive labor is inappropriately alienated by surrogacy because a surrogate mother must "divert [her labor] from the end which the social practices of pregnancy rightly promote—an emotional bond with her child."[10] It is not clear why the end which Anderson prefers for women's labor must be extinguished by money, but it is clear that her argument leaves women without money for their labor. Perhaps Anderson recognizes this, but sees it as a necessary trade-off for the preservation of familial bonds.[11] She does not explain though, why it is a trade-off; why markets and monetary exchange cannot coexist with expressions of affection in a realistic reflection of women's mixed motivations.

This is not to say that the anticommodification argument is insincere. But at least Radin readily admits that gut instinct plays a significant, perhaps deciding role in drawing a line between things essential to personhood that should not be commodified, and things that are less essential to personhood and therefore can be commodified.[12] These "gut instincts" must be informed by cultural gender understandings.

It certainly seems plausible that what makes us uncomfortable about selling female reproductive capacity, for example, is its subversion of the motherhood role, not just its potential to lead to exploitation. In contrast, consider the rather dull response to the sale of sperm.

The fact that we are more concerned about commodification of women's personhood does not mean that we have erred with respect to women; we might have erred with respect to men. Radin's work suggests this. But we must at least consider the gender line in the anticommodification discourse and its possible origins in gut instincts, including our own, which we might not want to trust. And in deciding whether we are right to permit partial commodification of "men's" personal attributes, such as wage labor, we need to ask which gut instinct is stronger: the one that permits wage labor, or the one that doesn't permit market analysis of home labor. The partial commodification of wage labor is acceptable to most people in a world of scarce resources that is as thoroughly organized around markets as our own. Much that is personal is created and produced on the market, and home labor is not special in that respect.

* * *

Conclusion

The commodification critique is often a conversation stopper. Because markets do not capture the entire experience in question, they are thought to threaten the existence of what they cannot describe. In the context of a phenomenon that is highly commodified, this argument might lead to fruitful discussions of the appropriate methods of preserving non-market understandings. In the context of [a] phenomenon that [is] almost entirely non-market, however, the objection to commodification seems much weaker, because it fails to consider the potential benefits that economic understandings can bring to the social relations surrounding that non-market phenomenon. Since many of women's activities have historically occurred outside of the market, a normative position against market reasoning about home activities is nearly equivalent to a normative position against market reasoning about women's activities. As long as women's economic power remains a central concern of feminist discourse, this aversion to market analysis is detrimental to feminist reform. Understanding the economic aspects of women's non-market activity is an important part of the transformative vision of a progressive feminism.

NOTES

1. Reprinted with permission from 9 Yale J.L. & Feminism 81, 96–99, 104–107, 120–121 (1997).

2. *See* Margaret Jane Radin, Contested Commodities 102–114 (1996).

3. *Id.* at 107.

4. *See id.* at 101.

5. *See* Viviana Rotman Zelizer, Morals and Markets: The Development of Life Insurance in the United States (1979).

6. See Cass R. Sunstein, *Incommensurability and Valuation in Law,* 92 Mich. L. Rev. 779, 815–816 (1994).

7. *See, e.g.,* Jean Bethke Elshtain, Public Man, Private Woman: Women in Social and Political Thought (1987); Frances E. Olsen, *The Family and the Market: A Study of Ideology and Legal Reform,* 96 Harv. L. Rev. 1497 (1983).

8. *See* Carol Sanger, *Separating from Children,* 96 Colum. L. Rev. 375, 451 (1996); Sharon Lerner, *The Price of Eggs; Undercover in the Infertility Industry,* Ms., Mar./Apr. 1996, at 28, 29, 34.

9. Think of a school teacher, for example. This is the lay understanding of altruism, not the economists' understanding of human behavior, which resists the existence of altruism.

10. Elizabeth Anderson, Value in Ethics and Economics 82 (1993).

11. *Id.* at 182–185.

12. *See* Radin, *supra* note 2, at 11–12.

3. COMMODIFYING
FAMILY RELATIONS

What's Wrong with
a Parenthood Market?

A New and Improved Theory of Commodification

Martha M. Ertman[1]

Most people believe parenthood should not be bought and sold.[2] A quarter century ago, Richard Posner and Elisabeth Landes defended, against a strong consensus, the economic efficiency of paying for babies in adoption.[3] Outraged readers decried their analysis, suggesting it epitomized the bloodless approach to human affairs that, they argued, fatally flawed legal economics.[4] But using a baby as a club to beat commodification over the head is misguided. Contrary to Margaret Jane Radin's claim that "conceiving of any child in market rhetoric wrongs personhood,"[5] a parenthood market, in some circumstances, can be a good thing.[6] Specifically, the sale of parental rights through the alternative insemination market facilitates the formation of families based on intention and function rather than biology and heterosexuality. Consequently, people who believe that same-sex couples and single parents can and do form families should reconsider their assumption that a parenthood market is always contrary to human flourishing.[7]

Yet dangers of the parenthood market, such as concerns relating to eugenics, access, paternal anonymity, and objectification exist alongside its potential benefits. Curiously, in the face of these plural meanings, legal scholarship tends to be either sharply skeptical or enthusiastic about commodification, rather than measured. Thus the sale of parental rights and obligations is an ideal case to illuminate the incomplete state of commodification theory. If selling parenthood, the quintessential instance of contested commodification, has both positive and negative aspects, we need to retheorize commodification to account for that range. This article's contribution to this effort is to articulate both the positive and negative effects of the alternative insemination market and to suggest that a highly contextualized approach to commodification, such as the one taken by sociologist Viviana Zelizer, accounts for these mixed valences better than other approaches.

If the market for parental rights has positive elements, in addition to its familiar downsides, then other, less controversial, markets may also have multivalent meanings. Currently, one rarely reads a defense of commodification per se in legal literature because the term itself carries such negative connotations that only commodification skeptics tend to use it. I seek to relieve the term commodification of some of its baggage and, in doing so, to encourage a more precise discussion of what marketization means in various contexts. In short, I address a question that existing commodification literature has largely ignored, namely the affirmative good that marginalized people may enjoy through markets, both literal and rhetorical. It is possible to enthusiastically embrace the benefits of commodification in particular circumstances without retreating to a bloodless, indeed merciless, legal economics that does not (and perhaps cannot) account for power disparities, nor the importance of alleviating them.

I begin by describing ways in which parental rights are already commodified through alternative insemination ("AI"). In focusing on reproductive technologies, in particular alternative insemination, I explore transactions that have clear positive import and pose relatively little danger to human flourishing, unlike, say, selling a baby through the online auction eBay. Adoption and reproductive technologies reveal a gap between the rhetoric condemning the sale of parenthood and people's actual practices. The blanket condemnation of the parenthood market as a species of slavery simply does not comport with the way we live and regulate these transactions.[8]

The next part elaborates on this point, describing in some detail the transactions involved in buying and selling sperm for alternative insemination. It illustrates how the market for male gametes operates as a relatively free market, "an economic activity in which buyers and sellers come together and the forces of supply and demand affect prices."[9]

One could respond to this analysis by determining to decommodify adoption and reproductive technology transactions to bring rhetoric condemning baby selling in line with legal and social practices. Because of the considerable benefits of marketizing parental rights and obligations, at least in the alternative insemination context, I reject the anti-commodification approach. However, recognizing the negative effects of the market reveals the need for a new and improved theory of commodification that can accommodate both benefits and drawbacks of commodifying parenthood in various contexts. One such theory, suggested here, combines the best of Posner, Radin, and Zelizer.[10]

Describing Parenthood Markets

Academic hand wringing about whether selling parenthood would be a good thing implies that we do not already buy and sell it. But the practice is alive and well in various guises, direct and indirect. People routinely exchange funds to obtain parental rights and obligations through adoption and reproductive technologies. Thus, there is a functioning market. In the case of reproductive technologies, especially in vitro fertilization and alternative insemination, this market is a relatively free market, operating as it does largely unhampered by legal regulation. At least in the case of alternative insemination the very fact that this market operates as a free market furthers human flourishing by allowing gay and single people to become parents.[11]

* * *

Reproductive Technologies

* * *

Alternative insemination, like adoption and other reproductive technologies, involves the exchange of money for parenthood. Sperm banks pay donors about $60 for each donation, and the donors agree to provide regular donations over a period of time.[12] Once a certain number of women conceive, usually between four and ten, the banks retire the donor. Prospective mothers pay between $120 and $275 for a vial, depending on the sperm bank and whether the sample is suitable for intrauterine insemination.[13] More than one vial may be required for each insemination, and most women inseminate for months before conceiving. Moreover, the sperm must often be shipped via overnight carrier from the cryobank in liquid nitrogen. Additional costs include a registration fee that some banks charge, tests to ensure the recipient's health, and doctor's visits for insemination. All told, alternative insemination can cost between $500 and $1000 for the first insemination and between $300 and $700 for each subsequent insemination.[14]

Seventy to seventy-five percent of women get pregnant using alternative insemination within six tries, a rate that is considerably higher than for IVF. Thus, assuming pregnancy on the sixth insemination and the possibility of conception at home rather than in a doctor's office, a woman may acquire parental rights through alternative insemination for between $1,000 and $4,500 (plus shipping costs of between $72 and $600).

* * *

The alternative insemination market differs from surrogacy and adoption in that AI is a literal market and a relatively free, open market. The free market aspects of alternative insemination transactions play a crucial role in making this branch of the parenthood market particularly beneficial to marginalized groups.

Markets, by definition, exist where supply and demand determine prices for the transfer of goods and services. Banks and recipients demand sperm, and donors and banks supply it. Suppliers (donors and sperm banks) transfer sperm on the condition of donor anonymity and indemnity for any injury or illness. Buyers (sperm banks and prospective mothers), in turn, demand medical and social information about the donor, further protections against disease transmission, and anonymity. All of these factors are necessary for the smooth functioning of the alternative insemination market. Moreover a relatively low price for the gametes and lack of regulation means that it is both an open market in which a large number of people can participate, and a free market that flourishes because of that comparative freedom from regulation. Taken together, these factors illustrate how the alternative insemination market makes positive contributions to both law and society. Of course, this relative lack of regulation also has potential drawbacks, including the lack of government oversight that could provide quality control and the lack of subsidies that could broaden the range of people who have access to parenthood through reproductive technologies.[15]

BUYERS AND SELLERS EXCHANGE MONEY FOR
MALE GAMETES

Alternative insemination generally involves at least two separate transactions. The sperm bank first purchases sperm from a donor and subsequently sells the sperm to a woman who uses it to become a mother. Both transactions (which I will refer to as the bank/donor and bank/recipient transactions) involve the exchange of money for goods and services. While the transactions differ in important respects, both transactions commodify gametes, and in doing so commodify parental rights and responsibilities.

* * *

The bank's provision of goods and services begins with the careful screening of potential donors. According to its promotional literature, California Cryobank, one of the largest sperm banks in the country, accepts fewer than five percent of the men who apply to be donors.[16] The application process takes three months and involves extensive medical tests as well as interviews about family background and behaviors that could result in transmission of disease. In addition, the banks test donors' blood in the application process, every three months, and upon "retirement" from the program, for diseases such as HIV, syphilis, and hepatitis, as well as genetic disorders such as Tay-Sachs disease, sickle cell disease, and cystic fibrosis.[17]

Also, sperm banks provide information about many other donor characteristics, including ethnicity, hair color, hair texture, eye color, height, weight, blood type, skin tone, years of education, occupation or major in college, and, in many cases, baby pictures and audio tapes of the donor's voice. At least one sperm bank matches photos of the mother's partner with prospective donors to increase the likelihood that the child will look like its other social/legal parent.[18] Banks also provide short profiles, often free of charge, and longer, multigenerational profiles of the donor's social and medical history, for a nominal fee.[19] Women wanting particular donor characteristics may use a sperm bank that recruits those donors, such as the Rainbow Sperm Bank, which, unlike many other banks, provides sperm from gay men.[20]

In addition to selling this medical and character trait information, the banks sell anonymity, the freedom to become a parent with little risk that the biological father will interfere with the intended family. Anonymity is crucial because family law often links biology to parental rights and responsibilities. Anonymity allows a donor to donate without risk that the donation will result in the financial or social responsibilities of father-hood and allows a recipient to conceive without the risk of unwanted in-tervention in the family by a stranger. The value of this aspect of the trans-action is demonstrated by the fact that while some donors contractually agree at the time of donation to have contact with the child or provide medical information that may become relevant, this agreement is gener-ally to have contact once the child reaches majority, when the family unit is less vulnerable to intrusion.

Both legal doctrine and the structure of the alternative insemination market contribute to anonymity in sperm sales. On a doctrinal level, statutes often terminate the donor's rights and responsibilities regarding the child. The 1973 Uniform Parentage Act ("UPA"), for example, pro-vides a measure of anonymity for both donors and recipients in alterna-tive insemination transactions by severing the parental rights and re-sponsibilities of a sperm donor when a physician is involved in the in-semination. While this provision applies only where the recipient is married to someone other than the donor, at least two states have ex-tended these protections to unmarried women.[21] The 2000 UPA further increases anonymity protections by removing the physician and marriage requirements, providing that "[a] donor is not a parent of a child con-ceived by means of assisted reproduction."[22] Thus, the 2000 UPA makes it easier for women, who are either single or partnered with women, to have children without being vulnerable to a donor's fatherhood claims and also provides donors with increased security from being held finan-cially or otherwise responsible for the child.

Contract law provides an additional basis for anonymity. Sperm bank contracts routinely provide for this anonymity. As California Cryobank's ("CCB") contract with its recipients ("Client") provides:

> Representations of Client: . . . Client agrees that client shall not now, or at anytime [sic] require nor expect CCB to obtain or divulge to Client the name of any Donor, nor any other identifying information contained in the files of CCB. Client also agrees not to seek this information from any other source. . . . It is the intention of the parties that the identity of the donor and Client shall be and forever remain anonymous. CCB has an Openness Pol-icy that allows requests for additional donor information from the adult child. Information, other than updated medical information, is provided only if there is mutual consent between the donor and adult child.[23]

* * *

ALTERNATIVE INSEMINATION AS A FREE, OPEN MARKET

Free markets are described as such because they are free from regulation, allowing unrestrained competition to determine prices. Open markets are those in which "anyone, or at least a large number of persons, can buy or sell."[24] As a general matter, markets are largely governed by private law, which tends to defer to parties' intent rather than judgments based on public response to particular arrangements.

Compared to other markets, the alternative insemination market is a relatively free market as it is subject to very limited legal regulation through statute or administrative rule. While some commentators think that public law should interfere with the operation of this market,[25] I think that the private law nature of alternative inseminations, on balance, furthers human flourishing because statutory regulations would likely reflect majoritarian bias against single parents and gay people. One important factor contributing to the positive implications of alternative insemination is that it is open to a wide range of people. Legal regulation might well limit access, both by banning certain people from participating in the market (such as single women or gay people), and by imposing requirements that could result in price increases that would practically exclude many people from parenthood. On the other hand, regulation could increase access by subsidizing assisted reproduction, and improve the quality of services by dictating minimum standards for obtaining, storing, and shipping samples, as well as the actual insemination.

* * *

A number of aspects of alternative insemination make it a particularly striking example of how privatization opens up possibilities for marginalized people to skirt the majoritarian moral bias of public law. First, both technologies and deregulation open the market to a wide range of people. The technologies mean that recipients in isolated areas can obtain sperm. As of 1993, more than 400 sperm banks provided specimens to more than 80,000 women each year, resulting in more than 30,000 pregnancies.[26] The number of banks, coupled with technological innovations, reflects a high supply of sperm, which translates to a relatively low price for this method of becoming a parent. The low price, in turn, makes alternative insemination a technology that most middle-class women can afford (unlike, for example, IVF or adoption). Moreover, access is facilitated by the possibility of insemination at the recipient's home. While some banks require a physician to authorize the sperm sale, at least one large bank refers clients to doctors, and will also send the sperm to the recipient's home once the doctor signs the appropriate form.

* * *

Mixed Valences of the Alternative Insemination Market

Considerable scholarly and popular commentary has focused on the dangers of marketizing parenthood.[27] This Part catalogues some evidence that supports this position and then identifies other ways in which the marketization of parental rights can further equality and human flourishing in ways that much of the commodification literature has not yet acknowledged.

Negative Implications of the Alternative Insemination Market

At least four aspects of the AI market could be described as negative. First, the donor selection process appears to be highly racialized, raising eugenic concerns. Second, poor women lack access to the market. Third, anonymity may deprive some children of the opportunity to know their biological fathers and also deprive them of potential financial support. Fourth and finally, a parenthood market might harm children by treating them like chattel. I address these concerns in turn below, concluding that while they are serious, especially with respect to objectification, they do not justify a blanket condemnation of the AI market, either because they are not unique to the AI market, or because addressing the concern would itself trigger other negative effects.

EUGENIC CONCERNS

The marketization of particular characteristics, such as race (especially whiteness as evidenced by archetypally white features such as blue eyes and blonde hair), a university education, and height, suggests that people who have these characteristics are more valuable than other people. The property value of whiteness is part and parcel of the legacy of white supremacy. While sperm is not priced on the basis of race, the alternative insemination market does seem to be racialized in other ways.

The California Cryobank's May 2001 Donor Catalog lists donors in sections based on the donor's race. At the top of each page is an italicized message explaining that the specimens listed below are from a particular racial group and further that they are stored and shipped with clear racial markings. The message at the top of the pages listing Caucasian donors, for example, states that specimens donated by Caucasian donors are stored in vials with "WHITE caps and are shipped in WHITE canes." Similarly, the catalog notifies sperm buyers at the top of the sections listing Black/African-American donors and Asian donors that these specimens, respectively, are stored in vials with "BLACK caps and are shipped in BLACK canes" and with "YELLOW caps and are shipped in YELLOW canes."[28] Further, the inventory of donors is mostly Caucasian (68%), with some Asian (17%), some with mixed race or "unique" racial designations (11%), and a handful of Black/African-American donors (4%). The general population, in contrast, is 75% Caucasian, 4% Asian, 3% mixed race and American Indian and Alaska Native, and 12.3% black/African-American.[29] Most striking in this large sperm bank's inventory is the over-representation of Asian donors and under-representation of African-American donors.[30]

While the seeming paucity of donors of color (especially Black/African-American) would give many people pause, further investigation indicates that the California Cryobank's inventory does not appear to be tailored to maximize replication of an Aryan ideal. A review of the catalog's other racialized designations of donors, such as hair color and eye color, suggests that blonde, blue-eyed donors are not in the majority. Of the 115 Caucasian donors listed, only 10% are blonde, and 23% are listed as having blue eyes.[31] Only 5% of the 115 Caucasian donors are listed as being both blonde-haired and blue-eyed.

* * *

It could be that sperm banks screen donors for racial characteristics based on perceived or actual higher demand for Caucasian, blonde, and/or blue-eyed donors. It is also possible that fewer African-American men seek to donate sperm, though it seems unlikely that those men would be so thinly represented in the donor pool, and also that Latino men would be virtually absent in a California donor pool. Although a social norm against discrimination might challenge banks' racial screening, it seems unlikely that racial screening would run afoul of legal rules. Only if the donors are characterized as employees, rather than independent contractors, could the banks be liable for engaging in employment discrimination on the basis of race.[32]

This analysis changes little when we consider the possibility that recipients, rather than banks, are discriminating on racial grounds in selecting Caucasian donors over donors of color. At least as a legal matter, women should be able to select the race of their child without state intervention.[33] Still, as a normative, cultural matter, some people might object when white women choose to have white babies through alternative insemination, in a market that monetizes whiteness and other characteristics as superior.[34]

But if we condemn would-be mothers for selecting donors who, they believe, will transmit what they deem to be socially optimal genes to their children, then we could ask the same question of both men and women who select their partners on similar grounds. If we scrutinize white single mothers' selection of white sperm donors, we should also critique white men who choose to marry white women or Harvard graduates who prefer to marry others who attended elite colleges. If this level of meddling seems ridiculous, it is hard to see how it is appropriate when the insemination occurs technologically rather than coitally.[35]

Moreover, while the concerns about sperm banks discriminating against donors of color are serious, the pricing of parental rights based on the child's race or other characteristics, if it does exist, is not unique to alternative insemination, nor even reproductive technologies generally. The adoption market for example, already differentiates fees based on children's characteristics.

ACCESS CONCERNS

A second negative element of the alternative insemination market is that many people do not have access to the market. As with other markets, buyers must have money to purchase the goods and services proffered by sellers. While most middle-class women can afford the $1,000 to $4,500 or so that alternative insemination may cost, working-class and poor women are left out.

Like eugenic concerns, problems of access are not unique to the alternative insemination market. Working-class and poor people have more limited access to all kinds of goods and services, from basic needs like housing to luxuries like beach vacations. Moreover the alternative insemination market is less exclusive than other markets for parental rights.

[A]doption can cost between $4,000 and $30,000, surrogacy fees alone can cost between $10,000 and $20,000, and in vitro fertilization can cost between $44,000 and $211,000, while alternative insemination can cost as little as $1,000 to $4,500.

To say the AI market should be terminated because poor and working-class people cannot access it would be to punish middle-class users of alternative insemination simply for being middle class and either single or gay. Specifically, a concrete good (extending parenthood to people otherwise excluded from that life experience) would be snuffed out to serve an end that is so grand (wealth redistribution) as to be aspirational rather than practical.

ANONYMITY CONCERNS

An additional element of the AI market that is vulnerable to criticism concerns the interest of children. Donor anonymity deprives children of the opportunity to know and enjoy the financial support of biological fathers. Moreover, it deprives donors of the possibility of knowing their biological children.

The prevalence of adopted children tracking down their birth parents illustrates the importance that some people place on knowing their genetic parents. However, not all adoptees seek this connection, and those who succeed in reconnecting with their birth families sometimes find that the fantasy of the perfect family was just that, a fantasy. Moreover, many children of divorced or single mothers have little or no contact with their genetic fathers. Given these considerations, it seems unfairly burdensome to impose a standard of two-biological-parent families for children conceived through AI that is not imposed on parents who conceive coitally.

* * *

The issue of whether a donor's human flourishing might be compromised by anonymity can be addressed quite quickly. Donors, unlike the children, are adults capable of making binding decisions. Donors apparently make their donations free of any kind of coercion, and could seek to have children that they know if they so desired. Indeed, donor forms often indicate that the donor prefers to stay anonymous because he does not know how a child produced through alternative insemination with a stranger would affect arrangements he anticipates making down the road with a future partner or child. This analysis, however, does not alleviate the one remaining concern, perhaps most serious among those addressed here, that the children themselves would be rendered commodities by the parenthood market.

OBJECTIFICATION CONCERNS

Importantly, purchasing gametes to conceive a child could cause the child to feel that he or she has been purchased like a new car. Radin claims that "conceiving of any child in market rhetoric harms personhood."[36] This statement asks us to consider whether the parenthood market, as manifested through adoption and reproductive technologies, treats children like chattel, thus harming their personhood.

However, this analysis suggests a monolithic market in which all transactions are interchangeable. Even transactions conventionally understood in market terms, such as insurance, car sales, and housing are governed by different rules that reflect the different contexts. Ambiguities in insurance contracts, for example, are construed against insurers. For their part, car buyers enjoy the implied warranty of merchantability as well as protection in their contractual relationships with financing institutions. Tenants, in turn, are protected by the implied warranty of habitability. The market for parental rights is just one more market with its own unique rules.

Becoming a parent invokes a raft of obligations quite different from those entailed in car ownership. Legally speaking, parents are obliged to, among other things, feed, clothe, shelter, and educate their child, keep the child out of wage labor, and refrain from discipline that rises to the level of abuse. From an ethical standpoint, parents have the duty to help the child develop a healthy sense of self, become an independent adult, and learn how to be a good citizen. While a car owner is obliged to maintain insurance and refrain from using the car to sell illegal drugs, that owner is also free to destroy the car if she chooses, or run it into the ground through lack of maintenance. Parents are obviously not free to do the same.

* * *

Positive Implications of the Alternative Insemination Market

While the market for parenthood has negative effects, it also has positive ones. These positive components of the AI market are both practical and theoretical.

* * *

The practical effect of new family structures is profound. While it is difficult, if not impossible, to estimate the number of new families that exist by virtue of AI, one can look to increases in single motherhood recorded by the Census and social science data to note the increasing numbers of children born to gay couples and single people. These families take various forms, including two same-sex parents, a gay male couple and a lesbian couple coparenting, a lesbian and a gay man coparenting, a single lesbian (or heterosexual woman) coparenting with a gay male couple, a heterosexual woman coparenting with a gay man, and a lesbian or bisexual woman coparenting with a heterosexual man.

The increasing prevalence of these new families is positive in several ways. First, as parenthood is an important social and personal experience, opening that option to previously excluded individuals facilitates human flourishing for those people and thus for society as a whole. Moreover, the importance of parenthood as a social responsibility means that people who can now become parents can become recognized as fuller citizens in the process. Of course, people should be recognized as citizens whether or not they are parents. But as a matter of equality, whether or not parenthood is properly considered a marker of citizenship, everyone should have access to it if some people have access to it. Finally, these new families undermine the traditional family, a form that is central to both gender and sexual orientation subordination.[37]

* * *

One important effect of new family forms is that they increase agency for women and gay people generally by undermining patriarchal understandings of family. As these new families live their lives, interacting with schools, neighbors, employers, employees, and other families, the social definition of what counts as a family inevitably evolves. To the chagrin of some social conservatives, family begins to mean the group that people choose rather than one ordained by nature or a divine authority.

The market is a key player in this transformation. If public law was the sole determinant of who could become a parent through alternative insemination or other reproductive technologies, then many gay people would likely be excluded from that opportunity. While American law leaves AI to the market, other countries regulate it, generally excluding gay people from becoming parents through AI.[38] Importantly, many of these bans allow opposite-sex unmarried couples to use reproductive technologies, revealing majoritarian bias against gay people as parents even in countries that recognize them as partners. While some jurisdictions, such as Holland, allow lesbian couples to alternatively inseminate, this rule excludes single lesbians from becoming parents through AI. The majoritarian moral bias of this regulation turns on its genesis in a public decision-making process. Since European health care is socialized, public bodies decide who has access to services such as AI. In the United States, in contrast, privatized health care leaves access issues to the market. As long as lesbians can purchase AI in the U.S. system, they may become parents by this method.

* * *

In addition to these practical, positive effects, the alternative insemination market has positive theoretical implications. Most important is that these new family forms, made possible by webs of contracts and a relatively free market, supplement our notions of family as natural with notions of family as intentional or functional. In short, alternative insemination, and reproductive technologies generally, contribute to the replacement of status-based understandings of family with contractual models.

* * *

Second, most scholarship on commodification assumes that women and other socially marginalized people will be the sellers of contested commodities, while men or other socially powerful people will be the buyers. But the alternative insemination market defies this generalization, inverting feminist concerns with the commodification of sex and reproduction. Feminists have articulated concerns that surrogacy harms women by tempting poor women to sell something precious they would not otherwise sell. Similarly, anti-prostitution and anti-pornography feminists contend that both the actual sellers and women generally are harmed when women sell their bodies for male sexual gratification. In each instance, the feminist concern is that poor women will be objectified by selling intimate parts of themselves out of economic necessity. In the alternative insemination context, in contrast, men are the sellers and women are the buyers. Men sell an intimate part of themselves, generated in an act that remains sexual even in the sterile environs of a doctor's office, to women. While the gametes are objectified, rendered commodities that are exchanged for value, so are the men, or at least the proceeds of their desire. Women, for a change, are the subjects in the transaction, rather than the objects.[39]

In sum, the alternative insemination market has both emancipatory and retrograde aspects. While the positive effects outweigh the negative ones, largely because most of the concerns about the market for parental rights are generalizable to markets generally, concerns about eugenics, access, anonymity, and objectification remain. What also remains is the need for a theory that accounts for this range of positive and negative effects.

Theoretical Grounding for a Multivalent View of Markets

[Richard Posner's defense and Margaret Jane Radin's critique of marketizing parenthood appear earlier in this volume. This article proposes a new theory of commodification that adds the best of Posner and Radin to sociologist Viviana Zelizer's "Differentiated Ties" approach to understanding commodification. By accounting for the ways that contractual analysis deepens our understanding of family, and also the ways that law can implement a regime of incomplete commodification, this theory transcends the conundrum of freedom versus equality in the classical commodification literature.]

* * *

Zelizer's Differentiated Ties Approach to Commodification

Zelizer critiques two models for understanding the exchange of money in intimate relationships, models she dubs "Hostile Worlds" and "Nothing But."[40] Adherents to the Hostile Worlds view of commodification see such a "profound contradiction" between intimate social relations and monetary transfers that "any contact between the two spheres inevitably leads to moral contamination."[41] Mary Lyndon Shanley's recent proposal that the State ban payment for any gametes epitomizes this approach.[42]

Her argument to ban payment for gametes draws a stark distinction between exchanges and gifts. Yet this distinction blurs upon close examination. Her gift morphs into exchange, as she would allow "inconvenience allowances" to promote gamete transfers.[43] The slippage is not surprising since, as Carol Rose has observed, gifts and exchanges routinely "melt together."[44] Despite the intuitive appeal of a stark separation between money and love, as both Zelizer and Rose demonstrate, the Hostile Worlds view is inadequate because it simply does not reflect the world in which we live.

Zelizer next demonstrates the weaknesses of what she calls Nothing But approaches to commodification. These arguments contend that intimate relations involving monetary exchanges are nothing but: (1) rational exchanges, indistinguishable from markets; (2) expression of cultural values; or (3) coercion.[45] Zelizer suggests these Nothing But approaches fail to explain the variable degrees of commensurability that people experience as they live their lives. While Hostile Worlds views money and love as mutually exclusive (complete incommensurability), she explains, the Nothing But approaches see everything as commensurable, as soon as we see the basis for commensurability: market, culture, or power.

Posner and Landes's approach to the parenthood market falls into the Nothing But camp, contending that the market for adoption is nothing but a market like any other. The critique of Posner's work shows the weakness of this approach. Many, even most, scholars do not see parenthood and cash as completely commensurable. Zelizer offers a view she calls Differentiated Ties to fill this gap, contending that her approach, unlike the Hostile Worlds or Nothing But approaches, accounts for degrees of commensurability.[46]

Zelizer's Differentiated Ties approach accounts for the ways that people mark their relationships with particular forms of payments, so that monetary exchanges, rather than tainting intimacy, can constitute an important part of intimacy. For example, one indication that a social engagement is a date is the act of treating, one person picking up the bill for both. But picking up the bill may also reflect hierarchy, as when the boss takes his assistant out to lunch for Secretary's Day. Moreover, important milestones in a romantic relationship are marked by financial transfers, such as designating the beloved as beneficiary of a life insurance policy or individual retirement account, signifying an engagement with a diamond ring, merging some or all finances in joint bank accounts and spending money on a wedding.

* * *

[The article then summarizes the antiessentialist theory of Diana Fuss,[47] using it to contend that views of commodification are incomplete if they assume commodification is all good or bad, just as views of men and women are incomplete if they assume, for example, that all men are violent or that all women are nurturing.]

The new and improved theory of commodification combines the best of Posner's, Radin's, and Zelizer's analyses with antiessentialist theory. It embraces Posner's insight that contract analysis allows us to think about intimate affiliation in new ways, and Radin's recognition that commodification can have plural meanings. It leaves behind, however, the essentialism in both commodification enthusiasm and commodification skepticism. In doing so, it accounts for the full range of consequences of commodification.

* * *

Conclusion

Many people wince at the mention of privatization, assuming that market mechanisms benefit powerful players at the expense of everyone else. This article questions this assumption, using the alternative insemination market to illustrate some weaknesses in contemporary commodification theory and propose a new and improved theory of commodification that, rather than being sharply skeptical or enthusiastic, accounts for multiple valances of commodification in any particular context. Zelizer's Differentiated Ties approach to marketization might be able to do the antiessentialist work required of such a theory. If this exercise in deciding what is wrong (and right) about the parenthood market opens up new possibilities for mining market mechanisms, a new generation of legal scholarship could result. At the very least, we might get a fuller articulation of what is wrong with selling parental rights and obligations (and legal economic rhetoric generally) than what we have now, namely something better than conclusory claims that rely on negative connotations of the term "commodification" instead of identifying precise dangers of the market.

NOTES

1. Reprinted with permission from *What's Wrong with a Parenthood Market? A New and Improved Theory of Commodification*, by Martha M. Ertman 82 N.C.L. Rev. 1 (2003).

2. Notable exceptions might be the sellers, buyers, transporters, and other intermediaries in the sale of mostly female babies in rural China due to poverty. Elisabeth Rosenthal, *Bias for Boys Leads to Sale of Baby Girls in China*, N.Y. Times, July 20, 2003, at A6.

3. Elisabeth M. Landes & Richard A. Posner, *The Economics of the Baby Shortage*, 7 J. Leg. Stud. 323 (1978).

4. *See, e.g.,* Elizabeth Anderson, Value in Ethics and Economics 172 (1993); Margaret Jane Radin, Contested Commodities: The Trouble with Trade in Sex, Children, Body Parts, and Other Things 137–40 (1996).

5. Radin, *supra* note 4, at 139.

6. Terminology is important in this discussion. I use "parenthood market" to mean a transfer of parental rights and responsibilities for a price. Posner and Landes used the phrases "market in adoption" and "free market in babies." *See* Landes & Posner, *supra* note 3, at 324. But Posner later altered his terminology, suggesting that the transaction is better described as the sale of parental rights. *See* Richard A. Posner, Economic Analysis of Law 167–70 (5th ed. 1998). He also has clarified that he "did not advocate a free market in babies." *See* Richard A. Posner, *Mischaracterized Views*, 69 Judicature 321, 321 (1986). Instead, he advocates a market that is regulated "less stringently than is done today." *See* Richard A. Posner, *The Regulation of the Market in Adoptions*, 67 B.U. L. Rev. 59, 72 (1987). Other scholarship, in contrast, uses the term "baby selling." *See, e.g.,* Radin, *supra* note 4, at 139. Not surprisingly, defenders of the market use the term "parenthood market" while detractors use the term "baby selling" to amplify their point. Defenders contend, as I do, at least in the case of alternative insemination, that parents are obtaining rights and obligations, while detractors see babies as objects being transferred for a price like inanimate objects or farm animals.

7. The phrase "human flourishing" echoes Margaret Jane Radin's language in her canonical critique of commodification. *See* Radin, *supra* note 4, at 64.

8. The specter of slavery is always in the background of discussions about the parenthood market and baby selling. Slavery and baby selling are not mutually exclusive; babies were among the black people enslaved and treated as commodities in the United States, and children are among the chief targets, along with women, of contemporary slave traders. Barbara Crosette, *What It Takes to Stop Slavery*, N.Y. Times, Apr. 22, 2001, at E4. But even assuming that we can think of the transfer of parental rights and obligations as baby selling, *see supra* note 6, commodification skeptic Margaret Jane Radin points out that it can be misleading to think about it as slavery. *See* Radin, *supra* note 4, at 138–39.

9. Merriam-Webster's Collegiate Dictionary 712 (10th ed. 1993).

10. *See* Viviana A. Zelizer, Pricing the Priceless Child: The Changing Social Value of Children (1985); Viviana A. Zelizer, The Social Meaning of Money (1994); Viviana A. Zelizer, *The Purchase of Intimacy*, 25 L. & Soc. Inquiry 817 (2000).

11. Facilitating this kind of family formation is positive both because parenthood is an important component of personhood and citizenship for many people and because irrational prejudice has barred gay and single people from being parents. Expanding people's options and countering invidious discrimination, generally speaking, furthers human flourishing. The only principled reason one could oppose these things is if gay people are inadequate parents. But empirical research demonstrates that children of gay and single parents fare as well as chil-

dren of heterosexuals and couples. *See* Raymond W. Chan et al., *Psychological Adjustment Among Children Conceived via Donor Insemination by Lesbian and Heterosexual Mothers,* 69 Child Dev. 443, 453–54 (1998); Judith Stacey & Timothy J. Biblarz, *(How) Does the Sexual Orientation of Parents Matter?,* 66 Am. Soc. Rev. 159, 167, 168–71 (2001).

12. At Pacific Reproductive Services, a sperm bank with offices in San Francisco and Pasadena, donors are paid between $60 and $80 per donation and contribute, on average, once weekly over a minimum one-year period. Pacific Reproductive Services, Becoming a Sperm Donor, at http://www.hellobaby.com/becomingspermdonor.html (last visited Nov. 3, 2003). This sperm bank pays more if donors are willing to be identified than if they remain anonymous.

13. New York State Task Force on Life and the Law, Assisted Reproductive Technologies: Analysis and Recommendations for Public Policy 255–56 (1998); California Cryobank, Inc., Service & Fee Schedule (March 2003), http://www.cryobank.com/fees_ds.cfm?page=9.

14. Rachel Pepper, The Ultimate Guide to Pregnancy for Lesbians 45, 51 (1999).

15. *See* Robin Marantz Henig, *Pandora's Baby,* Sci. Am., June 2003, at 62, 65.

16. California Cryobank, Inc., When You Succeed, We Succeed (promotional brochure), available at http://www.cryobank.com/pdf/fds.pdf, at 2 (last visited Nov. 3, 2003).

17. New York State Task Force, *supra* note 13, at 251 (1998).

18. California Cryobank, *supra* note 16, at 7.

19. *Id.* at 5; California Cryobank, *supra* note 13 (listing a $15 fee for a long donor profile, with a $5 discount if ordered online).

20. *See* Rainbow Flag Health Services, A Known Donor Sperm Bank, at http://www.gayspermbank.com (last visited Aug. 25, 2003); Gardiner Harris, *New Rules on Sperm Donations by Gays,* N.Y. Times, May 20, 2004, at A16.

21. Unif. Parentage Act 5(b) cmt. (noting that Colorado and Wyoming sever donor rights when women are inseminated with physician involvement, regardless of whether they are married).

22. Unif. Parentage Act 702, 9B U.L.A. 355 (2000).

23. Frozen Donor Semen Specimen Agreement of California Cryobank, Inc.

24. Alan R. Bromberg & Lewis D. Lowenfels, 4 Securities Fraud and Commodities Fraud 8.6 (1998).

25. *See, e.g.,* Marsha Garrison, *Law Making for Baby Making: An Interpretive Approach to the Determination of Legal Parentage,* 113 Harv. L. Rev. 835 (2000) at 852, 877, 896–920; *See generally* Mary Lyndon Shanley, *Collaboration and Commodification in Assisted Procreation: Reflections on an Open Market and Anonymous Donation of Human Sperm and Eggs,* 36 Law & Soc'y Rev. 257 (2002) at 273–75.

26. Karen M. Ginsberg, Note, *FDA Approved? A Critique of the Artificial Insemination Industry in the United States,* 30 U. Mich. J.L. Reform 823, 826 (1997); *See also* Office of Tech. Assessment, U.S. Cong., Background Paper, Artificial Insemination: Practice in the United States, Summary of a 1987 Survey 3 (1988).

27. *See, e.g.,* David Blankenhorn, Fatherless America: Confronting Our Most Urgent Social Problem 171–84 (1995) at 171–72; Radin, *supra* note 4, at 136–40; *See generally* Shanley *supra* note 25, at 271-273.

28. California Cryobank at 1–7. The catalog similarly notifies buyers that donors of mixed race or "unique ancestries" are stored in vials with "RED caps and are shipped in RED canes." *Id.*

29. U.S. Dep't of Comm., Profiles of Demographic Characteristics, 2000 Census of Population and Housing 1 (2000).

30. California's population includes more Asians than the general American population. *Compare* U.S. Census Bureau, California 2000: Summary Population and Housing Characteristics tbl.3 (2002) (documenting that Asians are 10.9% of California's total population), http://www.census.gov/census2000/states/ca.html (last visited Nov. 22, 2003).

31. While it is difficult to get reliable information on the prevalence of hair color, a hair color company, Clairol, estimates that 19% of American females are naturally blonde. Kristi Turnquist, *Oh, Lighten Up! More and More People are Dyeing To Be Blondes,* Oregonian, July 13, 2000, at E1.

32. *See, e.g.,* 42 U.S.C. 2000e-2 (1994).

33. *See Palmore v. Sidoti,* 466 U.S. 429, 433 (1984); *Loving v. Virginia,* 388 U.S. 1, 2 (1967).

34. Shanley, *supra* note 25, at 265–66, 272.

35. *See* Garrison, *supra* note 25, at 902–13.

36. Radin, *supra* note 4, at 139.

37. *See* Betty Friedan, The Feminine Mystique 33–69 (1997); Adrienne Rich, *Compulsory Heterosexuality and Lesbian Existence,* in The Lesbian and Gay Studies Reader 227, 232–34 (Abelove et al. eds., 1993).

38. Nancy D. Polikoff, *Recognizing Partners But Not Parents/Recognizing Parents But Not Partners: Gay and Lesbian Family Law in Europe and the United States,* 17 N.Y.L. Sch. J. Hum. Rts. 711, 719–26 (2000).

39. For a canonical feminist critique of the exchange of women between men, *See* Gayle Rubin, *The Traffic in Women: Notes on the "Political Economy" of Sex,* in Toward an Anthropology of Women 157 (Rayna R. Reitner ed., 1975).

40. Zelizer, *The Purchase of Intimacy, supra* note 10, at 817.

41. *Id.* at 818.

42. Shanley, *supra* note 25, at 271–73.

43. *Id.* at 275–76.

44. Carol M. Rose, *Giving, Trading, Thieving, and Trusting: How and Why Gifts Become Exchanges and (More Importantly) Vice Versa*, 44 Fla. L. Rev. 295, 296 (1992).

45. Zelizer, *The Purchase of Intimacy, supra* note 10, at 818.

46. *Id.* at 819.

47. Diana Fuss, Essentially Speaking: Feminism, Nature and Difference (1990).

Home Economics

What Is the Difference between a Family and a Corporation?

Teemu Ruskola

Rose is a rose is a rose is a rose.[1]   —Gertrude Stein

The absence of meaning is no doubt intolerable, but it would be just as intolerable to see the world assume a definitive meaning.[2]
—Jean Baudrillard

The spread of the rhetoric as well as practice of commodification has been subject to many critiques. While the critiques of commodification are myriad, there have been far fewer attempts at envisioning what the world would look and feel like if the rhetoric of commodification should give way—to what? That, of course, is the question. What *would* be an alternative to the way we currently organize the marketplace? In our present economic and legal understanding, the family is at least in theory the last surviving haven from the relentless spread of markets and commodification. Whether the family in fact constitutes such a haven is an entirely different question, as most contemporary observers recognize, yet conceptually we do not seem to have many other alternative paradigms for economic organization, except for the socialist model of a planned economy, and that paradigm certainly seems to have exhausted its political appeal for now. What, then, are we left with, given that we obviously cannot organize our entire economic system on the template of the family either?

Or can we? The notion of arranging an entire society on the ideological model of the family is in fact not simply an intriguing thought experiment. In the Neo-Confucian orthodoxy that obtained in China from the eleventh century to the collapse of the imperial state in 1911, the family *was* the paradigmatic governance model in affairs political, social, and economic. I first rehearse briefly a claim I have made in greater detail elsewhere, arguing that in late imperial China extended families often constituted what I call "clan corporations."[3] After de-naturalizing traditional Chinese kinship structures, I consider the investment of Anglo-American liberal theories in the integrity and distinctiveness of the corporation and the family, which I treat as paradigmatic units in the economic and intimate spheres, respectively. The governing logic of the economic sphere is that of reciprocity, while the intimate sphere operates—at least ideally— on the basis of altruistic kinship norms. I draw on Gary Becker's economic theory of the family to suggest that, prevailing ideologies aside, we can indeed interpret the modern American nuclear family as a kind of "family corporation" as well. In the end, there is no firm boundary between the "family" and the "corporation."

Family as Corporation (Part 1): Late Imperial China

Altruism offers its own definitions of legal certainty and freedom.[4]
—Duncan Kennedy

Many traditional Chinese extended families can be usefully interpreted as "corporations."[5] They were large kinship groups that stayed together, not necessarily merely (or at all) because of the members' affective ties but also (or even instead) as a means of accumulating capital and pursuing profit more effectively. As kinship groups, they were governed by family law, which performed many of the functions that corporation law performs in America today.

Before describing this traditional Chinese "corporation law," as we could call it, it is useful to contrast some of the background assumptions in traditional Chinese legal thought and modern American law.[6] Americans live in a legal system the basic unit of which is the category of the person. Every legal right and duty has to be held by a "person," no matter the conceptual stretch. Indeed, a central problem for Anglo-American corporation law has been how to justify the existence of collective entities, such as corporations, in a way that accords with liberal individualism. This in turn has given us the legal fiction of the corporation as a person in its own right.

In contrast, in the Confucian view, the collective was morally more real than the individual. Traditional Chinese corporate entities could hence take collective legal personality as a given. Instead, the main problem for Chinese business enterprises was Confucian hostility to profit-seeking in general.[7] In the Confucian scheme, even the larger political and social communities were conceptualized in terms of the family, and, as in family ideologies everywhere, one was not supposed to profit at the expense of family members.[8] Therefore, traditional Chinese corporation law focused on justifying to the state the *type* of collective entity that seeks profit at the expense of others, and then divide its profits unevenly among various classes of members/owners/workers. This is precisely why clan corporations insisted on characterizing themselves as extended families. As long as an entity constituted a kinship group, it enjoyed legal recognition. By implication, these clan corporations were governed by family law. Indeed, family was the paradigmatic form of private ordering, much like contract is the paradigm for private ordering in American law.

But just what does it mean to suggest that many Chinese clans are usefully understood as "corporations"? Most American corporate law academics focus on the fact that corporations have a centralized management structure that separates the corporation's owners from its managers. A corollary of this feature is the so-called agency problem, which has been the defining problem of American corporate law since at least the 1930s: Given the division of functions between the owners and the managers of a corporation, how can the owners, as principals, monitor the managers, who are—at least in theory—merely their agents?[9] Chinese clan corporations certainly met the core part of the definition of the corporation in that they had a centralized management structure.[10] In many clan corporations, kinship was a legal fiction that both required a separation of ownership and management and at the time sought to resolve the resulting agency problem by means of kinship norms.

Indeed, the kinship of Chinese clan corporations was often as much of a legal fiction as the personality of Euro-American corporations. The preeminent example of this was the legal merger of two clans. Since there are only about 400 Chinese family names, it was not uncommon for two unrelated clans in the same locale to have the same family name. Frequently, if they wanted to pool their capital together to set up a new business, they would combine their genealogies by fabricating a long-dead shared ancestor to whom they would begin offering sacrifices. Subsequently, the clan would draw up a contract for how to run their joint enterprise. The contracts were often quite detailed. Apart from instructions for carrying out sacrificial duties in the name of the clan's ancestors, they contained specifications on how to manage the general assets of the ancestral trust, as well as provisions on how to select full-time professional managers, how to select auditors, what the managers' and other officers' duties were, and so forth—basically, corporation bylaws in the form of trust instructions. In fact, often the parties would take the contract to the local magistrate, who would stamp it and promise to enforce its provisions, thus giving the rules the express force of law.

There are cases of a single clan adopting as many as three hundred members. Evidently, poor families that could not afford to hold on to their human capital ended up selling it to wealthy clan corporations. There is little question of the economic aspect of these transactions. The adoption contracts specified the price (higher for boys than for girls), and the sellers guaranteed title (by representing that the adoptee had not been kidnapped or obtained otherwise illegally) and assured that if something should "happen" to the adoptee subsequently, it would be of no concern to the sellers. Likewise, wives and concubines were, in many ways, bought and sold in the market for productive and reproductive labor. Marriage was, literally, a written contract that specified the economic terms of the transaction, including bride price.

The family metaphor not only justified the existence of clan corporations vis-à-vis the state, it also supplied a model for corporate governance in which ownership and management were separated. This separation in turn resulted in the same agency problem that afflicts the modern corporation. In the orthodox Confucian view, kinship relationships are paradigmatically hierarchical, with the senior kin exercising authority over the junior kin. In the context of a family business this means that while all property is owned by the family as a whole, family elders have the right to *manage* the property. Yet the elders also owe fiduciary duties of loyalty and care to those below them. Conceptually, this mirrors precisely the structure of modern American corporate law: managers have the authority to run the corporation, subject to a fiduciary obligation to do so in the interests of the shareholders.

Even after this summary reconstruction of a relatively sophisticated model of traditional Chinese corporation law, one may still ask, How well did this model work in practice? Not very well. To be sure, there are cases of clan members bringing successful suits against clan managers who sold off corporate property in their own names, for example. However, on the whole, clan corporations seem to have been run by small groups of wealthy well-educated men who, for practical purposes, ran the clans as their private empires. This is hardly surprising, given the social reality of kinship hierarchies. Indeed, the oft-quoted Confucian saying, "There is no parent who is not right," sounds rather like the Chinese version of the so-called business judgment rule of U.S. corporate law, which gives managers virtually unchecked discretion in running the corporation; with only moderate hyperbole, the business judgment rule could be paraphrased to say, "There is no manager who is not right."

Yet it seems that the failure of Confucian "corporation law" to live up to its potential is not—or at least not solely—the result of cynical abuse of power by those occupying the higher echelons of social hierarchy. Part of the problem lay in the very conceptualization of radical organic unity in the family. Constituting a single genealogical tree, the members of a Confucian clan were regarded as part of a single entity. To the extent that one thinks of the kinship group as literally "one body," in the Confucian idiom, the family head is virtually infallible. In the physical body, the head has decision-making power over the limbs, for example, but it is difficult to conceive that the head would purposely try to take advantage of or hurt the limbs. By definition, whatever benefits the head accrues to the benefit of the rest of the body as well. Hence, the head of a clan corporation was rarely limited by the need to act in the collective interest of the clan because, in effect, he *defined* that collective interest.

Nevertheless, despite certain striking structural similarities, traditional Chinese corporation law and modern American corporation law rest on diametrically opposed conceptual foundations. As I suggested above, fitting a collective entity such as the corporation into our individualistic mode of legal thinking has been a longtime problem for legal scholars. The most recent American theory of the corporation basically individualizes the corporation by viewing it as ultimately nothing more (or less) than a "nexus of contracts" among individual participants in the corporate venture.[11] Insofar as there are certain "mandatory" rules of corporation law that cannot be contracted around—such as fiduciary duties— even these rules are rationalized as representing the hypothetical contracts that the parties would have entered into had they had the opportunity and all requisite information to do so.

This view of the corporation as an essentially voluntary, artificial aggregate of individual constituents stands in sharp contrast to the Chinese clan corporation, which claimed to be an organic, real entity in its own right. Yet as even this brief account suggests, the Chinese clan corporation was in fact seething with contracts and all manner of self-seeking behavior that hardly accords with the pursuit of collective interest. The traditional Chinese clan was, indeed, a *kind* of corporation—or from the opposite perspective, the traditional Chinese corporation was a *kind* of family.

Family as Corporation (Part 2): Modern America

> In my research during the past six years, I have turned from an interest in old and new elite family organization in the Kingdom of Tonga to a not unrelated study of the achievement, in the face of considerable obstacles, of descent group organization among American families of great wealth.[12]   —George Marcus

But even if we agree that the Chinese case shows us that the family and the corporation can be difficult, even impossible, to distinguish, that case is of course a historically specific one. Can it tell us anything that might be of general theoretical interest? It is (perhaps) relatively easy to see the possibilities of applying a similar analysis to the intergenerational management of dynastic property even in the contemporary United States, as George Marcus suggests. But would it be possible, or productive, to apply a similar analysis to the more ordinary modern American nuclear family and its legal regulation?

At least on the surface, the histories of the family and the corporation in Anglo-American law are remarkably similar. Just as the corporation, as a legal concept, has evolved from a metaphysically real collective entity to a mere nexus of contracts, so has the family. In Blackstone's view, in marriage husband and wife became one person (although as Justice Black subsequently observed, "the one" was the husband).[13] Similarly, minor children were subsumed into their father's legal personality. Today, of course, the nuclear family is no longer viewed as a single corporate person: even after they enter into the marriage contract, both husband and wife remain legally distinct persons.[14]

Yet a similar historical trajectory from an entity-based conception to a contractarian understanding does not, alone, make the family an instance of the corporation. Presumably, what is unique about the corporation is that the participants in the corporate venture seek to maximize their *eco-*

nomic utility, while economic analysis seems misplaced in the case of the family. Indeed, while Law and Economics has marched from one doctrinal area to another, family law remains an area relatively untouched by economic analysis.[15]

The economist Gary Becker has, however, performed an extensive economic analysis of the family, which suggests that we *can* view the contemporary American nuclear family as a kind of closely held corporation —namely, a nexus of two contracts that is limited to one male and one female participant (given the current legal restraints on polygamy and same-sex marriage). Indeed, for Becker "marriage" is simply shorthand for "a written, oral, or customary long-term contract between a man and a woman to produce children, food, and other commodities in a common household."[16] This particular definition treats offspring as products of marriage, but elsewhere in Becker's analysis even children become partners in the nexus of contracts that is his economic family. For example, according to Becker the parental expectation that children care for them in their old age is "an implicit contract" between parents and children.[17]

Of course, family relationships are heavily regulated by the state, just as corporations are, which in turn means that they in fact do not constitute a perfectly free contractual association.[18] Becker's response to this is exactly the same as that of corporate contractarians. He too explains mandatory rules of family law as corresponding to the hypothetical contracts that the parties *would* enter into, in the absence of transaction costs and with access to complete information. For example, Becker argues that the state regulates divorce "to mimic the terms of contracts between husbands and wives and parents and children that are not feasible."[19] Taking the contractual metaphor to its ultimate conclusion, Becker posits implicit contracts even between parents and their "potential," unborn children, to justify their nonexistence![20] With the suggestion that even unborn children have somehow agreed not to be born, the metaphysical structure of Becker's economic family is eminently clear: It is contract all the way down.

Much as the key to corporate organization is the functional differentiation among various participants—most importantly, the differentiation between owners and managers—so in Becker's analysis the family, too, is founded on a division of labor, save that here the crucial division is based on sex, rather than ownership. Husbands perform wage labor in the marketplace, and wives care for the home and children. This differentiation implies divergent interests between husbands and wives, and it results in rather similar kinds of monitoring problems as does the separation of management and ownership in the corporation, namely "shirking, cheating, pilfering, and other malfeasance."[21] The sexual division of labor between market work and housework is justified on the same economic grounds as the division of labor in corporations—efficiency—and it has ultimately the same unpleasant side effect, namely unequal distribution of material resources.[22] (Indeed, Becker has no moral problems with same-sex couples, only that a lack of a sexual division of labor is liable to render same-sex couples relatively less efficient.)[23]

How does this kind of economic family—or, more tendentiously, "family corporation"—address its particular types of monitoring problems? They are resolved through altruism, which permits the spouses—at least in theory—to trust each other in performing their differentiated tasks. It turns out that even though the family members *are* individuals, rather than mere undifferentiated aspects of a single entity, their individual "utility functions" are, in the end, interdependent—economists' tender jargon for altruism.[24] Formally, this is a departure from corporation law, which imputes a *legal* fiduciary relation where no such relationship may exist psychologically, thereby seeking to create the conditions of actual trust that purportedly exist naturally in the family. Though distinct in form, the two solutions to opportunistic behavior are structurally analogous. Comparing the solutions, Becker suggests that altruism is "more common within households than within firms" simply because it happens to be "more efficient in small organizations."[25] The different solutions to the monitoring problems of the corporation and the family appear thus to be a function of the *size* of the economic entity, not a qualitative difference between kinds of entities.

Given this analysis, what *is* the fundamental difference between Becker's economic family and a business corporation? Both are joint undertakings to accomplish various corporate purposes. To be sure, households tend to be small, while corporations can be enormous. But, again, this means only that the family is best viewed as a kind of *small* corporation, whose monitoring problems are consequently best resolved by means of intrafamily altruism. Yet one might argue that the *capital* that spouses bring into a marriage is different from corporate capital in that it consists not only of financial capital but also of various kinds of human capital, such as cultural and symbolic capital.[26] But the argument fails, for corporations too rely on human capital as well as financial capital.

Alternatively, perhaps the family is distinguishable from the corporation by what it *produces*. In this view, corporations produce commodities while families produce psychic welfare. The U.S. Supreme Court has indeed insisted that marriage is an enterprise whose goal is the production of "a bilateral loyalty, not commercial or social projects."[27] But the Supreme Court aside, families most certainly seek to accumulate property and material well-being—many of them are just as devoted to making money as the most avaricious corporations are.

Besides, the work of corporations need not be limited to material production. In her poststructuralist rendering of Marx, Miranda Joseph advances a broader, performative understanding of production. In this analysis, corporations produce not only goods but also subjects, identities, and communities.[28] Given the loosening of corporate structures under the pressures of the New Economy, Joseph even sees a "way for older kinship structures to reinhabit production."[29] Certainly even the largest companies prefer to present themselves to the public as well as to their employees as families. Observing that corporations need not be just "cash-generating machines," Alan Schwartz similarly suggests that they can also function as "communities in and through which people pursue their good and from which they partly derive a sense of self."[30]

Indeed, the employment contract, a central component in the corporate nexus of contracts, is quite different from a contract for the sale of widgets. It is a relational contract, or a contract embedded in a long-term relationship that tends to generate its own norms. In Robert Gordon's felicitous phrase, partners to relational contracts "treat their contracts more like marriages than one-night-stands," the latter presumably being the sexual equivalent of a purely self-interested market transaction.[31] Like other kinds of contracts, employment contracts too of course vary from the temp's "one-night stand" with the corporation to the corporate "marriage" of a long-term employee. And just as both marriages and one-night stands can be either good or bad, so too can their corporate equivalents, whichever contractual form they may take.[32]

But perhaps there is one final line of argument in defense of the uniqueness of the family. Marriage is a relationship based on *sex*, a unique human good. Indeed, in Martha Fineman's critical observation, our conceptions of intimate association are peculiarly limited to what she terms the "sexual family."[33] Yet even conceding the dominance of this conventional conception, we can still view the family as a *kind* of corporation: a relatively small corporation specializing in (subsidized) heterosexual sex

—call it the "sexual corporation," to paraphrase Fineman. Furthermore, as Fineman pointedly observes, there is no ultimate reason that sex *should* be at the core of the definition of the family. Why should we care whether Donald and Ivana Trump, for example, ever had sex or whether their brief merger was purely economic? Besides, why *shouldn't* sex should be an object of explicit exchange in the contract that is marriage? As Linda Hirshman and Jane Larson argue, there is no *a priori* reason that exchanging "sex for support" could not be a fair trade.[34] Moreover, the exchange of sex is certainly not limited to the (putatively) intimate sphere: It occurs in corporations as well as in the White House. If it didn't, there would presumably be little need for sexual harassment law in the workplace, or for a constitutional procedure to impeach a president who engages in sexual acts in the Oval Office.

Economic Reciprocity or Altruistic Kinship?

> The "way of giving," the manner, the forms, are what separate a gift from straight exchange, moral obligation from economic obligation.[35]
>
> —Pierre Bourdieu

For an anthropologist, Becker's analysis of the family is hardly news. There is a long ethnographic tradition, going back to at least to Bronislaw Malinowski, describing the ultimately self-interested logic of gift exchange.[36] In a paradigmatic commercial exchange, the exchange of goods for goods, or money for goods, is simultaneous, while in a gift exchange the return gift is deferred.[37] Yet gifts, too, impose their own obligations of reciprocity. Nevertheless, one cannot give a return gift immediately. As an all too obvious *quid pro quo,* an immediate return gift would rudely expose the self-interested nature of the exchange and thus undermine the ultimate effect of exchanging gift: the creation of solidarity and goodwill between the participants. However, when the two kinds of exchange are viewed synchronically rather than diachronically, there emerges a functional equivalence between the exchange of ostensibly unmotivated gifts over time and self-interested spot exchanges on the market. In the latter, the economic logic is transparent, while in the former it is hidden.

Becker's study of the (admittedly rather outdated "traditional") American nuclear family makes a similar analytic move. A wife's caring for the home any one month and the husband's sharing (part of) his paycheck that month are surely gifts in the sense that neither party is explicitly basing his or her contribution on the express expectation of a *quid pro quo*. Yet, when these exchanges that occur over time are viewed as part of *one* transaction, a contract called "marriage," it appears that, as part of the traditional sexual division of labor, wives are providing housework and sexual services in return for maintenance. This insight is hardly novel. In *The Origin of Family, Private Property, and the State*, Engels expressly likens wives to workers,[38] and even more provocatively, Simone de Beauvoir characterizes a wife as a person "hired for life by one man," while a prostitute happens to have "several clients who pay her by the piece."[39] The difference, in this view, between marriage and prostitution is simply one between a relational contract and a discrete one. As perhaps the purest expression of this logic, Iranian law allows men to circumvent the prohibition of prostitution by entering into "temporary marriages" with women—say, into a one-hour marriage in return for the proper amount of cash.[40]

But even if the economic, or "objective," meaning of marriage is contractual exchange, the fact remains that, subjectively, most people do not *experience* their marriages as prostitution but love (or "love," as Becker uses the term only in scare quotes, to emphasize its extra-economic nature). An orthodox Marxian would no doubt view this subjective experience as reflecting simply the success of bourgeois ideology—people's "imaginary relationship" to "their real conditions existence," in Althusser's merciless definition of ideology.[41] Alternatively, it is useful to analyze the phenomenon in Pierre Bourdieu's sociological terminology. According to Bourdieu, a gift exchange is based on an active "misrecognition" of the *material* economy of the exchange that underlies the more apparent *symbolic* economy of altruistic sharing.[42] At the same time, this misrecognition is not simply epiphenomenal or superstructural. Rather, even in misrecognized relations that misrecognition constitutes "an integral part of the reality of those relations."[43] Similarly, in the case of the family we seem to suffer from a massive collective misrecognition of the material exchanges that place within it.[44] Furthermore, not only do we misrecognize kinship relationships as always already enchanted, but we also misrecognize corporations and economic relations as always already disenchanted. Yet despite *their* ideological representation as always and only material, corporations too have their own symbolic and affective economies.

If there is anything, then, that is evident from the family-corporation comparison, it is that the economic and intimate spheres are simply not as distinct as the two models would suggest. Just as the "family" is not oppositional to the "corporation," the "corporation" is not oppositional to the "family." Neither model represents a truth about social and economic organization. While one biologizes the organization of a socioeconomic unit by explaining its internal stratification as a function of the *natural* sexual division of labor, the other voluntarizes a socioeconomic unit by explaining its unequal functional differentiation in terms of *consensual* agreements.

In the final analysis, are we thus led to the conclusion that the only real difference between the family and the corporation is the fact that, at a minimum, kinship does have its basis in blood ties, even if any resulting sexual differentiation itself is socially, rather than biologically, determined? Even this is too strong a claim. Like the traditional Chinese, we too have families that are entirely creations of contract. Consider, for example, the husband and wife with an adoptive child, a family where no member is biologically related to any other. With advances in reproductive technology, the tenuousness of kinship is perhaps easier to see today, but kinship as a category has never been any more self-defining than our ideas about the corporation or of contract. One need only recall the remarkable ease with which slave-owning families in antebellum America absorbed their human capital into the idiom of the family.[45] In the end there is no "real" kinship to be found, or as Judith Butler puts it, "kinship can signify any number of social arrangements that organize the reproduction of social life."[46]

Beyond Objective vs. Subjective: Into the Political

Exchanges are peacefully resolved wars. . . .[47]   —Claude Lévi-Strauss

But even if neither families nor corporations can be reduced either to the objective logic of economic exchange or to the subjective experience of gifts freely given out of solidarity, economic and legal liberalism are premised on the notion that life consists of separate arenas, each of which is governed by a distinctive distributive logic. Ultimately, in the liberal schema all of social life is divisible into three macrospheres: (1) the political sphere of the state (where power is distributed on the fixed principle of one-person-one-vote), (2) the economic sphere of the market (consisting of voluntary exchanges governed by the laws of contract and property), and (3) the sphere of intimate personal relations (organized preeminently in families where the bonds of biology and interpersonal solidarity determine the intrafamily distribution of material and psychic welfare).[48]

The liberal ideology with regard to the first two spheres is highly individualistic. Exchanges in the market are governed by contracts among individuals, and even the political sphere is conceptualized metaphorically in terms of a hypothetical social contract among citizens. The family and the intimate sphere, in contrast, are a locus where affection, love, and intense identification with others make contractual exchanges inappropriate, posited as they are on the existence of competing self-interests. In this exceptional area where the boundary between self-interest and the interest of the other becomes blurred, there is little reason for the state and the law to interfere. To do so would in fact be counterproductive to the very intimacy that sustains the sphere since bargains are struck between strangers dealing at arm's length, not partners in a marriage.

At least in the conventional telling, the state was the first of these three spheres to claim autonomy. As recounted by Hobbes, for example, the signing of the social contract marked the separation of state from society and the creation of a distinct sphere of politics, which in turn signaled humanity's passage from the state of nature into civilization.[49] In contrast, the idea of the economic sphere of the market as an autonomous field of its own, parallel to but separate from the state, did not emerge until later —in the nineteenth century, if we follow, say, Karl Polanyi's periodization of the "economic and political origins of our time."[50] While Polanyi certainly recognizes that markets existed even earlier, the late nineteenth century witnessed the final victory of the utopian idea of a self-regulating, and ultimately self-destructive, free market, based on the novel idea that the desire to profit at others' expense was not only a morally permissible but a normatively *desirable* motive for economic action.[51] Before the emergence of the self-regulating market, the market was viewed primarily as an adjunct of the social, subject to whatever substantive regulation was viewed as socially proper, whereas in a world of self-regulating markets the social becomes an adjunct of the economic.[52] Not coincidentally, the idea of the sentimental family that sustains the intimate sphere emerged around the same time as the notion of the marketplace as an autonomous social field. As Michel Foucault puts it, the bourgeois family became "an obligatory locus of affection, love, and sentiment."[53] Within the private, nonstate social space, the sentimental family is the necessary counterpoint against which the free-reigning market ruled by self-interest defines itself.[54]

Even within the vocabulary of liberalism, then, our sole choices are not simply to try to invert the relationship between the economic and intimate spheres—by viewing either the economic as a function of the social (assimilating the corporation to the family) or viewing the social as a function of the economic (assimilating the family to the corporation). Instead, we can also draw on the model of the state and apply the logic of politics to both the economic and the intimate spheres. This has indeed been one of the central strategies of critical theory. In this analysis, neither the family nor the corporation is private. Rather, both are public, and, hence, political.

Even the vocabulary we still use reminds us that, prior to the rise of the ideological firewall separating the state from the marketplace, corporations were viewed as political and regulated as such. The very language of corporate governance is the political language of the state. To begin with, we speak of the "governance" of corporations, even though ordinarily we think that governance is the last thing that markets need, functioning as they do purportedly on "freedom." (One of the most notorious corporations of all time, the British East India Company, indeed *was* the government of India, quite literally.) In terms of titles, corporations are "governed" by "directors" and other corporate "officers."[55] Marx, for one, likened the factory to the army, and the term corporate "officer" certainly invokes the authoritative governance model of the military.[56]

The language in which we describe the family has changed more over time than the language of the corporation, but it is useful to keep in mind that Locke, for example, used the language of the (patriarchal) state to describe the affairs of the family, speaking of family "government," "paternal jurisdiction," and father's "authority to make laws" for the family.[57] We may not wish to turn today's family into a replica of the patriarchal state, yet even today it may be more useful to challenge the organization of both the corporation and the family by analyzing them in explicitly political terms.[58]

In the end, it should be clear that there is no "true" model of either the family or the corporation. The only absolute difference between the corporation and the family is the investment in the *idea* that they are, or must be, fundamentally different—that the family is not the corporation, nor is the corporation the family, and both stand apart from the state. For the purposes of this essay, I am agnostic on whether it is best to model the family on the corporation, or vice versa, or model both on the state, or perhaps seek to create a fourth model. Yet whichever model we choose, we must not think that we have made an ontological discovery about the nature of either the family or the corporation.

As models, both the "family" and the "corporation" are so self-referential that they are perhaps best understood as instances of the "hyperreal"—a concept that no fact can prove or disprove for the simple reason that it "has no relation to any reality whatsoever: it is its own pure simulacrum."[59] We appreciate only the economic aspects of corporation as being parts of its "real" constitution, and we accord the congratulatory label "family" only on those social configurations that accord with our highly idealized notions of kinship. In the tautology that too often passes for analysis, "families" are "families" and "corporations" are "corporations."

Or if Gertrude Stein had been a scholar of corporation law, "corporation is a corporation is a corporation is a corporation."

Conclusion

Ultimately, metaphors of contract and kinship aside, exploitation is possible everywhere, both in symbolic and economic guises, in the institutionalization of altruism in the family and in the institutionalization of profit in the corporation. As social and economic locations, both the family and the corporation are ambiguous, complex, and risky. The terms in which Adrienne Rich describes the family seem potentially equally applicable to the family *and* the corporation: "a battleground, open wound, haven and theater of the absurd."[60] Both are plagued by the same ultimate "agency problem": *Who* has agency? And, as Judith Butler reminds us, agency is always intimately linked to politics: "[T]he epistemological model that offers us a pregiven subject or agent is one that refuses to acknowledge that agency is always and only a political prerogative."[61] To truly reconceptualize corporation law and family law, we will need a more explicitly political analysis of both the corporation and the family. Commodified or not, neither location constitutes a safe haven.

NOTES

In addition to the conference and workshop re-theorizing commodification at the University of Denver Law School and American University, Washington College of Law, I have presented versions of this essay in several fora, including the conference New Economy at the Gonzaga School of Business at Emory University (cosponsored by the Social Science Research Council and the Center for the Study of Myth and Ritual in American Life); the conference Corporations, Capitalism, and Protest at the Baldy Center for Law and Social Policy at SUNY Buffalo; the International Economic Law Forum at the Center for the Study of International Business Law, Brooklyn Law School; the conference Marriage, Democracy, and Families at Hofstra University School of Law; and at Gayatri Chakravorty Spivak's seminar Multiple Narratives of the Politics of Culture at the University of Hawaii. I thank the following individuals in particular for having shared their work and criticisms, both at the above presentations and elsewhere: Michelle Adams, Keith Aoki, Nathaniel Berman, Ritu Birla, Mary Anne Case, Kandice Chuh, Rosemary Coombe, Adrienne Davis, David Eng, Martha Ertman, James Fanto, Martha Fineman, Melissa Fisher, Peter Halewood, Roberta Karmel, Paul Mahoney, Linda McClain, Arthur Pinto, Peggy Radin, Nancy Rosenblum, Gayatri Spivak, Katherine Stone, Leti Volpp, Joan Williams, and Steve Winter. Needless to add, not all of the above agree with my argument, but their questions have much improved it. I thank Dean Claudio Grossman of the Washington College of Law at American University for generous financial support in the preparation of this essay.

1. Gertrude Stein, *Sacred Emily*, in Writings 1903–1932: Portraits and Other Short Works 395 (1998).

2. Jean Baudrillard, Impossible Exchange 128 (Chris Turner trans., 2001).

3. The description of traditional Chinese "corporation law" in the first part of the essay is a summary of a more extended analysis in Teemu Ruskola, *Conceptualizing Corporation and Kinship: Comparative Law and Development Theory in a Chinese Perspective*, 55 Stan. L. Rev. 1599 (2000).

4. Duncan Kennedy, *Form and Substance in Private Law Adjudication*, 89 Harv. L. Rev. 1685, 1773 (1976).

5. I resort to the occasional use of scare quotes in referring to both "families" and "corporations" in order to draw attention explicitly to the provisional nature of both categories. However, even in places where the terms are not contained within quotation marks, it is only for reasons of style and convenience— not to suggest a difference between real and provisional families (or corporations).

6. I use the terms "late imperial China" and "traditional China" interchangeably, with full awareness of the conceptual biases in dividing Chinese history into "traditional" and "modern," where the latter term "usually refer[s] to the

period of significant contact with the modern West." Paul A. Cohen, Discovering History in China 58 (1985). In this essay, I use "traditional China" simply to denote a certain historical period, without implying any particular normative vision of history.

7. The term "Confucian," like "traditional," requires an immediate disclaimer. In this essay, the generic term "Confucianism" refers to the state ideology perpetuated by the imperial civil service examination system. On the one hand, this orthodox Confucianism, which grew increasingly rigid over time, stood in contrast to the philosophical Confucianisms in which it originated. On the other hand, it was also distinct from the Confucian officialdom's actual policies and administrative practices, which did not necessarily always conform to the state's professed ideals. Ruskola, *supra* note 3, at 1607 n18.

8. Needless to say, I am not suggesting that families are not in fact exploitative in many (if not most) places and times. However, exploitation of kin seems to operate, without fail, on the basis of various fictions of reciprocity—with the materially and psychologically subordinated family members receiving, at least in theory, care and protection from the superordinated kinfolk. As Marshall Sahlins observes, "[E]verywhere in the world the indigenous category for exploitation is 'reciprocity.'" Marshall Sahlins, Stone Age Economics 134 (1972).

9. The classic formulation of the agency problem derives from Adolf A. Berle, Jr. & Gardiner Means, The Modern Corporation and Private Property (1933).

10. Arguably, they fulfilled *all* the formal criteria of a modern "corporation." See Ruskola, *supra* note 3, at 1619–56.

11. The most radical contractarian interpretation of corporate law is Frank H. Easterbrook & Daniel R. Fischel, The Economic Structure of Corporate Law (1991).

12. George Marcus, *The Fiduciary Role in American Family Dynasties and Their Institutional Legacy,* in Elites: Ethnographic Issues (George Marcus ed., 1983).

13. United States v. Yazell, 382 U.S. 341, 361 (1966) (Black, J., dissenting).

14. There are other historical parallels as well. Mary Anne Case and Paul Mahoney, for example, observe that both marriage and corporation were initially relatively unregulated legal institutions, with increasing state control that culminated in the eighteenth century. Since then, Case and Mahoney observe, the state's involvement has generally decreased, although much more rapidly in the case of the corporation. Mary Anne Case & Paul G. Mahoney, "The Role of the State in Corporations and Marriage" (manuscript, October 1996). *See also* Paul G. Mahoney, *Contract or Concession? An Essay on the History of Corporate Law,* 34 Ga. L. Rev. 873 (2000).

15. *See, e.g.,* Foundations of Economic Approach to Law 410–11 (Avery Katz ed., 1998).

16. Gary S. Becker, A Treatise on the Family 43 (enlarged ed. 1991).

17. *Id.,* at 255.

18. Of course, despite the endless invocations of "freedom of contract" in American law and culture, *all* contracts are regulated by the state: among the most crucial tasks of contract law is to determine which promises can and cannot be enforced, to what extent, and under what circumstances. The point is simply that the marriage contract is regulated even more, and in more substantive ways, than ordinary common law contracts.

19. Becker, *supra* note 16, at 375. Regarding the state's inventions on behalf of children, Becker similarly argues that they typically "mimic the agreements that would occur if children were capable of arranging for their own care." *Id.,* at 363.

20. *Id.,* at 376–77.

21. *Id.,* at 48.

22. *Id.,* at 78–79.

23. *Id.,* at 330, 397.

24. *Id.,* at 278.

25. *Id.,* at 301.

26. Becker in fact describes families as "firms" with low ratios of " nonhuman capital." *Id.,* at 52–53. On "cultural capital," see Pierre Bourdieu, Outline of a Theory of Practice 171–83 (Richard Nice trans., 1977).

27. Griswold v. Connecticut, 381 U.S. 479, 486 (1965).

28. Miranda Joseph, *The Performance of Production and Consumption,* 16 Social Text 25, at 39–44 (No. 54, 1998).

29. *Id.,* at 43.

30. Alan Schwartz, *The Fairness of Tender Offer Prices in Utilitarian Theory,* 17 J. Legal Stud. 165, 196 (1988).

31. Robert W. Gordon, *Macaulay, Macneil, and the Discovery of Solidarity and Power in Contract Law,* 1985 Wis. L. Rev. 565, 569.

32. Indeed, the paradigmatic employment relationship may be changing from the "marriage" model toward the labor equivalent of a "one-night stand," with multivalent psychological and material implications for both employers and employees. *See* Katherine V. W. Stone, *The New Psychological Contract: Implications of the Changing Workplace for Labor and Employment Law,* 48 UCLA L. Rev. 519 (2001).

33. *See* Martha Albertson Fineman, The Neutered Mother, the Sexual Family, and Other Twentieth-Century Tragedies (1995).

34. Linda R. Hirshman & Jane Larson, Hard Bargains: The Politics of Sex 74 (1998). This is not to prejudge whether or not there may be good *sociocultural* reasons to subject gendered bargains to strict legal scrutiny.

35. Bourdieu, *supra* note 26, at 126.

36. *See* Bronislaw Malinowski, Crime and Custom in Savage Society (1926).

37. In a more sophisticated transaction, the parties can of course also exchange present promises of future performance in return for one another; what matters is the explicit nature of a *quid pro quo* exchange at a fixed point in time.

38. Friedrich Engels, *The Origin of the Family, Private Property, and the State,* in The Marx-Engels Reader 734 (Robert C. Tucker ed., 2d ed. 1978).

39. Simone de Beauvoir, Second Sex 619 (H. M. Parshley trans., 1974).

40. *See* Shahla Haeri, Law of Desire: Temporary Marriage in Shi'i Iran (1989).

41. Louis Althusser, *Ideology and Ideological State Apparatuses (Notes Towards an Investigation),* in Lenin and Philosophy and Other Essays 85, at 109 (Ben Brewster trans., 2001).

42. Bourdieu, *supra* note 26, at 105 ("the functioning of gift exchange presupposes individual and collective misrecognition of the truth of the objective 'mechanism' of the exchange").

43. *Id.,* at 136.

44. There is an extensive feminist literature analyzing the specific processes whereby the law "misrecognizes" (in Bourdieu's terms) the materiality of female labor in marriage. *See, e.g.,* Fineman, *supra* note 33; Joan Williams, *Un*bending Gender: Why Work and Family Conflict and What to Do about It (2000); Katharine B. Silbaugh, *Marriage Contracts and the Family Economy,* Nw. U. L. Rev. 93, 66–143 (1998); Reva B. Siegel, *Home as Work: The First Woman's Right Claims Concerning Wives' Household Labor, 1850–1880,* 103 Yale L.J. 1073 (1994).

45. *See, e.g.,* Elizabeth Fox-Genovese, Within the Plantation Household: Black and White Women of the Old South (1988).

46. Judith Butler, Antigone's Claim 72 (2000). Nor are our tenuous "kinship" practices necessarily any less commodified than those of traditional China —or the antebellum South, for that matter. The market for babies for private adoption *is* just that: a market where babies can be bought for money. Indeed, there is at least one (controversial) legal analysis that treats such commodification as normatively desirable. *See* Elisabeth M. Landes & Richard A. Posner, *The Economics of the Baby Shortage,* 7 J. Legal Stud. 323 (1978). Ironically, it is precisely *Chinese* babies that are a prize commodity in the American adoption market at this historical moment, much as we may be disturbed by the sale of babies in late imperial China. *See* David L. Eng, *Transnational Adoption and Queer Diasporas,* 21 Social Text 1 (No. 76, 2003).

47. Claude Lévi-Strauss, Elementary Structure of Kinship 67 (1969).

48. Probably the most elaborate effort to further divide these spheres of liberal justice into ever finer subspheres is Michael Walzer, Spheres of Justice: A Defense of Pluralism and Equality (1983).

49. Thomas Hobbes, The Leviathan (1651).

50. Karl Polanyi, The Great Transformation: The Political and Economic Origins of Our Time (1957).

51. *Id.*, at 68–76.

52. Indeed, as many observers have noted, the *homo economicus* of the marketplace is of quite recent historical provenance. *See, e.g.*, Sahlins, *supra* note 8; Marcel Mauss, The Gift: The Form and Reason for Exchange in Archaic Societies 32 (W. D. Hall trans., 1990).

53. Michel Foucault, History of Sexuality, Vol. 1, 108 (Robert Hurley trans., 1980).

54. Focusing on the constitutive interdependence of the definitions of family and market, Martha Ertman uses the term "private-private distinction" to describe attempts to demarcate a fixed boundary between the two, and indeed proposes borrowing the law of business organization—which recognizes a multiplicity of legal forms—to regulate intimate associations as well. *See* Martha M. Ertman, *Marriage as Trade: Bridging the Private/Private Distinction*, 36 Harv. C.R.-C.L. L. Rev. 79 (2001). *See also* Frances Olsen, *The Family and the Market: A Study of Ideology and Legal Reform*, 96 Harv. L. Rev. 1497 (1983) (analyzing the market-family dichotomy as a "structure of consciousness").

55. Indeed, while neoclassically oriented economists may be happy to reduce the corporation to a "nexus of contracts," institutional economists recognize the hierarchical structure of corporations. *See, e.g.*, Kenneth Arrow, The Limits of Organization 25, 64 (1974) (describing employment contract as employee's sale of her "willingness to obey *authority*" so that "what is being bought and sold is not a definite objective thing but rather a personal relation"); Oliver Williamson, The Economic Institutions of Capitalism 13 (1985) ("Rather than characterize the firm as a production function, transaction cost economics maintains that the firm is (for many purposes at least) more usefully regarded as a governance structure."). In the institutionalist account, corporations are thus not simply small nexuses of contracts in the even wider web of contracts that is the marketplace as a whole. Rather, corporations are islands of vertically structured hierarchy in an otherwise horizontally organized marketplace. In this view, then, corporations are not just part of the markets but, in an important sense, their very antithesis. *See generally* Oliver Williamson, Markets and Hierarchies (1975).

56. "An industrial army of workers under the command of capital requires, like a real army, officers (managers) and N.C.O.s (foremen, overseers), who command during labour process in the name of capital." 3 Karl Marx, Theories of Surplus Value 491 (1978), *quoted in* Dipesh Chakrabarty, Provincializing Europe 59 (2000).

57. *See, e.g.*, John Locke, The Second Treatise on Civil Government 39, 7, 38 (1986). To be sure, while Locke obviously found it useful to employ political analogies to explain familial relations, he did not consider patriarchal and politi-

cal authority the same. *See* Gordon J. Schochet, The Authoritarian Family and Political Attitudes in Seventeenth Century England: Patriarchalism in Political Thought 245 (1988).

58. Political analyses of the family are even rarer than those of the corporation. As Susan Moller Okin observes, family, unlike other economic arrangements, remains outside the purview of almost all political theories of justice. *See generally* Susan Moller Okin, Justice, Gender, and the Family (1989). Historically, however, activists for women's political rights were in fact deeply concerned with politicizing the family. *See* Reva B. Siegel, *She the People: The Nineteenth Amendment, Sex Equality, Federalism, and the Family,* 115 Harv. L. Rev. 947, 977–1006 (2002).

59. Jean Baudrillard, Simulacra and Simulation 6 (Sheila Faria Glaser trans., 1994).

60. Adrienne Rich, On Lies, Secrets, and Silence 218 (1979).

61. Judith Butler, *Contingent Foundations: Feminism and the Question of 'Postmodernism,'* in Feminists Theorize the Political 13 (Judith Butler & Joan Scott eds., 1992).

Hard Bargains

The Politics of Sex

Linda R. Hirshman and Jane E. Larson[1]

When women and men choose one another, sex, like other forms of human cooperation, benefits both. Sex thus resembles the classic of game theory called the Battle of the Sexes in which cooperation is everyone's preferred strategy, and the only issue is how a man and a woman will divide the surplus of their social cooperation. Yet our assurance that both men and women gain something by sexual cooperation cannot be the last word on the morality or politics of their dealings. Lovers will divide all the good and bad that their union creates and, in the world as we know it, will do so mostly by private bargaining. This heterosexual bargaining takes place between naturally and socially unequal players. Where the strong rule, the outcome of such an exchange is predictable: Weaker players face the choice of accepting a bargain of sex on bad terms, or having a solitary life on better terms but with no sex. Each is a hard bargain.

We propose to change these bargaining outcomes, specifically to divide the surplus of male-female sexual cooperation more equitably. We conclude from history that direct prohibition of sexual conduct is effective only at the margin, opens the door to arbitrary and discriminatory enforcement. By contrast, law has powerful oblique effects on heterosexual bargaining, often regulating indirectly what it cannot reach directly. Because the conventional model of sexual regulation has been prohibitory, in past regimes these bargaining effects have been mostly incidental rather than intended. We intend to invoke law's bargaining effects directly.

Game theory seeks to explain bargaining effects, working from the insight that the initial distribution of power between the players determines bargaining outcomes. A hungry person will work more cheaply than someone with savings in the bank. We can use that knowledge strategically to predict future bargaining outcomes and design legal reforms that will accomplish intended ends by structuring the largely hidden world of sexual bargaining.

Our proposal has two goals: to establish baselines that moderate the downward spiral of unequal bargaining, and to allow for wide play in sexual choice and preference. [T]his rough draft of a sex code demonstrate[s] our principal theoretical claim—that structured bargaining can regulate male-female sexual exchange in the interest of political and moral values of flourishing and equality, and at the same time assure individual autonomy and liberty.

* * *

Adultery

* * *

Like laws against fornication, making adultery unlawful restrains liberty in the interest of marriage. Ordinarily, such support for marriage would benefit women. But the ancient and common law definition of adultery strengthened the bargaining position of husbands and weakened that of wives and lovers. Prior to modern reforms, divorce law, for instance, allowed a husband to discard an adulterous wife (and denied her either a marital property share or child custody rights), but forbade the wife any parallel right to leave and punish a straying husband. So, too, the social tolerance for male infidelity allowed a married man to keep a mistress and yet plead no power to marry her, weakening that woman's sexual bargaining position as well as that of the wife. By contrast, wherever women tried to attack the double standard in law and custom—in the social purity movement, or in "fault" divorce rules that penalized adulterous spouses in marital property division—women's sexual bargaining power was enhanced and that of married men diminished.

* * *

If one spouse breaches a promise of sexual exclusivity, the wronged spouse suffers a personal loss to dignity and reputation, may experience emotional and mental distress, risks exposure to sexually transmitted disease, and may be deceived about his relationship to the children in the family. Yet these injuries are to the person and not to society. Framed as an injury to the person rather than the state, the most appropriate remedy for adultery is civil compensation, either in the form of a "bonus" in the division of marital property upon divorce or death, or a tort action for money damages available either during the ongoing marriage or after divorce.

It is conventional wisdom among legal scholars that the use of fault determinations at any stage of marital dissolution will encourage divorcing parties to perjure themselves. Before no-fault divorce reforms, commentators describe divorce proceedings as almost invariably corrupt and perjurious. This fear of perjury reflects a broader presumption that disputes between sexual intimates are categorically different from other human conflicts, and present unique and difficult problems not easily handled by the existing tools of legal truthfinding. Yet experience belies this conventional wisdom. Several states currently factor some element of fault into the division of marital assets at divorce. We propose that all states adopt the rule that adultery constitutes marital fault, and that fault affects property division at divorce or death.

The second prong of our proposal is to create a tort of adultery. This will, perhaps, generate even more skepticism. Perhaps compensation between spouses makes sense at death or after divorce, but if we presume a sharing model for marriage, is it meaningful to order one spouse to pay damages to another during an ongoing marriage? We argue that there is nothing incongruous about the transfer of assets from one spouse to another during an ongoing relationship. This legally describes, in fact, what happens in the designation of marital property under both common law and community property regimes, although these property interests ordinarily are not liquidated until the marriage ends in either death or divorce. Legal scholar Joan Williams proposes that family property routinely be divided during the course of a marriage, with the practical effect of giving each spouse greater power to manage that property unilaterally. A wealth of research shows that the degree of family decision-making power a spouse exercises depends on the amount of property he or she controls. Thus a transfer of assets from an adulterous spouse would shift power between married people and, given that men have a higher rate of marital infidelity, the greater measure of that shift would be from husband to wife.

NOTE

1. From *Hard Bargains* by Linda R. Hirschman and Jane E. Larson, copyright 1998 by Oxford University Press, Inc. Used with permission of Oxford University Press, Inc.

4. COMMODIFYING BODIES AND BODY PARTS

A Framework for Reparations Claims

Keith N. Hylton[1]

I am aware of two extant legal claims for reparations, the *Farmer-Paellman v. FleetBoston*[2] case in New York and the claim for compensation in Tulsa, Oklahoma. The *FleetBoston* complaint seeks compensatory damages, punitive damages, restitution, and an accounting of profits from American slavery. The Tulsa complaint seeks compensation for victims whose relatives were killed and property destroyed by angry white mobs that rioted though Tulsa's black community in 1921.[3]

My aim is to compare different reparations claims in terms of their goals and viability as tort suits. I contrast two approaches observed in the claims: a "social welfare" model and a "doing justice" model [and] conclude that reparations claims under the justice model are far more consistent with tort doctrine and likely to meet their goals as compared to the social-welfare-based claims.

Although both the *FleetBoston* and Tulsa complaints have been described as reparations claims, there are big differences between them. They reflect two distinct and in some ways conflicting policies behind reparations litigation. One approach is driven in large part by social welfare and distributional goals. The other approach is based on a desire to correct historical injustices, simply to "do justice."[4]

The justice approach views reparations lawsuits as efforts to identify uncorrected or uncompensated cases of injustice, and to seek "correction" in the Aristotelian sense of returning the parties to positions roughly similar to the preinjury setting. This involves identifying particular individuals or entities that committed bad acts, and particular victims who were injured; specifying the precise acts that led to injury, and the sums necessary to compensate victims for the injuries. The Tulsa complaint fits this description. The lawyers who filed the complaint have rounded up individuals who had their property destroyed and relatives killed or injured during the Tulsa riots. Another example under this category is the class action suit brought against the federal government in 1973 for the Tuskegee syphilis experiment. Yet another example is the Civil Liberties Act of 1988 providing compensation for Japanese Americans held in internment camps during World War II.[5] The statute compensates only direct victims—the individuals who were held in internment camps.

In contrast to the justice approach, the social welfare approach reflected in the *FleetBoston* complaint does not seek to do justice in any discrete case, but rather, aims for a significant redistribution of wealth. The complaint names several existing corporations as defendants, such as FleetBoston (a bank) and CSX (a railroad), including a reference to one thousand "Corporate Does" as additional defendants.[6] There are so many businesses that had a hand in slavery that the complaint could just as well refer to ten thousand Corporate Does. The plaintiff, Deadria Farmer-Paellmann, sues on "behalf of herself and all other similarly situated" persons.[7] This means she is suing on behalf of all African Americans whose ancestors were held as slaves in this country.

There is nothing controversial about doing justice. Most lawsuits claim to have that principle at their core. However, the social welfare approach is unusual in litigation. For at the core of the *FleetBoston* suit is a belief that reparations litigation will compensate or correct for years and years of inattention, or insufficient attention, to the welfare of African Americans. In short, proponents hope that *FleetBoston*-like lawsuits will force through the kind of broad redistribution of resources toward poor black citizens that could never be achieved through the political process.

* * *

Statistics and the Social Welfare Approach

* * *

The statistics show that the poverty rate among black families fell from nearly 50 percent in 1959 to 28 percent in 1969. It held steady at that level for the next twenty years. The most recent year in Table 1, 1999, shows the poverty rate for black families at 22 percent, a substantial decline relative to the stagnation of the previous three decades.

* * *

Families below Poverty Line in the United States (percent)

Year	Families White	Families Black	Families White Married	Families Black Married
1959	15.2	48.1		
1969	7.7	27.9		
1979	6.9	27.8	4.7	13.2
1989	7.8	27.8	5.0	11.3
1999	7.3	21.9	4.4	7.1

Source: U.S. Bureau of the Census.

Table 1 suggests a pessimistic outlook for the potential of social welfare–based reparations litigation. The most aggressive period of redistributional policy implemented by the federal government, 1969 to 1989,[8] coincides with more than twenty years of stagnation in the poverty rate for black families. For those who believe in the transformational potential of *FleetBoston*-like lawsuits, this is a disappointing fact.

* * *

The relative poverty rates of married families to general families suggest most of the difference between black and white family poverty rates can be explained by family structure—specifically, the low rate of marriage among black families below the poverty line.

That the black poverty rate appears to be so largely influenced by family structure has to be considered a discouraging piece of information for proponents of the social welfare model of reparations litigation. The problem is that reparations lawsuits cannot do much to change the marriage rate in poor black families.

* * *

A Framework for Claims

Distinguishing Reparations Claims from Ordinary Tort Claims

Two features distinguish reparations claims from ordinary, run-of-the-mill tort lawsuits. One is a credible assertion by the plaintiffs that they

faced an insurmountable *legal barrier* in the past, such that it would have
been impossible to seek a remedy in the courts at the time of the initial injury. This is true of both the Tulsa and *FleetBoston* complaints. The Tulsa
riots were initiated by lynch mobs who claimed to be searching for a
black man accused of assaulting a white woman. In that period, when
racist lynchings were common, black residents of Tulsa would have rationally assumed that no court would seriously consider a lawsuit seeking compensation for injuries caused by a lynch mob. In the *FleetBoston*
complaint, the claim of a legal barrier is obviously more credible: slavery
was formally sanctioned by law until its abolition in 1865.

The second feature distinguishing reparations claims from ordinary
tort lawsuits is *passage of time*. The claims are typically brought long
after relevant statutes of limitations for torts as well as many crimes have
passed. The passage of time problem presents several legal difficulties.
First, there is the problem of *identification*. The identities of the victims
and injurers are hard to determine,[9] though the importance of this problem varies with the type of reparations claim. The Tulsa complaint involves identifiable victims. The injurers in the Tulsa case are to some extent identifiable. Some of the vandals and killers are probably still alive,
perhaps living quietly in Tulsa. If you accept plaintiffs' claims that the city
and state governments are partially responsible, which seems plausible
when a group launches a pogrom and goes unpunished by the state, then
those entities still exist and can be sued. However, the local and state governments have surely changed since the days of the Tulsa riots. They are
formally the same entities that were in existence at the time of the riots,
but in terms of the characteristics relevant to the lawsuit they are vastly
different from their predecessor regimes.

* * *

Perhaps the more troubling identification problem in *FleetBoston* is that
it appears to be a matter of chance that some corporations have been
identified as successors.[10] One assumes there were many more firms involved in slavery than the number that appear as named defendants on
the *FleetBoston* complaint. Suppose the named defendants (including the
Corporate Does) were all held liable. Should their liability be capped, as
in the market share liability cases, by their degree of responsibility in creating the harm?

The identification problem on the part of plaintiffs in the *FleetBoston*
case is even more severe. Who are the descendants of the victims of slavery? What should be done about African Americans who cannot trace an

unbroken blood line through other descendants of slaves? Should an African American multimillionaire who can trace an unbroken blood line to slavery be considered within the plaintiff class?

The second problem connected to the passage of time is described as *causation* or *proximate cause* in the law. The law requires proof of a causal link between the plaintiff's injury claim and the defendant's breach of the legal standard. For now, it should be enough to say that it will not be easy to prove that a particular plaintiff's position today is the direct result of slavery several generations ago.

The third problem connected to the passage of time is that of *prescription of legal rights*. I refer to statutes of limitation. They exist in part because of the reasons mentioned above—identification and causation, both of which become difficult to prove as time passes. They also exist because the deterrent effect of the law is likely to be weak, relative to the cost of its implementation, as more time passes between initial injury and enforcement of the law.

* * *

Conclusion

When thinking about reparations claims, one should avoid the mistake of viewing them as all the same, having the same difficulties in terms of identification of plaintiffs, causation, and prescription of legal rights. In fact, reparations claims vary along many legal dimensions, creating a rich array in terms of their consistency with settled law. This article has set out a framework for evaluating the likelihood that these claims will prevail in court, primarily in the hope that it might help clarify the issues in debates over the wisdom of reparations litigation.

NOTES

1. Reprinted with permission from 24 B.C. Third World L. J. 31 (2004).

2. Complaint and Jury Trial Demand, Farmer-Paellman v. FleetBoston Fin. Corp. (E.D.N.Y. 2002) (No. CV 02-1862).

3. For a recent news account, see Tatsha Robertson, *Quest for vindication: Survivors of 1921 Tulsa race riots hail suit for reparations*, Boston Globe, Feb. 26, 2003, at A1 and A17; Lyle Denniston, *Lawyers hope Tulsa case can lay foundation for more claims*, Boston Globe, Feb. 26, 2003, at A16. For a full his-

torical treatment, see Alfred L. Brophy, Reconstructing the Dreamland: The Tulsa Riot of 1921—Race, Reparations, and Reconstruction (2002).

4. This view of reparations claims brings them within the class of recent criminal trials of former Klansmen for murders committed in the 1960s. See, e.g., Rick Bragg, *Former Klansman Is Found Guilty of 1966 Killing*, N.Y. Times, March 1, 2003, at A11.

5. See 50 U.S.C.A. § 1989.

6. Complaint and Jury Trial Demand at 1, Farmer-Paellman (No. CV 02-1892).

7. *Id.* at 1.

8. Admittedly, the civil rights and great society legislation began during the mid-1960s, but it is unlikely that they had much of an impact on relative wealth levels by 1969. Thus, the 1969–1989 period covered by the Census data probably provide a reliable measure of the effects of redistributional policies.

9. For discussions of the identification problem, see Mari Matsuda, *Looking to the Bottom: Critical Legal Studies and Reparations*, 22 Harv. C.R.-C.L. L. Rev. 323 (1987).

10. This version of the identification problem—inability to get substantially all of the responsible injurers in court—has emerged as a barrier to market share liability claims. See, e.g., Skipworth v. Lead Industries Association, 690 A.2d 169 (Pa. 1997).

National Organ Transplant Act (NOTA)

42 U.S.C.A. §274e (1993)

§274e Prohibition of Organ Purchases
(A) Prohibition
It shall be unlawful for any person to knowingly acquire, receive, or otherwise transfer any human organ for valuable consideration for use in human transplantation if the transfer affects interstate commerce.
(B) Penalties
Any person who violates subsection (a) of this section shall be fined not more than $50,000 or imprisoned not more than five years, or both.
(C) Definitions
For purposes of subsection (a) of this section:

(1) The term "human organ" means the human (including fetal) kidney, liver, heart, lung, pancreas, bone marrow, cornea, eye, bone, and skin or any subpart thereof and any other human organ (or any subpart thereof, including that derived from a fetus) specified by the Secretary of Health and Human Services regulation.

(2) The term "valuable consideration" does not include the reasonable payments associated with the removal, transportation, implantation, processing, preservation, quality control, and storage of human organ or the expenses of travel, housing, and lost wages incurred by the donor of a human organ in connection with the donation of the organ.

(3) The term "interstate commerce" has the meaning prescribed for it by section 321 (b) of Title 21.

(Pub. L. 98-507, Title III, §301, Oct. 19, 1984, 98 Stat. 2346; Pub. L. 100-607, Title IV, §407, Nov. 4, 1988, 102 Stat. 3116.)

Increasing the Supply
of Transplant Organs
The Virtues of an Options Market

Lloyd R. Cohen[1]

An Options Market in Organs

The morally acceptable solution to the problem of acquiring a greater proportion of potentially transplantable organs is for people to sell their own organs for delivery after their death. Unlike your mother, you do have a moral claim to a property right in your body and therefore may sell parts of it. There is a long history of the legal and widespread sale by people of their own blood, semen, hair, and saliva. How would such a market operate?

[T]he major organs of those who die of disease are usually unsuitable for transplantation; the best organs are retrieved from victims of traumatic head injuries and cerebral hemorrhage. By the time these people arrive at the hospital they are usually in a state of permanent unconsciousness. Therefore if we are to acquire these organs by contract with the original owner and possessor it must be via an options market in which individuals in good health grant an option to an organ procurer to harvest their organs for delivery after death.

In its appearance and functioning, the proposed market would be but a slight variation on the current system of contingent organ donation. People could be offered the opportunity to sign a short and simple organ sales contracts when they receive their driver's license, buy insurance, file a tax return, walk down the street, or through the mail. The only substantial difference from the current system is that the vendor will be promised remuneration in return. The appropriate sales campaign would be extensive rather than intensive. It would seek to inform as many people as possible as cheaply as possible. It is my belief that for virtually no potential vendor will this prove to be a terribly complex or difficult decision to make. Once they understand what is being offered the vast majority will assent and a small minority will not.

[T]he problem with our current system of organ acquisition is *not* that people in general have a strong antipathy to organ donation that must be overcome through some sort of highly elaborate and creative campaign. It is rather that: (1) *nothing* is being offered to them in exchange; and (2) no clear, routine, commonly understood and shared mechanism exists that transfers the moral and legal right to this valuable property from the decedent to the recipient. The principal goal of the contract is to offer a small incentive to potential vendors and to routinize and formalize the changing claim to the organs by transferring them across a market.

Nothing more personal and something considerably less elaborate is required than the mailing one receives from the Publishers Clearing House Sweepstakes. Pertinent information, such as name, sex, date of birth, social security number, beneficiary, and limitations on which organs may be harvested, would be placed in a computer file that could be accessed by telephone or computer. In that respect it would function much like the National Organ Procurement and Transplantation Network.

NOTE

1. From Lloyd Cohen, *Increasing the Supply of Transplant Organs: The Virtues of an Options Market*. Austin: R. G. Landes; Heidelberg: Springer-Verlag, 1995. Reprinted with permission.

Futures Markets in Everything

Noam Schieber[1]

Even for an institution accustomed to P.R. fiascos, the Pentagon hit something of a milestone this year with its aborted Policy Analysis Market, or PAM. The idea was to find an efficient way of collecting a wide range of expert opinion about threats to national security. To do this, the Pentagon created a futures market—a cross between a betting pool and a stock market—in which government officials and other experts would buy and sell "assets," or futures, linked to developments in the Middle East. An asset might be, say, an imminent terrorist attack in Jordan. If experts believed that such an event was likely, they'd snatch up the asset, and its value would rise. Though individual investors would stand to benefit, the real beneficiary would be U.S. policy makers, who'd get otherwise diffuse opinion distilled into a single, easy-to-interpret number: the price of a future.

Congress didn't see it that way. This summer, shortly after an enterprising Senate staff member came across a sample bet—on the assassination of Yasir Arafat—on a Pentagon contractor's Web site, two Democratic senators held a press conference to denounce the idea as "stupid" and "morally wrong." PAM and its chief Pentagon advocate, Adm. John Poindexter, were promptly put out to pasture.

But the principle behind PAM is the very same principle behind the Democrats' criticism of the war in Iraq: the importance of basing national security decisions on expert opinion (especially when that opinion is at odds with the opinions of administration high-ups). Democrats wonder why the administration's prewar intelligence wasn't challenged more aggressively by the C.I.A. Well, a market involving lots of people with access to intelligence clearly would have challenged it. What C.I.A. analyst

357

with knowledge of Iraq would have bet money that we'd discover an advanced nuclear program after the war?

The beauty of futures markets like PAM is that they're among the most meritocratic institutions ever devised. You bet on the chance that event X will occur on date Y and regardless of where your office is or the size of your security detail, you make money if you're right and lose money if you're wrong. In 1997, Hewlett-Packard set up a similar market with midlevel sales managers who, in the normal course of things, might have shaded their estimates on the high side to please their superiors. The advantage of the company's futures market was that it was anonymous, meaning no one could be punished for hazarding an honest opinion. Factor in the profit motive, and it's no surprise that honesty is exactly what the market elicited. About 75 percent of the market's forecasts over the next three years proved better predictors of actual sales than the company's official forecasts.

Authority isn't the only bias that futures markets are designed to overcome. You might think people would be blinded by their partisan affiliations when trying to predict, say, the outcome of a presidential election. But the Iowa Electronic Markets, a futures exchange run by the University of Iowa business school, proved better at predicting the results of the last four presidential elections than 75 percent of the 600 polls conducted during that period. A futures market created by two European academics helped overcome partisan loyalty among soccer fans, correctly predicting the outcome of 15 of 21 games in the Euro 2000 tournament. And futures markets have even helped sort hype from reality in Hollywood. Traders on the Hollywood Stock Exchange, a movie industry futures market, in which bets are made with play money, correctly picked the winners in six of eight top Oscar categories in 2001; they went eight for eight the year before.

Still, meritocracy isn't democracy. Like any market, a futures market is only as good as the information it processes. Robin Hanson, a professor of economics at George Mason University, likes to distinguish between naive investors (so-called sheep) and investors who base decisions on hard evidence (so-called wolves). Get too many sheep and not enough wolves, and it's possible that you end up with bad predictions. Which, in the end, may have been the real flaw in the Pentagon's PAM experiment. The original model for PAM was limited to people with access to the best available information. But thanks to some bureaucratic red tape, the idea of using government analysts was junked in favor of opening the market to the general public. Unfortunately, when it comes to national security, there may not be enough lay people out there with good information— and the people who do have information (that is, the bad guys) have little incentive to share it.

NOTE

1. Copyright 2003, Noam Schieber. Reprinted by permission. Originally published in New York Times Sunday Magazine, Dec. 14, 2003, at 51.

D.

Retheorizing Commodification

To Commodify or
Not to Commodify
That Is Not *the Question*

Joan C. Williams and Viviana A. Zelizer[1]

> [P]hilosophical problems . . . are, of course, not empirical problems;
> they are solved, rather, by looking into the workings of our lan-
> guage . . . not by giving new information, but by arranging what
> we have always known. Philosophy is a battle against the bewitch-
> ment of our intelligence by means of language.[2]

Is commodification a good thing? Many feminists think so. Martha Ertman has argued in favor of commodifying marriage, and Katharine Silbaugh has defended the commodification of women's household labor.[3]

Other feminists disagree. A particularly articulate example is the
philosopher Elizabeth Anderson, who argues that women's household
labor should be valued through "love, honor and appreciation" rather
than through market norms.[4] "When women's labor is treated as a commodity," she argues, "the women who perform it are degraded."[5] Commodification of women's labor can result in the exploitation of women,
in Anderson's view, when women's noncommercial motivations are exploited by rational self-interested maximizers.[6]

Leading commodification theorist Margaret Jane Radin, agrees.[7] Focusing on sexuality and reproduction, Radin has expressed concern that
commodification hurts women,[8] "If the social regime permits buying and
selling of sexual and reproductive activities, thereby treating them as fungible market commodities given the current understandings of monetary

exchanges, there is threat to the personhood of women, who are the 'owners' of these 'commodities.'"[9]

The landscape gets less tidy still when one considers conversations outside feminism. Influential queer theorists, notably Alexandra Chasin, have explored the ways in which queer "politics and . . . market activity are interdependent systems, having grown up with each other and reinforced each other. . . ."[10] Theorist Miranda Joseph agrees, noting that while "hijacking the corporate means of production of the discursive value of commodities can be a powerful intervention," such "hijacking" also can have negative effects on queer politics.[11]

Similar ambiguity exists with respect to the commodification of racial and ethnic identities. bell hooks argues that when such identities "become commodified as resources for pleasure," the culture and bodies of dominated groups become "an alternative playground [for] . . . members of dominating races. . . ."[12] Other influential scholars of race have explored the market's liberating potential, as in Regina Austin's study in this volume of Kwanzaa as a means of empowering the African-American community. Still others have examined how black cultural traditions, from rhythm and blues to hip hop, have been co-opted for the financial benefit of whites.[13]

Meanwhile, in the intellectual property arena, debates rage over commodification of indigenous identities and products, including DNA, the Internet, and rights to publicity.[14] Many intellectual property commentators have noted the insistent march toward propertization, but sharp disagreements have arisen over whether the increasing scope of intellectual property rights will incentivize creativity or help destroy it.[15] In contexts as diverse as whether Amazon should be allowed to patent "one click" shopping,[16] whether DNA sequences and life forms should be patentable,[17] and who should own the traditional assets of indigenous peoples (from artwork[18] to plants with medicinal properties[19] to religious symbols),[20] some argue in favor of increased commodification while others oppose it.[21]

Is commodification a good or a bad thing? People of goodwill appear to disagree. This article neither defends commodification nor attacks it. Instead, we argue that "to commodify or not to commodify" is the wrong question. We begin with a brief look at why people tend to frame a wide variety of disparate social issues in terms of an on-off decision about whether or not to commodify. We then describe a new approach, Differentiated Ties, which we apply to four different arenas: care work; subordinated identities; intellectual property; and human beings (or parts thereof).

To Commodify or Not to Commodify: The Wrong Question

Hopes and worries about commodification both derive from a worldview that divides the landscape into separate, antagonistic spheres.[22] In one sphere is a world of cool calculation and market mediation; in the other is a world of sociable sentiment and reciprocal relations. This conventional bifurcated vision obscures our understanding of how economic life —the production, distribution, and consumption of valuable goods and services—actually operates. Division of the world into dichotomous domains rests on a number of proposed distinctions: capitalist firms versus the informal economy; perfect versus imperfect markets, serious versus trivial economies, male versus female economic activity.

The culprit is neither blind masculine prejudice nor momentary confusion. The culprit is an intellectual tradition more than 200 years old. Since the nineteenth century, social analysts have repeatedly assumed that the social world organizes around competing, incompatible principles: *Gemeinschaft* and *Gesellschaft,* ascription and achievement, sentiment and rationality, solidarity and self-interest.

Two complementary, but partly independent, arguments prevail. We can call them the theories of *separate spheres* and of *hostile worlds.* Separate spheres theories identify two distinct domains that operate according to different principles: rationality, efficiency, and planning on one side; solidarity, sentiment, and impulse on the other. We should, according to this theory, expect different results and satisfactions to emerge from the two dichotomous spheres.

Hostile worlds theories maintain that when the separate spheres come into contact they contaminate each other. Their mixing, says the theory, corrupts both spheres. Invasion of the sentimental world by instrumental rationality desecrates and desiccates it, while introducing sentiment into rational transactions threatens inefficiency, favoritism, cronyism, and other forms of corruption. By this account, a sharp divide exists, and should persist, between intimate social relations and economic transactions, marking any contact between the two spheres as moral contamination. In this view, intimacy thrives only if people erect effective barriers around it. Thus, goes the reasoning, orderly social systems keep the realms apart.

Hostile worlds and separate spheres theories gained force in the context of nineteenth century industrial capitalism. Although earlier theories often assumed the coexistence of solidarity and self-interest, both advocates and critics of industrial capitalism adopted the assumption that industrial rationality purged solidarity, sentiment, and intimacy from markets, firms, and national economies at the same time that "home sweet home" became a shelter from the harsh realities of workaday economic activity. Whether commentators deplored capitalism's advance, celebrated it, or treated it as a necessary evil, advocates as well as critics agreed that the world of intimacy and the world of economics were hostile worlds, and that any mixing would lead to contamination. In the hostile worlds view, sentiment within the economic sphere generates favoritism and inefficiency, while rationality within the sentimental sphere destroys intimacy, sincerity, and solidarity. Strong segregation of the spheres preserved each sphere from degradation.[23]

The hostile worlds theory reappears in contemporary critiques of commodification. Over and over again we hear that the expansion of market activity to an ever-widening range of goods and services and to the world's diverse cultures is producing a stultifying subjection of spontaneity, creativity, and particularity to a single rational standard. From Robert Kuttner's *Everything for Sale*,[24] to Robert Lane's *The Loss of Happiness in Market Democracies*,[25] to Jeremy Rifkin's *The Age of Access*, social critics fret over what Rifkin calls the "clash of culture and commerce."[26] "When most relationships become commercial relationships," Rifkin worries,

> what is left for relationships of a noncommercial nature . . . when one's life becomes little more than an ongoing series of commercial transactions held together by contracts and financial instruments, what happens to the kinds of traditional reciprocal relationships that are born of affection, love, and devotion?[27]

Nothing remains but cold instrumental rationality.

The theoretical stakes are high. On one hand lies the notion that social life divides according to separate, dichotomous organizing principles; on the other hand lies the notion that contact between these two worlds corrupts them. At issue are the value, potency, and compatibility of different economic activities. The separate spheres doctrine alleges a divide between serious economic phenomena, such as those engaged in by firms and corporations, and supposedly trivial, sentimental economies, such as households, microcredits, immigrant roscas, remittances, pawning, gifts, and consumption.[28]

As descriptions and explanations, theories of separate spheres and hostile worlds fail badly. Actual studies of concrete social settings, from auctions to households, do not yield descriptions of spheres neatly separated, nor of segregated hostile worlds.[29] We can bridge the gap between intimacy and impersonality by recognizing the wide variety of differentiated ties that cut across particular social settings. Instead of living in segregated spheres, people participate in dense networks of social relations that intertwine the intimate and economic dimensions of life.

Within high-powered corporations, for example, we discover personal networks of patrons and clients that cut across formal departmental boundaries; in households we discover extensive ties to external agents of production, distribution, and consumption. In households, members maintain distinct economic ties not only to each other but also to employers, to local merchants, to doctors, to credit card companies, to telephone companies, and to the U.S. government. In corporate and household settings, people are constantly managing and distinguishing multiple sets of distinctive social relations. They manage different ties simultaneously rather than moving them from one sealed chamber to another.

All this may seem mysterious or abstract. Yet struggles over distinctions and classifications become dramatically visible in legal disputes. Notice, for example, how various relatives and companions of World Trade Center victims have contested who has the right to compensation for loss of the victim's services, income, and attention.[30] They appear to believe that it is appropriate to intermingle their most intimate feelings of personal loss with economic motivations concerning appropriate levels of compensation.

In short, the vivid traditional picture of two separate spheres—a harsh and hostile market where individuals treat one another instrumentally and are driven by self-interest, and a warm and intimate sphere where people treat one another in a caring fashion and driven by altruism—has two drawbacks. First, it presents a distorted picture of the market, by erasing the relational dimension of many commercial relationships.[31] Second, it presents a distorted picture of intimate transactions, by erasing the economic dimension of intimate relationships.[32] If the conventional picture so clearly is inaccurate, why is it so pervasive? The answer lies in intellectual history.

The Intellectual History of Separate Spheres and Hostile Worlds

In the feudal world, the domains of sentiment and of economics were explicitly linked; indeed, the assumption was that personal fealty to one's lord was the necessary prerequisite of a successful economic relationship.[33] As liberal ideologies began to emerge in the early modern period, initially they still did not embed the hostile worlds and separate spheres imagery of a private sphere of caring altruism set off against a public sphere of individuals in hot pursuit of economic self-interest, and self-interest alone.

Indeed, until well into the nineteenth century, self-interest was seen as properly limited by boundaries set by "the virtues of liberalism," as defined by religion, republicanism, and Scottish moral philosophy.[34] The virtues of liberalism waned as the nineteenth century progressed and liberalism flattened into what historians call possessive individualism. Possessive individualism embraced behavior that traditionally had been decried as selfishness, through a celebration of rational self-interested maximizers pursuing their own self-interest to create the "good life," newly redefined as a life of economic plenty rather than one dedicated to pursuit of the common good in political life.[35] Neoclassical economics is one expression of a new orthodoxy that stood in sharp contrast to the earlier view (held by republican theorists from James Harrington to Thomas Jefferson) of a public sphere defined in terms of politics rather than economics, with virtue defined in political terms as the quality that enabled citizens to pursue the common good, thereby preserving the republic from a descent in to monarchy or tyranny.[36]

As self-interest colonized the public sphere, virtue was depoliticized and relegated to a separate sphere newly defined as the province of women. Intellectual historians have documented the depoliticizing of virtue, and its consignment to the domestic sphere.[37] Domesticity, in turn, functioned as the dangerous supplement of possessive individualism, with women providing both a refuge and a critique of the "bank note world" of exploitative nineteenth century capitalism.[38] Legal historians also document how the onset of domestic ideology erased the economic dimension of marriage, so that legal recovery for the value of wives' labor—which had been seen as uncontroversial—became contested and often impossible.[39] Complementing the notion that men and women inhabited separate spheres was the hostile worlds premise that any intermingling of economic and intimate relations would contaminate intimacy, properly

altruistic, with self-interested behavior.[40] Commodification anxiety policed the sharp and supposedly impenetrable boundaries between the hostile worlds of family and market, as when courts refuse to grant wives
economic entitlements at divorce, anxious that doing so would introduce
strategic behavior into an otherwise-altruistic family sphere.[41]

This brief description shows that the possessive individualism and domesticity, its dangerous supplement, are not just descriptions of a preexisting reality. Instead, they are *just one way of looking of the world*
through a particular ideological lens framed by possessive individualism
on the one hand and the ideology of domesticity on the other. What does
this intellectual history mean for contemporary commodification theory?
The simple on-off question about whether or not to "commodify" perpetuates the assumption of two distinct and hostile worlds: one where
commodification is always appropriate; the other where it never is. A
more useful approach is to recognize that many market transactions have
elements of emotion and sociability, and that many intimate transactions
have economic dimensions—so much so that the Hamlet question of
whether "to commodify or not to commodify" only serves to confuse us.

From Hostile Worlds to Differentiated Ties

The Hamlet question is precisely the view that economic sociology is
challenging. This growing field confronts the assumptions of neoclassical
economics, including the assumption of an economic sphere governed by
dry and dispassionate rational choice and set off against the rest of life.
In a cautious version of their challenge to the neoclassical model, economic sociologists have repeatedly demonstrated that market transactions take place in the context of institutions and social ties that constrain
and stabilize them. For example, entrepreneurs or consumers engaging in
high-risk transactions regularly depend on others with whom they have
already established reliable connections through friendship, kinship, or
long association. A closer look shows that what appear to be self-con-
tained market transactions always involve meaningful, negotiated interpersonal relations, such as transfers of money, that, far from predeter-
mining an impersonal gray quality to the social relations involved, instead
take their meaning from the interpersonal setting in which they occur.[42]

Economic sociology shows that we need to steer away from the question of "to commodify or not to commodify," and appreciate instead that

people strive to define the moral life in a wide variety of social contexts that involve *both* economic dimensions *and* socioemotional relationships. This model of Differentiated Ties allows us to recognize the existence of the complex social ties that cut across particular settings.[43] In all sorts of situations, from predominantly intimate to predominantly impersonal, people differentiate strongly among various kinds of interpersonal relations, marking them with distinctive names, symbols, practices, and media of exchange.

Ties themselves do vary from intimate to impersonal, from durable to fleeting, but ties as such cut across social settings. As a consequence, virtually all social settings contain mixtures of ties that differ in these regards. Participants in intimate relations often differentiate ties in two ways. Ties first are differentiated based on specific relationships, for example, mother-daughter bonds or relationships with one's physician. Second, people adopt economic practices—forms of payment, routines for shared work, joint participation in shopping, and so on—to conform to their understandings of the relationship at hand.[44]

Differentiated ties form in all arenas of social life, including schools, armies, churches, corporations, and voluntary associations. Patron-client relations operate within firms, for example, just as friendship networks often organize a great deal of inequality within schools.

Changing from Separate Spheres and Hostile Worlds to Differentiated Ties does not necessarily make the answers easy. As Wittgenstein pointed out long ago, philosophy does not provide easy answers. Its goal is help us ask right questions.

A Brief Look at Existing Theory

Many contemporary commentators track separate spheres and Hostile Worlds assumptions. Nancy Folbre worries that market notions of self-interested exchange may "corrode ties of affection and obligation."[45] Elizabeth Anderson expresses commodification anxiety when she worries that compensating women's work will degrade the women who perform it.[46] Commodification anxiety also frames debates among legal scholars. Margaret Jane Radin begins from the Hostile Worlds tradition, her discourse, framed in reaction to law and economics' universal commodifiers, advocating the sale of virtually everything, including babies, organs, and justice.[47] Radin ultimately moves beyond the Hostile Worlds paradigm even as she remains trapped by it, noticing that many human interactions involve not full commodification or none at all but, instead, "incomplete commodification."[48]

In the view of Katharine Silbaugh, incomplete commodification means that no "*spheres* [exist] where the market is completely banished or completely dominant."[49] In contrast, Radin perpetuates Hostile World premises, as when she argues:

> The way to a less commodified society is to see and foster the non-market aspect of much of what we buy and sell, to honor our internally plural understandings, rather than to erect a wall to keep a certain few things completely off the market and abandon everything else to market rationality.[50]

Note how Radin's analysis preserves a yearning for a world free from commodification even as she senses the artificiality of a model that posits dichotomous worlds.

"There Is Nothing So Practical as a Good Theory"[51]

For the remainder of this essay we attempt to show how Differentiated Ties clarifies the muddy waters of commodification debates.

Where Marketization Is Not the Issue: Valuing Domestic Work versus Marketizing Care Work

In contexts involving care work, the issue often is not whether to marketize (i.e., to allocate a certain set of social relations to the market) but whether to assign appropriate value to women's work by revisiting the question of who owns what within the family.[52] Thus Katharine Silbaugh argues in favor of taking "the economics of home labor seriously,"[53] and of "importing economic reasoning" to transform our understanding of care work. In the face of women's disproportionate poverty, she argues, "Concern over women's lives becoming entirely commodified seems by comparison an abstract worry."[54] Silbaugh proposes to link care work with economic entitlements in a broad range of contexts, advocating Social Security and broad privately financed post-divorce entitlements for homemakers,[55] and broad publicly financed entitlements for "welfare" mothers, to name only a few.[56]

Note that in these contexts, Silbaugh and others involved in the care work debate[57] are not proposing to shift a set of intimate relationships into the market sphere, as do advocates of markets for babies. Courts' anxiety over commodification only serves to confuse the issue, for advocating post-divorce and other entitlements does not entail bringing market norms and institutions into the family.[58] The operative issue is not *whether or not* the husband's wage should be owned within the family; the question, instead, is *who should own it*. Should we preserve the unilateral ownership traditionally allocated to the husband, or should we shift to a regime of joint ownership shared by the spouses, on the grounds that the husband's wage typically reflects not only his market work but also the flow of family work from his wife—which supported his ability to devote his energies one-sidedly to market work.

Note how the term "commodification" blurs the distinction between proposals to bring market institutions and strategic, self-interested behavior into family life, and proposals to end domesticity's erasure of women's economic contributions. To clarify this distinction, we propose to shift in this context from the term "commodification" to the term "marketization." The new term allows us to avoid confusion between feminist proposals to recognize the economic dimension of care work, and proposals to introduce market norms and institutions into new arenas of social life.

Where Marketization Is Liberatory

Debates over the commodification of lesbigay identities, unlike much of the commodification debate in feminism, *do* indeed involve marketization. Often marketization will seem *liberating* because it signals public acceptance of the existence and legitimacy of lesbigay identities. Where subordination is accomplished through erasure, marketization can be an important step in the right direction. For example, if mainstream media carry an advertisement targeted to lesbians or gays, mainstream Americans thereby acknowledge their existence.[59]

Marketization also sometimes holds the potential to protect lesbigay access to privileges readily available to privileged heterosexuals. This explains queer theorists' embrace of the commodification of sperm and eggs because they trust the impersonality of the market more than the social attitudes of social workers who would otherwise be in charge of allocating opportunities for parenthood.

When Marketization Is Oppressive: The Market Delivers Many Things Efficiently, Including Race, Gender, and Class Privilege

On the other hand, in other contexts marketization seems oppressive because it bring us face to face with race, gender, and class privilege in ways that seem an affront to our commitments to equality and human dignity. Consider the transnational market for organs. Kidneys sell for $10,000 to $15,000 in Egypt, and for $1500 in India, where a cornea fetches $4000.[60]

Markets often work *too well*: among the many things they deliver efficiently are race, gender, and class privilege. To have the rich drink tastier coffee than the poor does not seem a big deal. To have the poor selling their corneas is another matter.

Markets for nonreplaceable human organs, and for babies, seem distasteful because adopting market norms in these contexts confronts us with "preferences" that reflect racism and class brutality. In the market for babies, for example, black babies can be expected to cost less than white babies (and do).[61] Moreover, when a cornea fetches $4000, some parents in India will go blind so that people in richer countries don't have to. This kind of commodification brings us uncomfortably close to brutal power disparities that should be limited.

Indeed, consigning some social relations to the market may seem an affront to human dignity. Doesn't allowing parents to sell corneas, or allowing black babies to sell for less than white, undermine our cultural commitment to equality as well?

Radin worries that, in some contexts, marketization "transform[s] the texture of the world" by sullying our sense that life is a pearl without price.[62] Commodification anxiety in this context involves a clash between two strains of the liberal tradition, one of which has not yet been introduced. In contrast to possessive individualism's obsessive focus on economic self-interest, an alternate strain of liberalism stresses the need to limit market norms in order to preserve human dignity. The liberal dignity strain, often associated with Kant, also is embedded in human rights law, constitutional law, and the Judeo-Christian religious tradition.[63]

Differentiated Ties in this context offers a proposal to examine closely whether any or all of the benefits of the market can be garnered in ways that preserve our aspirations to respect human dignity. Radin discusses similar issues when, in her analysis of the "double bind," she suggests that both commodifying or refusing to commodify can be oppressive in some contexts, as where the woman "chooses" prostitution or to sell her kidney because her only alternative is for her and her children to starve.[64] Radin's "double bind" is nothing more than the recognition that, because of the oppressive social conditions within which markets operate, both marketizing, and refusing to do so, often will perpetuate existing patterns of oppression.

Differentiated ties proposes that our focus should shift away from the Hamlet question toward an examination of the social conditions that frame market exchanges. Particularly in an age when globalization has precipitated a race to the bottom, le doux commerce is, all too often, "exploitative in the extreme," to quote Miranda Joseph in this volume.[65]

When Is the Issue Not Whether to Marketize but Who Controls the Process and the Proceeds?

Indian arts and crafts are going to be sold, native plants made into medicines, and blue corn sold. In each context, the key issue is not whether or not to marketize but who controls the process and the proceeds of marketization. In this volume, Regina Austin discusses commodification of racial identity in the context of Kwanzaa, pointing out the liberatory potential for commodification of African-American culture if blacks control the process and profits. Other scholars have examined the process by which black music has been changed slightly and turned into profits for white musicians and their handlers: examples include Elvis Presley, the Beatles, and Eminem.[66]

Parallel issues arise with respect to indigenous people both in the United States and abroad. For example, an indigenous community spends generations developing a certain plant with medicinal properties. Then a Western company "discovers" the plant, patents its medicinal properties, and drives up the price, so that the indigenous people who developed it now can no longer afford it. This pattern has been repeated in India, Africa, and other developing countries.[67] Similar problems have arisen in the United States. Native Americans have developed blue corn over many generations, only to have European-Americans buy the seed and produce blue-corn chips and other products with no benefit coming to the community that originated it.[68] In each of these contexts, the issue is not whether to marketize but on who controls the process and the profits of marketization.

The solution may be to have the Amazon tribe itself patent the medicine, or to create a regulatory regime that allows consumers to know which crafts are the genuine article or a licensing regime so that anyone who produces "genuine" crafts will have to pay a licensing fee. While these solutions may be hard to structure, the point is that we need to spend our energy designing regimes that allow subordinated peoples to control the process and the profits of marketization instead of anguishing over the Hamlet question.

Marketization as Imperialism

In other contexts involving subordinated identities, the issue is whether an indigenous community (domestic or transnational) should be forced to treat its cultural artifacts within the intellectual framework defined by a Western property regime, at the expense of traditional ways of living and being that do not revolve around market norms. These issues emerge when a traditional community is not concerned solely with who controls the process and the proceeds of marketization; it wants to resist marketization altogether. For example, an Australian merchant spots an attractive Aboriginal pattern reproduced in a fine-art painting, and incorporates it into inexpensive rugs made by a factory in Vietnam. Aboriginal artists are upset because their traditions prohibit the images in question from being freely reproduced; perhaps they do not relish having European-Americans walking on their sacred symbols.[69] Or Native Americans resist commodification of petroglyphs, which they regard as sacred.[70]

Sometimes indigenous people oppose marketization because they do not want their cultural products turned into commodities; the marketization itself is felt as a violation. In these instances, marketization is a problem because it rips the objects from their original, often sacred, context and shoves them unceremoniously into the rough-and-tumble arena of market norms. This is one of the rare cases where "to commodify or not to commodify" is indeed the right question (although it is far clearer when formulated as "to marketize or not to marketize"). The question asked by a Differentiated Ties analysis is whether an indigenous community should be entitled to resist converting social ties defined by indigenous traditions into a Westernized property regime governed by individualistic self-interested behavior. The solution often lies in preserving indigenous traditions by giving control over cultural symbols to the community as a whole, rather than to any one individual, thereby eliminating the ability of any one individual unilaterally to marketize the objects in question. Sometimes this is accomplished through legal channels;[71] elsewhere it occurs informally, as when an indigenous community simply hides its symbols or their meanings.[72]

Intellectual Property: Differentiated Ties and Hohfeldian Property Theory

The raging debates over intellectual property are rarely incorporated into the commodification debate. They should be. Intellectual property debates address a range of issues relevant to traditional commodification debates.

Should life forms be turned into commodities? The Supreme Court resisted the marketization of life forms until 1980, when it approved the granting of a patent for an oil-eating form of bacteria on the grounds that it was a product rather than a nonpatentable "product of nature."[73] By 1988, the Patent and Trademark Office granted a patent on a genetically engineered mouse, in a decision that expressly excluded human beings from patentability.[74] The explosion in propertization of life forms and cyberspace is a small part of "an explosion of cases in which courts have relied on trademark-like rubrics to uphold claims to exclusive rights in names, faces, voices, gestures, phrases, artistic style, marketing concepts, locations, and references."[75]

The striking thing about these debates within intellectual property is that they have the potential to eschew the on-off "to commodify or not to commodify" model, and draw instead on property theory that stretches back to legal scholar Wesley Hohfeld in the early twentieth century. Contemporary property theorists influenced by Hohfeld argue that property involves not an on-off decision about whether or not a person has absolute ownership over a thing; instead, property defines social relationships that shift both over time and according to context, so that what it means to "own property" in one context may be quite different from what it means to "own property" in a different context.[76]

Sounds like Differentiated Ties. The convergence of Hohfeldian analysis and Differentiated Ties is striking. This convergence, upon reflection, makes sense, given that commodification debates often involve a decision about whether gene sequences, indigenous designs, life forms should be recognized as property—as well as decisions what "having property" should mean in a given context.[77] Both Hohfeldian theory and differentiated ties ultimately send the same message: we should abandon the Hamlet question, and ask instead how we want to structure social relationships that involve elements of both economics and identity.

Conclusion

This essay has shown the importance of bringing together different conversations about commodification that, until now, have never engaged with one another in a sustained way: feminists' discussions of care work; race theorists' discussions of the commodification of racial identities; queer theorists' discussions of the commodification of queer identities; debates over the commodification of babies, bodies, and body parts; and intellectual property lawyers' discussions of the commodification of indigenous identities and products and of the creeping propertization of intellectual property law.

We have traveled a long distance from the Hamlet question. In place of a unified analysis focused on the question of whether or not to commodify, we have identified six themes that help spell out specific dimensions of Differentiated Ties analysis.

1. When the issue is not marketization but ending domesticity's erasure of the economic dimension of family work.
2. Marketization is liberatory where it signals public acceptance of the existence and legitimacy of subordinated identities, notably in the context of the lesbigay community.
3. Marketization is often oppressive because among the many things the market delivers efficiently are gender, race, and class privilege.
4. Sometimes marketization is inevitable, and the issue is who controls the process and the proceeds?
5. Marketization as imperialism. In other contexts involving indigenous communities, the issue often is whether they should be forced to treat their cultural artifacts within the intellectual framework

defined by a Western property regime, at the expense of traditional ways of living and being that do not revolve around market norms.

6. Differentiated ties and contemporary property theory. Once we shift to a Differentiated Ties approach, we can draw on Hohfeldian property theory, with its useful focus on the quality of the social relationships formed instead of the traditional on-off approach that asks "is it property or not" or whether to commodify or not?

"Philosophical problems . . . are . . . solved by rearranging what we have always known."[78] Once this rearrangement breaks the "bewitchment of our intelligence," practical problems remain. We can best address them by abandoning the question of whether or not to commodify and focus instead on an often-painful assessment of how to create differentiated interpersonal ties that are just, equal, socially beneficial, and satisfying to their participants in both their material and their symbolic dimensions.

NOTES

Grateful thanks for excellent research assistance to Sarah Kenney and Natalie Maxwell.

1. Some portions of this paper adapt passages from Viviana A. Zelizer, "Intimate Transactions," in The New Economic Sociology: Developments in an Emerging Field 274 (Mauro F. Guillén et al. eds., 2002), and "Dangerous Dualities," Keynote Address at the Radcliffe Institute's Women, Money and Power Conference (Oct. 2002).

2. Ludwig Wittgenstein, Philosophical Investigations I at 46e ¶ 109 (G. E. M. Anscombe trans., 1970).

3. Martha M. Ertman, *Marriage as a Trade: Bridging the Private/Private Distinction,* 36 Harv. C.R.-C.L.L. Rev. 79 (2001); Katharine Silbaugh, *Turning Labor into Love: Housework and the Law,* 91 Nw. U. L. Rev. 1 (1996).

4. Elizabeth Anderson, *Is Women's Labor a Commodity?,* 19 Phil & Pub. Aff. 71 (1990), *quoted in* Katharine Silbaugh, *Commodification and Women's Household Labor,* 9 Yale J.L. & Feminism 81, 85 (1997). *See also* Elizabeth Anderson, Value in Ethics and Economics 150–58 (1993).

5. Anderson, *supra* note 4, at 150–58.

6. See id.

7. Silbaugh, *supra* note 4, at 83.

8. See generally Margaret Jane Radin, Contested Commodities (1996) (developing a philosophical analysis of commodification).

9. See id. at 127.

10. See generally Alexandra Chasin, Selling Out: The Gay and Lesbian Movement Goes to Market 15–19 (2001).

11. Miranda Joseph, *The Performance of Production and Consumption,* 54 Social Text 37 (1998).

12. bell hooks, Black Looks: Race and Representation 23 (1992).

13. See generally Tricia Rose, Black Noise: Rap Music and Black Culture in Contemporary America (1994).

14. See generally James Gleick, *Patently Absurd: Once the Province of a Nuts and Bolts World, Patents Are Now Being Applied to Thoughts and Ideas in Cyberspace,* New York Times Sunday Magazine, March 12, 2000, at 44–49, available at http://www.sciencemag.org/cgi/content/full/280/5364/698; Andrew Kimbrell, *Biocolonization: The Patenting of Life and the Global Market in Body Parts, in* The Case Against the Global Economy (Jerry Mander & Edward Goldsmith eds., 1996); Sandra Lee Pinel & Michael J. Evans, *Tribal Sovereignty and the Control of Knowledge, in* Intellectual Property Rights for Indigenous Peoples: A Sourcebook (Tom Greaves ed., 1994); Jessica Litman, *Breakfast with Batman: The Public Interest in the Advertising Age,* 108 Yale L.J. 1717, 1725–35 (1999); Carol Rose, *Several Futures of Cyberspace and Folk Tales, Emission Trades and Ecosystems,* 83 Minn. L. Rev. 129, 144–63 (1998); Keith Aoki, *Neocolonialism, Anticommons Property, & Biopiracy in the (Not-So-Brave) New World Order of International Intellectual Property Protection,* 6 Ind. J. Global Legal. Stud. 11, 46–58 (1998); Michael Heller & Rebecca Eisenberg, *Can Patents Deter Innovation? The Anticommons in Biomedical Research,* Science, May 1, 1998; Margaret Jane Radin, *Property Evolving in Cyberspace,* 15 J.L. & Com. 509 (1996); Rosemary J. Coombe, *Embodied Trademarks: Mimesis and Alterity on American Commercial Frontiers,* 11 Cultural Anthropology 202 (1996); Maggie Chon, *Postmodern "Progress": Reconsidering the Copyright and Patent Power: Introduction,* 43 DePaul L. Rev. 97, 97–104 (1993).

15. See, e.g., James Boyle, Shamans, Software, and Spleens : Law and the Construction of the Information Society (1996) (arguing that justice and efficacy are harmed as a result of there being too many property rights in our society).

16. See Gleick, *Patently Absurd, supra* note 14 at 44–49.

17. See Kimbrell, *supra* note 14, at 131–45.

18. See Chilkat Indian Village IRA v. Johnson, No. 90-01 (Chilkat Tribal Court, Nov. 3, 1993), *in* Curtis J. Berger & Joan C. Williams, Property: Land Ownership and Use 1166 (4th ed. 1997) [hereinafter Berger & Williams, Property] (analyzing whether Native American artifacts belong to the tribe as a whole or can be sold by an individual tribal member).

19. See, e.g., Aoki, *supra* note 14, at 46–58.

20. See Pinel & Evans, *supra* note 14, at 43–55 (advocating property rights for indigenous people).

21. Compare id. (advocating property rights for indigenous people) *with*

Aoki, *supra* note 14, at 46–58 (questioning whether the Western notion of "property" is the best analytic to handle contemporary problems).

22. For codification of views concerning *consequences* of commodification, see Ivan Cohen, *The Price of Everything, The Value of Nothing: Reframing the Commodification Debate*, 117 Harv. L. Rev. 689 (2003).

23. Viviana A. Zelizer, *Circuits within Capitalism, in* The Economic Sociology of Capitalism (Richard Swedberg & Victor Nee eds., forthcoming 2004).

24. See generally Robert Kuttner, Everything for Sale: The Virtues and Limits of Markets (1999).

25. See generally Robert E. Lane, The Loss of Happiness in Market Democracies (2001).

26. Jeremy Rifkin, The Age of Access: The New Culture of Hypercapitalism Where All of Life Is a Paid-For Experience 112 (2000).

27. Id.

28. Zelizer, Dangerous Dualities, *supra* note 1.

29. See, e.g., Charles Smith, Auctions: Social Construction of Value (1989) (analyzing the process of creating value through auctions); Viviana A. Zelizer, *Intimate Transactions, supra* note 1.

30. See Zelizer, Dangerous Dualities, *supra* note 1.

31. See generally Viviana Zelizer, The Social Meanings of Money: Pin Money, Poor Relief, Paychecks, and Other Currencies (1995).

32. See Zelizer, *Intimate Transactions, supra* note 1, at 274.

33. See Berger & Williams, Property, *supra* note 18, at 113–15 (describing the feudal system in relation to land ownership, explaining that "[i]n feudal England, a person's social status generally depended on the extent of his land holdings and, equally relevant, on the tenure by which he held. In these arrangements we recognize the feudal vision of property as social glue to cement the social interdependencies in the 'great chain of being.'").

34. James T. Kloppenberg, *The Virtues of Liberalism: Christianity, Republicanism, and Ethics in Early American Political Discourse, in* James T. Kloppenberg, The Virtues of Liberalism 21–37 (1998).

35. See C. B. McPherson, Political Theory of Possessive Individualism: From Hobbes to Locke (1964).

36. See Daniel T. Rodgers, *Republicanism, in* A Companion to American Thought 584 (Richard Wightman Fox & James T. Kloppenberg eds., 1995). *See generally* J. G. A. Pocock, The Machiavellian Moment: Florentine Political Thought and the Atlantic Republican Tradition (1975).

37. See, e.g., Ruth H. Bloch, *The Gendered Meanings of Virtue in Revolutionary America*, 13 Signs: J. Women Culture & Soc'y 37, 54 (1987). *See also* Joan C. Williams, *Rorty, Radicalism, Romanticism: The Politics of the Gaze, in* Pragmatism in Law and Society 155–80 (Michael Brint & William Weaver eds., 1991).

38. See Joan C. Williams, *Domesticity as the Dangerous Supplement of Liberalism,* 2 J. Women's Hist. 69, 69–76 (1991); Nancy Cott, The Bonds of Womanhood: 'Women's Sphere' in New England, 1780–1835 68–69 (1977).

39. See generally Jeanne Boydston, Home & Work (1990).

40. See Joan C. Williams, *Un*bending Gender: Why Family and Work Conflict and What to Do about It 117–18 (2000).

41. See id. at 117–19.

42. On economic sociology, see, e.g., Richard Swedberg, Principles of Economic Sociology (2003); The Handbook of Economic Sociology (Neil J. Smelser & Richard Swedberg eds., 1995).

43. See Zelizer, *Intimate Transactions, supra* note 1, at 274.

44. See id.

45. Nancy Folbre, *Holding Hands at Midnight: The Paradox of Caring Labor,* 1 Feminist Econ. 73 (1995).

46. See, e.g., Anderson, *supra* note 4, at 150–58.

47. See Silbaugh, *supra* note 4, at 87 (discussing the work of Gary S. Becker, Richard Posner, Lloyd R. Cohen, and others).

48. Radin, *supra* note 8, at 108–18.

49. Silbaugh, *supra* note 4, at 88 (emphasis in original).

50. Radin, *supra* note 8, at 107.

51. See generally Kurt Lewin, Field Theory in Social Science (1951), *quoted in* Kay Deaux & Marianne LaFrance, *Gender,* 1 The Handbook of Social Psychology 788, 807 (Daniel T. Gilbert et al. eds., 1998).

52. See generally Joan Williams, *Do Wives Own Half? Winning for Wives after Wendt,* 32 Conn. L. Rev. 249 (1999) (advocating for a revisitation of the intersection of property law and family life to develop a proper method of allocating assets post-divorce, to account for women's domestic work).

53. Silbaugh, *supra* note 4, at 83.

54. Id.

55. See, e.g., Silbaugh, *supra* note 3, at 38–42, 56–68. See also Martha Ertman, *Commercializing Marriage: A Proposal for Valuing Women's Work through Premarital Agreements,* 77 Tex. L. Rev. 17 (1998); Joan C. Williams, *Is Coverture Dead? Beyond a New Theory of Alimony,* 82 Geo. L.J. 2227 (1994).

56. See Silbaugh, *supra* note 3, at 67–79.

57. See Symposium, *The Structures of Care Work,* 76 Chi.-Kent. L. Rev. 1389 (2001).

58. E.g., O'Brien v. O'Brien, 66 N.Y.2d 576, 581 (N.Y. 1985) (wife worked several jobs simultaneously and passed up an opportunity to get a teaching certificate that would have qualified her for a higher salary); In re Graham, 574 P.2d 75, 77 (Colo. 1978) (en banc) ("An advanced degree is a cumulative product of many years of previous education, combined with diligence and hard work."); Borelli v. Brusseau, 16 Cal. Rptr. 2d 16 (Ct. App. 1993) (refusing to enforce an

oral contract between husband and wife upon the death of a rich, elderly husband, leaving his young widow without the riches he had promised in return for her care prior to his death).

59. See Danae Clark, Commodity Lesbianism 191 (2000).

60. See *Trading Flesh around the Globe, Time,* June 17, 1991, at 61.

61. See Patricia J. Williams, *Spare Parts, Family Values, Old Children, Cheap,* 28 New Eng. L. Rev. 913, 914–20 (1994).

62. Margaret Jane Radin, *Market Inalienability,* 100 Harv. L. Rev. 1849, 1887 (1987).

63. Joan C. Williams, *The Rhetoric of Property,* 83 Iowa L. Rev. 277 (1998).

64. Margaret Jane Radin, *The Pragmatist and the Feminist,* 63 S. Cal. L. Rev. 1699, 1699–1701 (1990).

65. See also Albert O. Hirshman, The Passions and the Interests (1997). See also Carol M. Rose, *Giving, Trading, Thieving, and Trusting: How and Why Gifts Become Exchanges and (More Importantly) Vice Versa,* 44 Fla. L. Rev. 295 (1992).

66. See, e.g., http://www.210west.com/archives/pop_culture/000064.php (quoting Sam Preston of Sun Records: "Find me a white man who can sing the blues, and I'll make a million dollars."); Vince Guerrieri, *The Elvis of Rap and the Eminem of Rock,* 210 West Magazine, *available at* http://www.210west.com/archives/pop_culture/000064.php (July 7, 2003) (describing the rise to stardom of Elvis and Eminem, two white men from modest means, through the use of "race music" or "rhythm and blues"); *Essay: Crossing Over, at* http://www.pbs.org/newshour/essays/jan-june03/page_1-15.html (Jan. 15, 2003) ("Yes, Eminem —AKA Marshall Mathers, AKA Slim Shady—pop culture's bad boy flavor of the moment. He takes the old complaint about white performers stealing black music, and puts it right back in our faces. 'Yes, I know what I am,' he says. 'I've got a right to rap the blues. Nobody knows the troubles Slim Shady has seen, and I'm going to tell them. I am the latest white guy to get rich off a black sound, and you're making me a success—or your kids are. So, deal with it.'").

67. See Aoki, *supra* note 14, 47–53.

68. See Pinel & Evans, *supra* note 14, at 43, 45–46.

69. See Milpurrurru v. Indofurn Pty Ltd. 54 FCR 240 (1994).

70. See Pinel & Evans, *supra* note 14, at 43, 48–50.

71. See Chilkat Indian Village IRA v. Johnson, No. 90-01 (Chilkat Tribal Court, Nov. 3, 1993), *in* Berger & Williams, Property, *supra* note 18, at 1166 (analyzing the ability of a Native American tribal member to sell tribal artifacts to a museum versus the tribe's collective right to retain the artifacts for its personal use).

72. See Pinel & Evans, *supra* note 14, at 52.

73. Anthony Kimbrell, *Biocolonialization: The Patenting of Life and the*

Global Market in Body Parts, in The Case against the Global Economy and for a Turn toward the Local 133–34 (Jerry Mander & Edward Goldsmith eds., 1996).

74. See id. at 135.

75. Litman, *supra* note 14, at 1717.

76. See, e.g., Wesley Newcomb Hohfeld, *Fundamental Conceptions as Applied in Judicial Reasoning*, 26 Yale L.J. 710 (1917).

77. See Joseph Singer, Property Law: Rules, Policies, and Practices (3d ed. 2002); Berger & Williams, Property, *supra* note 18, at 14–20 (providing different interpretations of Hohfeld's analysis).

78. Ludwig Wittgenstein, Philosophical Investigations I at 46e ¶ 109 (G. E. M. Anscombe trans., 1970).

The Multivalent Commodity

On the Supplementarity
of Value and Values

Miranda Joseph

> As a value, [the commodity] remains the same no matter how many metamorphoses and forms of existence it goes through; in reality, commodities are exchanged only because they are not the same and correspond to different systems of needs.
>
> This double, differentiated existence must develop into a *difference*, and the difference into *antithesis* and *contradiction*.[1]

Any attempt to determine the pros and cons of commodification depends of course on one's definition of commodification. What is a commodity? What is commodification? As many of the essays in this volume demonstrate, a debate over the pros and cons of the commodification of particular goods often means a debate over the impact on diverse human "values" of treating particular goods as having a "value" commensurable with money or as separable, "alienable," from particular individuals or communities. This assessment of commodification, to the extent that it is at all negative, takes what might be called a Romantic anticapitalist approach. That is, it tends to consider only one side of the commodity, exploring the implications of the abstraction of value from its particular embodiment and context, the effect of treating a good as equivalent and fungible, but not the role of the commodity as a particular embodiment of abstract value.

From my Marxist perspective, this approach overlooks a number of key issues, particularly the implication of commodities in a larger economic and social system. That is, in the fashion of the liberal political economists that Marx critiques, it fails to address the connections between exchange (the marketplace) and production, thus missing what might be seen as the most crucial implications of commodification. As Moishe Postone argues, Romantic anticapitalists participate in the fetishism of commodities, taking that visible form of value, and especially money, to be the root of all evil.[2] While attacks on money and abstraction can be found in Marx (for instance, in the *Economic and Philosophic Manuscripts of 1844*)[3] and persist in the Marxist literature, I argue that an adequate analysis of commodification must begin (as Marx does in the opening chapter of *Capital Volume 1*)[4] with an articulation of the dual character of the commodity as simultaneously particular and abstract. From that base, I offer an account that does connect the exchange of commodities with their production. And, through a poststructuralist reading of Marx's account of the commodity, I propose that value and values must be seen as supplementary.[5] This approach, I suggest, makes it possible to trace the complicity of race, ethnicity, gender, nation, and sexuality with capital.

This reader is the product of a multiyear multifaceted effort to rethink commodification, inspired in large part by the works of Viviana Zelizer and Margaret Jane Radin. I have likewise taken these scholars' texts as a jumping-off point, exploring the definitions and conceptualizations of commodities and commodification that they offer, marking what I see as the insights and limitations of their approaches. Finally, I attempt to cast my poststructuralist Marxist view of commodities and commodification in contrast, as correcting for some of the limitations, building on the insights and providing what I would argue is a fuller account—and what is certainly a different account—of the implications of commodification.

In proposing a fundamentally different definition of the commodity and commodification, I propose to shift the terrain of the discussion, from a debate over the implications of the market exchange of particular goods to a discussion of the social and economic system in which commodities are produced as well as exchanged, and from a Romantic anticapitalist critique of abstraction to an examination of the implications of the multivalence of the commodity. Two things are at stake in this shift in terrain. First, our fundamental evaluation of commodification, which turns out to be systemically, not incidentally, related to exploitation and domination. Second, our strategies for intervening on behalf of social justice, which, as it turns out, not only require us to use our (cultural, communal) values to hold the line against the depredations of value but to examine and critique those values, those communal formations, as well for the role they play in capitalism.

The urgency of this shift in approach is the urgency of adequately grasping the social, political, and economic dynamics of our world in which *globalization* names a renewed effort to extend and intensify the reach of commodification. Globalization generates ever-greater concentrations of wealth for the few, while producing ever-more-severe poverty and displacement for the many. It proceeds by elaborating stark racial, gendered, and national divisions of labor. The project of engaging more people more fully in globalization entails the deliberate deployment and transformation of cultural particularities in the production and exchange of commodities. While I do not have the space here to lay out a full theorization of the relationship between culture and economy, domination and exploitation, values and value,[6] I do hope to at least sketch an approach that is more incisive than that offered by liberal theorists.

In *Contested Commodities*, Radin sets out to explore the "meaning—and attendant normative evaluation," the morality, of commodification and particularly the commodification of goods "related to persons and the nature of human life," such as babies, sex, and body parts.[7] Taking modern market society as a given, her goal is to provide standards for discerning the appropriate legal regulation of commodification in such problematic cases. Her choice of this question and her approach to it, however, are constrained by her definitions of the commodity and commodification. Like many of the contributors to this volume, Radin's definitions are market-centered. She states, "One of the earmarks of commodification, perhaps its central one, is that of *sale*."[8] Her discussion, predictably, focuses on the issues of *commensurability* and *alienability,* with significantly greater attention to the issue of alienability. She explains, "Market-inalienability is a [in fact *the*] focus of this book because it often represents an attempt to prevent commodification, or at least expresses an aspiration for noncommodification."[9]

Radin's consideration of the implications of commodification is also shaped by her conceptualization of commodification as a process. She argues that "'commodification' denotes a particular social construction of things people value. . . . Commodification refers to the social process by which something comes to be apprehended as a commodity."[10] I take no issue with her claim that commodification is a social (by which she means, specifically, discursive) construction. In fact, I read Marx as proposing that discourse is an integral part of materiality and that material social practices are always in a sense discursive.[11] But Radin's version of social construction is idealist rather than materialist (though she claims to have learned it from Marxists). To say that something is socially constructed—that it is not simply a natural fact but a particular way of making the world meaningful—is a crucial first step in generating a critique. However, as Michael Taussig has pointed out, such a statement is only an invitation, an invitation to investigate and account for the social process —the history, the practices, the social relations—from which this construction emerges and which it helps to sustain or transform.[12] And it is here that there seems to be a gap or problem in Radin's theorization of the commodity.

Radin does not offer an account of the social process by which commodification has emerged as a dominant discourse, the dominant mode of understanding, relating to, and interacting with the goods we produce and consume. Absent such an account, commodification, as a way of apprehending things, appears to be a matter of subjective or even idiosyncratic choice. While Radin contests the liberal notion of subjects as abstract, offering instead a notion of personhood in which persons are constituted through a dynamic relation with particular contexts,[13] she nonetheless seems to situate the social process of commodification inside the heads of individual subjects. She suggests that such individual subjects will be influenced by their particular "culture"[14] but in doing so, begs the question of social (cultural) construction as a process. She refers to nomadic societies[15] as well as our market society as "cultures"[16] in a way that naturalizes and dehistoricizes those political economic arrangements and the cultural formations that are entailed by them, where what is needed is precisely an account of the historical and structural emergence of those social formations.[17] While she gives the law a role in regulating commodification and thus appears to think that the social process is in part external to persons, as it turns out, she gives the law this role not because she sees it as constitutive but rather because she wants the law to reflect and respect personhood.

Because Radin defines the commodity and commodification in this way, her assessment of the morality of commodification takes the form of the question: Does treating x or y as alienable, commensurable, and fungible correspond to our values? Her insightful response to this question, about which I will have more to say below, is that our answer is (or can be) simultaneously yes and no. That is, we can and do simultaneously view things as commodities and in other ways. She goes further, however, and attempts to create a foundation for arguing that we and perhaps the law should value certain things in their particularity, rather than solely as commensurable, alienable, and fungible. To make this argument she borrows from Martha Nussbaum the notion of "human flourishing" as a political goal, which entails a set of "conditions in which a good human life can be chosen and lived."[18] In developing this notion, Nussbaum generates both a list of human features (such as mortality, the human body with its needs for food and drink, and cognitive capability) and a list of conditions allowing for the development of those features (such as being able to have good health, adequate nourishment, use of the five senses, and use of imagination and reason) that she intends to be "nonrelative," "acceptable cross culturally.[19] While Radin takes issue with some of the specifics of Nussbaum's lists, she likes the general idea, which fleshes out her own view of personhood as dynamically context-dependent and clearly suggests that personhood cannot be reduced to a single dimension of commensurable value. For the law to reflect and respect personhood, then, it must reflect and respect values other than value.

The limits of both Radin's question and her answers become clear as she discusses the cases of contested commodification with which she is most concerned. Radin is centrally concerned with what she calls "double bind" cases in which social conditions of inequality and poverty would seem to make neither commodification nor the banning of commodification moral. For example, while some (relatively privileged) people may find it immoral to sell sex or body parts, others might, from another perspective, see it as immoral to prevent a desperately poor person from selling sex or body parts in order to feed her children.[20] In presenting these cases, Radin, apparently unwittingly, makes clear the limits of the Nussbaumian universal human rights argument she puts forward, demonstrating the ways that it can, and most often does, operate as the universalization of particular dominant norms at the expense of the oppressed. But more important, although her example suggests that a genealogy of morals might link morality (values) with economic interests (value), her question—Does treating x or y as a commodity correspond to our values?—presupposes that values and value are independent of each other. Consequently, she is able to offer no theorization of this relationship.

Further, by focusing solely on the life of the commodity in the marketplace, she undermines her own efforts to explain the relation between the market and the conditions producing the double binds with which she is concerned. In particular, how is the desperate poverty that might drive a person to sell sex or body parts systemically connected to commodification? While she does take up this question toward the end of the book, her discussion, for the most part, presumes that all market players are equally powerful individuals. Where they are not equally powerful, and thus engage in "desperate exchanges," she views their desperation as external to and independent of the market itself, a social problem that may impinge on a discussion of commodities but is not integral to it. That she considers social problems like poverty to be distinct from and independent of commodification is made most clear, in fact, by her assertion that

> cases of contested commodification in the real world are "mixed" and not "pure." When we worry about baby-selling or kidney selling, for example, concerns about commodification are mixed up with concerns about the effects of poverty, sexism and racism on the would-be sellers, as well as concerns about harm to innocent third parties (the babies who are sold).[21]

Radin's fundamental presumption that the market is a realm of equality (with exceptions created by externalities) not only fails to account for any relation that might exist between poverty and commodification but also fails to account for the obvious fact that while individuals do participate in the market as sellers of labor (or body parts or babies) and as buyers of consumption goods, those individuals generally do not interact in the market with other individuals but, rather, with corporations.

From a Marxist perspective one might say that Radin views the commodity only in relation to the C-M-C circuit of exchange, in which commodities are exchanged for money in order that money can then be exchanged for other commodities.[22] She does not address the M-C-C'-M' circuit in which money is exchanged for commodities that are used in a production process such that commodities of greater value are produced, which are then sold for the purpose of realizing that greater value as money so the process can begin again.[23] In other words, she does not address the fact that commodities are produced and exchanged for the purpose of accumulating capital. For Marx, it is this circuit that drives the marketplace, and an examination of this circuit, especially the production process by which commodities magically gain greater value, can explain the inequalities of power both within and outside the market.[24]

The magic by which commodities gain greater value is the super-adequation of labor-power. Labor-power can produce greater value (surplus value) than is required to reproduce that labor-power. In other words, the use value of labor-power is greater than its exchange value. In the capitalist mode of production, the mode in which commodity exchange—production for exchange is not merely incidental but dominant, that surplus value is appropriated by the owners of the means of production, those who purchase labor-power along with other commodities and deploy those commodities to produce new commodities for sale. As Marx argues in the *Grundrisse*:

> The right of property undergoes a dialectical inversion, so that on the side of capital it becomes the right to an alien product, or the right of property over alien labour, . . . and on the side of labour capacity, it becomes the duty to relate to one's own product as to alien property.[25]

Certain preconditions must exist in order for the production process to occur in this way. First, an adequate quantity of use values must have been already accumulated by those who will enter the production process as capitalists, that is, as owners of the means of production. Second, labor must be free in a double sense. First, the laborer must be free from relations of obligation or dependence (such as slavery or serfdom) and thus free to sell her labor. Second, the laborer must be free of, lacking, the means of production and thus find it necessary to sell her labor-power for wages.[26] "Desperate exchanges" in this understanding are not then exceptional or externally determined. Instead, every sale of labor-power for wages is in effect a desperate exchange since the laborer lacks the means of production and would be unable to survive except by such a sale.

In an established capitalist system, these preconditions tend to reproduce themselves. As the capitalist appropriates the surplus value generated by the direct producers, returning to the direct producers only that portion of what they produce (in the form of wages) necessary to their own reproduction, the capitalist gains ever greater control over the means of production, leaving the laborer ever more dependent on wages for survival. But the establishment of the capitalist mode of production, and its ongoing expansion, (that is, the "social process" of commodification—the process by which things come to be understood as commodities—is viewed as truly social, as emergent from social practices and historical processes) depend on what Marx calls "so-called primitive accumulation." At the beginning of *Capital,* Vol. One, Part 8, Marx explains,

> So-called primitive accumulation, therefore, is nothing else than the historical process of divorcing the producer from the means of production. ... And this history, the history of their expropriation, is written in the annals of mankind in letters of blood and fire.[27]

In thinking of commodification as "so-called primitive accumulation," two points are crucial to emphasize. First, that this is not a matter of introducing economic processes into relations that were previously noneconomic but, rather, of changing social relations to fit a new mode of production. Second, that the shift to capitalism, to exploitation, is ongoing and ongoingly aided by domination.

Viewing the market only as a C-M-C circuit, Radin finds little traction for her argument when she finally does take up the question of the relationship between commodification and what she calls "social oppression."[28] Radin asks whether "commodification, subordination and maldistribution" are linked because they are all "forms of objectification of persons?"[29] That "objectification" *per se* should be considered bad depends on a Kantian subject/object binary, which she explicitly recognizes as problematic and, in fact, unsustainable,[30] thus undermining the argument she proceeds to make for a very weak set of links. Rather than theorizing any systematic relationship among these forms of objectification, she merely observes that "the kinds of oppressive objectification corresponding to each 'ism' often occur together."[31] She casts the synergy among "commodification, sexism and racism, and great inequalities of wealth," toward which "the market culture" inexplicably "tends,"[32] as an historical accident, suggesting that sexism and racism are "lingering"[33] anachronisms from some earlier moment and implicitly not integral to contemporary capitalism. Finding that, in the real world, these things do occur together, but not finding any systemic connection, she in effect raises this issue only to dismiss it. Her answer does not redirect the discussion but rather reaffirms her basic approach of attempting to sort out reforms (but not transformations) of commodification with reference to universal standards of human flourishing.

In offering her "both yes and no" answer to the morality question she poses, Radin casts herself as a reasonable voice between the "universal commodifiers" (the law and economics school) who see everything as alienable and believe that the best society results from treating everything as a commodity, and the "humanist Marxists" who, she claims, oppose all commodification, because they see any market-alienability as a pernicious virus infecting every aspect of human society and thus producing human alienation.[34] While I am not in a position to question her characterization of the Chicago law and economics theorists, I do recognize her characterization of Marxists as a caricature, one that is well-founded in the Marxist literature but nevertheless mistakes certain parts of a Marxian argument for the whole and thus reduces Marxism to Romantic anticapitalism.

In characterizing Marxist views of commodification, Radin appropriately focuses on Lukács, who does offer one of the most elaborate Marxist theorizations of commodification, arguing that the "riddle of the commodity-*structure*" can answer all social riddles for the historical moment in which he writes. For Lukács, "commodity-relations" are the social relations of production and consumption that are masked by commodity fetishism (the appearance that commodities have an inherent value and have relationships with one another, when in fact their value is socially determined and it is their human producers who have relationships with one another). He says, "[T]he problem of commodities must not be considered in isolation or even regarded as the central problem in economics."[35] Considered in this way, "the structure of commodity-relations" can "yield a model of all the objective forms of bourgeois society together with all the subjective forms corresponding to them."[36]

In place of the Kantian subject/object binary opposition, Lukács approaches the relation between subjects and objects as adialectic. In his discussion of that part of the M-C-C'-M' circuit in which commodities must be turned back into money, he examines the attempts by capitalists to produce and control consumer desire (an issue taken up by Zelizer, as I will discuss below, and a central arena of study for numerous Marxist and post-Marxist cultural studies scholars).[37] In his discussion of production, he is concerned with the impact of particular production processes on the subjectivity of the producer. In both cases, Lukács focuses on the abstract side of commodification, the abstraction of quantitatively equivalent value from qualitatively distinct use values. Concerned primarily with the commodification of labor, Lukács expresses Romantic concerns for the loss of organic unity of the individual and the community because labor is not only abstracted (treated as a commensurable value) in the context of market exchange but also becomes, through Taylorization and industrialization, fragmented and fungible as it is put to use in production.[38] Mistaking the features of a specific historical moment of capitalism, industrial mass production, for essential features of capitalism, Lukács overreads (as did Marx himself and any number of other Marxists) the impact of abstraction on particularity. A Marxist account of the commodity-structure, which I will detail below, does not necessarily imply the argument that all human relations are subject to the virus-like objectification, abstraction, and reduction to alienable, fungible commensurables that Lukács asserts and that Radin attributes to all Marxists. A poststructuralist reading of Marx's account of the commodity structure does, however, imply that all human relationships are likely to be mobilized as sites of capital flow and deployed in the process of systematically enriching the few at the expense of the many.

Radin's analysis does provide a useful argument against reductionist economisms of both the left and the right, suggesting as it does that the economy is not simply and unidirectionally determining of all social relations. She recognizes the potential multivalence of any particular good as simultaneously an abstract exchange value (worth a certain amount of money and thus commensurable and fungible with other commodities) and particular, valuable in ways that may be incommensurable, at least in the money economy. This recognition is a major step toward theorizing the relationship of values to value and ultimately, the supplementarity of values with value in the accumulation of capital.

But where Radin would say that insofar as a good is a commodity it has only one meaning and that any other meanings it might have are independent of its being as a commodity, Zelizer takes us much closer to an account of the relation between values and value by showing that it is the commodity itself that is multivalent. Zelizer makes this case in a particularly strong way by describing the multivalence of the commodity that would seem to be most abstract, most commensurable and fungible—money itself.[39]

Zelizer takes on the "powerful ideology . . . that money is a single, interchangeable, absolutely impersonal instrument—the very essence of our rationalizing modern civilization."[40] Further, she contests the pervasive Romantic narrative—a narrative offered by both conservative and progressive scholars, a narrative fundamentally structuring of the discipline of sociology—that money has progressively destroyed community, "replacing personal bonds with calculative instrumental ties, corrupting cultural meanings with materialist concerns."[41] Against this view, Zelizer argues that money is endlessly particularized, "earmarked"—by, for instance, being placed in distinct locations or formed into alternative currencies such as gift certificates, food stamps, or gambling chips—based on the source (honest or "dirty," earned or received as a gift, etc.) or the use to which it is put (various particular household expenses, gifts, etc.). She also notes that money is gendered (with clear distinctions between husbands' and wives' monies, for instance) and classed (earmarking is done differently in different classes, and the poor engage in contests with charitable agencies over the deployment of money) as well as ethnically specified (as becomes apparent in the contests of ethnically identified poor people with government attempts to standardize their spending).[42] Particularized in diverse ways, money is not only incorporated into social relationships, she suggests, but, in fact, becomes the instrument for elaborating precisely the kinds of personal and communal ties that are supposedly destroyed by money (though the particular relationships may in fact be different ones, transformed by an expanded market).

Zelizer argues, "'Earmarking' . . . lies at the heart of economic processes."[43] Focusing on the elaborate differentiations of money within the specific contexts of domestic spending, gift giving (in which she includes not only sentimental gifts but also year-end bonuses offered by corporations), and government-sponsored welfare policies (what she calls "charity"), Zelizer ultimately argues that these cases are not exceptional but, rather, indicate that the "social differentiation of money is pervasive. . . . Not just individuals but organizations and even the government distinguish among forms of legal tender or other monies."[44] Further, she points to the differentiation of money in the marketplace (rather than in relation to consumption, as in most of her examples) through instruments such as "overnight repurchase agreements, Eurodollars, money market mutual-fund shares, savings bonds, commercial paper"[45] and the fragmentation of markets (indicating not only niche marketing of consumption goods but also divisions of the labor market by gender, race, and ethnicity).[46]

In the course of demonstrating the impact of social relations on the meanings of money, Zelizer suggests that the elaboration of particularized money coincided with an expansion of the commercial economy and, further, that the elaboration of particularized money was deliberately promoted by governments, corporations, and consumer magazines seeking to train subjects to be proper consumers. While contesting the claim that subjects are homogenized as they are incorporated into a consumer economy and encouraged to buy mass-produced commodities, she nonetheless acknowledges an aspect of the subject/object dialect that Lukács (and many other theorists) have identified, namely the need to control consumer desire as part of the capitalist effort to realize the capital embodied in commodities. In effect, she points out that the particularization of abstract value as use values in the body of particular commodities, the relationship of value to values, is not accidental or incidental, but necessary. Value and values are not autonomous, as Radin would have them. And Zelizer also crucially notes that efforts to bring value and values together, the specific regimes for the particularization of money, are sites of contest and power struggle. Marx's theory of the commodity offers a structural account of such struggles and further, by attending to labor-power as a commodity, enables us to see the social implications of the supplementarity of value with values in production, where Zelizer focuses on consumption. Marx, like Zelizer, defines the commodity as multivalent. In the first chapter of *Capital,* Marx describes the commodity as simultaneously a use value and a value.[47] In doing so, he defines the commodity as joining two different orders of value. But this joining turns out to be no simple matter. The relation between value and use value might be read as "supplementary." Derrida defines supplementarity this way:

> The supplement adds itself, it is a surplus, a plenitude enriching another plenitude. . . . But the supplement . . . adds only to replace. It intervenes or insinuates itself *in-the-place-of*; if it fills, it is as if one fills a void. . . . its place is assigned in the structure by the mark of an emptiness.[48]

A supplementary reading notes the void, the absent center, of any structure, suggesting that a given structure cannot be by itself coherent, autonomous, self-sustaining, or what Spivak calls "continuous."[49] The structure constitutively depends on something outside itself, a surplus that completes it, providing the coherence, the continuity, the stability that it cannot provide for itself, although it is already complete. But at the same time this supplement to the structure supplants that structure. Insofar as the structure depends on this constitutive supplement, the supplement becomes the primary structure itself. Its own logic becomes, or at least may become, dominant or destabilizing, a blockage to the continuity, a sign of crisis or incompleteness.

Marx argues that *value,* the "exchange relation of commodities, is characterized precisely by their abstraction from use value."[50] Marx also, and more famously, defines *value* as "abstract socially necessary labor." As *value*, he says, commodities "do not contain one atom of use value."[51] *Value* is what remains when use value, the particularity and concreteness of the commodity, is "subtracted," that is, when particularities become irrelevant in a given moment of exchange. Marx suggests that *use values* are merely "material bearers" of value: "As old Barbon says, 'one sort of wares are as good as another, if their value be equal.'"[52] Marx would seem here to be dismissing use value as irrelevant to capital accumulation. However, in the *Grundrisse* Chapter on Money, as well as in Volume Two of *Capital*, the significance of use values to the circulation of value as capital becomes very clear, as Gayatri Spivak has pointed out.

In *Scattered Speculations on the Theory of Value*, Spivak notes that the common reading of the "labor theory of value" describes the determination of capital as a chain of increasing abstraction, grounded positively in labor.[53] In this reading, labor is represented by value, which is in turn represented by money, which then appears transformed as capital. However, Spivak argues that this chain is discontinuous, open at each moment of representation or transformation. It is open at the origin in the sense that value is not only determined positively by labor, but also determined negatively, differentially, as an abstraction from use value. Likewise, for money to represent value, it has to be separated from its own being as a commodity. However, if money is not simply to be hoarded, this separation, the abstractness of money, must be negated as it is exchanged for commodities. And finally, the transformation of money into capital depends not only on prior accumulations of (abstract) capital but, as I noted above, on "so-called primitive accumulation," the separation of labor from the means of production through domination, and, further, on the super-adequation of labor, its ability to produce surplus value, that is, its use value.[54] So, while the determination of capital would seem to be a continuous and therefore independent chain of representation and transformation, in fact, at each stage, the movement towards abstraction—that is, the predication of capital itself—depends on the intervention of other orders of value, or on an investment in particular use values.

The indeterminateness of capital, its openness to determination by use value, is an opening to determination by social relations and "values" in exchange, production, and consumption. Marx says, "Nothing can be a value [that is, exchangeable] without being an object of utility."[55] But utility is socially and historically determined:

> Every useful thing is a whole composed of many properties; it can there-
> fore be useful in many ways. The discovery of these ways and hence the
> manifold uses of things is the work of history.[56]

Likewise, the production process itself is dependent on historically particular social relations. Production, as Marx says, is "conditional on reproduction processes outside the reproduction process of the individual
capital."[57] That is, the producer must be able to obtain the necessary materials (raw and otherwise) for his production process. While Marx is
here referring to the dependence of one capitalist upon other capitalist
producers, the dependence of capital on other orders of value is also made
especially obvious by the fact that, for Marx, the important commodity
is labor power. For production to be possible, a process of social distribution must assign some but not all, at birth, to wage labor and distribute
the members of society among the different kinds of production.[58] And,
as "the object is not an object in general but a specific object which must
be consumed in specific manner,"[59] consumption as well can occur within
only a particular social formation, in which particular desires for particular commodities, produced by particular acts of labor, are operative.

This reading of the theory of value suggests that the particularities of
historically and socially determined use values, which include particular
social relations and "values," supplement the discontinuous circuit of abstract value, enabling its circulation. While Marx's structural account of
the value/use value relation makes it impossible to posit "community,"
"culture," "family," or "values" as offering a pure or resistant alternative
to capitalism, this account does make it possible to trace the complicity
of race, ethnicity, gender, nation, and sexuality with capital.

But Marx's discussion of the relation between value and use value em-
phasizes not only or even primarily their complicity. Instead, he generally
describes them as contradictory or antagonistic:

> The simple form of value of the commodity is the simple form of the ap-
> pearance of the opposition between use-value and value which is con-
> tained within the commodity.[60]

In the simple equation of two commodities (x coats = y linen) each commodity can only be either in the role of the relative form or the equivalent
but not both. The relative form would seem to express only value, while
the equivalent form appears to express only use value. But in the process

of exchange, a given commodity must metamorphose from its appearance as value into use value and vice versa. (In every exchange, a thing that is not useful to its owner, and that, in fact, represents only value to its owner, is sold to someone for whom it does have a use value.) "The commodity itself is here subject to contradictory determinations. At the starting point it is a non-use-value to its owner; at the end it is a use value."[61] The realization of capital depends on the resolution of these opposed determinations through successful exchange. Should the metamorphosis of value and use value fail, capital accumulation will fail. For instance, if useless goods are brought to market they will not be purchased. Conversely if useful goods are not brought to market, do not participate in the social exchange process, they will fail to have value.[62]

The development of technologies for overcoming the obstructions presented by the necessary embodiment of capital is a history that hardly needs repeating here.[63] The most interesting developments for my purposes are those technologies that increase the mobility of labor (so-called "guest worker programs" would be an obvious current example) because they indicate that the contradiction between abstraction and particularity must be solved for social formations as well as for material commodities.[64] The solution to such contradictions is not solved once and for all through the enforced conformity of the particular with the universal (as Romantic accounts would have it) but is, rather, a constant struggle, engaged through ongoing rearticulations of social formations and values.

Taken together, the necessary relation between the exchange and production of commodities and between value and values, has tremendous implications for our understanding of commodification and our strategies for resisting the domination and exploitation that it entails. If on the one hand, we must recognize that communities and identities that we value are positively constituted through participation in production and consumption, we must also recognize that such social formations are inevitably linked to exploitative and oppressive social formations. So for instance, while gay/lesbian community in the United States has in recent years been largely constituted through commodity consumption, and many communal events, such as film festivals, and so on, are sponsored by corporations seeking to promote such consumption, we must recognize that the commodities we consume and the profits that support our events are often derived from the labor of women working in factories in export processing zones all over the world, women whose labor is exploited in large part through the deployment of patriarchal gender and sexual norms. Our freedom depends on their oppression. Further, much of the "community-building" work that we do in our families or non-profit organizations must be read as complicit in the process of constituting subjects for capitalism.

Recognizing that values, as well as value, are crucial to capital accumulation, it is clear that Radin's strategy of having the law respect values as well as value does not begin to address the problem. The only solution is one that accounts for the supplementary relation of value and values. But in fact, the very complicity of social formations with capital provides us with a huge diversity of opportunities for resistance. Precisely because particular social formations (values) are necessary to the flow of capital, they can become sites of crisis. While mobilizations that recognize the importance of values to the circulation of capital are themselves often deeply conservative and oppressive, as is the case with various religious fundamentalist antimodernization movements, it is my hope that they need not be. In other words, it is my hope that by attending to the relationship between their values (and strategies) and the circulation of value, feminist, queer, and antiracist movements might organize themselves against rather than through capitalism. The question then might be, how does the pursuit of marriage rights facilitate or disrupt the flow of capital in this particular historical moment? Further, recognizing the complicities, the links, between communal formations and capital, gives us leverage by enabling us to see connections with potential allies who may be constituted and positioned very differently in the circuit of capital but with whom we might nonetheless find common cause. It is only through such social movements, informed by a comprehensive analysis of the imbrication of our communal values with value, that we can intervene in the power balance between people and capital.

NOTES

Many thanks to Martha Ertman for including me in this project and for her helpful editing of this essay.

1. Karl Marx, The Grundrisse 141, 147 (Martin Nicolaus trans., 1973).

2. Moishe Postone, *Anti-Semitism and National Socialism, in* Germans and Jews since the Holocaust 309 (Anson Rabinach & Jack David Zipes eds., 1986).

3. Karl Marx, Economic and Philosophic Manuscripts of 1844 135–40 (Martin Milligan trans., 1988).

4. Karl Marx, Capital Vol. One 125 (Ben Fowkes trans., 1977).

5. My reading is poststructuralist in the sense that it aims to elicit neither a political program nor a teleological narrative but, rather, through attention to the openings in Marx's texts, seeks to elicit his structural analysis of capitalism as itself an open process, open specifically to the social. While giving proper poststructuralist attention to signification, I recognize capitalism as potentially the most powerful generator of meanings. *See* Miranda Joseph, Against the Romance of Community (2002) (The reading of Marx I offer here is drawn from my book, which reworks Marx's most fundamental argument—that social relations are constituted through production—in order to account for the complexity of contemporary identities and communities.) Several paragraphs toward the end of this essay are borrowed directly from Against the Romance of Community. *Id.* at 29.

6. *See id.* (in which I do attempt such a full theorization).

7. Margaret Jane Radin, Contested Commodities: The Trouble with Trade in Sex, Children, Body Parts and Other Things xii (1996).

8. *Id.* at 15.

9. *Id.* at 20.

10. *Id.* at xi.

11. *See* Joseph, *supra* note 5, especially Chapter Two, "The Performance of Production and Consumption," at 35. My argument is an attempt to move beyond the materiality/discourse binary that undergirds endless debate among Marxists over the relationship between the economic base and the superstructure of ideas, political systems, etc. in constituting social practices. *Id.* at 30–35.

12. Michael Taussig, Mimesis and Alterity: A Particular History of the Senses xvi (1993).

13. Radin, *supra* note 7, at 56–57, 60–63.

14. *Id.* at 58.

15. *Id.*

16. *Id.* at 75.

17. *Id.* Radin accounts for her naturalization of market society by way of her pragmatism, which explicitly accepts the "culture" we have and builds what she calls "nonideal theory" on that basis. However, as Radin herself says, certain reform efforts merely stabilize a bad situation and it seems to me that the limits of her account are such that her practical proposals will be reforms of this sort. A pragmatist, even more than a utopianist, needs an adequate account of the situation in which she or he wishes to intervene.

18. *Id.* at 64.

19. *Id.* at 64–69; *See also* Martha C. Nussbaum, *Human Functioning and Social Justice: In Defense of Aristotelian Essentialism,* 20 Political Theory 202 (1992).

20. Radin, *supra* note 7, at 51.

21. *Id.* at 8.

22. Marx, Capital Vol. One, *supra* note 4, at 200.

23. *Id.* at 248.

24. It is worth noting here that, in general, Marxists are not particularly concerned with commodification, or at least not with commodification in the market-centered sense in which Radin uses the term. While Marx opens *Capital* with a discussion of the commodity, he does so because the commodity is the form of appearance of wealth in capitalism, a form of appearance that functions to mystify the social and productive human relations under capital, and that must thus be analyzed and demystified, to reveal those human relations that are really the matter of concern. When Marxists refer to commodification they are generally using the term as a metonym for the entire capitalist mode of production. That is, the term indicates not merely that some good is being produced for sale that was previously produced for use, but also that some arena of social life is now subject to the extraction of surplus value, to exploitation, and further that the ideological regime or "phenomenological matrix" of "commodity fetishism" is operative, such that relations between people appear as relations between things and that the value of a commodity, which is really a product of human labor, appears to be inherent in the commodity itself. Rosemary Hennessy, Profit and Pleasure: Sexual Identities in Late Capitalism 95 (2000).

25. Marx, *supra* note 1 at 458.

26. Karl Marx, Capital Vol. One, *supra* note 4, at 270–73.

27. *Id.* at 874–75.

28. Radin, *supra* note 7 at 154.

29. *Id.* at 155.

30. *Id.* at 155–56.

31. *Id.*

32. *Id.* at 158–59.

33. *Id.* at 158.

34. *Id.* at 80–83.

35. Georg Lukács, History and Class Consciousness 83 (Rodney Livingstone trans., 1968).

36. *Id.*

37. *See, e.g.,* Jean Baudrillard, The Mirror of Production (1975); Wolfgang Fritz Haug, Critique of Commodity Aesthetics: Appearance, Sexuality and Advertising in Capitalist Society (1986); Max Horkheimer & Theodor W. Adorno, Dialectic of Enlightenment (John Cumming trans., 1972) (especially the chapter on the culture industry); and various essays by Herbert Marcuse.

38. Lukács, *supra* note 35 at 88–90.

39. Viviana A. Zelizer, The Social Meaning of Money: Pin Money, Paychecks, Poor Relief, and Other Currencies (1997).

40. *Id.* at 1.

41. *Id.* at 2.

42. *Id.* at 204 (summarizing arguments made across the book).

43. *Id.* at 208.

44. *Id.* at 200.

45. *Id.* at 206.

46. *Id.* at 207.

47. Marx, Capital Vol. One, *supra* note 4 at 125. In fact, the kinds of value that Marx suggests can be embodied by the commodity are much more diverse than this binary opposition of value and use value, as I discuss in Joseph, *supra* note 5, at 35. *See also* Marx, Economic and Philosophic Manuscripts of 1844, *supra* note 3 at 135–40.

48. Jacques Derrida, Of Grammatology 145 (Gayatri Chakravorty Spivak trans., 1976).

49. Gayatri Chakravorty Spivak, In Other Worlds 158–62 (1987).

50. Marx, Capital Vol. One, *supra* note 4 at 127.

51. *Id.* at 128.

52. *Id.* at 126, 127.

53. Spivak, *supra* note 49 at 158–62.

54. *Id.*

55. Marx, Capital Vol. One, *supra* note 4 at 131.

56. *Id.* at 125.

57. *Id.* at 154.

58. Marx, The Grundrisse, *supra* note 1, at 96.

59. *Id.* at 92.

60. Marx, Capital Vol. One, *supra* note 4, at 153.

61. *Id.* at 207.

62. Marx describes these potential failures at length in *Capital,* Vol. Two, where he discusses the time and space obstacles in the circuits of capital (to the circulation of capital). Marx, Capital Vol. Two (David Fernbach trans., 1978).

63. Any technology that increases the turnover time of capital (the speed with which the capital initially invested can be turned back into capital for further investment) is a technology that is aimed at overcoming the obstructions presented by the necessary embodiment of capital. Examples include the invention of the steam engine, the refrigerated railcar or the airplane, various credit instruments, the "liquidation sale," and electronic funds transfers.

64. For more on labor mobility, see Saskia Sassen, The Mobility of Labor and Capital: A Study in International Investment and Labor Flow (1988).

Afterword

Whither Commodification?

Carol M. Rose

The word "commodification" is a kind of verbal giveaway, like "bourgeois," or "deconstruct" or "utility function." When you use a word of this sort, you convey a certain set of analytical categories or rather commitments—commitments that separate you from some other people who might well be interested in the same subjects but who think about them in very different terms. I would be willing to bet, for example, that the word "commodification" never appears in the entire *oeuvre* of the neoclassical economist Milton Friedman. By the same token, the scholars who have a lot to say about commodification are not likely to have much truck with utility functions, though neoclassical economists do. Indeed, the very word "commodification" conveys serious doubts (not to say scorn) about market economics, especially the most imperialistic versions of law-and-economics, which purport to reduce all human institutions, motives, and actions to the comparisons of supply and demand.[1]

It is particularly interesting, then, to see that the language of commodification has started to penetrate the enemy camp. The word "commodification" makes an unexpected appearance in Richard Posner's contribution to this volume, where this quintessential guru of law-and-economics mentions the c-word several times, with a straight face albeit rather skeptically.[2] Less skeptical are James Salzman and J. B. Ruhl, two legal scholars who are comfortable with market-friendly economic thinking but who nevertheless have published an article critiquing the "commodification" of environmental law."[3] A particularly startling surprise has emanated from the Nike Corporation, which, in case you didn't know it, is one of the world's largest producers of athletic shoes. When Nike de-

cided to sever its connections with the mass-market retail shoe distribu-
tor Foot Locker, a Nike spokesperson explained that one problem was
that Foot Locker was "commodifying" sneakers.[4] Come again? How's
that? What exactly *is* a sneaker if not a commodity?

These instances of linguistic cross-dressing hint that market-friendly
economic theory may be drawing just a bit closer to commodification theory, however warily. In a way, this should not be a surprise. One of the
commodification pieces designated as classic in this volume is Calabresi
and Melamed's 1972 article "One View of the Cathedral," which generally took its cues from economic reasoning. But this economics-influ-
enced duo argued quite explicitly that markets might not work for everything, and they focused in part on the question of inalienability—that is,
legal constraints on the buying and selling of certain goods and services.[5]
When Peggy Radin popularized the term "commodification" in 1987,[6]
she too was addressing inalienability, even though she thought that economists' explanations were mighty thin.

Perhaps it is no wonder, then, that a number of the new essays in this
book suggest that the reconsideration is mutual. Commodification theory
itself seems to be taking a second look at markets and even issuing a few
plaudits amidst the usual chorus of Bronx cheers. To be sure, Miranda
Joseph sees commodification as part of a larger self-aggrandizing capitalist project, while Michael Sandel and Tanya Hernández, taking a somewhat less wholesale approach, still think commodification has gone too
far when it comes to buying and selling such matters as sex or military
service. But Ann Lucas thinks there is something to be said for selling sex
after all. Martha Ertman thinks it might be a nifty idea to sell reproductive materials. Deborah Stone has some nice words to say about the commodification of caregiving, and Katharine Silbaugh thinks a dose of market talk could do some good in evaluating women's housework. Alexandra Chasin, while not very happy about the matter, can't help but notice
that merchants and entrepreneurs have made the market sizzle for
gay/bi/lesbian chic. Three cheers for commodification? No. But perhaps
one or two.

What, then, has happened to commodification theory to result in this
mixed message about markets? Consider the early use of the term.
Radin's "commodification" was a rather awkward term, but it was probably a good deal easier to say than "commoditization," Arjun Appadurai's kindred appellation,[7] and besides that, the word's verbal thumbing-
of-the-nose at markets clearly struck a nerve. After Radin's major article

on "market inalienability," whole choruses of market-critical scholars started to use the language of commodification (and its kissing cousin "incommensurability")[8] to attack what they saw as the simpleminded nostrums of law-and-economics for torts, criminal law, family law, constitutional law, and pretty much every other legal subject.

Moreover, the commodification critique was never just a matter of scholarly theorizing. Lots of other people apparently share the basic intuition that one cannot reduce everything to market terms. We have all heard the adages: You can't buy love. The best things in life are free. Money isn't everything. And so on. Business people (like that Nike spokesperson) know this too. There is something about cold cash that drives out the atmospherics. That is why, as one former realtor told me, realtors never say, "What kind of house would you like?" Instead they say, "What kind of a home (or as my informant said, a hooooome) would you like?"

But of course one does buy houses, or homes, just as one buys Nike shoes. Does that make houses (hooooomes) or shoes (Nikes) commodities? Yes. And no. Joan Williams and Viviana Zelizer apparently find the conundrum of commodity *vel non* so frustrating that they want to change the subject and to talk instead about what they call Differentiated Ties.[9]

Williams and Zelizer's attitude reflects some unfinished business in commodification theory. Things are both commodities and not commodities. Markets seem inappropriate for some things, but then again, maybe markets are pretty useful for exactly the same things. It is interesting that several of the essays in this volume return to some of Appadurai's ideas about "commoditization" (awkward language and all), and particularly to the idea that over time, things slip in and out of the status of commodity.[10] But when? And when not? This is the set of questions that the new commodification theory seems to be addressing.

Since much commodification theory already seems to be headed in the direction of a reassessment of markets, in the remainder of this essay, I am going to suggest some ways that commodification theory might borrow from the erstwhile opposing team. My plan is to take up some of the major themes of "classical" commodification theory—all of them contained in Radin's first big article on market inalienability—and then to explore how in each case, the new commodification theorists are already capturing, reworking, and even liberating analogous but market-friendly approaches to the same themes, and how they might do even more of this work.

Rethinking the Double Bind:
The Perspective of the "Second Best"

One of the most striking discussions in Radin's major article *Market Inalienability* came toward the end, after she recounted a whole set of reasons that a society might not want to permit the commodification of sexuality, children, bodies, and body parts. At the end of it all, she forthrightly addressed the daunting problems that poverty poses for an anticommodificationist position. Radin named the general problem "the double bind": a poor person is in danger of holding a commodified view of her own body if she sells, say, a kidney, but because of her poverty she is in trouble too if she is forbidden to sell it.[11] You cannot tell a poor person who wants to make some money by commodifying one of her body parts that she has to starve instead. Commodification may be bad, but starving is worse. To cope with these unpleasant realities, Radin argued for what she called "incomplete commodification" in goods like sexual services, i.e., permitting some sales but under tight restrictions.[12]

This double bind analysis has been a subject of numerous elaborations in the commodification literature, perhaps nowhere more than in the discussion of prostitution and the sale of body parts. But in general, Radin's double bind suggests a way of thinking that market-friendly economists developed some time ago, even though the problems they discussed were normally not so emotionally charged as sales of sexuality and body parts. The concept is that of the "second best," and like most economic thinking, the second best is an attempt to compare things. In the law and economics literature, second-best analysis has often focused on the appropriate response to monopolies or to regulatory regimes. For example, a law and economics scholar might argue that the "first-best" solution to some situation would be no regulation at all (what a surprise!), but given some X set of regulations, the second-best option might be a further set of Y regulations that offset some of the problems created by X.[13]

Despite commodification theorists' aversion to many kinds of purportedly incommensurable comparisons, the general idea of the second best is one that has some resonance, in no small part because the concept lends itself to a reverse twist that in a sense gets a little revenge on the economists. The reverse twist is this: instead of *regulations* acting as a major context for second-best thinking, commodification theorists can identify *markets* as the context for second best. That is, in a first-best world there would be no market for a particular good or service, and any transfers would be at most gifts; but the actual fact of markets forces the consideration of what might be second best. On this analysis, it is markets themselves that create the second-best problem (take that, economists!).

To take the typical problem, sexual relations: in a first-best world, one might think, sexual relations would form a seamless whole with love, which of course cannot be bought but is instead freely and passionately *given*. For the moment, I will sideline any critiques of this rather romantic and perhaps unadventurous notion, and simply suppose it to be true.[14] We live, nevertheless, in a second-best world with respect to this eternally interesting subject. As we all know, sexual services are in fact bought and sold. Even women have started to buy them from men, apparently rather gleefully, as Tanya Hernández's article on female sex tourists so vividly illustrates.[15]

Given the fact of a market for sex, how might commodification theory use the concept of the second best? Here the question becomes, as it was for Radin, what is the second-best legal strategy where there actually are market exchanges in this kind of activity? Different theorists might answer differently, of course. Some (like Radin earlier and Hernández more recently) clearly think that the proper legal strategy is to prohibit or severely hedge sales of sexual services, some for paternalistic reasons (psychological, physical, and/or economic damage to the participants themselves), others for reasons relating to the effects on third parties (illness, nuisance, graft, spread of commodified attitudes, etc.).

Nevertheless, other commodification theorists might well think that the appropriate second-best strategy is a relatively free market. Let us concede for the sake of argument that first best is love. Second best, nevertheless, is getting paid. More specifically, second best is not having to pay a pimp or a corrupt cop for the protection and contract enforcement that the law refuses to provide to sex workers. Who does well out of a prohibition model? Pimps and corrupt cops, that's who. The prostitute might be better off if she were not a prostitute at all. But given that she is, and given that she doesn't have a whole lot of other choices, a freer market might let her keep the money and get out of the trade sooner if she so desires. Radin's discussion of sexual services flirted with second-best analysis, but Ann Lucas's and Martha Nussbaum's chapters in this volume now push the point much further, and with great aplomb.[16]

Consider the applications of second-best thinking in other areas where markets seem quite awful but nevertheless exist as a fact. In the notorious article on baby-selling by Elisabeth Landes and Richard Posner, there is implicit a point that is often overlooked: there already *is* a market for babies. It just isn't a very efficient market or one that is conducted in cash, at least overtly. Instead, it is conducted in the currency of groveling to social workers, though as Pat Williams points out, the latter seem to want some money too.[17] A more straightforward market for babies at least could get more money to the birth mothers, and less to the intermediaries in the so-called helping professions.[18] Organ transfers are another case in point. At the moment, there is an active though illegal market for organs from live donors, though it is generally kept pretty quiet. There are some health benefits to such markets by comparison to prohibition (fresher organs, timed sequences of operations), but even putting those benefits to one side, a more straightforward market might get more of the money to the original owners of the organs, instead of forcing would-be purchasers to pay large sums to clandestine fixers, corrupt bureaucrats, and career-nervous surgeons.[19] Or take a quite different subject, the location of locally unwanted land uses (so-called LULUs) like sewage treatment plants and sanitary waste fills. If LULU siting were based on a genuine reverse auction, in which the would-be facilities managers have to hike up their bids until some neighborhood agrees to act as a host site, these facilities might well wind up in low-income neighborhoods, as critics complain. But LULUs tend to wind up in low-income neighborhoods anyway, through a political market (of influence and favors) in which the poor are at a great disadvantage because they are not as organized or powerful as the middle-class neighborhoods. With an auction system, at least the poorer neighborhoods could receive some compensation.[20] In all these cases, first-best (arguably) would be perfect love, or perfect health, or a perfectly trash- and waste-free environment. But in a second-best world where there actually are implicit markets, all-out commodification might just start to look more attractive—more attractive, that is, than the fake processes that disguise the market, drain off the money to intermediaries, and let the most disadvantaged parties hang out to dry.

Obviously, there are well-known problems with explicit markets in all these areas, particularly when the person doing the selling isn't selling his own or her own goods: parents can sell their kids into the sex trade, husbands might force wives to sell kidneys, neighborhoods could sell landfill space upwind of uncompensated neighboring communities. These forced transfers are not to be dismissed lightly, and indeed, market inalienability might be a superior choice where such problems are too difficult to monitor and solve. But thinking about commodification in a second-best framework allows one to compare bad situations while acknowledging that some other (unattainable) situation would be ideal. Looked at this way, commodification is not always the worst-best. Sometimes it is just second best—in a world in which first best isn't feasible, and other options are even worse than second best.

Now, the second-best approach that I see just under the skin of commodification analysis presumes that the absence of markets would be first best, at least for a given set of subjects. Says who? Sometimes markets looks pretty good, as Ann Lucas's article points out, even with subjects as intimate as sex. Big, impersonal, alienated free markets have some attractions too. But when, and when not? Another kind of market-friendly theory suggests some directions in which commodification theorists might take this question.

Rethinking the Gift/Market Dichotomy: The Perspective of Social Norm Theory

One of the major contributions of Radin's classic analysis of commodification was her refinement of the concept of inalienability. As she pointed out, there is a pure form of inalienability in which the goods or services at issue are never allowed to be transferred at all—matters like the electoral franchise, and (at least in a post-bounty world) the obligation to military service. But a second and especially important form of inalienability permits transfer by gift but not transfer by sale and purchase. Here some of her examples were sexual services and body parts. Goods like these, in the gift-but-not-sale category, are not necessarily inalienable strictly speaking. They are inalienable only in *markets*, or to put it in adjectival form, they are market-inalienable. It was this gift vs. sale distinction that led Radin to the concept of "commodification," that is, with some goods, the objection was not to transfers but to *commodified* transfers.[21]

From a certain perspective, the distinction between gift and market transfers seems rather thin. In 1925, Marcel Mauss's classic work *The Gift* suggested that his fellow anthropologists were making too much of a purported difference, since gifts and market exchanges were really a lot alike. After all, both gift-giving and market dealings normally involve reciprocal exchanges, and in societies without cash-mediated markets, the complexities of gift-giving mimic the market, including concepts of debt and even interest.[22]

So, is there any difference between gift exchange and market exchange? Well, yes and no. Among commodification theorists, Viviana Zelizer has been most notable in pointing out that yes, there are similarities between nonmarket and market exchanges, but no, as a social matter they are still not the same. She has famously described, for example, the lengths to which people will go to disguise a gift of money as something else. With careful folding, a five-spot can be made to look like a belt decoration.[23]

Zelizer's work points in the direction of what legal scholars now term "law and social norms," an area of legal scholarship that is generally friendly to law-and-economics thinking but that criticizes its psychological and social bases. Robert Ellickson, whose 1991 book *Order Without Law* propelled social norms into the legal limelight, is like Zelizer in pointing out that gifts involve reciprocity and that gift-givers even keep mental accounts of who owes what to whom, but that there nevertheless are occasions on which gifts are appropriate but cash is not. Bringing the bottle of wine to the dinner party will be just fine, and may even be expected, but paying its price in cash would offend the host.[24]

One of the critical differences between gift exchange and commodified exchange is the *size* of the relevant community in which exchange takes place, or at least its potential size. Dollars are just as green, no matter who plunks them down. If you have the cash, you can be anyone in the world but you can still buy the hairdryer or the bar of soap; and if not, not.[25] Gift exchange, on the other hand, operates within more limited ambits. Its context, it seems, entails embeddedness in a culture—even a culture of two—where social norms govern. That is why gifts need not be exactly equal or symmetrical. The parties know each other, and they keep similar mental accountings in which the giver of the lesser gift still has a debt, to be made up next time or to be advanced in the "currency" of admiration and respect. And if one of the immediate parties should lapse in her reciprocal obligations, she will be reminded by the surrounding and observing community, which uses advice, gossip, and ostracism to enforce the prevailing social norms.[26]

All the complicated understandings of gift exchange make sense in a community web of densely intertwined and mutually observed interactions. But cash markets, it seems, can dispense with these social interactions. They depend not on well-understood relationships or community social norms but, rather, on impersonal law. Hence communitarians see market transactions as hard, distant, unfeeling, and cold by comparison to gift exchanges, where everyone has to be a member of the relevant community, and as it were, in the know.

How aggravating, then, to find that a community's culture may show up in a big, impersonal cash market. How distressing, for example, to see the spiritual designs of Aboriginal groups adorning pimply mainstream adolescents' tee-shirts.[27] How annoying to find the earrings and fashions of proud gays and lesbians being sported by straights who never paid their dues.[28] How irksome to see the cultural icons of Kwanzaa, the glories of Kenta cloth, bedecking a blue-haired, middle-aged white woman from the suburbs.[29] (Alas, I confess that I am that blue-haired middle-aged white woman.). Cash markets, it would seem, drive out the intimate meanings and cultural synergies of gift exchange, and instead dilute social norms in a cold bath of literal and figurative alienation.

The gifts-vs.-markets issue needs some addenda, however. Here is a first addendum, concerning a *wealth/meaning trade-off*. In gift exchange, the community of exchange is likely to be rather limited, contained within the ambit of the controlling social norms. In markets, on the other hand, there are all kinds of potential bidders out there for your stuff, and if there are more bidders, the chances are better that your stuff will bring in a bigger return. But here's the trade-off: sales in a larger cash market can dissipate the cultural meanings that infuse your stuff in the smaller gift-exchange community. Those tie-dyed tee-shirts of the 1960s were way cool as long as only hippies wore them, but they got pretty tepid when the over-30 set started to appropriate the designs. Gay bars can lose their cachet for the regulars when too many eager straights show up.[30] Kenta cloth—not to speak of hip-hop gestures—start to look creepy and alien and even like something of a power grab in the hands of suburban white folk, as bell hooks argues.[31]

The trade-off, in short, is money versus meaning. What is more, there is a collective action problem at the heart of the meaning/money trade-off. Meaning is a collective good, whereas money is likely to go to individuals. When individuals sell a few culture-laden items to outsiders, their individual sales may cumulatively spell the end of the community's collective good of iconic meaning. This is the reason that communities might want to have some say about individuals' sales of cultural goods.[32]

On the other hand, money is nothing to sneeze at, even for the collectivity, and the paternalistic concern of outsiders may be just that—paternalism, and unwanted too. You think that it ruins the tribal group's authenticity when tourists buy tickets to see the rain dances? You bemoan the ways that the dances themselves have changed, just to please the tourists' insatiable demand for what they obtusely think is authentic?[33] Tough. Mind your own business. Meaning and money might trade off against each other, but who is to say that meaning should always trump money? Besides, as Sarah Harding points out with respect to Native American artifacts, money may become a part of meaning, where commodification is a part of a thing's history.[34]

Here's a second addendum to the gifts-markets dichotomy. This addendum concerns *asymmetries in access to market exchange,* asymmetries that have been much noted among commodification theorists, particularly with respect to family structure. Typically the wife specializes in matters of gift exchange while the husband sells his services in the market, and both develop their skills accordingly. No wonder that at divorce, he has a wider range of options. He can offer his human capital in the wider employment market, whereas her human capital is, as the economists would say, firm-specific, which is another way of saying that the only major bidder for her services is the husband she is divorcing, hardly an ideal situation for her. No wonder either that feminist critics—and market economists too—often call for a market-based assessment of the household work that she has done.[35] Anticommodificationists resist such efforts, for the usual reasons: marketizing Mom's housework and child care would drain meaning out of loving relationships. But some others think a dollop of commodification would be a good thing, particularly as a way of evening the score as between Mom and Dad.[36] In any event, these asymmetries once again highlight the point that the locus of gift exchange is a relatively limited community—here a family—whereas the locus of the market exchange is potentially worldwide. If one (Mom) deals with the limited community of gift exchange, and the other (Dad) deals in the global marketplace, he's bound to have more economic options when they stop getting along.

The third addendum to the gift-market dichotomy follows directly, and it concerns a *certain comparative advantage of commodification.* There are times when commodification does not seem like a second best, to revert to the economists' terminology. Commodification can be first best. To be sure, if markets are disallowed and only gift exchanges are allowed, those gift exchanges will be thick with community meaning. Ugh, says Martha Ertman, get your thick meaning out of my hair.[37] As her article suggests, when exchanges are subject to social norms and community surveillance, the participants may be subject to stifling intrusion, particularly in matters so delicate and so socially fraught as reproduction. Neighbors, government officials, and self-appointed moralists think they have a right to intrude in nonmarket exchanges. But not in markets. As Michael Sandel points out, for better or worse, markets are nonjudgmental.[38] You can buy this sperm or that egg for indifferent, cold cash. No wonder some prefer markets: by comparison to the cloying heat and friction of social norms, the cool, smooth market is liberating, empowering, insouciant. Viva commodification!

And one final addendum to the gift-market dichotomy revolves about the *social norms of markets*: who says markets are so alienated from norms and trust? No doubt a turn from gift exchange to market exchange can entail the loss of community meanings, along with the disruption of relationships based on understanding, local knowledge, and trust. But social norm scholarship suggests that markets themselves are rather more complicated than we might have thought, and that they may be norm-based and norm-generative rather than norm-destructive. The economic historian Avner Greif has traced the ways in which medieval merchants leveraged home-town, small-group relationships to give themselves the mutual assurances they needed to trade on an international scale.[39] Contract theorists—and Teemu Ruskola in this volume—point out that many or even most commercial relationships last over long time periods, during which the participants come to know and to trust one another.[40] Lisa Bernstein's work is packed with examples of the ways in which merchants in varied commodities—diamonds, cotton, hay—overlay their market dealings with consultations, behavioral norms, chatter, and chiding.[41] Even eBay, presumably the most impersonal and universal of markets, has devised indices through which the participants can report on one another, publicizing which buyers and sellers are prompt, honest, and competent, and which are slowpokes and slackers.[42] In many if not all these contexts, market participation fosters new communities of interest among former strangers, even though these new communities of interest may disrupt the older communities of birth, status, and locality. But what's the matter with that?

In an interesting way, the key to what we might call market-communitarianism is the economists' bugbear, transactions costs. One cost of transactions, for example, is imperfect information. In some markets, information is not much of a problem. As sociologists have pointed out, where product information is obvious on the face of the product, and where the relevant transactions can occur simultaneously, little social structure may be expected to unfold among the participants. But where market participants must take risks, as when they buy goods of untested quality or sell goods before payment is delivered, they need institutional structures to assure them. In these situations of imperfect information, trading relationships are much more likely to effloresce into dense social networks and long-term relationships, even among persons who were initially complete strangers.[43]

Not that market-communitarianism is all sweetness and light, however. Amy Chua's important work on market-dominant minorities all over the world underscores the importance of social organization for trade.[44] It is precisely the social organization of some social groups that permits them to dominate the trading activities of the countries in which they reside—the Ibo in Nigeria, the overseas Chinese in Indonesia, the Indians in east Africa. But Chua also describes the pathologies that may emerge. The members of market-dominant social groups trust one another, but they don't trust the rest of the society, so that unlike eBay, the market-dominant minority group is closed. In turn the outsider-majorities may hate and distrust market-dominant insider-minorities, and they may well blame them for local social ills, sometimes with disastrous results.

In a sense, one could see Chua's market-dominant minorities as the modern-day inheritors of Avner Greif's medieval merchants. They are groups that rest on the dense-packed norms of gift-exchange among themselves, and that have leveraged those small-scale social talents into commodity-based skills in a wider trading market. But whatever the status of medieval and modern market-dominant minorities, the scholarship of social norms has simply blasted out of the water the notion that markets are cold, distant, and asocial. Quite the contrary, none but the simplest of markets can function without social organization, trust, and norms. No wonder, then, that in the theories of social norms, we can see a certain convergence between market thinking and commodification theory.

Rethinking Fungibility:
The Perspective of the In Rem *Theory of Property*

One of Radin's concerns about market rhetoric is its implicit rejection of the uniqueness of things. Market rhetoric assumes that everything can be traded for everything else, and that through the medium of money, all is fungible. According to Radin, this attitude represents an impoverished view of human activity.

Radin's analysis of market rhetoric and fungibility has recently received some unexpected support from a couple of market-friendly property scholars, Thomas Merrill and Henry Smith. Merrill and Smith are among a group of authors who have gotten interested in the differences between property and contract, and they have written a series of articles that attempt to refine those differences, which they think have been blurred in law and economics scholarship.[45] Interestingly enough, their analysis also enlightens readers about the relationship between markets and fungibility.

In distinguishing property from contract, Merrill and Smith argue that as a general matter, contracts involve only a small number of persons who can actually work out the terms of the deal, and for that reason contracts can be quite complicated. In any event, the contract will be all over when the immediate participants finish with it. Property, on the other hand, can easily survive its current owners. A given piece of property may be bought and sold over and over, and the more durable the goods, the more times those goods will show up in the market. What this means, according to the new theory, is that property's legal consequences attach to the thing (*in rem*) as opposed to the persons involved (*in personam*), as in contract law. And most importantly, the legal categories of property have to be kept simple, so that new generations of owners have a pretty good idea about what they are getting, and so that current buyers and sellers don't go crazy trying to search out a lot of weird relationships that might affect the purchase.

What does all this say for commodification theory? The point to notice is that the *in rem* theory is really about property that circulates in big markets, that is, commodifiable property. This property has to be simple because simplicity reduces information costs. The theory assumes a big universe of buyers and sellers over time, who cannot possibly all know one another or know anything about the history and context in which the purchased thing once appeared. Thus the *in* rem theory tells us why market-alienability and fungibility go together: idiosyncrasies are not allowed because big markets bring strangers to the goods, and strangers cannot be asked to figure out the idiosyncratic twitches of prior owners.[46]

But of course not all resources lend themselves to simplification or fungibility. Take environmental resources: most are notoriously complicated.

That is one reason that it has been so hard to figure out workable "tradable rights" schemes for most of them. For example, wildlife habitat in one location and topography is very difficult to compare to wildlife habitat elsewhere, since different plants and animals thrive in different topographies and weather patterns.[47] Generally, only the simplest and most fungible of environmental goods (or bads) have proven tractable to trading schemes. Similarly, for works of art, there is certainly a thriving art market, but the artworks themselves are far from fungible. No one cares if you buy a bottle of orange juice and carelessly drop it on the floor, but lots of people would care if you did the same with a Rodin sculpture. You can always get another bottle of orange juice, but a Rodin sculpture is a lot harder to replace. Speaking of Rodin, the artist himself or herself may have a special investment in the artwork, and might be particularly concerned if you painted the sculpture chartreuse.

Inalienability or incomplete inalienability is one way to manage these real-life complicated properties that do not fit easily into the legally simple, marketable categories that the *in rem* theory proposes. A very common form of incomplete alienability results from regulation. An example is the Endangered Species Act's prohibition on "taking" endangered animals, which means killing or otherwise disrupting them.[48] A property owner can sell her acreage, but generally, neither she nor the new owner can wriggle out of this "take" prohibition by paying something; effectively the public has a permanent and inalienable wildlife easement over the property. Artists' so-called moral rights in works of art are another instance of incomplete alienability.[49] These moral rights give artists the authority to prevent alterations of their works of art, even post-sale; the artists' cannot alienate this entitlement, presumably because too many would simply bargain away their rights, leaving the artworks to the not-always-tender mercies of the purchasers. The United States to date has been rather reluctant to enact many moral rights into its intellectual property law, but European countries are much more favorably inclined.[50]

There are also nonregulatory ways to restrict alienability. Restrictive covenants on real estate are a form of partial restraint on alienation, allocating rights to neighbors over one another's use of property. Restrictive covenants also illustrate another interesting phenomenon, namely that property may be made practically inalienable by the *proliferation* of property rights themselves. Michael Heller has written at length about the "anticommons," a situation in which there are so many and such diverse legal interests in a particular resource that no one can reassemble the whole, a situation that becomes pathological when it means that the property can never be used.[51]

Nevertheless, the complex/inalienable end of the property spectrum is not always pathological, even for economic thinkers. In fact, complexity can be a way to enforce inalienability, just as inalienability can be a way to manage complexity. True enough, according to the *in rem* theory, property that is marketed has to be relatively simple. But not everyone wants his or her property to be marketable, and for such people, complication can be a part of a conscious plan to foil the market. I know someone whose family has long had some land in the Rocky Mountains. In an effort to keep the property in the family, the current generation of family owners are dividing up the property among so many members of the newer generations that (they hope) the property can never be sold to an outsider. Somewhat similarly, Stuart Banner's work on property relations in settlement-era New Zealand describes the complicated layerings of use rights among Maori landholdings, where one family had the fruit of a tree, another the fowling rights, and a third the rights to the bark.[52] The twofold effect of this proliferation of overlapping rights was that (a) outsiders couldn't understand them and (b) as a consequence they were discouraged from buying the properties. Matters changed later on, when the English settlers managed to force some simplification onto Maori land claims and then proceeded to buy them apace.

Note that complexifications of this sort tend to act not just as limits on the alienability of property, but also as limits on *change*. The sculpture subject to moral rights is not likely to get daubed chartreuse. The endangered species habitat will remain as it is. The Rocky Mountain property will not only stay in the family but it will stay roughly in its current configuration, since the larger the number of family members, the less likely it is that they will agree on any drastic changes. The Maori properties continued in their multiple uses as long as they remained complicated— and changed dramatically once they became legally simple.

This pattern suggests a basic conservatism running through the language of "market-inalienability," "anticommodification," and "incommensurabilities," and it suggests a reason that law and economics scholars are impatient with this kind of talk. Despite the nickname of the dismal science, market-oriented economists tend to like things that are dynamic, optimistic, breezy. They don't like to be reminded that matters are more complicated, and they don't like to delay change by accounting for all the little wrinkles. The *in rem* theory of property demonstrates what commodification theorists already knew about market alienability and market rhetoric, namely that market rhetoric is simple and oblivious to nuances, made for bulls in china shops. It has to be, or big markets won't work. But the *in rem* theory also illustrates why market economists get irked with commodification theory. Inalienability, complexity, and stasis are all part of the same anticommodification package. Which is to say, anticommodificationists seem like a bunch of fuss-budgets and Nervous Nellies.

Clearly some of the new commodification theorists in this volume suggest a similar view. Inalienable rights may protect important matters, but markets open up possibilities. How much easier it would be for gays and lesbians to have babies if they could just buy reproductive materials, and not mess around with snoopy bureaucrats![53] Who can fail to sympathize, just a little bit, with the young ladies whose gender-bending experiments include the purchase of sexual services from men![54] Who does not find it just a bit refreshing that the seller of Kwanzaa clothing is completely indifferent to black and white, and instead cares only about green?[55] In short, markets serve up ways to get rid of old stuff and acquire new stuff —and that means figuratively as well as literally. The new commodification theory has more than a whiff of recognition of the market's enormous potential for experiment and novelty. Sometimes, liberation comes in the form of a money price.

Rethinking Market Rhetoric: The Perspective of "Doux Commerce"

One of Radin's major contributions to commodification theory was her attentiveness to the *rhetoric* of the market. As she pointed out, marketizing some human activities inappropriately makes us talk about them differently, and talking about them differently can make us *think* about them differently, sometimes to the detriment of others, sometimes to the detriment of ourselves. Your children may be frightened and confused if they hear you talk about the market for babies. Juries may be inured to the pain, terror, and humiliation of muggings or rapes when they hear these crimes described as "market bypass."[56] When you buy what are euphemistically called sexual services, you may fool yourself into thinking that sex can be separated easily from the personal and emotional content that normally gives sex its *gravitas*. Radin's complaint, in short, was that the application of market rhetoric to noncommodifiable matters coarsens our understanding of these matters, leading us into mistakes, loosening our moral grasp, and undermining our ties to others. And so it seems that, just as commodified properties necessarily take on a simplified and flattened *in rem* legal character that is good against an undifferentiated world at large, so does market rhetoric itself take on an *in rem* quality, simplifying and flattening all nuance, idiosyncrasy, and sentiment, not only for the speaker of this rhetoric but for hearers as well.

Both before and after Radin's work, others have echoed these complaints about the rhetoric of markets in contexts that the writers deemed inappropriate. From a conservative perspective, this is the problem with the language of contractual marriage. Contract obligations in this intimate setting, it is said, could make the married partners talk and think of their individual entitlements, undermining the moral foundation of sharing that should permeate their relationship.[57] Market ideas for environmental protection suffer a similar criticism. Talk of pollution entitlements, it is said, hollows out the moral obligation to do the right thing, because this talk encourages the idea that those with the cash can buy the right to inflict damage on others.[58] And in perhaps the most famous study of all, Richard Titmuss argued that the sale of blood undermines the altruistic voluntary blood donations that are likely to be of higher quality.[59] In all these areas, market speakers, seemingly like Shylock, shockingly mix the "spheres" in which money reigns with those in which money means nothing.[60]

But clearly marketization and commodification are more subtle than this. Deborah Stone, writing in this volume about paid caregivers, gives us the most succinct and charming statement: "Love creeps in." Ann Lucas suggests that love or at least affection even creeps into prostitution, where clients and sex workers come to think well of one another. Richard Posner argues that just about everyone admires and respects our professional military service personnel, and that we are not concerned that the soldiers are volunteers for pay.

In all these examples it appears that commodification of a good or service has not markedly diminished people's abilities to think beyond the cold cash to the nuance of the relationship or service. To be sure, most would probably acknowledge that the cash is an impediment to be overcome. Surely the call girl (or call boy) suffers a moment of anxiety or embarrassment while a favorite client fumbles for his wallet. On the other hand, had it not been for the cash, the call girl and client would never have met at all. Neither would the care-needy and the care worker. Neither would the Kwanzaa bookseller and the interested customer.

If the new commodification theorists have noticed this pattern, in which commerce creates new relationships among former strangers, they are not alone. Eighteenth-century economic thinkers noted that commerce brings people together who otherwise would not encounter one another at all, and they argued that far from coarsening speech and thought, commerce makes manners gentle, patient, and other-regarding.[61] A business person wants to sell you something, not start a fight with you. To make the sale, he or she needs to find you and pay attention to what you want, in order to meld your interests with his or hers. Notice that "she" and "hers" are very much a part of the discourse of commerce. Travelers to Holland, the most commercial country of early modern Europe, noticed the great freedom of Dutch women, who could participate in commerce in a way unthinkable in the military pursuits of the aristocracy.[62] Subsequent historians have somewhat controversially linked the burgeoning late-eighteenth-century global trade to the rise of philanthropy, including the antislavery movement.[63] The reason is that commerce introduced traders to others all across the globe, and got them interested in the well-being of people very unlike themselves.

All this gooey sentimentality about gentle commerce may seem a bit hard to take in the light of the antiglobalization movement of the last several years, in which capitalist expansion is presented in its most hardhearted and exploitative light.[64] The economic historian Albert Hirschman, whose work over the last generation has reminded everyone about the *doux commerce* theories of the eighteenth-century economic theorists, also observes that commerce invites far less favorable descriptions.[65] These appear notably in the work of Karl Marx, but among others as well, as for example in Alexandra Chasin's warnings that the great slut commerce may lure gays and lesbians away from wider social concerns.[66] But on the whole, commodification theory may be mirroring the mood swings that Hirschman has described with respect to theories of commerce, with anticommodificationist concerns in the ascendancy in the early years, followed by a more open interest in markets among the newer commodification theorists. Again as Stone puts it, we can scarcely fail to see that love creeps in.

And yet, to return to the theme of rhetoric, might we be better off if market-created love could avoid using the language of cash? Might we actually benefit more if we could enjoy markets in intimate, complex, or unique goods, while pretending we were doing something else and talking about commodities some other way? Well, perhaps so. Perhaps we would be happier with a veil drawn across the rhetoric of commerce. And no doubt the first people to notice this are the people who are trying to sell you something, the Nike executives worried about Foot Locker's commodification of Air Jordans, or the real estate broker's offer to find you a suitable hooooome.

Hence I would like to suggest that while there is probably something to be said for disguising commodification with some other rhetoric, these disguises can be overdone. Funeral directors are notorious for their dislike of talking to you about the cost of the coffin. Tour operators and dance instructors would rather not tote up the final bill, as if the fun were not for sale.[67] But it is. Moreover, the law reflects that fact, and forces "anticommodificationist" fun merchants to fess up to the tab.

More radically, there can be times when commodification rhetoric has its uses even where things are *not* for sale. In environmental law, much ink has been spilled over the technique of "contingent valuation," the effort to find shadow prices that assess the value of nonmarket goods like scenery and wildlife.[68] There are few explicit values for these good things, so economists have tried to come up with other valuation methods. They ask people, How much do you spend to visit a national park where you might see or hear a wolf? How much *would* you spend to know that the experience was available to you? How much just to know the wolf was there? These so-called contingent valuations have drawn fire from both right and left—from the right because they seem so loaded with uncertainty and hypothetical thinking, from the left because they seem so, well, so inappropriate to the wonders of nature, great and small.[69]

My view is that these critiques are taking market rhetoric far too literally. In a sense, contingent valuation is metaphoric, the best we can do when we have no explicit way to assign values. In a commercial society, the absence of money value for something makes its value look like zero. But everyone knows that this is wrong. There is a value to eighty-mile visibility, clear water, and live fish in the clear water. It is precisely the jarring quality of contingent valuation—the let's-pretend market language, the mixing of "spheres"—that makes the point. Much the same may be said of the claims for reparations that Keith Hylton's contribution describes, that is, for race-based injuries in the sometimes-distant past. As Hylton points out, the strongest legal claims are for identifiable personal and property losses, fitting as they do most easily into the conventional categories of compensatory justice. But in some ways, the more outré claims for slavery reparation are more interesting rhetorically. Frail and unwieldy though they may be as a legal matter, these demands for money compensation make up a jarringly pointed call for justice too, albeit of a type not easily addressed by the tort system.[70] As in the language of the so-called market for ideas or the market value of spousal services, the very terms of cold cash and commodification wake us up to the fact that a great deal is at stake.[71]

In a sense, using commodification rhetoric in this way is quite like the extension of rights language to unexpected subjects and objects, such as animal rights, children's rights, and "standing" for trees. This linguistic extension too has drawn fire from both right and left, in part on the ground that rights-talk corrupts our thinking. But rights-talk, like market-talk, draws on our rather limited metaphoric resources to make clear that something important is at stake.[72] It is the very mixing of spheres that gives these analogies their power, and of course their danger.

Conclusion

Whither, then, commodification, or rather commodification theory? One can never be certain that the future will be like the past, of course. But observing the trends in commodification theory over the last several years, it seems clear that some commodification theorists are at least somewhat more comfortable with markets, and more intrigued with the market's possibilities for novelty, liberty, and self-fashioning—not to speak of money. To be sure, no one who talks a great deal about "commodification" is likely to be wholly uncritical of markets. The language is still a signal, and the signal still says, You can't buy happiness. But then again, let's check eBay one more time. . . .

NOTES

For helpful comments on earlier drafts I wish to thank Hanoch Dagan, Reva Siegel, Henry Smith, and Kenji Yoshino.
    1. Commodification anxiety may be a species of a more general distrust of inappropriate mixing of "spheres"; see Kenji Yoshino, *The Lawyer of Belmont,* 9

J. L. & Humanities 183, 184–88 (1997) (discussing Michael Walzer, Spheres of Justice (1983)). See also Note, *The Price of Everything, the Value of Nothing: Reframing the Commodification Debate*, 117 Harv. L. Rev. 689, 696 (2003) (discussing Walzer's "spheres").

2. Richard A. Posner, *Community and Conscription*, New Republic, May 5, 2003, this volume.

3. James Salzman & J. R. Ruhl, *Currencies and the Commodification of Environmental Law*, 53 Stan. L. Rev. 607 (2000).

4. Maureen Tkacik, *In a Clash of Sneaker Titans, Nike Gets Leg Up on Foot Locker*, Wall St. J., May 13, 2003, at A10, col. 4.

5. Guido Calabresi and A. Douglas Melamed, *Property Rules, Liability Rules, and Inalienability: One View of the Cathedral*, 85 Harv. L. Rev. 1089 (1972), this volume. See also Susan Rose-Ackerman, *Inalienability and the Theory of Property Rights*, 85 Colum. L. Rev. 931 (1985).

6. Margaret Jane Radin, *Market-Inalienability*, 100 Harv. L. Rev. 1849 (1987) [hereinafter Radin, *M-I*]; for her more recent reflections on the subject, see Margaret Jane Radin, Contested Commodities: The Trouble with Trade in Sex, Children, Body Parts and Other Things (1996), this volume.

7. Arjun Appadurai, *Introduction: Commodities and the Politics of Value, in* The Social Life of Things: Commodities in Cultural Perspective 3, 15 (1986), this volume. Appadurai credits the term to another author in the same volume: Igor Kopytoff, *The Cultural Biography of Things: Commoditization as Process, id.* at 64.

8. *See, e.g.,* Symposium, *Law and Incommensurability*, 146 U. Pa. L. Rev. 1169 (1998).

9. Joan Williams & Viviana Zelizer, *To Commodify or Not to Commodify: That Is Not the Question*, this volume. Katharine Silbaugh's article takes a similar position with respect to household labor: *Commodification and Women's Household Labor*, 9 Yale J. L. & Feminism 81 (1997), this volume.

10. Sarah Harding, *Culture, Commodification, and Native American Cultural Patrimony*, this volume; Ann Lucas, *The Currency of Sex: Prostitution, Law and Commodification*, this volume. *See also* Thatcher Freund, Objects of Desire: The Lives of Antiques and Those Who Pursue Them (1993) (tracing an antique's history).

11. Radin, *M-I, supra* note 6, at 1915–18.

12. *Id.* at 1915–18; *but see* Lucas, this volume (criticizing Radin's version of "incomplete commodification").

13. *See, e.g.,* George Mundstock, *The Trouble with FASB*, 28 N.C. J. Int'l L. & Comm. Reg. 813 (2003) (explaining economic theory of the second best, citing as "classic exposition" Richard G. Lipsey & Kelvin J. Lancaster, *The General Theory of Second Best*, 24 Rev. Econ. Stud. 11 (1956)).

14. *See* Katherine M. Franke, *Theorizing Yes: An Essay on Feminism, Law,*

and Desire, 101 Colum. L. Rev. 181, 206–7 (2001) (noting that female sexuality need not always be "warm, fuzzy, soft-focused" but sometimes edgy, dangerous, and willing to confront shame and "objectification").

15. Tanya Katerí Hernández, *"Sex in the [Foreign] City"—Commodification and the Female Sex Tourist,* this volume.

16. *See* Martha Nussbaum, *Taking Money for Bodily Services,* in Sex and Social Justice (1999), this volume; Ann Lucas, *The Currency of Sex,* this volume. Radin herself now refers to these kinds of problems as those of "nonideal theory"; *see* Margaret J. Radin & Madhavi Sunder, *Introduction,* this volume.

17. Patricia J. Williams, *In Search of Pharaoh's Daughter,* in The Rooster's Egg: The Persistence of Prejudice (1995), this volume.

18. Elisabeth M. Landes & Richard A. Posner, *The Economics of the Baby Shortage,* 7 J. Legal Stud. 323, 326, 336–39, 347 (1977), in this volume.

19. Michael Finkel, *Complications,* N.Y. Times, May 27, 2001, sec. 6 (Magazine) at 26, col. 1 (describing extensive international trade in kidney replacement); *see also* Lloyd R. Cohen, Increasing the Supply of Transplant Organs (1995), this volume (supporting markets in organs); cf. Emanuel D. Thorne, *When Private Parts Are Made Public Goods: The Economics of Market Inalienability,* 15 Yale J. Reg. 149 (1997) ("exhortation" for inalienable organs might have advantages over market).

20. *See, e.g.,* Michael B. Gerrard, Whose Backyard, Whose Risk: Fear and Fairness in Toxic and Nuclear Waste Siting 86–90, 178–80 (1994).

21. Radin, *M-I, supra* note 6, at 1853–55.

22. Marcel Mauss, The Gift: Forms and Functions of Exchange in Archaic Societies 1, 3, 40 (1967) (English translation of Essai sur le don, forme archaique de l'échange, 1925); *see also* Appadurai, *supra* note 7, at 10–12 (chiding fellow anthropologists for romanticizing gift over market); for some other potshots at the gift/market distinction, *see also* the mercilessly slashed version of my 1992 article, *Giving, Trading* etc., this volume.

23. Viviana Zelizer, The Social Meaning of Money 105 (1994).

24. Robert C. Ellickson, Order Without Law: How Neighbors Settle Disputes 78, 225–29 (1991) (describing numerous neighborly in-kind exchanges and strategies to even up implicit obligations).

25. This is not to say, of course, that prejudice does not affect markets, as for example in the efforts of homeowners to prevent sales of housing to minority racial groups. *See* Carol M. Rose, *Shelley v. Kraemer,* in Property Stories (2004).

26. For a fascinating account of complex reciprocal labor exchange in a remote Peruvian agrarian area, *see* Paul B. Trawick, The Struggle for Water in Peru: Comedy and Tragedy in the Andean Commons 98–108 (2003). For gossip in norm-enforcement, *see* Ellickson, *supra* note 24, at 232–36.

27. For similar situations, *see* Madhavi Sunder, *Property in Personhood,* this volume.

28. *See* Dereka Rushbrook, *Cities and Queer Space: Staking a Claim to Global Cosmopolitanism*, this volume.

29. Regina Austin, *Kwanzaa and the Commodification of Black Culture*, this volume.

30. *See* Rushbrook, *Cities and Queer Space: Staking a Claim to Global Cosmopolitanism*, this volume.

31. *See* Austin, *supra* note 29; and hooks, *Eating the Other*, in Black Looks: Race and Representation (1992), this volume.

32. *See* Sunder, *Property in Personhood*, *supra* note 27 (concerning group efforts to control culture). Williams and Zelizer, *supra* note 9, argue that it is critical to locate the property right appropriately; hence if meaning is a collective good, the collectivity might be the appropriate decision maker about sales. Collective "ownership," however, poses major alienability problems; *see* discussion of inalienability and stasis, *infra*.

33. For a fascinating account of Turkmen carpet weavers' modifications to satisfy purchaser demand for "authentic" design (thereby undermining the whole idea of authenticity), *see* Brian Spooner, *Weavers and Dealers: The Authenticity of an Oriental Carpet, in* The Social Life of Things, *supra* note 7, at 195, 214–35.

34. Harding, *Culture, Commodification and Native American Patrimony,* this volume.

35. To cite some of the authors appearing elsewhere in this volume, see Joan Williams, *Un*bending Gender: Why Family and Work Conflict and What to Do about It 125–27 (2000) (giving feminist case for recompense); Martha M. Ertman, *Commercializing Marriage: A Proposal for Valuing Women's Work through Premarital Security Agreements*, 77 Tex. L. Rev. 17 (1998) (same); Richard A. Posner, Economic Analysis of Law 151–54 (6th ed. 2003) (giving market economists' analysis).

36. *See* Silbaugh, this volume. For a cross-section of the various views on this subject, see *Symposium on Divorce and Feminist Legal Theory,* 82 Geo. L.J. 2119 (1994).

37. Martha M. Ertman, *What's Wrong with a Parenthood Market? A New & Improved Theory of Commodification*, 82 N.C.L. Rev. 1 (2003), this volume.

38. Michael J. Sandel, The Moral Limits of Markets (1998) this volume.

39. Avner Greif, *Reputation and Coalitions in Medieval Trade: Evidence from the Maghribi Traders,* 49 J. Econ. Hist. 857 (1989).

40. Teema Ruskola, *Home Economics: What's the Difference Between a "Family" and a "Corporation"?* this volume; for early theoretical discussions of the real-world importance of long-term or "relational" contracts, *see* Ian MacNeil, *The Many Futures of Contract,* 46 S. Cal. L. Rev. 691 (1977); and Stewart Macaulay, *Elegant Models, Empirical Pictures, and the Complexities of Contract* 11 L. & Soc'y Rev. 507 (1977).

41. Lisa Bernstein, *Private Commercial Law in the Cotton Industry: Creating Cooperation Through Rules, Norms, and Institutions,* 99 Mich. L. Rev. 1724 (2001); *Merchant Law in a Merchant Court: Rethinking the Code's Search for Immanent Business Norms,* 144 U. Pa. L. Rev. 1725 (1996) (discussing practices of the Nat'l Grain & Feed Assn.); *Opting Out of the Legal System: Extralegal Contractual Relations in the Diamond Industry,* 21 J. Legal Stud. 115 (1992).

42. eBay encourages both buyers and sellers to report on their experiences with one another, whether positive or negative, through a "Feedback Forum" that results in a "profile" for each user. The profile is then available to subsequent buyers or sellers. For a complete description, see http://pages.ebay.com/help/feedback/feedback.html. eBay describes this system as one that helps to "create a trustworthy community for everyone" (at http://pages.ebay.com/help/sell/basics.html, item 7).

43. *See* Peter Kollock, *The Emergence of Exchange Structures: An Experimental Study of Uncertainty, Commitment and Trust,* 100 Am. J. Soc. 313 (1994) (describing psychology experiment in behavior that established trading relationships).

44. Amy L. Chua, *The Privatization-Nationalization Cycle: The Link between Markets and Ethnicity in Developing Countries,* 95 Colum L. Rev. 223 (1996).

45. Thomas W. Merrill & Henry E. Smith, *What Happened to Property in Law and Economics?* 111 Yale L. J. 357 (2001); same, *The Property-Contract Interface,* 101 Colum. L. Rev. 773 (2001); same, *Optimal Standardization in the Law of Property: The Numerus Clausus Principle* 110 Yale L.J. 1 (2000); *see also* Henry Hansmann & Reinier Kraakman, *Property, Contract and Verification: The Numerus Clausus Principle and the Divisibility of Rights,* 31 J. Legal Stud. 373 (2001), Carol M. Rose, *What Government Can Do for Property (and Vice Versa), in* The Fundamental Interrelationships Between Government and Property 209, 213–15 (1999).

46. Austin, *supra* note 29, also notes that commodification involves a flattening of cultural character.

47. Salzman & Ruhl, *supra* note 3.

48. Endangered Species Act, 16 U.S.C. sec. 1531–44, sec. 1538 (forbidding any person to "take" endangered species; "take" defined in sec. 1532 (19) as "harass, harm, pursue, hunt, shoot, wound, kill, trap, capture, or collect," or attempt any of these acts).

49. For the concept of moral rights in intellectual property, and its varying legal treatments, *see, e.g.,* Thomas F. Cotter, *Pragmatism, Economics, and the Droit Morale,* 76 N.C. L. Rev. 1 (1997).

50. For the concept and legal treatment of moral rights in intellectual property, *see, e.g.,* Cotter, *supra* note 49.

51. Michael A. Heller, *The Tragedy of the Anticommons: Property in the Transition form Marx to Markets,* 111 Harv. L. Rev. 621 (1998); Michael A. Heller and Rebecca S. Eisenberg, *Can Patents Deter Innovation? The Anticommons in Biomedical Research,* 280 Science 1243 (1998).

52. Stuart Banner, *Two Properties, One Land: Law and Space in Nineteenth-Century New Zealand,* 24 Law & Soc. Inquiry 807, 811 (1999).

53. Ertman, *supra* note 37.

54. Hernández, *supra* note 29.

55. Austin, *The Commodification of Black Culture and Kwanzaa,* this volume.

56. Richard A. Posner, *An Economic Theory of the Criminal Law,* 85 Colum. L. Rev. 1193, 1199 (1985).

57. *See, e.g.,* Milton Regan, *Spouses and Strangers: Divorce Obligations and Property Rhetoric,* 82 Geo. L.J. 2119 (1994) (taking baleful view of compensation efforts). But see Carol M. Rose, *Rhetoric and Romance,* 82 Geo. L.J. 2409 (1994) (criticizing Regan's *Spouses and Strangers*); Marjorie Maguire Schultz, *Contractual Ordering of Marriage: A New Model for State Policy,* 70 Cal L. Rev. 204 (1982) (favoring contracting); Reva B. Siegel, *Home as Work: The First Woman's Rights Claims Concerning Wives' Household Labor, 1850–1880* 103 Yale L.J. 1073 (1994) (sympathetic presentation of early compensation efforts)

58. Michael J. Sandel, *Editorial, It's Immoral to Buy the Right to Pollute,* N.Y. Times, Dec. 15, 1997, at A23.

59. Richard M. Titmuss, The Gift Relationship: From Human Blood to Social Policy 225 (1971), this volume.

60. On closer analysis, Shylock is the one character who knows the difference. *See* Yoshino, *supra* note 1, for a brilliant analysis of *The Merchant of Venice*'s pervasive confounding of money with love.

61. Albert O. Hirschman, The Passions and the Interests 54–63 (1977).

62. *See, e.g.,* Peter C. Sutton, *Dutch Treat,* N.Y. Rev. Books, Feb. 17, 1994, at 31, 32 (reviewing James A. Welu, et al., Judith Leyster: A Dutch Master and Her World (1993).

63. Thomas Haskell, *Capitalism and the Origins of Humanitarian Sensibility (Part 2),* 90 Am. Hist. Rev. 547, 549–59 (1985). For the controversy about the relationship of capitalism to abolitionism; *see generally* Capitalism and Abolitionism as a Problem in Historical Interpretation (Thomas Bender, ed., 1992).

64. *But see* Linda Y. C. Lim, *Women's Work in Export Factories: The Politics of a Cause, in* Persistent Inequalities: Women and World Development 101, 116–18 (Irene Tinker, ed., 1990) (comparing women's multinational factory employment favorably to patriarchal dominance, criticizing feminist opposition to this work).

65. Hirschman, *supra* note 61, at 54–63; *see also* Albert O. Hirschman,

Rival Interpretations of Market Society: Civilizing, Destructive, or Feeble, 20 J. Econ. Lit. 1463 (1982).

66. Alexandra Chasin, Selling Out: The Gay and Lesbian Movement Goes to Market (2000), this volume.

67. *See, e.g.,* Vokes v. Arthur Murray, Inc. 212 Sol 2d 906 (Ct. App. Fla. 1968) (permitting suit to cancel expensive dance lesson and trip contracts, on grounds of sales pattern of excessive flattery).

68. For the pros and cons, see the Symposium on Contingent Valuation, 8 J. Econ. Perspectives 3 (1994).

69. *Id.; see also* Donald J. Boudreaux, Roger E. Meiners, & Todd J. Zywicki, *Talk Is Cheap: The Existence Value Fallacy,* 29 Envt'l. L. 765 (1999) (conservative criticism of contingent valuation as too uncertain); John M. Heyde, *Comment, Is Contingent Valuation Worth the Trouble?* 62 U. Chi L. Rev. 331 (1995) (criticizing contingent valuation from left as inappropriate for natural wonders).

70. Keith N. Hylton, *A Framework for Reparation Claims,* 23 B.C. Third World L.J. 31 (2004), this volume.

71. *See* Carol M. Rose, *Environmental Faust Succumbs to Temptations of Economic Mephistopheles, or, Value by Any Other Name Is Preference* 87 Mich. L. Rev. 1631, 1642–46 (1989) (reviewing Mark Sagoff, The Economy of the Earth (1988)) (arguing that critics of contingent valuation overlook its shock value).

72. *See* Mary Ann Glendon, Rights Talk: The Impoverishment of Political Discourse (1991) (conservative critique of "rights talk" for focusing too much on individual claims, ignoring corresponding duties, need for balance and political conversation); Mark Tushnet, *An Essay on Rights,* 62 Tex. L. Rev. 1363, 1382–84 (1984) (leftist critique of the "reification" of rights); *cf.* Kimberlé Williams Crenshaw, *Race, Reform, and Retrenchment: Transformation and Legitimation in Antidiscrimination Law,* 101 Harv. L. Rev. 1331, 1364–66 (1988) (criticizing critiques of rights, arguing the great importance of rights rhetoric for "dispossessed people").

About the Contributors

Arjun Appadurai is Provost and Senior Vice-President for Academic Affair and John Dewey Professor in the Social Sciences at the New School University. His numerous publications such as *Modernity at Large: Cultural Dimensions of Globalization* (1996) and *Anthropology of Consumption: a Transnational Perspective* (1994) focus on the anthropology of globalization, ethnic violence, consumption, space and housing, international civil society, and urban South Asia.

Regina Austin is the William A. Schnader Professor of Law at the University of Pennsylvania Law School. She is a leading authority on economic discrimination and critical race feminism. Her work on the overlapping burdens of race, gender, and class oppression has been widely recognized for its insight and creativity. Her books include *Black Genius: African American Solutions to African American Problems* (1999), coauthored with Walter Mosley, Manthia Diawara, and Clyde Taylor.

Guido Calabresi is Sterling Professor Emeritus of Law and Professorial Lecturer in Law at Yale Law School. As both a judge on the U.S. Court of Appeals, Second Circuit, and a legal scholar he has written more than one hundred articles, nearly eight hundred opinions of varying lengths, and four books. Calabresi's classic works include *The Cost of Accidents: A Legal and Economic Analysis* (1970), *A Common Law for the Age of Statutes* (1982), and *Ideals, Beliefs, Attitudes and the Law* (1985).

Alexandra Chasin teaches at the University of Geneva and has co-chaired the Board of Directors of the International Gay and Lesbian Human Rights Commission.

Lloyd R. Cohen is Professor of Law at George Mason University School of Law. He has published on a variety of applications of economics to law, including a market in transplant organs, marriage and divorce, wrongful death, tender offers, free riders, and holdouts.

Martha M. Ertman is Professor of Law at the University of Utah, S.J. Quinney College of Law. She has written law review articles about the commonalities between domestic relations and commerce, contending that contractual models can improve the legal rules governing intimate affiliations.

Sarah Harding is an associate professor and Co-Director of the Institute for Law and the Humanities at Chicago-Kent College of Law. A 1989 Rhodes Scholar, she has written about comparative constitutional law, property law, and the legal treatment of cultural objects.

Tanya Kateri Hernández is a professor of law and justice and Frederick W. Hall Scholar at Rutgers University School of Law. She has written law review articles focusing on comparative race relations. She is a senior editor for the *Oxford University Press Encyclopedia of Latino/a History and Culture* and an editorial board member for the *Latino Studies Journal.*

Linda R. Hirshman is the author of *A Woman's Guide to Law School* (1999) and coauthor, with Jane E. Larson, of *Hard Bargains: The Politics of Sex* (1998).

bell hooks is Distinguished Professor of English at City College in New York. Her writings cover a broad range of topics on gender, race, teaching, and the significance of media for contemporary culture. Some of her works include *Ain't I a Woman: Black Women and Feminism* (1981), *Talking Back: Thinking Feminist, Thinking Black* (1989), *Yearning: Race, Gender, and Cultural Politics* (1990), and *Reel to Real: Race, Sex, and Class at the Movies* (1996).

Keith N. Hylton is Professor of Law the Boston University School of Law. He has written law review articles on antitrust, litigation theory, labor and corporate law, and the book *Antitrust Law: Economic Theory and Common Law Evolution* (2003).

Miranda Joseph is Associate Professor of Women's Studies at the University of Arizona and author of *Against the Romance of Community* (2003) as well as journal articles and book chapters. Her research brings together Marxist and poststructuralist theory to explore the mutually constitutive relationship between community and capitalism.

Elisabeth M. Landes has been a practice leader at Lexecon, a leading international economics consulting firm. She has published numerous journal articles in the fields of labor economics and industrial organization.

Jane E. Larson is Professor of Law at the University of Wisconsin Law School and coauthor with Linda R. Hirshman of *Hard Bargains: The Politics of Sex* (1998). Her numerous other publications focus on women's legal history, feminist legal theory, conflict of laws, land use, and property.

Ann Lucas is Assistant Professor of Justice Studies at San Jose State University. Her scholarly interests include the legal regulation of prostitution, drugs, and victimless crime.

A. Douglas Melamed is Co-Chair of the Antitrust and Competition Practice Group at Wilmer Cutler Pickering Hale and Dorr LLP. A former Acting Assistant Attorney General, Antitrust Division, U.S. Department of Justice, he has written numerous articles on antitrust and on law and economics.

Martha C. Nussbaum is the Ernst Freund Distinguished Service Professor of Law and Ethics at the University of Chicago Law School. She is the founder and Coordinator of the new Center for Comparative Constitutionalism and is author and editor of many influential books including *Women and Human Development: The Capabilities Approach* (2000) and *Upheavals of Thought: The Intelligence of Emotions* (2001).

Richard A. Posner is a judge of the U.S. Court of Appeals for the Seventh Circuit and Senior Lecturer in Law at the University of Chicago Law School. Judge Posner has written an extraordinary number of books, including *Economic Analysis of Law* (6th ed. 2003), *Law and Literature* (1988), *Sex and Reason* (1992), *Overcoming Law* (1995), and *The Problematics of Moral and Legal Theory* (1999), as well as many articles in legal and economic journals. His writing has explored the application of economics to a variety of subjects including family law, primitive law, racial discrimination, jurisprudence, and privacy.

Margaret Jane Radin is William Benjamin Scott and Luna M. Scott Professor of Law, Stanford Law School, and author of *Contested Commodities* (1996) and *Reinterpreting Property* (1993) as well as over thirty journal articles. A preeminent property theorist, she has written extensively about commodification and electronic commerce, as well as property as a right and as an institution, leading the critique of Chicago school law and economics approaches.

Carol M. Rose is the Gordon Bradford Tweedy Professor of Law and Organization at Yale Law School. A leading scholar on property theory, she has written *Property and Persuasion* (1994) and *Perspectives in Property Law* (2000, coedited with Robert Ellickson and Bruce Ackerman) in addition to publishing numerous articles on environmental law and property. She has contrasted market-based versus community-based strategies in addressing the uneasy relationship of commerce to the environment.

Dereka Rushbrook is a graduate associate and doctoral candidate in the Department of Geography at the University of Arizona. Her area of scholarly interest includes development, Latin America, and social theory.

Teemu Ruskola is Assistant Professor of Law at American University. He specializes in contracts and commercial law, Chinese law and comparative law, and law and identity and has written law review articles on the interplay between social, legal, and cultural constructs in China.

Michael J. Sandel is the Anne T. and Robert M. Bass Professor of Government at Harvard University and a Rhodes Scholar. His publications include *Liberalism and the Limits of Justice* (2nd ed. 1997) and *Democracy's Discontent: America in Search of a Public Philosophy* (1996) in addition to numerous articles in scholarly journals, law reviews, and general publications.

Noam Schieber is a reporter at the *New Republic*. He has written for the *New York Times Magazine*, the *Washington Post*, *Slate*, *Salon*, the *Wash-*

ington Monthly, the *Chicago Tribune,* and the *Christian Science Monitor,* in addition to appearing on national television and radio.

Katharine Silbaugh is Associate Dean for Academic Affairs and Professor of Law at Boston University School of Law. She coauthored with Judge Richard Posner *A Guide to America's Sex Laws* (1996), and is also the author of numerous journal articles on the work-family conflict.

Deborah Stone is Research Professor of Government at Dartmouth College and author of *Policy Paradox: The Art of Political Decision Making* (1997). She has also written many journal articles on social policy, especially in the area of health, welfare, and families.

Madhavi Sunder is Professor of Law at the University of California, Davis School of Law. She has written numerous law review articles in the area of law and culture, property, intellectual property, and women's international human rights.

Richard M. Titmuss (1907–1973) was Professor of Social Policy at the London School of Economics. He authored many books, including *The Gift Relationship* (1970), *Income Distribution and Social Change* (1962), and *Commitment to Welfare* (1968), which cover diverse subjects such as social class inequalities, the national health service, and blood donation.

Joan C. Williams is Distinguished Professor of Law and Director of the Program on WorkLife Law at University of California–Hastings College of Law and author of Un*bending Gender: Why Family and World Conflict and What to Do about It* (2000) and *Land Ownership and Use* (4th ed. 1998). Her prolific output of scholarly articles on feminist jurisprudence, property, and ways that work and family conflict has received widespread mainstream attention.

Patricia J. Williams is the James L. Dohr Professor of Law at Columbia University School of Law. Among her numerous writings are the acclaimed books *The Alchemy of Race and Rights: A Diary of a Law Professor* (1993) and *Seeing a Color-Blind Future: The Paradox of Race* (1998). She is the recipient of a recent MacArthur Fellowship for her provocative work on U.S. race relations and her innovative interdisciplinary approach to writing.

Viviana A. Zelizer is Lloyd Costen '50 Professor of Sociology at Princeton University and author of *Pricing the Priceless Child* (1985), *Morals and Markets* (1994), and *The Social Meaning of Money* (1997), in addition to numerous journal articles. Her work focuses on historical analysis, childhood, economic processes, and economic sociology—specifically the various interpretations of money.

Index

Abel, Emily, 276

Abortion, 54, 56

Adoption, 46–57; abortion, 54, 56; adopted *vs.* natural children, 53–54; adoption agencies, 47–48; affordability, 309, 313; agency fees, 48–49; alternative insemination (AI) compared to, 306; altruism, 94; baby breeding, 55–56; black markets, 50, 51–53, 57n7; buyer's queue, 47; child abuse, 54; in China, 327; commissioned adoptions, 91–92; contracts, 52; costs, 313; effects of baby shortage, 49–51; freedom of contract, 2; gray markets, 49, 92; incentives to relinquish parental rights, 51; independent adoptions, 47, 49–50, 57n7; legal baby markets, 51, 53–56, 68–70, 303; marginalized groups, 309; market-clearing price, 47, 50; middleman function, 50, 54, 65; money in, 60, 61–62, 64–65, 68–70, 73, 304–305; newborn *vs.* older children, 55; nonrelative adoptions, 48; personal report of adopting a child, 68–70; prices for babies, 50, 51, 52–53, 55, 312, 313; property rights, 55; race and, 55, 68–70, 312; repetitive business relations, 52; seller's queue, 47; surrogate-parenting agreements and, 58–59, 61–62, 73; in United States, 48–49, 68–70; of unwanted children, 92

Adultery, 346–347

Advertising: diversity in, 194–195; *Ellen* "Coming-Out Episode," 218–219; for gay public spaces, 202; of prostitution, 250, 263; visibility of gays and lesbians in, 215–216

African Americans: economic advancement, 180; *Farmer-Paellman v.*

FleetBoston Fin. Corp., 348–350; Kwanzaa, 183–190, 373; poverty rates, 349–350; reparations for slavery, 348–353; sex tourism, 238n28

Afrocentricity, 181–182

Age of Access (Rifkin), 365

Alienability: of cultural patrimony, 158; debates about, 81; in economic and cultural studies, 10–13; entitlements, 78; of human blood, 108; of human organs, 354–355; objections to extending its reach, 122; property rights, 414, 424n32; of public rights, 23

Alternative insemination (AI) market, 303–323; access by poor women, 312–313; adoption compared to AI, 306; as an open market, 309–310; benefits, 303, 314–317, 417; California Cryobank (CCB), 307, 308, 311; as a contested commodity, 124, 304; costs to buyers, 305–306, 312–313; dangers of, 303–304, 310–314; Differentiated Ties and, 317–319; donor anonymity, 307–308, 313–314, 321n12; eugenic concerns, 310–312; feminist concerns, 316; as a free market, 309–310; gays and lesbians in, 14, 15, 305, 315; human flourishing and, 309, 313–314, 315; lack of regulation, 306; majoritarian moral bias and, 316; marginalized groups in, 306, 309; multivalent view of, 317–319; negative implications, 310–314; new family structures, 314–316; objectification of children, 314; positive implications, 314–317; reproductive technologies, 305–306; sperm banks, 307–308, 309, 311, 321n12; sperm-selling, 124; subject/object in, 316; surrogacy

Body parts, 11
Bourdieu, Pierre, 333, 334
Butler, Judith, 335, 338

C-M-C circuit of exchange, 388, 390
Calabresi, Guido, 403
California Cryobank (CCB), 307, 308, 311
Calvert et al., Johnson v., 71–76
Cambodia, prostitution in, 22–23
Canada, prostitution in, 263
Capital accumulation, 388, 395, 398
Capitalism: commodification in, 389;
   Kwanzaa, 187, 188, 373; possessive individualism, 367–368; racism, 372, 390;
   rights, 214; Romantic anticapitalism,
   384, 391; sexism, 390
Capitalist societies, 38
Care work, 271–290; accountability in,
283; altruism, 274–275; bureaucracy in,
282–287; caregiver's relationship with
clients, 273, 277–278, 281–282,
288n16; child care (*see* Child care); citizenship, 271; commodification of, 274,
278; compassion, 281–282, 285–286;
contracts for, 284–285; costs, 282; Differentiated Ties and, 370–371; EEC
(early education and care), 284; elder
care, 129, 272, 283–284; eligibility for
public assistance, 276–277; exploitation
of women, 278–279; by families, 271;
family day care providers, 275–276,
281; foster care, 47–48, 50–51, 108;
human flourishing and, 271–272; love
for strangers, 274–278; loyalty,
272–273; market motivations, 277; measurement of services, 283–284; misrecognition of, 334; money for, 4–5,
262, 274–278, 282–283, 291–292,
342n44, 362, 366, 369–371, 411; motivation for, 274–275; one's own kids,
280, 411; payer's power over caregivers,
285–286; as politics, 286; profit motive,
282–283; progress in, 283–284; race
and, 281; reciprocity in, 273–274; sacredness of, 287, 365; self-interest,
287n9; of the sick/disabled, 272,
283–284; unionization of, 279; work
and, 279–282, 293–296, 366
Cases: *Johnson v. Calvert et al.,* 71–76; *In
the Matter of Baby M,* 58–67; *Min-*

nesota v. Bachmann, 293–296; *Moore v.
Regents of the University of California,*
96–105; *U.S. v. Corrow,* 156–163
Cell lines, patents on, 98, 102–103
Channels of Desire (Ewen and Ewen),
196–197
Charlie's Angels (film), theme from, 235
Chasin, Alexandra, 363, 403, 419
Chicago school of economics: new commodification theorists, 15; pervasiveness
of commodification, 10, 391; universal
commodification, 9, 10, 82
Child care: commodification of, 129, 272,
284–285; as education, 284; by immigrant nannies, 288n16; for one's own
kids, 280
Child sex tourism, 223, 236n3
Children: child abuse, 54, 236n3; child sex
tourism, 223, 236n3; contract with parents, 330; exchange value of, 13; foster
care, 47–48, 50–51; markets in, 1,
46–76, 303–323; nurturing of, 124; objectification in alternative insemination
(AI) market, 314; paid adoption of unwanted children, 92; rights in, 75; separation from a birth parent, 63–64
China, clan corporations in, 325–329
Chrysler Corporation, 218–219
Chua, Amy, 413
Cities, 204–205
Citizenship, 124, 271, 315
Civic virtue, 125–126
Class: asymmetry in economic power and
status in female sex tourism, 235; "creative class," 204; differences among gays
and lesbians, 217; double bind and, 92;
enlistees in the volunteer army, 130–131;
marketization of, 312–313, 372; poor
people as objects of commodification,
11, 388; poor women, 73–74, 92; surrogate-parenting agreements and, 65,
73–74, 92
Closely held corporations, families as, 5,
330–335
Co-optation, 179
Coercion, 122–124. *See also* Double bind
Cohen, Lloyd, 355–356
Commensurability, 124, 318, 385, 404
Commercialization: commodification
and, 179; of human tissue, 96–105;

porations, 337–338; foster care, 47–48, 50–51; as "hyperreal" entities, 338; intimacy and, 336–337; language for describing, 337; marriage as close corporation, 5, 330–335; new family structures, 314–316; politics in, 337; work's conflict with, 279–282, 291–292

Families as corporations, 324–344; Becker on, 325, 330; in China, 325–329; clan corporations, 326–329; as a closely held corporation, 330–335; contracts, 328–329, 335; division of labor, 330–331; functional differentiation among participants, 330; management structure, 326–329; material exchanges within, 334; output, 332; self-referentiality, 338; sex, 333; size of the enterprise, 331; in United States, 329–333

Family day care providers, 275–276, 281

Fanon, Franz, 231

Farmer-Paellman v. FleetBoston Fin. Corp., 348–350

Fashion, taste makers in, 41

Fatherhood, 124, 307–308

Female sex tourism, 222–242; asymmetry in economic power and status, 235; dating and, 224–225, 235; dominance theory of sex tourism, 232–233; double bind in, 224, 234–235; escapism of, 233; gender relations, 17–18, 226–234; gender role reversal in, 233; human flourishing and, 223, 224, 226–234; incomplete/partial commodification in, 234–235; inequality, 236; instrumental motivations in, 234–235; interracial sex, 226; motives of sex providers, 225–230; prostitution and, 225; racialized fantasies, 226–227, 236; romance tourism, 223, 225, 232–233; validation of female sexual attractiveness, 231–232; validation of masculinity, 228–230; wealth in, 231, 234; White female tourists, 230–234; Whiteness, 233, 242n71, 242n72; women of color tourists, 238n28. *See also* Prostitution

Fineman, Martha, 332–333

Firth, Raymond, 39–40

FleetBoston Fin. Corp., Farmer-Paellman v., 348–350

Folbre, Nancy, 369

Foner, Nancy, 273

Foster care, 47–48, 50–51

Foucault, Michel, 337

Franck, Thomas, 167

Franke, Katherine, 232, 422n14

Fraud, 1, 52

Free markets, 50, 309–310

Freedom of choice, 79, 126–127

Freedom of contract, 2, 3

Friedman, Milton, 130, 402

Fungibility, 87, 226, 251, 413–417

Fuss, Diana, 318

Futures markets, 357–359

Gambia, sex tourism in, 226, 227, 228

Gays and lesbians, 199–220, 303–323; acceptance of, 201, 315, 371; activist groups, 199, 217; alternative insemination (AI) market, 14, 15, 305, 315; black culture, 207; casual/anonymous sex, 267n26; class differences among, 217; clubs/bars, 205–208; commodification of gay/lesbian identity, 20, 200; community of, 201, 213; cosmopolitanism, 202, 203–204; demographic characteristics, 202, 210n15, 215; diversity and, 202; *Ellen* "Coming-Out Episode," 218–219; gay-friendliness of cities, 204–205; growth of gay and lesbian movement, 199–200, 213, 397; Harlem clubs (New York City), 207; marketed by cities, 202, 208; marketization, 371–372; movies about, 201; niche market, 202, 210n15, 214–218; parenthood, 315, 320n11; pride events, 208; public spaces, 199–212; *Queer Eye for the Straight Guy* (TV show), 20; Simmons Market Research Bureau, 215; Sydney, gay pride parade in, 208; symbols of, 217; television shows about, 201; visibility in advertising, 215–216; Yandelovich (research firm), 215

Gender relations: capital and, 396; contractual models of families, 316; equal sharing in sexual relations, 89; female sex tourism, 17–18, 226–234; Hostile Worlds view of commodification, 4–5; household labor, 291–292, 294, 299–302, 362; intimacy as bargaining, 345–347; markets and, 372; women's

Law-and-economics literature *(continued)*
82–83. *See also* Chicago school of economics
Left, the, 128
Lesbian Avengers, 199
Lesbians. *See* Gays and lesbians
Lévi-Strauss, Claude, 335
Liberalism: dignity strain, 372–373; individualism, 336; macrospheres in, 335–336; markets and, 372; nineteenth-century *vs.* modern, 128–129; possessive individualism, 367, 372
Liberty, 4, 17, 128, 249
Life insurance, 298
Lind, Michael, 129, 130
Locally unwanted land uses (LULUs), 407
Locke, John, 3, 337, 343n57
Loss of Happiness in Market Democracies (Lane), 365
Love: lost in markets, 243; in markets, 418, 419; money and, 243, 274–279, 318, 418, 419; as noneconomic, 334; prostitution and, 243; for strangers, 274–278; work and, 279
Loyalty in care work, 272–273
Lucas, Ann: prostitution, 16, 403, 418; second-best analysis, 406, 408
Lukács, Georg, 391–392, 394
LULUs (locally unwanted land uses), 407

M-C-C'-M' circuit of exchange, 388, 391
MacKinnon, Catharine, 89, 232
Made in America (film), 182
Madonna (Madonna Ciccone), 14
Male gametes, market in, 14, 301, 307–308
Male prostitutes, 225–230, 257, 418
Male sex tourists, 222–223, 224–225, 226, 240n56
Malinowski, Bronislaw, 333
Manners, 409, 419
Maori landholdings, 416
Marcus, George, 329
Market compartmentalization, 82–85
Market-dominant minorities, 413
Market-Inalienability (Radin), 10–11, 25n16, 67n8, 164, 237n9, 248–249, 403–404, 405
Market rhetoric, 417–423
Marketization: class, 312–313, 372; com-

modification and, 371; control over, 373–374; definition of, 2; in Differentiated Ties, 370–375, 376; gay and lesbian identities, 371–372; as imperialism, 17–19, 191, 224, 374–375; of military service, 2, 124–127, 130–132, 408; as a nonissue, 370–371; of race, 1, 372; spread of, 122–127. *See also* Commercialization
Markets: altruism, 4; "as if" reasoning about, 298; autonomy of, 336; coercion in, 122–124; complexity hindering markets, 414–415; corruption by, 122–127; in culture, 21–22; definition of, 2; desperate exchanges in, 11, 14, 86, 90, 122, 388–398; in economic sociology, 368–369; effect of Internet on, 9–10; fair bargaining conditions, 123; free markets, 309–310; freedom of choice, 126–127; freedom of contract, 3; futures markets, 357–359; gay niche market, 202, 210n15, 214–218; hegemony of, 23; homogenization of culture, 12–13; in human capital theory, 292; imperfect information in, 412–413; intimacy, 4–5, 301, 317–318; justification of, 3; laissez-faire markets, 10, 17, 90; liberalism and, 372; locus of, 411; love in, 418, 419; moral agents in, 14, 216; objections to, 122–127; options markets, 355–356; potential for experiment and novelty, 417; role of, 82–83; second best, 405–406; self-interest, 5; separate spheres view of commodification, 366; in sex tourism, 224; social norms of, 412; society and, 336; transaction costs, 412–413
Marriage: to Becker, 330; as close corporation, 5, 330–335; as a commodity context, 37; division of property in, 291, 345, 347; divorce, 291–292, 346–347, 370–371; gifts in, 411; marriage contracts, 334, 341n18, 418; personhood, 329
Martinez, Angel, 280
Marx, Karl: bourgeois ideology and, 334; capital accumulation, 388, 395; on commodities, 2, 34–35, 81–82, 384, 394, 400n24; *doux commerce* theories, 419; factories to, 337; on freedom of contract, 3; money and, 384; primitive accu-